Middle Classic Mesoamerica: A.D. 400–700

ESTHER PASZTORY, EDITOR

middle classic mesoamerica: a.d. 400-700

COLUMBIA UNIVERSITY PRESS   NEW YORK   1978

Library of Congress Cataloging in Publication Data
Main entry under title:

Middle Classic Mesoamerica, A.D. 400–700

  Bibliography: p.
  1. Indians of Mexico—Antiquities—Addresses,
essays, lectures.   2. Indians of Central America—
Antiquities—Addresses, essays, lectures.   3. Mexico—
Antiquities—Addresses, essays, lectures.   4. Central
America—Antiquities—Addresses, essays, lectures.
I. Pasztory, Esther.
F1219.M758   972   77-23837
ISBN 0-231-04270-1

Columbia University Press
New York   Guildford, Surrey
Copyright © 1978   Columbia University Press
All rights reserved
Printed in the United States of America

acknowledgments

Grateful acknowledgment is made to the following institutions, publishers, and individuals:

To the Carnegie Institution of Washington and Harvard University, Peabody Museum of Archaeology and Ethnology for permission to reproduce fig. 156 from *Excavations at Kaminaljuyu,* publication 561, by A. Kidder, J. Jennings, and E. Shook, 1946. Pasztory, fig. 9, p. 115.

To The Cleveland Museum of Art. Pasztory, fig. 6, p. 113. The Cleveland Museum of Art, Gift of Hanna Fund, 54.857.

To The Connecticut Academy of Arts and Sciences. Miller, fig. 1, p. 64. Reproduced by permission of The Connecticut Academy of Arts and Sciences from *Studies in Classic Maya Iconography* by George Kubler, *Memoir Vol. 18,* 1969. The Shoe String Press, Hamden, Connecticut.

To the Denver Art Museum for permission to reproduce Escuintla ceramic tripod. Hellmuth, fig. 9, p. 78.

To Dover Publications, Inc., for permission to reproduce pl. 40a from

P. Kelemen, *Medieval American Art,* vol. 1, 1969. Cohodas, fig. 11, p. 103.

To Dumbarton Oaks Research Library and Collection, Washington, D.C. for permission to reproduce fig. 44 from "A Possible Focus of Andean Artistic Influence on Mesoamerica" by M. Badner in *Studies in Pre-Columbian Art and Archaeology,* no. 9, 1972, fig. 12 from "The Iconography of the Art of Teotihuacan" by G. Kubler in *Studies in Pre-Columbian Art and Archaeology,* no. 4, 1967, and Teotihuacan mural from Tetitla. Pasztory fig. 2, p. 113 and fig. 30, p. 126; Miller, fig. 2, p. 64.

To The Ethnic Arts Council of Los Angeles and Mr. and Mrs. Robert Kuhn for permission to reproduce fig. 2a from "Rituals Depicted on Veracruz Pottery" by H. von Winning in *Ancient Art of Veracruz,* 1971. Hellmuth, fig. 10, p. 78.

To the Instituto Nacional de Antropologia e Historia, Mexico. Photos 360, 362, and 419 from *Arquitectura prehispanica* by I. Marquina, 1964.

Cortesía: INAH, México. Cohodas, fig. 6, p. 94, fig. 7, p. 95, and fig. 12, p. 103; fig. 9 from *Proyecto Cholula* by I. Marquina, 1970. Cortesía: INAH, México. Pasztory, fig. 2, p. 110; fig. 346 from *Urnas de Oaxaca* by A. Caso and I. Bernal, 1952. Cortesía: INAH. México. Pasztory, fig. 7, p. 115; Pasztory, fig. 14, p. 118. Cortesía: INAH. México; supplement figs. 4, 3, and 2 from *Arquitectura prehispanica* by I. Marquina, 1964. Cortesía: INAH. México. Pasztory, figs. 34, 35, and 36, p. 140.

To Merle Greene Robertson for permission to reproduce pls. 8, 13, 52, and 15 from *Ancient Maya Relief Sculpture*, 1967. Pasztory, fig. 10, p. 116, fig. 17, p. 121, and figs. 23 and 24, p. 126; pls. 132, 121, 189, and 156 from *Maya Sculpture from the Southern Lowlands, Highlands, and Pacific Piedmont*, 1972. Pasztory, fig. 5, p. 113, fig. 11, p. 118, fig. 16, p. 119, and fig. 18, p. 122; fig. 7 from "The Iconography of the Panels of the Sun, Cross and Foliated Cross at Palenque: Part II" by M. Cohodas in *Primera Mesa Redonda de Palenque*, 1974. Pasztory, fig. 26, p. 126.

To the Milwaukee Public Museum for permission to reproduce pl. 60e from *Bilbao, Guatemala*, publication 12, by L. Parsons, 1969. Pasztory, fig. 21, p. 124.

To the Smithsonian Institution, National Museum of Natural History, for permission to reproduce figs. 11a and 11b from "Stone Monuments of Southern Mexico" by M. Stirling, *Bulletin 138*, 1943. Pasztory, fig. 4, p. 113, and fig. 8, p. 115.

To the Tikal Project, University Museum, University of Pennsylvania, for permission to reproduce West wall of Structure 5D-57, Central Acropolis, Tikal and East end, upper zone of Structure 5D-57, Central Acropolis, Tikal. Miller, fig. 3, p. 65 and fig. 4, p. 66.

To the Universidad Nacional Autonoma de Mexico for permission to reproduce fig. 44 from *La escultura de Uxmal* by M. Foncerrada de Molina, 1965. Pasztory, fig. 25, p. 126.

The University Museum, University of Pennsylvania for permission to reproduce the illustrations on pp. 33 and 32 from "Tikal: A Handbook of the Ancient Maya Ruins" by W. R. Coe in *Expedition* 8(1) 1965. Pasztory, figs. 12 and 13, p. 118.

To the University of Oklahoma Press for permission to reproduce pl. 242 from *Maya Cities: Placemaking and Urbanization*, by George F. Andrews. Copyright 1975 by the University of Oklahoma Press. Cohodas, fig. 10, p. 102.

To the University Presses of Florida for permission to reproduce the photograph of the north-central panel of the Tajin ball court from *Sculptures of El Tajin* by M. Kampen, 1972. Pasztory, fig. 27, p. 128.

To the University of Texas Press for permission to reproduce fig. 10 from "Archaeology and Prehistory in the Northern Maya Lowlands" by E. W. Andrews IV in *Handbook of Middle American Indians*, volume 2, edited by R. Wauchope, copyright © 1965 by University of Texas Press. Cohodas, fig. 15, p. 104.

To the Vanguard Press for permission to reproduce fig. 55 from *Burning Water* by L. Sejourne, 1956. Pasztory, fig. 29, p. 128.

GORDON F. EKHOLM

ſorewordo

THROUGHOUT THE YEARS, our understanding of Mesoamerican culture history has slowly evolved as the result of varied kinds of archaeological investigations—chief among them being the attempts to establish archaeological sequences in all of the several cultural regions or centers. Such sequences are, of course, fundamental to dealing with a large and complex cultural entity such as Mesoamerica, for which there are no written historical records, except for the latest periods. To me, the outstanding advances have been those breakthroughs through which relationships between culture sequences in separate regions have become apparent and the obviously interrelated processes of development of the whole larger area have become clarified.

One such breakthrough resulted from the Carnegie Institution's excavations at Kaminaljuyu in the early 1940s, from which it became clear, all of a sudden, that the early Classic Maya cultures were contemporary with the developmental peak at Teotihuacan. Another breakthrough occurred at the Round Table Conference of the Sociedad Mexicana de Antropologia in 1941, which revealed that there was a Tula that could be identified with the historic Toltec and that this was clearly related to and contemporary with the appearance of Mexican elements at Chichen Itza in Yucatan. These happenings may not seem so important at this present time, but they were spectacular developments when they occurred. They were the first signs of a kind of logic in Middle American archaeology, a logic that became crystallized in 1943 with Kirchhoff's notable concept of Mesoamerica.

These briefly stated recollections are prompted by my thinking that the major papers in this symposium volume are evidence of another similar kind of breakthrough in understanding the larger framework of Mesoamerican culture history. They emphasize the importance of the Middle Classic period as a time when highly significant interchanges appear to have been taking place between culture centers in highland Mexico and the Maya regions, and, even more specifically, in the inbetween regions of central Veracruz, Oaxaca, and southern Guatemala. They suggest new alignments that, even though they will be subject to modification in the future, will probably be proven correct.

In my opinion, the special value of this volume rests on the emphasis that is given to viewing Mesoamerica, or at least large parts of it, as a whole. This emphasis is based on the underlying assumption that a complex, advanced culture such as Mesoamerica—a "civilization," if you will—is not a collection of distinct cultures that happen to be grouped in relative proximity to each other, but is rather a larger functioning and developing unit whose parts are interrelated in many ways. This kind of emphasis is to be expected in a symposium organized by and including persons whose backgrounds are in art history rather than in anthropological archaeology. It has long been my feeling that the views engendered by the discipline of art history have been too seldom applied to the study of pre-Columbian America and that any increase in their application would be of great value. With the publication of this volume, a larger audience will be able to judge whether this assessment is correct.

ESTHER PASZTORY

preface

THIS COLLECTION of essays differs from most books published on Mesoamerica, because it is a comparative study of art and cultural history during a certain important time period. Usually, each region or culture is examined separately, with the emphasis on the continuity of local traditions rather than on the interrelationships between cultures in different regions. While the focus on separate cultures has resulted in a great deal of new information, cross-cultural comparison is essential to the reconstruction of the history of the area as a whole. The purpose of this book is threefold: to explore the usefulness of a new chronological division, the Middle Classic period, in Mesoamerican history; to analyze some of the cultural and artistic developments in this period; and to emphasize the importance of comparative approaches in both archaeological and art historical investigations.

The Middle Classic period in Mesoamerica was the subject of a symposium held by the University Seminar on Primitive and Pre-Columbian Art at Columbia University in 1973. The purpose of the symposium was to discuss the significance of a recently proposed time period in Mesoamerican chronology that is still controversial. The participants in the symposium, Marvin Cohodas, Gordon Ekholm, Nicholas Hellmuth, George Kubler, Arthur Miller, Lee Parsons, and William Sanders agreed that there were good reasons to divide the Classic period into three, rather than two, phases, but they disagreed on the actual dates, events, and sociocultural processes that should determine the new chronology. Since some of the ideas presented contradicted the usually accepted reconstructions of the Classic period, it was felt that these papers needed to be published to generate more discussion. Other scholars interested in this period were asked to contribute papers on subjects not covered in the symposium but relevant to the problem. The aim has been not to achieve a unanimity of opinion or a resolution but to stimulate reevaluations of Mesoamerican history from new perspectives.

The Middle Classic period was a crucial 300-year time span in the history of Mesoamerica. It was a time of both climax and change. It corresponded to an intense period of trade and cultural contact between political groups, which resulted in the rise of several sophisticated and eclectic centers, but also contributed to the temporary or permanent decline of others. It was, in general, in the political, intellectual, scientific, and artistic realms, a period of ferment and experimentation, of brilliant achievements side by side with sudden collapse. By contrast, both the years before A.D. 400 and after 700 showed a higher degree of regional isolation. While some of the cultures after A.D. 700 went on to even greater accomplishments in the Late Classic period the tendency was for the consolidation and elaboration of ideas and institutions rather than innovation. There is a parallel to this situation in the history of Europe from the fifteenth to the seventeenth centuries: the Middle Classic period with all of its achievements, contradictions, and upheaval, is comparable to the "Renaissance" of the fifteenth and sixteenth centuries, while the Late Classic period of consolidation is comparable to the baroque civilizations of the seventeenth century.

The book is divided into three parts. Part I is an introduction to the problems of the Middle Classic period and a synthesis of the major historic events. The papers in part II deal with the concept of the Middle Classic period and its possible usefulness in Mesoamerican archaeology and art history. Parsons, Sanders, and Paddock discuss the archaeological aspects of the problem, while Miller, Hellmuth, Cohodas, and Pasztory concentrate on developments in the arts. The essays collected in part III, while not directly concerned with a definition of the Middle Classic period, deal with materials and problems relevant to it. Holien, Sharp, and Matos present different approaches in the cross-cultural interpretations of archaeological finds and works of art and add further descriptive material to the subjects covered in the more theoretical papers of part II.

I would like to thank the American Council of Learned Societies for having supported travel in Mexico and Guatemala in connection with the research for this book. Various parts of the manuscript were read and commented on by Gordon Ekholm, John Paddock, Marvin Cohodas, and Clemency Coggins. I am indebted to them for valuable criticism and suggestions. I would further like to thank my students, Magali Carrera, Marilyn Goldstein, and Wendy Schonfeld for editorial assistance.

contents

ACKNOWLEDGMENTS   v

FOREWORD   vii
GORDON F. EKHOLM

PREFACE   ix
ESTHER PASZTORY

PART ONE: INTRODUCTION   1
Historical Synthesis of the Middle Classic Period   3
ESTHER PASZTORY

PART TWO: THE MIDDLE CLASSIC CONCEPT   23
The Peripheral Coastal Lowlands and the Middle Classic
Period   25
LEE A. PARSONS
Ethnographic Analogy and the Teotihuacan Horizon Style   35
WILLIAM T. SANDERS
The Middle Classic Period in Oaxaca   45
JOHN PADDOCK
A Brief Outline of the Artistic Evidence for Classic Period
Cultural Contact between Maya Lowlands and Central Mexican
Highlands   63
ARTHUR G. MILLER

Teotihuacan Art in the Escuintla, Guatemala Region   71
NICHOLAS HELLMUTH
Diverse Architectural Styles and the Ball Game Cult: The Late
Middle Classic Period in Yucatan   86
MARVIN COHODAS
Artistic Traditions of the Middle Classic Period   108
ESTHER PASZTORY

PART THREE: MESOAMERICA BETWEEN A.D. 400–700:
PROBLEMS AND CROSS-CULTURAL STUDIES   143
Analogues in Classic Period Chalchihuites Culture to Late
Mesoamerican Ceremonialism   145
THOMAS HOLIEN AND ROBERT B. PICKERING
Architecture as Interelite Communication in Preconquest
Oaxaca, Veracruz, and Yucatan   158
ROSEMARY SHARP
The Tula Chronology: A Revision   172
EDWARD MATOS MOCTEZUMA

BIBLIOGRAPHY   178

INDEX   191

Middle Classic Mesoamerica: A.D. 400–700

PART ONE

introduction

ESTHER PASZTORY

historical synthesis of the middle classic period

Introduction

HISTORIANS APPROACH the past in one of two ways: they focus either on the uniqueness of events or on the repetition of certain patterns of events. Those who are interested in the content of past epochs seek to reconstruct the past and to interpret its significance, while those who are interested in the patterns of events seek to establish rules or axioms that explain why these events occurred. This essay belongs to the first category. It is an interpretive reconstruction of the cultural history of Mesoamerica between A.D. 400 and 700. Relevant archaeological information is synthesized and related to trends in artistic representation. It is assumed that works of art reflect the attitudes and preoccupations of the societies in which they were made and that historians of another time and place can rediscover those motivating forces. Like much of historical interpretation, this essay is frankly subjective. Assertions about the attitudes and world views of ancient cultures are not readily testable. The usefulness of such interpretations derives from the meaning they give to the chaos of historical facts, even if only temporarily.

The term "Mesoamerica" is used to refer to the high cultures of southern Mexico, Guatemala, British Honduras, western El Salvador, and Honduras, prior to the Spanish conquest. The land of this Mesoamerican area is extremely varied (ranging from jungle lowlands to arid highlands), and the basic subsistence of its ancient inhabitants varied a great deal according to altitude and rainfall. Like Europe, Mesoamerica was never culturally and politically unified into a single state; in all periods it was divided into different ethnic groups, which spoke different languages and had different cultures and values. Nevertheless, the separate Mesoamerican political and ethnic groups were usually in contact with each other through trade, war, and intermarriage, and they shared a basic ideology. The major ethnic and cultural groups of Mesoamerica are usually placed in one of two large groups, the Maya in the south and the "Mexicans" in the north. The Mexican group includes the cultures of the Oaxaca highlands, the Gulf coast, and Central Mexico, while the term "Maya" refers to the cultures of the Guatemala highlands, the rain forest of Guatemala and Mexico, and the Yucatan peninsula (fig. 1).

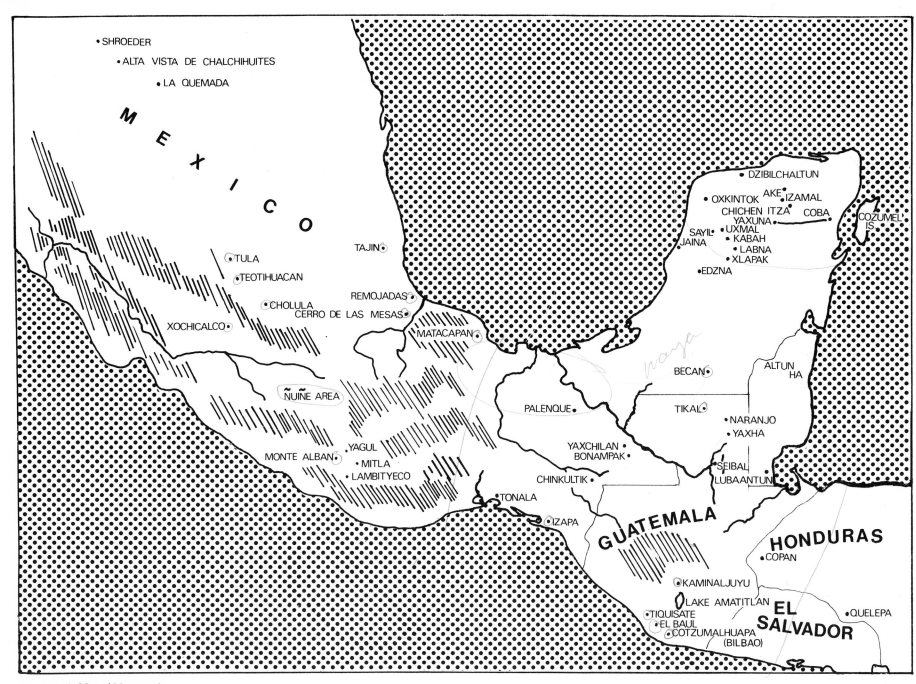

1. Map of Mesoamerica.

Archaeological excavations have shown that the culture history of Mesoamerica began many centuries ago. By the second millennium B.C., Mesoamerica had been settled by villagers who farmed corn, squash, beans, and a variety of root crops. Their artifacts included stone tools, ceramic vessels, and clay figurines of fine workmanship and aesthetic appeal. Mesoamerican history is divided into three broad periods: Preclassic or Formative, 1500 B.C.–A.D. 250; Classic, A.D. 250–900; and Postclassic, A.D. 900–1519. The anchor in this chronological division is the Classic period, which is dated by inscriptions on Maya monuments that have been correlated with the Christian calendar. This period is usually described as the florescence of Mesoamerican civilization, particularly in the arts, writing, and astronomy. The cultures of the Preclassic period are thought of as leading up to the achievements of the Classic from relatively humble village beginnings. The Postclassic period represents to some extent a cultural decline, since it encompasses the abandonment of the Maya lowlands, the disappearance of many of the Maya intellectual achievements, and an apparent shift towards more secular and militaristic values.

The use of the terms "Classic, "Preclassic," and "Postclassic" has become standard in Mesoamerican archaeology. The major shortcoming of this system is that these terms have dual meanings that give rise to ambiguities in description. They refer both to absolute time periods and to cultural stages in evolution. As a cultural stage, the Classic in Mesoamerica is often defined as a time of cultural climax, characterized by urbanism, great art styles, and intellectual achievements. Since the several Mesoamerican cultures do not start or finish periods of climax at the same time, some may be Classic in date but Preclassic or Postclassic in character, a distinction that is blurred by the period designation. Although ambiguity may always be avoided through precision of language, it would be clearer to adopt a different terminology and refer to the time periods by more neutral, less suggestive names. The possibility of adopting a new period terminology for Mesoamerica, similar to the system used in Peruvian archaeology, of Early, Middle, and Late periods, has been recently discussed.[1] In Peruvian history, periods of regional isolation alternate with periods of intense commercial or military interaction. The periods of pan-Peruvian contacts are described as "horizons," and the periods of regional isolation

as intermediate periods within the Early, Middle, and Late rubric. Thus, in Peruvian terminology, emphasis is placed less on the growth and climax of cultures than on the changing nature of the interrelationships between them. While this terminology has not been generally used in Mesoamerican studies, Sanders and Parsons suggest that the middle years of the Classic period in Mesoamerica in particular should be considered a "middle horizon," between two intermediate periods of relative regional isolation.[2] In this essay, the names "Classic," "Preclassic," and "Postclassic" will be retained for the sake of convenience, since the proposed new terminology has not yet been generally accepted (fig. 1).

The chronology of Mesoamerica, in particular the history of the Classic period, hinges on the problem of correlating Maya dates with the Christian calendar, a task that has not yet been completed to everyone's satisfaction. Two major correlations are used at present, which place Maya dates 260 years apart. The Spinden correlation dates the Classic period from 10 B.C. to A.D. 640; the first C_{14} dates from the Maya area in the 1950s supported this correlation. Subsequent C_{14} dates were closer to the Goodman-Martinez-Thompson (GMT) correlation, which places the Classic period between A.D. 250 and 900; this correlation is used by most Mesoamericanists and Mayanists. The question is not settled, however, since several scholars believe that the GMT correlation does not correspond to the situation in the Yucatan Maya area. E. Andrews IV (1965b) uses a modified Spinden correlation for this region. The generally accepted GMT correlation will be used in this essay, but with the understanding that the "dates" so provided are not facts but interpretations for which other alternatives are possible.

The traditional division of the Classic period into Early and Late phases is essentially based on dated Maya monuments and ceramic sequences. The lowland Maya erected stone stelae with dated inscriptions ranging from A.D. 250 to 900. Almost no dated monuments were erected in the Maya area, between A.D. 534 and 613, a hiatus that is generally thought to reflect political instability. Both this hiatus and the fall of the Central Mexican state of Teotihuacan, an event that until recently was believed to have occurred at around that time, have been viewed as manifestations of a period of shifting balances of power.

Table of Mesoamerican time periods.

PERIOD	MAYA LONG COUNT		DATES		CENTRAL MEXICO	OAXACA	GULF COAST	FAR NORTH	GUATEMALA HIGHLANDS	PACIFIC SLOPE	MAYA LOWLANDS	NORTHERN MAYA
POST CLASSIC	GMT Correlation	AZTEC HORIZON	1521	LATE	aztec IV / III	MA V	isla de sacrificios 3					
			1350	MIDDLE	aztec II / I		isla de sacrificios 2	calera	chinautla			decadent
			1150	EARLY	tula - mazapan		isla de sacrificios 1	rio tunal	amatle 3	peor-es-nada	eznab	modified florescent
			900									
CLASSIC	10.4.0.0.0. 909	TEOTIHUACAN HORIZON		LATE	xometla / coyotlatelco / oxtoticpac		tajin III	las joyas	amatle 2	santa lucia	tepeu 3 imix / tepeu 2	
	9.13.0.0.0. 692		700									
	9.8.0.0.0. 593			MIDDLE (late)	metepec IV	MA IV	tajin II	ayala / retono	amatle 1		tepeu 1 ik	florescent (puuc)
	hiatus 9.5.0.0.0. 534 ad		550	MIDDLE (early)		MA IIIb	upper remojadas 2	calicha / alta vista	esperanza	laguneta	tzakol 3 muluc	
	9.0.0.0.0. 435 ad		400		xolalpan IIIb			aurora				early II
				EARLY	tlamimilolpa IIIa / miccaotli II / tzacualli I	MA IIIa / MA II-IIIa	tajin I / upper remojadas I	miraflores / verbena-arenal / canutillo	mejor-es-algo	tzakol 2 / tzakol 1 cimi / matzanel	early I	
	8.14.0.0.0. 317 ad		100 AD									
PRECLASSIC		OLMEC HORIZON		LATE	patlachique tezoyuca / ticoman	MA IIa	lower remojadas		providencia / sacatepequez	ilusiones	chicanel cauac / chuen	
			500 BC	MIDDLE	zacatenco / guadalupe	MA I	el trapiche 3 / el trapiche 2		las charcas	algo-es-algo	mamom tzec / eb / xe	
			1000 BC	EARLY	ixtapaluca	san jose mogote	el trapiche 1		arevalo			
			2000 BC									

(Vertical side labels within columns: TEOTIHUACAN HORIZON; MONTE ALBAN; CHALCHIHUITES – ALTA VISTA – SCHROEDER; KAMINALJUYU; SANTA LUCIA COTZUMALHUAPA; XACTUN – KAMAKAL; TEOTIHUACAN; MONTE ALBAN; KAMINAL)

2. Table of Mesoamerican time periods.

The apparent correspondence of events in the Maya area and in Central Mexico seemed to confirm the view of a period of turbulence dividing the Classic into Early and Late segments.

Recent excavations in several regions of Mesoamerica have raised doubts about such a simple framework. The revised chronology for Teotihuacan indicates that the city did not fall at the end of the sixth century but lasted until after A.D. 700, and therefore its collapse could not have been the cause of the hiatus in the Maya inscriptions. The Maya site of Tikal, moreover, has been shown in recent excavations not to have been abandoned in the sixth and seventh centuries, although several buildings with marked foreign influences were erected there during that time. While these buildings are sometimes described as Mexican or Teotihuacan in style, they have characteristic Veracruz architectural profiles, indicating strong contact with the Gulf region, not with Teotihuacan. The Classic period in Monte Alban, Oaxaca—Monte Alban III—has also been dated from A.D. 300 to 900, but recent excavations of the nearby site of Lambityeco indicate that Monte Alban IV was under way by the seventh century, and that Monte Alban, like Teotihuacan, had collapsed by the eighth century. In the Pacific Slope region, the sculptures of the site of Bilbao, which were formerly dated to the end of the Classic period and related in style and subject to the Postclassic, have been redated between the years A.D. 450 and 700, contemporary with Classic Teotihuacan (Parsons 1969). All these changes in regional chronological sequences indicate that the middle segment of the Classic period is far more complex than had been supposed up till now. Much of the new content of Classic period sites cannot be simply divided into early and late segments. The division of the Classic period into early and late subperiods emphasizes the cultural differences within the period, thus obscuring the similarities of that transitional time. Clearly, the content of the Classic period cannot be examined without some evaluation of the period terminology that is being used.

The term "Middle Classic" has been used occasionally in the past by Kubler (1962), but it has been proposed anew by Parsons in order to single out the central 300 years of the Classic period (1969). Parsons views the time between A.D. 400 and 700 as characterized by extremely intense cross-cultural communication, which is manifested by the wide distribution of trade wares and prestige and ceremonial objects, as well as by the diffusion of architectural and art styles and iconography. By contrast, both the years before A.D. 400 and after A.D. 700 show a higher degree of regional isolation. In art styles, the period between A.D. 700 and 800 is one of consolidation and regional development, showing less eclecticism than in preceding centuries. The designation of a new term, "Middle Classic," is a recognition of the similarities in cultural content and processes that link the late part of the Early Classic period to the early part of the Late Classic period. As suggested by Parsons, the Middle Classic period includes the realignment of the balance of power in Mesoamerica that occurred during the second half of the sixth century, an event that was used to separate the Early and Late Classic periods. This event is still a significant point of change, and Parsons uses it to subdivide the Middle Classic period into an early and a late phase.

The early phase of the Middle Classic period, from A.D. 400 to 550 coincides with the greatest expansion and influence of the Central Mexican state of Teotihuacan, and for that reason Parsons refers to it as the Teotihuacan phase. The late phase, from A.D. 550 to 700 is marked by the absence of direct Teotihuacan influences and by the rise of centers such as Tajin, Xochicalco, Nuine, and Cotzumalhuapa, located between the Teotihuacan and Maya areas. These sites have some traits that Parsons considers Teotihuacan related, and for that reason he calls the late phase Teotihuacanoid. Parsons's most novel suggestion involves redating some supposedly Postclassic Toltec structures at Chichen Itza to the seventh century, because of strong stylistic and iconographic similarities to the arts of Tajin, Xochicalco, and Cotzumalhuapa. The Postclassic date of Toltec Chichen art and the relationship between Tula and Chichen Itza through the ethnohistoric legends of Quetzalcoatl and Kukulcan have been among the chief pillars of Mesoamerican chronology, so to tamper with them is to invite the collapse of the entire edifice. It is, therefore, understandable that so far Parsons's hypothesis has received little attention and even less support. Should Parsons be correct in his dating of Toltec Chichen, a major reevaluation of our definitions of both the Classic and Postclassic periods in Mesoamerica would be necessary.

The Postclassic period is thought to begin in Mesoamerica at about A.D. 900, after the fall of the Classic Maya. Its characteristics include defensive locations on hills, an emphasis on military subjects in art, and art styles similar to those of Toltec Tula. Recent dates for sites such as Xochicalco and Bilbao show that many of these traits were already present during the Classic period and that the Postclassic period often differs from the Classic in degree rather than in kind.

While the traditional view of the transition between the Early and Late Classic was usually of a period of political change and lessened artistic activity—a breather between two peaks of achievement—the suggested changes of dates in Oaxaca, the Pacific Slope, and Yucatan would crowd the sixth and seventh centuries with an almost greater amount of cultural activity than occurred either before or after. One may well ask what will remain in the late periods if so many of the sites dated to the Late Classic and Postclassic periods are now to be dated to the Middle Classic? There should be no problem with the idea on a theoretical level. It may be easier to conceive of cultural developments taking place at a relatively even pace during a long time span than to visualize a pattern of intense activity alternating with periods of quiescence. Yet, wherever historical information is available, it is evident that cultures sometimes go through bursts of creativity in phenomenally short periods of time and that an irregular pattern is far more frequent than a uniform rate of development.

Complexity of cultural interaction and a high degree of innovation are characteristic of the Middle Classic period. This is evident in the number of important sites and regions competing for trade and influence, in the wide spread of trading networks, in the great increase in imported goods, in the presence of highly eclectic art styles, in the development of syncretism in iconography, and in innovations in architecture, engineering, and possibly science and mathematics. These traits are not random but interrelated. The increase in commercial contact between regions results not only in the exchange of luxury goods but also in an increased exposure to other artistic traditions, religious cults, social and political systems, and ideologies. The eclectic art styles, in which a single work may show influences from three or four regions, indicate the degree of receptivity to new ideas. Exposure to foreign ideas eventually leads to the reevaluation of local tradition from a more cosmopolitan point of view. Eclecticism is particularly evident in local artistic content in which motifs from different regions are not only juxtaposed but also synthesized. Deities of different regions are equated with one another. The reexamination of local artistic content is accompanied by more systematic representations of the cosmos, which reveal a self-conscious articulation of concepts. The need to deal with so many outside ideas stimulates not only more systematic organization but also willingness to experiment locally with new ideas. Innovation is particularly evident in architecture and engineering; veneer masonry, concrete vaults, aqueducts, causeways, roads, thin walls, large interiors, round walls, and round buildings all make their appearance in the Middle Classic period. After A.D. 600 there appears to be a major change from religious to more secular values. Secularism, which may be defined broadly as a questioning of tradition and a willingness to change and experiment, is a result of increased communication in all levels of society.

Not all regions of Mesoamerica participate equally in these general developments. Teotihuacan appears to be the commercial power that initiated the intense trading patterns that lead to both Central Mexican and Maya preeminence in the first half of the Middle Classic period. By the middle of the sixth century, competition from many centers in the peripheral coastal regions and Yucatan eclipse Teotihuacan influence and cause disruptions in the Maya region. For a century or more the peripheral regions control trade and build flourishing rival centers of eclectic magnificence. Their success undoubtedly lies in their less tradition-bound practices and more expansionist outlook. It is not surprising that most of the innovations in architecture and engineering and many of the syncretistic tendencies occur at these peripheral centers. Their spurt of creativity declines after A.D. 700, when the lowland Maya centers regain their former position, but the Late Classic Maya are deeply influenced by the peripheral cultures both in ideology and material culture. The catalysts in the events of the Middle Classic period appear to be the expansionist cultures of the peripheral regions that wrest commercial power from the more established centers for a brief period, but whose influence transforms all of Mesoamerica into a more competitive and secular society.

Archaeologists have demonstrated the intensity of commercial contact during the Middle Classic period by the finds of imported objects at many sites. Still, much of the evidence for the ideological transformation of Mesoamerican society in this period is in the style and iconography of architecture and artistic traditions. In the following pages I will detail some of the historical events of the Middle Classic period in the light of present archaeological interpretation and analyze the major changes in architecture, monumental art style, and iconography that are pan-Mesoamerican in nature.

Teotihuacan Influence, A.D. 400–550

During the Early Classic period in Mesoamerica, many local centers coexisted without one achieving dominance over the others. After about A.D. 400, however, Teotihuacan influence can be noted in nearly all regions of Mesoamerica. This influence reached its peak between A.D. 400 and 550 and declined considerably thereafter.

The Central Mexican state of Teotihuacan was by far the largest, most efficiently organized society in Mesoamerica in the Early Classic period. From a modest village in 200 B.C., Teotihuacan had grown by A.D. 300 into a capital city of 22½ kilometers square with a population of 45,000. Separated into four quarters by two great avenues meeting at right angles, the city was further subdivided into residential blocks on a grid plan. The density of residential population at Teotihuacan increased to 100,000–200,000 inhabitants during the years A.D. 300–600 (Millon 1973, p. 44). While intensive agricultural practices, such as irrigation, provided the subsistence base for the state, the eventual influence of Teotihuacan probably resulted from its highly developed craft specialization, its trade, and its market system.

Teotihuacan-style artifacts have been found in foreign contexts, but their significance is still a matter of dispute. When the Guatemala highland site of Kaminaljuyu was excavated in 1946, Teotihuacan-style ceramics were discovered in some burials, and the temple bases were found to be imitations of Teotihuacan architecture (Kidder, Jennings, and Shook 1946). The practice of alternating sloping and vertical panels, called *talud* and *tablero*, was introduced into Teotihuacan architecture in the Miccaotli phase, A.D. 200–300, and was standard throughout the city until A.D. 700. While foreign ceramics in a burial can be explained as indications of commercial ties, foreign architectural styles suggest more intensive contact. Kidder, Jennings, and Shook have suggested that Kaminaljuyu became a Teotihuacan colony during the Early Classic Esperanza phase.

Since 1946, Teotihuacan influences on other regions in Mesoamerica have been studied from many different points of view.[3] Influences have been noted on both material and nonmaterial aspects of culture. A distinction is usually made between those artifacts actually made in Teotihuacan and those imitating Teotihuacan types, styles, and iconography. Even non-Teotihuacan-style items are believed to have been traded by Teotihuacan merchants. Of objects made at Teotihuacan, the most widespread are green obsidian projectile points and ceramic tripod vessels decorated in relief or painted in fresco. The examples of Teotihuacan stylistic and iconographic influence may be divided into two categories: local artifacts that are imitations of Teotihuacan objects, such as ceramic tripods, incense burners, or figurines; and Teotihuacan-derived designs that are incorporated into local art works, such as the designs from Teotihuacan vessels found on Maya stelae. Teotihuacan architecture was influential in Mesoamerica in style, planning, and settlement pattern. At a number of sites, Teotihuacan architectural profiles are imitated directly; at many others, the local types of platform articulation are strongly influenced by the Teotihuacan *talud* and *tablero* model. The placement of streets or compounds at right angles to one another and the nucleation of the residential population around an elite center, which occur at a number of sites in the Middle Classic period, are frequently ascribed to Teotihuacan influence.

In the nonmaterial realm, Teotihuacan influences have been recognized in both sociopolitical and religious institutions throughout Mesoamerica. Teotihuacan is thought to have increased social stratification and the power of foreign ruling groups either through conquest and the imposition of its own hierarchic structure (Borhegyi 1965) or through stimulus diffusion (Sanders and Price 1968). The wide spread of Teotihuacan iconography has been interpreted as indicative of the spread of Teotihuacan religious cults. Several authors have suggested that Teotihuacan was the first culture in Mesoamerica to systematize religious belief and to develop a religion of high gods, rather than of deified ancestors, which could appeal to many different populations (Borhegyi 1965, 1971, M. Coe 1966). The Teotihuacan religious cults are thought to have been spread directly by missionaries or indirectly through exposure and voluntary acceptance.

Conclusions regarding the nature of Teotihuacan influence depend on interpretations of the nature of the Teotihuacan state itself. Was Teotihuacan a conquest state with colonies in Guatemala and Veracruz? Or was it a commercial empire with trading networks throughout Mesoamerica, manned by professional merchants, but exercising no political control over foreign centers? Recent interpretations have tended to support the second hypothesis. Teotihuacan influence on different regions appears to vary in kind, a situation not consistent with the possibility of Teotihuacan having a well-integrated empire with colonies. Instead, a pattern of commercial ties of varying intensity is slowly emerging. Webb (1973) has shown that the merchandise for Teotihuacan's long-distance trade essentially consisted of luxury goods—precious stones, feathers, rubber, cacao, ceramics, and textiles—and that in some instances trade developed as a form of ceremonial exchange. Some aspects of Teotihuacan influence are still difficult to explain: e.g., if there was no Teotihuacan empire, why were the gods of Teotihuacan, many of them warrior gods or deity images carried by warrior figures, represented in many parts of Mesoamerica during the sixth century?

The dates of Teotihuacan contact with the different regions of Mesoamerica vary considerably. That some regions closer to Teotihuacan should have established trading contacts quite early is hardly surprising. Oaxaca and Veracruz, for example had intensive trading relationships with Teotihuacan by A.D. 300, while the Maya area remained more isolated until the end of the fourth century. Relative proximity, however, may not be the only factor to account for the timing of noticeable influence, since certain areas, such as Chalchihuites in the far north, a source of important raw materials, was reached as early as A.D. 300. In general, however, the impact of Teotihuacan culture culminated between A.D. 400 and 550 and declined afterwards.

Several recent interpretations of the rise of Maya civilization in the Early Classic period credit Teotihuacan with providing an outside stimulus and example (Sanders and Price 19678; Webb 1973). Prior to the time of obvious Teotihuacan influence, the Early Classic centers of the Guatemala highlands, Peten lowlands, and Yucatan were small, elite centers consisting of temples and palaces, with the populations living in scattered hamlets. Most examples of Teotihuacan influence have dates subsequent to A.D. 400, but recent excavations at Altun Ha, British Honduras (Pendergast 1971) and Becan, Mexico (Ball 1974a) have unearthed caches containing Teotihuacan-type obsidian in third-century contexts.

Greater nucleation of the population, more intensive trade, and more ambitious building programs accompany Teotihuacan commercial contacts in the Maya area. The site of Kaminaljuyu in the Guatemala highlands undergoes a rapid increase in size and density between A.D. 400 and 600. Sanders suggests that Teotihuacan merchants may have established trading wards, intermarried with the elite of Kaminaljuyu, and practiced their own religious cults. The Kaminaljuyu population was resettled around a new civic center built in part in Teotihuacan style in about A.D. 550. By that year, however, the tombs contain fewer objects imported from Teotihuacan; in fact, direct Teotihuacan contacts appear to have diminished. Sanders believes that the conquest of Kaminaljuyu by a Teotihuacan merchant group was not an example of colonization, but rather a private undertaking. Soon after Teotihuacan contacts cease, Kaminaljuyu also declines in importance.

Teotihuacan contacts with the lowland Maya of the Peten may have been through Kaminaljuyu rather than direct. The Early Classic florescence of sites such as Tikal and Uaxactun is associated with trading relationships with the highland regions of Mesoamerica. At Tikal, the peak of activity in the Early Classic period occurs between A.D. 380 and 480. Coggins (n.d.) suggests that the second and third rulers of Tikal—"Curl Nose" (d. 426) and "Stormy Sky" (d. 457)—came from a Kaminaljuyu family with strong Teotihuacan connections. The ties to Teotihuacan were strongest during the reign of Curl Nose. Between A.D. 457 and 681 there is no evidence of Teotihuacan contacts. Teotihuacan iconographic traits are again found during the reign of Ruler A—"Sky Rain" (accession A.D. 681) a descendent of Stormy Sky, who establishes a Teotihuacan-Maya dynasty at Tikal.

The Peten Maya area is not a region rich in natural resources or raw materials for which other areas would compete, and even basic necessities, such as stones for grinding corn, often had to be imported. The area is mostly tropical forest, cultivated by the rotating field system, which encourages scattered settlement patterns. Although ridged fields have been found in the Maya area, it is not yet known how extensive the practice of this form of intensive agriculture was. The tropical forest is unsuited to irrigation agriculture. As has been pointed out, the Peten Maya had neither the subsistence base nor the control over desirable raw materials for trade that would stimulate great population concentration, specialization, and state development (Rathje 1971). The change of the minor Peten centers into nearly urban civilizations during the fifth century is attributed by Rathje to their participation in a pan-Mesoamerican trade in elite goods that was to a large extent in the hands of Teotihuacan merchants. In return for the exotic and necessary goods, the Maya could trade fine arts and crafts and provide teachers in intellectual fields such as writing and astronomy. Teotihuacan had no writing and calendar systems comparable to those of the Maya and did not adopt the Maya systems. But the residents of Teotihuacan were interested in the Maya systems, as is evidenced by the presence of Maya-style inscription fragments from mural paintings at Teotihuacan (Villagra 1952).

Teotihuacan contacts with the Peten Maya are evident in a number of Teotihuacan-style artifacts found in burials and in Teotihuacan motifs on Tikal and Uaxactun works of art. There are, however, no examples of Teotihuacan-style buildings, and no indication that Teotihuacan groups ever politically controlled the Peten. Nevertheless, the fate of the Peten Maya centers seems to have been bound up with the commercial power of Teotihuacan, since, after the decline of Teotihuacan, significant changes occurred in the Peten Maya area. At the end of the sixth century, there was a hiatus in the erection of dated monuments at many lowland sites, and massive fortifications were maintained both at Tikal and at Becan—a recently excavated site—indicating an increase in warfare and in large-scale measures taken for self-protection (Ball 1974a, p. 2).

The lowland centers between the Maya and Teotihuacan, on the Gulf coast of Mexico and the Pacific coast of Guatemala, also experienced a period of expansion, in part as a result of Teotihuacan contacts in the fifth century. Because of their important local natural resources and initiative, however, they were to become commercial rivals of Teotihuacan. This region, which Parsons has labeled the Peripheral Coastal Lowlands, lies between the two major cultural areas. Its inhabitants were, therefore, in a good position to be middlemen in trade. The area has a number of highly desirable natural resources, among them rubber and cacao. Rubber was used for making the ball for the Mesoamerican ball game, which was probably invented in the Peripheral Coastal Lowlands and which spread during the Middle Classic period to many other parts of Mesoamerica. More important than rubber, which had primarily a ceremonial function, cacao was used in Mesoamerica both for making a beverage and as a form of currency. Its latter use could have made cacao an especially important item of trade. Cacao is best cultivated in soil with good drainage and high annual rainfall, conditions that are present in the Peripheral Coastal Lowlands. Thus, this area was in a position to control an extremely important trade resource in Mesoamerica, even though it may not have been the first to distribute the crop.

In the fourth and fifth centuries, however, none of the Peripheral Coastal Lowlands sites could rival Teotihuacan in size and elaboration, and Teotihuacan influences were strong throughout the region. A Teotihuacan structure with a *talud* and *tablero* platform has been found at Matacapan (M. Coe 1965, p. 704), a Veracruz site that may have had commercial ties with Teotihuacan groups that were as close as those of Kaminaljuyu. Close commercial contacts between Veracruz and Teotihuacan are also indicated by the many Veracruz-style objects that have been found at Teotihuacan, dating from the Tlamimilolpa through the Xolalpan phases, A.D. 300–600. Nor have Veracruz-style objects been restricted to Teotihuacan. Artifacts such as mirrors, ball game paraphernalia, and classic Veracruz scroll designs have been found in many parts of Mesoamerica, from Queretaro in the north (Ekholm 1945) to Costa Rica in the south (Stone and Balser 1965). These objects are usually thought to have been spread by Teotihuacan merchants who picked up Veracruz items on their travels (Borhegyi 1965).

This concept goes back to old ideas of the Teotihucan population's supposed migration south to Guatemala and El Salvador after the fall of Teotihuacan in A.D. 500. In an ambitious attempt to interpret the archaeological excavations of the Classic period in relation to sixteenth-century ethnohistoric accounts, Jimenez Moreno has suggested that the Pipil population known from Guatemalan ethnohistoric sources are the descendants of the sixth-century Teotihuacan migrants (1966, p. 65). These migrants were believed to have settled first in Veracruz, where they became "Tajinized," and to have subsequently migrated to the Guatemala highlands, Pacific Slope, and as far as Central America and possibly even Colombia and Ecuador. Borhegyi (1965) has further suggested that "Tajinized-Teotihuacan-Pipil" migrants brought the Veracruz ball game and its paraphernalia to Guatemala. Teotihuacan is now known to have lasted as a major center at least until A.D. 750, so theories postulating large-scale migrations of Teotihuacan refugees to account for Teotihuacan influences in the fifth and sixth centuries are no longer accepted. Instead, commercial contacts are suggested; but Veracruz influences are still thought to have been carried through Teotihuacan merchants (Parsons 1969).

The above interpretation is questionable for a number of reasons. First, the strong influence of Veracruz art style on Teotihuacan sculpture, mural painting, and pottery between A.D. 300 and 500 may not be merely a sign of aesthetic appreciation of the style itself, but could also indicate the prestige of contemporary Veracruz centers. Veracruz influences are far more widespread in Teotihuacan art than are either Maya or Oaxaca influences. Second, it seems more likely that the ball game and its paraphernalia were spread from Veracruz, where the cult was widespread, than by Teotihuacan groups who never emphasized the cult despite intensive exposure to it. (To assume that Teotihuacan merchants had become "Tajinized" is to beg the question of their cultural affiliation.) Third, even if Teotihuacan initiated or controlled long-distance trade for a time, in the absence of political control, commercial competition was bound to emerge. The break in Teotihuacan relations with the Maya highland area around A.D. 550 probably indicates changes in trade routes, in traded objects, or in trading agents, which could have occurred if Teotihuacan had experienced competition ready to take over. Some Veracruz-style objects may have been carried by Teotihuacan traders, but they were probably mostly distributed concurrently by Veracruz traders. The Classic period sites in

Veracruz have not been as extensively excavated as either Teotihuacan or Kaminaljuyu, and less is known about their influence on the rest of Mesoamerica. The wide spread of Veracruz art style and of Veracruz ball game paraphernalia suggests that some Veracruz centers may have been nearly as important commercially as Teotihuacan.

Parsons shows that the northern area of the Peripheral Coastal Lowlands, or Veracruz, was influential in the south between A.D. 400 and 550. The major building activity of Cerro de las Mesas in Veracruz coincides with the fifth- and sixth- century florescence of Teotihuacan and the Peten.[4] Widespread commercial contacts are evident from the discovery of a cache of nearly 800 objects in a major Early Classic mound (M. Coe 1965, p. 702). In that offering, Teotihuacan-style cylinder tripods, Olmec jade heirlooms, and Oaxaca- and Maya-style carvings were found side by side. While Cerro de las Mesas declines after A.D. 550, other Veracruz centers, such as El Tajin, increase in importance.

The Classic development of the southern segment of the Peripheral Coastal Lowlands also coincides with Teotihuacan influences in the fifth century. Thousands of Teotihuacan-inspired cylinder tripods have been found in the Escuintla area near major Classic period sites that still need excavation. Teotihuacan influences are evident in art style and iconography at Escuintla, but they are always combined with local features. Veracruz influences are equally strong, as suggested by fragments of yokes, *hachas,* and pyrite mirrors and by a general preoccupation with the ball game theme. After the Guatemala highland center of Kaminaljuyu declines in importance, Bilbao emerges as the leading center in Guatemala. Most of the architecture and sculpture at Bilbao dates from the fifth to the eighth centuries. Thus, the Peripheral Coastal Lowland sites are stimulated by a period of Teotihuacan and Veracruz trade contact, but their fates are more independent of Teotihuacan, and several of them become major commercial centers as the power of Teotihuacan contracts in the sixth century.

The highland Oaxaca valleys are neither as large nor as ecologically favorable as the valleys of the Central Mexican area, and this region has never supported states comparable to those of Central Mexico. Since the important Peripheral Coastal Lowland trade routes connecting northern and southern Mesoamerica bypass the mountainous

Oaxaca region, Oaxaca is somewhat isolated from other centers. Monte Alban was an innovating center during periods I and II; in period III it was isolationist and removed from the eclectic trends evident elsewhere in Mesoamerica. Teotihuacan contact with the Oaxaca area appears to have been one of stimulus without political control. The greatest building activity at Monte Alban, the largest tombs, and the finest sculptures date from the end of period IIIa and the beginning of IIIb (A.D. 300–500), a period coeval with Teotihuacan contact. We know from the recent Teotihuacan mapping survey that Monte Alban had unusually close connections with Teotihuacan. A Monte Alban residential section has been discovered in the western part of Teotihuacan (Millon 1973; pp. 40–43), and a Monte Alban urn of the period of transition from II to IIIa (A.D. 200–300) was excavated in this area. Teotihuacan influence on Monte Alban is of greater scope and intensity than Oaxaca influence on Teotihuacan. Teotihuacan influences are seen in Monte Alban architectural profiles, terra-cotta urns, and mural paintings. Very few Teotihuacan objects have been found imported to Monte Alban. The decline of Monte Alban begins around A.D. 600 and culminates in its abandonment after A.D. 700. A similar decline is not evident at all Oaxaca centers, since a number of Classic period sites, such as Lambityeco in the south and Huayuapan in the north, continue to grow during the seventh and eighth centuries. But these sites are in contact with the new centers of influence in Veracruz and Yucatan, rather than with Teotihuacan.

The Yucatan Maya region has not been discussed so far because of problems in both cultural and temporal classification. Certain characteristics found in Yucatan, such as the use of masonry vaults, relate this region to the Classic Maya, while other traits, such as architectural mosaic decoration, link it with the intermediate area—the Peripheral Coastal Lowlands and Oaxaca. Parsons (1969) considers the Yucatan area to be a subarea area of the Peripheral Coastal Lowlands, with which the Yucatan centers had intense commercial contacts during the latter part of the Classic period. But Yucatan's cultural relationships cannot be determined until there is greater agreement on its temporal development. Most Mesoamericanists place the Puuc and related styles contemporary with the Late Classic period and the Toltec Chichen style contemporary with the Postclassic Toltec. Parsons suggests that both styles have their beginnings in the seventh century. E. W. Andrews IV (1965b), however, believes that even the Puuc development does not occur until the end of the Late Classic and Early Postclassic. The more usual Late Classic date for the Puuc will be accepted here, and a Late Classic date for Toltec Chichen will be discussed as a possibility.

Yucatan was of marginal importance during the Preclassic and Early Classic periods in Mesoamerica. From the Late Classic to the Postclassic periods, on the other hand, the region was densely populated and involved in both maritime and overland trade. One of its natural resources traded was salt from the sea. A major item of trade during the Early Classic period appears to have been shells, such as *strombus gigas,* which are found in the Caribbean Sea. These were used in ceremonial contexts at Teotihuacan and were exported to the Guatemala highlands and as far as Nayarit in Western Mexico. Despite the evidence of a trading relationship, primarily in shells, Yucatan does not appear to have been strongly influenced by Teotihuacan culture. Although one structure at Ake and another at Dzibilchaltun have Teotihuacan-type *taluds* and *tableros* (Marquina 1941), no Teotihuacan influence has yet been noted in Yucatan ceramics and terra-cottas. Yucatan did have strong connections with the Peten Maya during the Early Classic period; they are evidenced by the presence of Peten trade wares in Yucatan and the diffusion of both sculptural and architectural styles. The hiatus, evident in the erection of monuments in the Peten, is not present in Yucatan, where many monuments were erected during the second half of the sixth and many during the seventh century. Despite considerable Peten influence, the Yucatan centers do not appear to have been politically or commercially dependent on the fortunes of the Peten and continued to flourish during this period. By the beginning of the eighth century, the direction of influence appears to have been reversed, with Yucatan exerting its influence over the lowland Maya, as can be seen from Yucatan-style inscriptions at sites such as Yaxchilan.

The far north and west of Mesoamerica remained largely unaffected by major cultural developments in the south until the Classic period. Then, however, southern influences became very strong in the states of Zacatecas and Durango and reached as far as the American Southwest (Kelley 1971; p. 801).[5] Unlike southern Mesoamerica, the mountainous interior valleys of Zacatecas and Durango and the coast of Sinaloa were inhabited by village populations without elite centers, until the Early Classic period. The first such centers were placed in defensible locations and built in southern architectural styles during the Classic period, suggesting that they were established by, or in response to, invading colonists from the south. Kelley suggests that the southerners colonized the area in order to control and work mines for semiprecious stones, such as turquoise and jadeite. Excavations at the site of Alta Vista in the Chalchihuites area have shown two periods of contact with the south: first, when the site was established during the Canutillo phase (A.D. 1–250), at which time a ball court was constructed; and second, the Alta Vista phase (A.D. 250–500), when another group of southerners, whom Kelley tentatively identifies as Teotihuacan in origin, invaded the area. The ground plans for the stone and adobe temples and courts at the site seem to have derived their inspiration from Teotihuacan town-planning principles. Similarly, the cloisonné-decorated pottery of Alta Vista has technical parallels in certain fresco-decorated Teotihuacan vessels. Alta Vista and its mines were abandoned around A.D. 500, and a portion of the population moved to the northwest Durango sites, such as Schroeder, which remained active throughout the Late Classic and Early Postclassic periods. Kelley (1971; p. 793) has demonstrated that meaningful southern influence on the American Southwest occurred only after the end of the Alta Vista phase.

Information from the Chalchihuites area of the far north shows that during the Classic period, southern influences arrived first with a group of people who brought with them the ball game and ball-game-related architecture, most likely not of Teotihuacan origin. Around A.D. 300, this group was succeeded by invaders, possibly from Teotihuacan, who retained their ascendancy until around A.D. 500. The timing of the decline of the site indicates Alta Vista's special relationship with Teotihuacan, since this decline is contemporary with the decline of Teotihuacan influences elsewhere in Mesoamerica. As in the Peripheral Coastal Lowlands, the abandonment of this Teotihuacan-influenced site was not a consequence of the decline of the area as a whole, and other centers flourished even after A.D. 550.

As some foregoing examples indicate, Teotihuacan played an important role throughout Mesoamerica in the fifth and sixth centuries. Because of its size, organization, and commercial needs, that state was able to control long-distance trade routes for about a century and a half. These trade routes were not necessarily initiated by Teotihuacan, and evidence from the far north and the valley of Mexico indicates that Teotihuacan may have taken over some trade routes previously established by other cultures, particularly those from the Peripheral Coastal Lowlands. Most Teotihuacan contact seems to have consisted of trade with local elite groups, an activity that could range from ceremonial gift exchange to more strictly commercial endeavors. In some areas, such as the far north, Teotihuacan may also have established colonies. The dispute over whether Teotihuacan exerted its influence through trade or conquest may therefore be moot. In any event, Teotihuacan contact tended to increase regional intercommunication and consequently to enhance the wealth and effect the cultural florescence of some of the centers located along the long-distance trade routes. The diffusion of Veracruz cultural elements alongside those of Teotihuacan by the sixth century indicates that this region was already competing with Teotihuacan. This competition may have been partially responsible for the later decline of Teotihuacan influence.

It is conceivable that Teotihuacan started out controlling trade routes by peaceful means, such as alliances and intermarriages with local rulers, activities that assured benefits to both sides. The presence of martial gods and warrior themes on Teotihuacan-influenced art around A.D. 500, however, suggests that, whether or not there was a desire to colonize a large area, some military effort may have been needed to protect Teotihuacan's "sphere of influence" from rival groups. By A.D. 550, Teotihuacan and the centers commercially allied with it had entered a period of disruption and decline. The nature of the disruption indicates that it probably involved military defeats but defeats that did not lead to subjugation by any other single center. Military defeats are suggested because of the abruptness of the termination of certain activities, such as the erection of stelae in the Maya area, and by the concurrent decline or abandonment of a number of separate centers throughout Mesoamerica between A.D. 500 and 550.

Because no one site seems to have benefited from the decline of Teotihuacan, it is possible that Teotihuacan was defeated either by a temporary alliance of several groups or simply as a result of having become overextended along too many fronts. While there were population shifts around A.D. 550 in almost all areas of Mesoamerica, there is no evidence of massive depopulation comparable to the lowland Maya decline after A.D. 800 Despite a major loss in its outside prestige, Teotihuacan continued to increase in population and to prosper locally for more than another century. This suggests that rivals could disrupt the Teotihuacan commercial monopoly, but that they could not and did not wish to set up either a political or commercial empire in its place.

The disturbance at the end of the sixth and beginning of the seventh centuries in the Maya area foreshadows the collapse of Maya civilization in the tenth century (Willey 1974). It is quite conceivable that the political and economic causes of the earlier hiatus and collapse were similar. Webb (1973) has suggested that the decline of the Maya resulted from a change in trade patterns: secular goods gradually replaced exotic and ritual goods in long-distance trade, and, in the exchange of practical items, ease of transport and cost became more significant than they had been in ceremonial exchange. According to this theory, the lowland Maya region was progressively bypassed, and economic power accumulated in the states on its peripheries. Webb has attributed the sudden collapse of the Maya cities to armed conflict with those peripheral sites. A similar sequence of events could have taken place on a smaller scale during the late sixth and early seventh centuries. The rise of peripheral centers during these centuries is evidence of a changing network of trade routes, which occurred to the detriment of old, established centers such as Teotihuacan and Tikal. Willey (1974) has suggested that the old, established centers of the early Middle Classic period probably had highly centralized political structures that were inflexible in the face of changing trade conditions and left too many newer centers out of their exclusive trading relationships. Two major results of the hiatus disturbances were that trade routes shifted from core to peripheral areas, and that many more centers became actively involved in trade.

The Rise of Peripheral Centers,
A.D. 550–700

During the second half of the Middle Classic period, Teotihuacan clearly lost its dominant position in Mesoamerica and became one of numerous rival cities. Many new eclectic centers grew up—particularly on the peripheries of the Early Classic centers—such as Xochicalco in Morelos, Palenque in Chiapas, and Copan in Honduras. The most expansive and innovative area in Mesoamerica at this time was the region composed of the Gulf Coast and Yucatan, both of which exerted considerable influence throughout Mesoamerica, even beyond the boundaries of Teotihuacan influence. It was at this time, for example, that certain aspects of Mesoamerican culture were introduced into the American Southwest and possibly the Caribbean.

Teotihuacan remained a flourishing center during the second half of the Middle Classic period. Important complexes, such as the Palace of the Butterflies, were erected during the Metepec phase (A.D. 650–750). Teotihuacan trading relationships continued to prosper in some areas; there is evidence of trade with Oaxaca and Puebla during this period. On the other hand, the intensification of contacts with Tajin in Veracruz and the Yucatan indicates the increasingly prominent role of these areas in the seventh century (Rattray n.d.). Signs of change at Teotihuacan are manifested by a decrease in the number of ceremonial vessels and incense burners and by less exacting standards of craftsmanship. The presence of a number of Metepec phase Teotihuacan sites outside Teotihuacan, such as Azcapotzalco, probably reflect a weakening of Teotihuacan centralization and political authority. Recently, Millon has expressed the view that Teotihuacan did not decline seriously prior to its collapse.* The burning of the city, around A.D. 750, was not random, but restricted to important ceremonial areas, which indicates that it was done by insiders rather than invaders unfamiliar with the city. Whatever crisis overtook Teotihuacan around A.D. 750, it was of such magnitude that the city never recovered.

Three Central Mexican sites peripheral to Teotihuacan became im-

*Rene F. Millon 1974: personal communication.

portant in the seventh century: Cholula in Puebla, Xochicalco in Morelos, and Tula in Hidalgo. In many ways the history of Cholula parallels that of Teotihuacan. Cholula was also founded during the Preclassic period and had a time of cultural florescence between A.D. 400 and 700, but it was abandoned—in part the result of heavy rains and floods—somewhat earlier than Teotihuacan, in A.D. 700 (Dumond and Muller 1972). Teotihuacan influences were strong in Cholula architecture, painting, and ceramics between A.D. 200 and 500. Between A.D. 500 and 700 Cholula became less associated with Teotihuacan and more an eclectic center strongly influenced by Veracruz and Oaxaca (Muller 1973). It established an especially close relationship with Veracruz, as a number of monumental stelae ornamented with Classic Veracruz-style scroll borders erected at this time indicate.[6]

The major occupation of Xochicalco, a site built on a hilltop, probably for security reasons, dates from the latter part of the sixth through the seventh centuries, when the city had trading relationships with Veracruz, Oaxaca, and the Maya area. A single excavated offering at the site included stone yokes, a Maya-style jade, a Teotihuacan-style figurine, and a Xochicalco-style relief (Saenz 1964). Seventh-century eclecticism is particularly evident in Xochicalco art, in which Teotihuacan, Monte Alban, Piedras Negras, and Veracruz elements are synthesized. Xochicalco's rise was probably due to its favorable position to control trade routes between southern Mesoamerica and the valley of Mexico and to its independence from Teotihuacan. After major changes in trade routes and political alignments in A.D. 700, Xochicalco declined, and by the end of the Classic period, it had ceased to be a major center.

The abandonment of Teotihuacan and Cholula and the decline of Xochicalco after A.D. 700 may be related in part to the growth of a new major center in Central Mexico, Tula in Hidalgo. Tula reached its cultural climax during the Early Postclassic period, but a recently excavated early temple complex, Tula Chico, was found to contain both Metepec- and Coyotlatelco-related pottery. According to Matos, the Tula ceremonial center was begun between A.D. 650 and 750. In the late Middle Classic period, Tula was probably one of several emerging Central Mexican centers that sought to control trade and natural resources at the expense of Teotihuacan. Among the important natural resources in the Tula area were the obsidian mines of Pachuca, which originally had been exploited by Teotihuacan.

There is evidence of warfare and strife in Central Mexico throughout the late Middle Classic period. Old, established centers, such as Teotihuacan and Cholula, were abandoned, and new centers were built in defensive locations. Cerro Zapotecas, a hilltop site in Cholula, was first occupied as a place of refuge during the troubled seventh century (Mountjoy n.d.). Both Xochicalco and the ceremonial center of Tula were built on defensible hilltop positions.

The historical significance of the late sixth and early seventh centuries in the Maya area is still not well understood. It was at this time that the central Peten sites lost their position of primacy and a number of peripheral Maya sites first became major centers. The pattern noted for Central Mexico—the decline of the major Early Classic centers and the growth of peripheral centers—was thus repeated in the Maya area. During the Early Classic period, the population in the Peten was larger than in the peripheral regions. During the temporary decline of the Peten, the peripheral regions were repopulated, and a number of new centers emerged (Molloy and Rathje 1974). As in Central Mexico, some of the new centers were most influential only during the unsettled seventh century. Unlike Teotihuacan, the central Peten sites revive in the eighth century and survive for another 200 years.

After a late sixth-century hiatus, another great phase of prosperity began at Tikal around A.D. 700: dated stelae were again carved; several major temple pyramids—such as Temples I and II— were built; and the major causeways were begun. The preceding period, between A.D. 550 and 700, is known mainly from ceramic remains and a few building projects, including three foreign-style structures, 5D-43, 6E-144, and 5C-53 (W. Coe 1965, p. 40). These platforms were at first thought to be Teotihuacanoid in style, since their profiles are articulated by a variation of panels and slopes. In view of the break in relations with Teotihuacan by the middle of the fifth century, however, these seventh-century platforms are not likely to have been built by Teotihuacan groups. And the structures are not in pure Teotihuacan style. The panels were finished with flaring cornices, a molding not used at Teotihuacan but present in Oaxaca and Veracruz as early as the seventh century. The axial placement of 5D-43 across from the center line of a ball court at Tikal, and the presence on 5D-43 of graffiti representing the ball game, suggest a functional and symbolic relationship between these two buildings, a feature not characteristic of Teotihuacan plans, where ball courts are unknown. Both the moldings and emphasis on the ball court are Gulf coast characteristics and suggest either the presence of non-Maya foreigners or the local acceptance of foreign cults. The resurgence of building activity after A.D. 700 marks the cessation of foreign influences and a revival of local Maya traditions. Molloy and Rathje (1974) suggest that Tikal recaptured its leading position through warfare and conquest and maintained its power because of the respect in which its old dynastic lineage was held. The rulers of the new centers wished to acquire status by marrying into the royal families of the Peten.

Prosperity returned to Tikal under Ruler A (accession A.D. 681, d. 733) who claimed to be the descendant of Stormy Sky, his family having lived in exile during the reigns of several usurpers and a time of troubles at Tikal (Coggins n.d.). Ruler A's ancestry and insignia combine Maya and Teotihuacan traits in emulation of Stormy Sky (Kubler 1976; Miller 1976). There are, however, other elements in the art associated with Ruler A that are close to Piedras Negras and Dos Pilas, both newer centers in the west. With his ambitious building projects, Ruler A is very similar to the rulers of the peripheral Maya centers who come into their own during the seventh century, and he had the extra benefit of being able to claim an ancient hereditary right to effect these projects. Ruler A and his son, Ruler B, are responsible for at least three of the largest pyramid temples (Temples I, II, IV) and for the monumental causeways that link the scattered building complexes of Tikal.

A number of Maya sites outside the Peten first gained prominence during the seventh century. The history of three sites, Palenque, Piedras Negras, and Copan, illustrate this development. At Palenque, a site located near the western periphery of the Maya region, the major sculptural and architectural undertakings date from A.D. 600 to 700. Recent studies of the Palenque inscriptions indicate that two rulers were responsible for the site's dramatic rise. Lord Pacal reigned for sixty-eight years and was buried in the crypt of the Temple of the Inscriptions, which is dated A.D. 683. Lord Chan Bahlum reigned

eighteen years and in A.D. 692 had his accession commemorated by the building of a group of three temples, the Temples of the Sun, Cross, and Foliated Cross (Mathews and Schele 1974). The eighth-century rulers of Palenque did not erect monuments of comparable magnitude.

Palenque is often noted for the grace and beauty of its architecture and sculpture, which were influential at a number of lowland Maya sites. Novel both in style and iconography, Palenque art is not directly derived from Peten Maya traditions. Palenque is also unusual among Maya centers because of the number of its practical achievements in architecture and engineering: an aqueduct, bridge, and a several-story tower have been found at the site. In addition, Palenque's architects used thinner walls and more slender supporting pillars to create greater interior spaces. In the light of the slight degree of emphasis Mesoamerican cultures generally placed on practical, technological innovations, the architecture of seventh-century Palenque stands out as being remarkably innovative and experimental.

Piedras Negras, a city located in the Usumacinta valley, also became important during the late sixth and early seventh centuries. The early art of Piedras Negras was eclectic, and many stylistic and iconographic elements had non-Maya sources or parallels. Besides Peten and Palenque traits, Piedras Negras art and architecture had similarities to the art of Xochicalco, Cotzumalhuapa, and Teotihuacan (Parsons 1969, p. 168). The themes on seventh-century Piedras Negras sculpture frequently deal with warriors and warfare, a preoccupation that may have reflected the unsettled conditions of the period.

Copan, a city on the banks of the Motagua River in Honduras, also rose to prominence during the seventh-century (Robicsek 1972, pp. 172–73). The first center in the area may have been built as early as the fifth century, but it was subsequently abandoned. During the late sixth and early seventh centuries, several minor centers competed with one another for supremacy, but by the middle of the seventh century, the Copan ceremonial center had emerged at the expense of the others. The art of seventh-century Copan, like that of Piedras Negras, is strongly eclectic. Some seventh-century monuments, such as Stela 6, include iconographic details that could be of Central Mexican derivation. Although both Copan and Piedras Negras reached their cultural peak in the eighth century, this development had its beginnings in the seventh century.

In the Yucatan Maya region, the seventh century was a period of cultural vitality. At least three very different major cultural areas developed concurrently: the eastern region centered around Coba; the western or Puuc region centered around Uxmal; and the central region centered on Chichen Itza. The architecture and sculpture of Coba, a large site situated near four lakes, appears to have been derived from the Early Classic Peten Maya, but Coba achieved its greatest importance during and after the hiatus in the Peten. Nearly thirty stelae were erected at Coba during the seventh century (Marquina 1964, p. 792). Coba was the center of sixteen causeways or *sacbe*, which link minor sites with the major centers. One causeway, 62.3 miles long, connected Coba with Yaxuna, a site near Chichen Itza. Shorter *sacbe* are also frequent in the central and western regions of Yucatan. Although these roads are usually thought to have had a ceremonial significance, their potential commercial and political uses should not be underestimated.

The sites of the Puuc region in western Yucatan, such as Uxmal, Labna, and Sayil, which are generally better known archaeologically than Coba and the east, go back to the sixth and seventh centuries (Foncerrada de Molina 1965, p. 48).[7] Puuc architecture is characterized by major innovations in construction and ornamentation, such as veneer masonry over a concrete core and stone mosaic decoration. The origin of stone mosaic decoration, found in a seventh-century context in Oaxaca and later in Veracruz, is not known, although the richness and variety of forms found in Yucatan during the Middle Classic period suggest that Yucatan may be its source. According to Sharp, the idea of assembling a design from mass-produced elements, as is the case in stone mosaic ornamentation, may have been inspired by Teotihuacan, where *incensarios* were ornamented by *adornos* made in molds. Early Puuc-style structures, however, also have eclectic and heterogeneous ornaments. For example, in the first stage of the Temple of the Magician at Uxmal, some of the reliefs have lowland Maya parallels, some of the deity faces suggest Central Mexican sources, and a number of mosaic patterns are shared with Oaxaca. The zenith of Puuc architecture came during the eighth century, when many of these heterogeneous and eclectic characteristics disappeared and stone mosaic design was purified and elaborated. Ceramic finds indicate that the Puuc region had significant commercial ties with the Peten until A.D. 700. After that time, the Peten trade wares were rarely found in the north (Brainerd 1956). In other words, during the seventh century, the Puuc centers were characterized by widespread eclectic influences as well as by local innovation and experimentation.

The third major region of Yucatan was the central area in which the largest center was Chichen Itza. The Puuc-style structures of Chichen are usually thought to be Classic in date, while the Toltec-style structures are believed to be Postclassic. A Classic date for some of the Toltec-style buildings, however, is by no means improbable: Toltec-style structures underlie some Puuc-style buildings, and they share stylistic and iconographic traits with seventh-century Puuc designs and with Middle Classic Cotzumalhuapa and Veracruz designs (Parsons 1969, pp. 172–84; Cohodas n.d.). If some Toltec Chichen structures were built in the seventh century, then at least three very different eclectic cultures were flourishing in Yucatan at the same time.

The Peripheral Coastal Lowland centers became even more eclectic in the second half of the Middle Classic period. The international aspect of their cultural traditions is particularly evident in ceramic works from the Escuintla region of the Pacific Slope of Guatemala. The archaeological context of most of these vessels is unknown, but a sixth- to seventh-century date is likely on the basis of cross dating with the foreign designs. Hellmuth has shown that motifs derived from Monte Alban, Teotihuacan, Veracruz, and Yucatan are often found side by side on both Escuintla incense burners and tripod vessels. The most important Pacific Slope centers were Bilbao in the south and Tonala in the north. The predominant iconographic theme on Escuintla vessels, and Bilbao and Tonala sculptures is the ceremonial ball game, the major religious cult of the Peripheral Coastal Lowlands. El Tajin, a site in Veracruz comparable in size and complexity to the major Early Classic sites, first emerges during the seventh century. Although the foundation of the site goes back to the Early Classic period, most of its architecture and sculpture date from A.D. 600–900 (Garcia Payon 1971, pp. 505–42). So far, there is little agreement on the sequence of buildings at the site, so that early and late characteristics are difficult to distinguish. A mixture of lowland Maya, Oaxaca, Pacific Coast, and Yucatan characteristics, Tajin-style architecture and sculpture are among the most eclectic in Mesoamerica. Flaring cornices and stone mosaics are Tajin characteristics shared with Oaxaca and the Puuc region, while Tajin narrative relief sculpture is similar to the art of Bilbao and Chichen Itza.

In Oaxaca, Monte Alban slowly declined and was eventually abandoned during the late Middle Classic period. Here too, the seventh century marked the emergence of peripheral centers, such as Lambityeco in the south, which departed significantly from the Classic Monte Alban traditions and had no Teotihuacan relationships. The architecture at Lambityeco is ornamented with stone mosaic comparable to Puuc architecture. The presence of trade relations with the Gulf coast and Yucatan area is indicated by finds of Fine Orange pottery and local imitations of Maya pottery, such as Puuc slate wares. Paddock has given the name Nuine to the artistic tradition of northern Oaxaca during the Middle Classic Period, in which Oaxaca, Veracruz, and Teotihuacan stylistic elements are combined (1966a pp. 176–200). It is an eclectic style comparable to that of Xochicalco in Morelos. Very little excavation has been undertaken in the area, but C$_{14}$ dates and ceramic parallels suggest a Middle Classic date. All of this evidence seems to indicate that the dominant foreign influences on both southern and northern Oaxaca during the second half of the Middle Classic period originated in the Gulf Coast and Yucatan regions.

According to Kelley (1971, p. 784), a major cultural change occurred in the far north of Mesoamerica after A.D. 550. He has noted that during this period some of the population of Alta Vista moved further north, to the Schroeder site. Architecturally, the Schroeder site is quite different from Alta Vista. A ball court and a circular platform are important structures at Schroeder that have no parallels at Alta Vista. Kelley has suggested that Mesoamerican influences on the Hohokam area of the American Southwest first began during the second half of the Middle Classic period, during the local Ayala phase (A.D. 550–700). These influences include the ball game, the ball court with floor markers, rubber balls, and pyrite mosaic mirrors.

Throughout the far north as well as on the western peripheries of Mesoamerica, Veracruz and Xochicalco cultural traits were very strong during the first half of the Late Classic period. Veracruz and Xochicalco influences were stronger and more widespread in this period than Teotihuacan influences had been in the previous centuries. Many of the sites of the far north have not been sufficiently explored and dated. Although many are thought to date from the Toltec or Postclassic periods, there is little doubt of the importance of the Classic occupation of the area, which is revealed wherever there has been intensive excavation. For example, the site of La Quemada, located near Alta Vista is usually thought to have Toltec affiliations (Marquina 1964, pp. 243–49), even though most of the architecture's characteristics have Classic prototypes. Particularly striking are the thirteen raised causeways connecting building groups at La Quemada, which are similar to the causeways of Xochicalco and the Puuc area. Little is known of the late Middle Classic period in the Michoacan region, but finds there of several sculptures in a style similar to that of Xochicalco and Classic Veracruz indicate that the area was in close contact with southern Mesoamerica (Chadwick 1971, p. 678).[8]

Although Mesoamerican influences in the Caribbean are not as precisely dated as those in the American Southwest, there is a strong possibility that Mesoamerican contacts with both areas occurred at about the same time. Ball courts and ball-game-related objects similar to yokes have been found in Puerto Rico and other Caribbean islands (Ekholm 1961).[9] The function, style, and iconography of these objects are related to Gulf coast traditions of the Middle Classic period.

Besides contact with the Caribbean, there is evidence of increased trade relationships between Mesoamerica and Central America. The designs of the Ulua marbles from Honduras and the incised slate disks from Costa Rica are derived from Classic Veracruz scroll decoration (Stone and Balser 1965). The aim of trade with Central America was probably to acquire gold, which first appears in Mesoamerica during the Late Classic period. The fragment of a Central American gold figure was placed under a Copan stela dedicated in A.D. 782. (Robicsek 1972, p. 86), and a variety of imported and reworked gold pieces were found in the Chichen cenote, along with Classic period offerings in the styles of Piedras Negras and Cotzumalhuapa (Lothrop 1952).

The second half of the Middle Classic period began with the decline of a number of great Early Classic centers, such as Teotihuacan,

Tikal, and Monte Alban, accompanied by disturbances throughout Mesoamerica. The crisis appears to have begun at Teotihuacan and to have affected the other cities in turn. The decline of some large centers clearly benefited the many small peripheral centers that grew up in all areas. The areas most favorably affected by the changes were the Peripheral Coastal Lowlands and Yucatan. The fact that many new centers were established on defensible hilltops indicates that these changes were accompanied by warfare and some population displacements.

It is possible that some of these growing centers may have caused Teotihuacan to suffer a military defeat or other setback in its prestige. In any event, seventh-century dominance by the Peripheral Coastal Lowlands and Yucatan is evident from the spread of characteristics associated with those areas: the ball game cult with its customary paraphernalia, ball court architecture, the Classic Veracruz scroll style, the Cotzumalhuapa narrative carving style, stone mosaic architectural decoration, and the building of roads. Strong Veracruz influences came hard on the heels of the withdrawal of Teotihuacan both at Cholula and Tikal, but they were not as intense or of so long a duration as previous Teotihuacan influences. Many Peripheral Coastal Lowland traits were probably spread as a result of trade or were local imitations of the prestige cults and styles of the period. For example, ball court architecture and objects associated with the ball game cult became widespread in almost all areas of Mesoamerica during the late Middle Classic period. Their prevalence probably indicates the far-flung trading contacts and the prestige of Peripheral Coastal Lowland centers and their major cult of the ball game, rather than any actual political unification.

There is no question that interregional trade was even more extensive and intensive during the late sixth and seventh centuries than in preceding centuries. At this time, Mesoamerican cultural patterns were introduced in regions as far away as the American Southwest, the Caribbean, and Central America. Aside from the land routes, there is evidence of maritime trade around the Yucatan peninsula and more intensive communication along the Usumacinta, Pasion, Sarstun, and Motagua river systems. In all areas, the association of late Middle

Classic trade with the introduction of architecture and objects related to the ball game suggests that the expansion of Mesoamerican commercial frontiers was in the hands of groups originating from or having close contacts with the Peripheral Coastal Lowlands. Although commercial reasons may have been paramount, the building of road systems in Yucatan during the seventh century is likely to have been dictated to some extent by political and military needs. Road systems on such a scale for solely ceremonial purposes are not known anywhere in the world, thus suggesting that the Yucatan road systems were in some way utilized to exert political control.

Little of the political situation that existed during the second half of the Middle Classic period can be conclusively reconstructed, although a number of tentative conclusions may be drawn from the available evidence. After a brief time of disturbances, new trade contacts were reestablished, and many new, smaller centers began a period of prosperity and cultural florescence. This period of expansion and relative peace does not seem to have been the result of the domination of a single center but rather of the establishment of a stable network of commercial and political alliances between a number of smaller centers. Some of the eclectic artistic traditions may give evidence not only of widespread trade but of a particular pattern of alliances. Similarities in public architectural styles, for example, suggest contact between regions more intensive than just simple trade.

The presence of *talud* and *tablero* profiles in foreign contexts is often interpreted as evidence of unusually strong contacts with Teotihuacan. Similarly, the appearance in Yucatan, Oaxaca, and Veracruz of patterns of stone mosaic decoration should be interpreted as evidence of more than trade relationships. It is not unlikely, for example, that the elite of these areas involved formed alliances and intermarried at various times. Some foreign artistic traditions may have been borrowed to demonstrate visually the prestigious contacts of a local elite group with a distinguished foreign group. This process may be illustrated by Lambityeco in Oaxaca. That culture is basically a continuation of Monte Alban IIIb; however, evidence of the introduction of stone mosaic and stucco modeling into architectural decoration and the introduction of dynastic subject matter into art (Rabin 1970) indicates that there were strong commercial or other ties with the Gulf coast. The elite of Lambityeco may very well have cemented a commerical relationship by a marriage alliance, and the new forms of architectural ornamentation and dynastic iconography may have been a public recognition and glorification of that alliance.

The predominance of dynastic subjects in Mesoamerican art after A.D. 600 is not merely a secular trend but probably a reflection of political realities. In the unsettled sixth and seventh centuries, some measure of political stability was probably achieved through networks of commercial and perhaps military alliances cemented by marriage ties that were made public by representations in works of art. The establishment of such alliances is difficult to reconstruct from the material remains, since it is not easy to determine whether the widespread motifs in question had political, religious, or purely artistic significance. Interpretation becomes especially difficult when individual centers had eclectic and heterogeneous artistic traditions. Further advances in the decipherment of the historical content of Maya inscriptions may eventually reveal the specific nature of the relationships between various contemporary centers.

The cultural eclecticism of the dominant centers of the late Middle Classic period has been noted by Parsons (1969). Some elements of this eclecticism may merely indicate specific commercial and political interrelationships between individual areas. To some extent, however, the eclecticism is related to the development of new sites. Since the new centers were in most cases relatively young and had no great past heritage, they tended to synthesize traditions out of the art of other, older societies with which they desired to establish real or fictitious relationships. The eclecticism of the new centers is evident mainly in works of art, but it probably extended to nonmaterial aspects of culture, such as religious cults and intellectual traditions. The mixing of traditions throughout Mesoamerica in the late Middle Classic period resulted in a tendency toward cultural leveling and syncretism. Despite the political fragmentation that existed during the period, the predominant Mesoamerican centers were cosmopolitan and international in character. The less tradition-bound character of the newly emerging seventh-century centers also accounts for the many innovations in architecture and engineering that were, from a practical and technological viewpoint, quite significant. No comparable array of architectural innovations is known to have occurred in any of the later periods of Mesoamerica.

In sum, the inhabitants of the dominant centers of seventh-century Mesoamerica may be considered self-made men: they emerged from insignificant backgrounds and were eager to acquire the trappings of civilization, often displaying the eclecticism of the newly rich. Since they had no stake in strong traditions, they were willing to take risks, and engaged in experimentation and innovation. Their achievements in commerce, science, and art opened up new horizons. They achieved success through drive and intense motivation; their descendants, however, tended to be less strongly motivated and either lived off or elaborated on the material and intellectual wealth of their parental heritage.

Notes

1. Price recommended the use of a new chronological framework for Mesoamerican archaeology at a School of American Research Advanced Seminar in Santa Fe in 1972.

2. Recently, Tolstoy (1974) has employed a chronological framework using the terms "period" and "horizon" rather than Classic, Preclassic, and Postclassic.

3. Teotihuacan influence was discussed at the XI Mesa Redonda on Teotihuacan in 1966. See especially the articles by Paddock and W. Coe.

4. The only dated Cerro de las Mesas stelae were erected in this period, in A.D. 468 and 533.

5. Teotihuacan influences appear to have been less strong but may be found in the Nayarit-Jalisco-Colima region of the shaft-tomb-making cultures. Objects such as Teoti-huacan-style incense burners, Fine Orange pottery, and *strombus gigas* shells have been found (Bell 1971, p. 720).

6. Hills surrounding Cholula were occupied after the abandonment of the city. Cerro Zapotecas is a defensible hilltop site with a ball court built in the beginning of the seventh century. The site was probably a refuge during the unsettled political period. When Cholula was reestablished in the Early Postclassic period, Cerro Zapotecas was abandoned (Mountjoy and Peterson 1973).

7. E. W. Andrews IV (1965b) preferred a late date for Uxmal and the Puuc structures: A.D. 950–1050 according to the GMT correlation, or A.D. 650–900 according to the Spinden correlation. The Spinden correlation was preferred by Andrews. The recent C_{14}

dates from Uxmal and other Puuc structures in Yucatan range from the sixth to the ninth centuries. Mexican archaeologists generally date the Puuc structures A.D. 600 to 900, an interpretation that I follow.

8. Two largely unexcavated sites, Las Ranas and Toluquilla, may further indicate the intensity of Veracruz influences in the north. Both of the sites were built on hilltops, characteristic of the far north, but the many ball courts, and the finds of Veracruz-style stone yokes in the area indicate cultural stimuli from the Gulf zone. These sites are now thought to be Postclassic, but the Veracruz parallels suggest that they may be Classic in origin.

9. At present, all dated ball game objects are no earlier than A.D. 800–1000 in the Caribbean, and therefore considerably later than the Middle Classic period. However, there is much evidence that these stone objects were kept and venerated for a long time after their original purposes were forgotten. At the time of the conquest, they were used as sacred images no longer associated with the ball game. Since the ball game cult had its greatest popularity in Mesoamerica during the Middle Classic period, I suggest that it may have been first introduced into the Caribbean at that time.

PART TWO

the middle classic concept

LEE A. PARSONS

the peripheral coastal lowlands and the middle classic period

IN PREVIOUS STUDIES, I have stressed the Middle American "cotradition" (Parsons, n.d.; 1969). This concept of interrelated cultural regions had been more or less tacitly accepted under the rubric "Mesoamerica," but I have tried to set forth in some depth the cotradition as a working hypothesis for the northern area of Nuclear America. To illustrate this kind of synthesis, I analyzed the Teotihuacan horizon and, in order to embrace the period in question in all of its ramifications, I introduced the term "Middle Classic"—the subject of this symposium. This period is visualized, however, as more than the late Early Classic time of intensive Teotihuacan expansion, in that it overlaps the beginning of the conventional Late Classic period as well. It includes phases 3 and 4 (Xolalpan and Metepec) at Teotihuacan, Tzakol III and Tepeu I in the Peten, Esperanza and Amatle I at Kaminaljuyu, and Laguneta at Bilbao (Parsons 1967b; 1969). Moreover, I divided the Middle Classic period (ca. A.D. 400–700) into two phases: the first was one of commercial contact, or "Mexicanization," radiating from Teotihuacan, and the second one of consolidation and absorption of widespread influences, which resulted in the development of the important hybrid cultures that highlight the Late Classic period in Middle America.

This paper will focus primarily on the pragmatic reality of an extensive region that heretofore has not been visualized fully as an integral sphere of pre-Columbian interaction. I have proposed labeling the region "Peripheral Coastal Lowlands," as opposed to the Mexican highlands to the west and the Maya lowlands to the east (Parsons n.d.; 1967a; 1969). I formerly considered the Coastal Lowlands a subregion of the greater Maya lowlands. Although it is closely allied to the Maya area, I now think the Coastal Lowlands should be treated as a discrete region. I believe that a tripart regional division of Middle America (fig. 1) usefully elucidates our present state of knowledge of the area's archaeology. Although such a division does not conform to modern political boundaries, it does conform to related environmental and cultural units.

Too much of our thinking has been shackled by the frontiers of recent political states and by the tendency of field workers to confine their studies to these artificial regions. Some of us think of Mexico versus Guatemala or of southern Guatemala in contrast to central Guatemala, and we have restricted our efforts to the archaeology of particular states, such as Veracruz or Chiapas. These modern entities do correspond in part to pre-Columbian cultural regions, but their present-day boundaries obscure the full extent and direction of ancient affinities. Studies that pay closer attention to natural environmental regions, such as the Gulf coast or the Guatemala-Chiapas highlands, are treating areas that approximate pre-Columbian cultural units more sharply. Also, broad, two-part divisions of Middle America (Mexican as opposed to Maya, or northwestern versus southeastern) do approximate the ancient cultural scene, but introduce arbitrary confusion in dealing with the intermediate regions. The *Handbook of Middle American Indians,* for example, places southern Veracruz (and even Oaxaca) in a southern division, with central Veracruz in a northern division. Coe's two-volume (1962; 1966) popular survey treats the Gulf coast Olmec culture and the Pacific coast Izapan culture in the "Mexico" volume; the "Maya" volume minimizes Olmec coverage and repeats the Izapan. Thus, it seems that the recognition of a third major region peripheral to, and intermediate between, the Mexican and Maya regions is highly desirable for reasons other than the strictly geographical.

Peripheral Coastal Lowlands

We combine as one long, continuous Peripheral Coastal Lowland region both the Gulf coast of Mexico (Veracruz and western Tabasco) and the Pacific coast of Chiapas, Guatemala, and El Salvador—the Gulf side being joined to the Pacific side by the low-lying Isthmus of Tehuantepec (fig. 1). The 2,000-foot (600-meter) contour may be taken as a guide for the inland limit to this coastal zone, which includes both the upland piedmont and the lowland alluvial plain. This entire region was formerly unified environmentally by predominant rain forest cover in the upper reaches and by gallery forest and savanna in the coastal fringe. The indigenous resources of the Coastal Lowlands that were especially exploited by man included, in addition to tropical and

marine food products, rubber, bird feathers, jaguar skins, sea salt, and seashells. Cultivated cacao and cotton were also of paramount importance to the region. All of these resources were sought by highland cultures, which led to patterns of trade established in Middle Preclassic times (Parsons and Price 1971). Undoubtedly, highland people were particularly covetous of the Coastal Lowlands as a source of rubber, for the pan-Middle American ball game, and cacao, for both an elite beverage—a sacred symbol—and (at least in later periods) chocolate-bean currency.

This Coastal Lowland strip is a cultural as well as an environmental unit. Successive civilizations developed there, and aspects of each diffused north and south within its confines. The coastal corridor provided easy passage for trade and communication in both directions. Long-distance contracts between the exclusively Mexican and Maya regions, which were especially characteristic of the Teotihuacan and Toltec horizons in Middle America, of necessity had to pass through the Coastal Lowlands. Although contacts continuously occurred with the adjoining Mexican highlands and Maya lowlands, this corridor was peripheral to both and maintained an individual identity. Recent archaeological work in the Pacific sector demonstrates the corridor's close affinity to the Gulf coast sector in all time periods. Therefore, it is no longer feasible to view the corridor solely as a frontier of the southern Maya.

While the environmental cohesiveness of the Peripheral Coastal Lowlands is readily appreciated, the cultural-historical integration of the region requires exposition. I would like to indicate both the continuity of cultural traditions from the Preclassic to the Classic and the spatial interrelationship of prehistorically contemporary cultures in the Coastal Lowlands. The Preclassic picture will be summarized, while the Middle Classic situation will be discussed in more detail from the viewpoint of the Coastal Lowlands.

Prelude:
The Preclassic Period

The Middle Preclassic period (1200–500 B.C.) was dominated by the incipient civilization we call "Olmec," and the heartland of the Olmecs

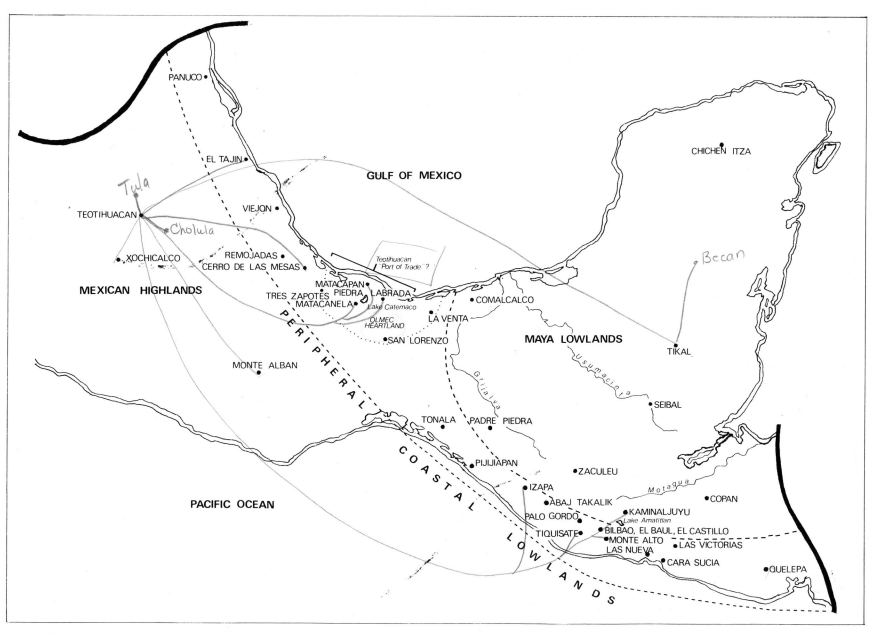

1. **Map of the Peripheral Coastal Lowlands in Mesoamerica.**

PANUCO

EL TAJIN

GULF OF MEXICO

CHICHEN ITZA

Tula

TEOTIHUACAN

VIEJON

Cholula

Teotihuacan
"Port of Trade"?

Becan

XOCHICALCO

REMOJADAS
CERRO DE LAS MESAS

MEXICAN HIGHLANDS

MATACAPAN
TRES ZAPOTES PIEDRA LABRADA
MATACANELA Lake Catemaco

COMALCALCO

OLMEC
HEARTLAND

LA VENTA

MAYA LOWLANDS

TIKAL

SAN LORENZO

MONTE ALBAN

PERIPHERAL

Grijalva

Usumacinta

SEIBAL

TONALA PADRE PIEDRA

COASTAL

PIJIJIAPAN

ZACULEU

Motagua

IZAPA

PACIFIC OCEAN

ABAJ TAKALIK

COPAN

PALO GORDO

KAMINALJUYU
Lake Amatitlan

LOWLANDS

TIQUISATE

BILBAO, EL BAUL, EL CASTILLO
MONTE ALTO
LAS NUEVA

LAS VICTORIAS

CARA SUCIA

QUELEPA

(in the La Venta-San Lorenzo-Tres Zapotes district) was centralized in the area we now call the Peripheral Coastal Lowlands (fig. 1). The distribution of stelae and rock carvings in generally accepted "pure" Olmec style extends from Viejon in central Veracruz, through Pijijiapan and Abaj Takalik in coastal Chiapas and Guatemala, to Las Victorias in western El Salvador. This distribution pattern implies that the major part of the Coastal Lowland region was under the direct aegis of the heartland district, at least by late Middle Preclassic times. Substantial Olmec penetration into the Mexican highlands is manifested by the rock carvings in Morelos and the cave paintings in Guerrero. Also, the stela at Padre Piedra in highland Chiapas indicates Olmec contact with the southern Maya region by way of the Grijalva valley. Both of these extensions of the Olmec style suggest that there existed reciprocal Middle Preclassic trade routes connecting the Coastal Lowlands with adjacent areas.

In the immediate post-Olmec, Late Preclassic, period (500–200 B.C.) widespread "Olmecoid" manifestations, which cluster in the Coastal Lowlands at such sites as Tres Zapotes and Monte Alto can be documented (Parsons *in preparation*). There also are significant Olmecoid offshoots at Monte Alban in Oaxaca and Kaminaljuyu in the southern Guatemala highlands. By the Late Preclassic period, Kaminaljuyu was established as an important extension of Coastal Lowland traditions, and it continued to maintain itself as a leading center through Middle Classic times. Situated in the valley of Guatemala, Kaminaljuyu had a commanding position over the Pacific coast and enjoyed convenient access to the Atlantic watershed via the Motagua valley.

The terminal Preclassic period (200 B.C.–200 A.D.) in the Coastal Lowlands is characterized by the innovative Izapan civilization. Although Izapa on the Pacific coast of Chiapas is surely the type site, a high concentration of the style continues southward along the coast to Kaminaljuyu, where the Miraflores (Verbena) and Arenal phases express subregional variants of the Izapan style. The Izapan cultural horizon also influenced Coastal Lowland sites to the north in the vicinity of Tres Zapotes and to the south as far as Quelepa in eastern El Salvador (E. Andrews V. 1970, fig. 2). In addition, the Izapan horizon had a profound effect on the Maya lowland area (Parsons 1967a; 1973).

It has become increasingly clear that the Izapan-Miraflores art style is ancestral to the Classic Maya, and that it is developmentally transitional between the Olmec and the Maya. The fact that this Preclassic development took place in the peripheral zone outside the central Maya area should be emphasized. One author has partially attributed the remarkable elaborations of iconography and symbolism produced during the Izapan period in the Coastal Lowlands to extra-continental influences—the Chavin culture of Peru (Badner, 1972). Be that as it may, and however innovative the Izapan horizon was, a continuity of cultural tradition from Olmec, through Olmecoid, to Izapan and Maya can be perceived in the evidence from the Coastal Lowlands (Parsons *in preparation*). In more than one respect, the entire Coastal Lowland region may have been "proto-Maya" during the Preclassic period. We have the lexicostatistical hypothesis that the Huaxtec language of northern Veracruz diverged from the proto-Maya tongue some 3,600 years ago (Vogt 1964). This could imply that by the time of the Olmecs much of the Peripheral Coastal Lowlands was already occupied by proto-Maya speakers. The region did not become significantly "Mexicanized" until the Middle Classic.

In the Middle Classic period, the Classic Veracruz civilization emerged to dominate the northern sector of the Coastal Lowlands, while the southern sector correspondingly became distinctively Cotzumalhuapan. Like the Maya, the two Coastal Lowland civilizations inherited certain aspects of the Terminal Preclassic Izapan art style—namely, its emphatically narrative quality as well as specific features of its content. While the Cotzunalhuapa style of the southern sector was more strongly Mexicanized, the art of both sectors retained such Izapan themes as the diving god, the death manikin, the trophy head cult, and the "tree of life" (see appendix, items C-4, 5, 7, 10). (For these themes at Izapa, note particularly Stelae 2, 50, 21, 5.) The Classic Veracruz style also evolved its unique interlaced scroll signature—the basic motif possibly being derived from the Izapan tradition. And the grotesques in Classic Veracruz art, such as human eyes and noses amidst scroll patterns (Proskouriakoff 1954, p. 82), are also integral to the earlier Izapan style, where human noses are attached to profile dragons and monster heads are worked into complex compositions. During the Middle Classic period, there was also a considerable interchange of culture traits between the northern and southern centers of civilization in the Peripheral Coastal Lowlands, and there are intermediate zones reflecting this phenomenon.

Ebb and Flow:
The Middle Classic Period

Before reviewing the events characterizing the Middle Classic, I would like to list some principal cultural traits shared by various sites in the Peripheral Coastal Lowlands during that period. (See annotated appendix, with a compilation of forty traits under the headings: A) architecture, B) artifacts, C) art styles and themes, D) style traits and motifs, and E) deities.) Many of these traits are of Teotihuacan origin, others demonstrate Classic Veracruz-Cotzumalhuapa relationships, and a few are restricted to shared Pacific Coastal traits.

As defined previously (Parsons 1969, pp. 159–64), phase I of the Middle Classic (ca A.D. 400–550) was the era of Teotihuacan control. The most prominent distant colony of that civilization was, of course, Kaminaljuyu, where architecture, tomb contents, and stone sculpture testify to the domination of Central Mexico. At that time, north-to-south movements may have passed through the central Veracruz region, where such items as ball game paraphernalia (yokes and *hachas*) and slate-backed mirrors were added to the classical Teotihuacan ceramic complex and transmitted southward (appendix, items B-1, 2, 4, 5). Teotihuacan intrusion into the Pacific coast region is demonstrated by the cylindrical tripod vases appearing in graves at Izapa (Lee and Lowe 1968, p. 22) and in the Tiquisate district (Shook 1965, fig. 2). There also are indications of Teotihuacan's interest in the cacao-growing piedmont region of southern Guatemala (Parsons 1969, pp. 138–41). In the fifth century, Teotihuacan culture also penetrated the central Peten, as shown by stone carvings and tomb contents at Tikal and other Classic Maya sites.

Rather than elaborating on the above well-established early Middle Classic manifestations, I would like to propose a possible focus of Teotihuacan settlement in a sector of the Coastal Lowlands that has been generally overlooked. I am referring to a small, but suggestive, body of evidence from the sites of Matacapan, Matacanela, and Piedra Labrada in the Los Tuxtlas region of southern Veracruz (fig. 1). M. Coe (1965, p. 704) noted that there were Teotihuacan-style architecture and ceramics at Matacapan. Blom and La Farge (1926, figs. 24, 26, 38) were the first to report stone sculpture from the other two sites, which, according to present judgment, may be attributed to Teotihuacan influence. From Matacanela came two stone boxes and one circular stone basin (Parsons 1969, pl. 57h-j); their raised rectangular borders, pecten shells, and ring motifs point to stylistic inspiration from Teotihuacan (Parsons 1969, p. 140). Stela 1 from Piedra Labrada (Melgarejo 1960) is also clearly of Teotihuacan derivation. Although M. Coe (1957, p. 600) discussed Stela 1 in the context of Cycle 7 monuments, he also credited Caso with identifying the upper glyph as the Teotihuacan "reptile's eye." According to von Winning's (1961) analysis of that glyph, the "reptile's eye" is surely the correct attribution. Furthermore, the superfix on the Piedra Labrada glyph, in the form of a tied flame bundle (*xiuhmolpilli*), is a Teotihuacan symbol (von Winning 1965a, fig. 4). Thus, future excavations in the Lake Catemaco-Los Tuxtlas upland zone should reveal a Teotihuacan center, or centers, of sufficient magnitude to be considered "ports of trade," or mercantile way stations, on the Aztec model (Chapman 1957). They are conveniently situated between highland Teotihuacan and its Kaminaljuyu outpost, as well as between Teotihuacan's central Peten destinations. In another paper (Parsons and Price 1971), we misinterpreted the port of trade concept when applying it to Kaminaljuyu. The Lake Catemaco zone, however, may have served just such a function in the Middle Classic period.

I have portrayed phase II of the Middle Classic (ca. A.D. 550–700) as a time when many diverse influences were interchanged, and new cultural foci in Middle America were formed, the Teotihuacan hegemony being disrupted (Parsons 1969, pp. 164–69).

Toward the end of this period, the Classic Veracruz sculptural style became fully developed, with the addition of ball court architecture and the stone *palma* to the yoke-*hacha* complex. (Proskouriakoff analyzed the style and assigned the *palma* and Tajin-carved ball court panels to the Late Classic period.) Both the Tajin stone sculpture and the "Remojadas" ceramic complex of the Gulf coast region reflect a mixture of exotic stimuli. Mayoid features may be perceived in the figurine types and stone carving of south-central Veracruz (Proskouriakoff 1954, p. 73). Maya and Tajin elements also reached Teotihuacan and Xochicalco; and Teotihuacan physiognomy can be observed in Remojadas ceramic sculpture. It is also probable that Veracruz traits—such as certain architectural features—diffused to the Campeche-Yucatan region (Parsons 1969, p. 173). Not discussed before is the possibility that, in this time period, a phallic cult was introduced into the Puuc region from Veracruz. (For phallic themes at Tajin, see Tuggle 1968 and Garcia Payon 1962.) Later, I will point out Cotzumalhuapa influence in the Classic Veracruz sculptural style.

The Pacific coast region during the late Middle Classic period is characterized by the Cotzumalhuapa culture and by narrative compositions in stone sculpture (Parsons 1969, p. 141). Active narrative themes emphasize ball game rituals and human sacrifice. Monuments 1–8, 18, and 21 at Bilbao epitomize the narrative style and have archaeological associations with the period (Parsons 1969, pp. 141, 142). Foreign cultural traits on the Pacific coast were traced to the Teotihuacan, Zapotec, and Tajin regions, while Cotzumalhuapa features diffused in the opposite direction to Tajin and the Yucatan peninsula (Parsons 1969, p. 170).

New finds of monumental stone sculpture permit us to expand the limits of the Cotzumalhuapa region in the Middle Classic period. Whereas we formerly fixed the extremes of Cotzumalhuapa occupation between the sites of Palo Gordo and La Nueva on the Pacific coast of Guatemala, we now may extend them to Abaj Takalik on the west and to Cara Sucia, El Salvador, on the east (fig. 1). In addition, there was significant highland occupation in the Antigua basin (see Girard 1973 for a new Late Classic Cotzumalhuapa stela there). Four unusual sculptures from Kaminaljuyu (Stelae 13 and 23, Monuments 10 and 12) may also be attributed to the Middle Classic period (Parsons 1969, pls. 54d, 55c; Villacorta 1927, pp. 45, right, 48, left). A full description and illustration of this expanded corpus of Middle Classic sculpture will be incorporated into a separate study (Parsons *in preparation*).

Although the northern and southern sectors of the Peripheral Coastal Lowlands were becoming regionally specialized during the late Middle Classic, relationships between the two continued, and the corridor remained a channel for widespread contacts. A special component of Teotihuacan IV culture diffused southward along the coast—hourglass-and funnel-shaped incense burners with mold-made, appliqué *adornos*. This type of artifact has not only been found at Kaminaljuyu (Kidder, Jennings, and Shook 1946, fig. 201,i,j), but also at coastal sites south of Tiquisate and Monte Alto. These incense burners are abundantly represented in Lake Amatitlan offerings too (Borhegyi 1966). In this period, architectural ball courts were conspicuous adjuncts to ceremonial centers, and horizontally tenoned stone heads became widely distributed in the Pacific coast region (Appendix, items A-8, 9).

Ceremonial stone ball game paraphernalia are distributed in greatest concentration throughout the Peripheral Coastal Lowlands. Since stone *palmas* are unknown for southern Guatemala, I have suggested that the plain yokes and thin *hachas* (and pyrite mirrors) were introduced prior to the evolution of the *palma* form in Veracruz, or, prior to the late Middle Classic. Also, the Classic Veracruz ornate style of scroll decoration on yokes, in vogue at the end of the Middle Classic, did not appear in the south. Although some decorated yokes are known there, they are not of diagnostic Classic Veracruz style.

On the other hand, there is a strong suggestion of Cotzumalhuapa narrative-style influence in the low-relief sculpture at Tajin and in Veracruz stone *palma* decoration. While one might propose independent collateral derivation from the Izapa horizon for some of these correspondences, direct south-to-north contact and diffusion during the late Middle Classic seems probable also. The following themes are common to both the Cotzumalhuapa and Classic Veracruz styles: human sacrifice (decapitation, heart removal, and limb amputation); death (including death manikins and death's heads); trophy head cult; ball game rituals (associated with human sacrifice); diving god (associated with supplicating figures or sacrificial offerings); eagle and jaguar complex; eagle or vulture receiving sacrificial offerings (associated with sun symbols); the "tree of life" emanating from death figures; and consulting, gesticulating figures with attendants (appendix, items C-3–11). The specific clustering of these thematic traits and their emphasis—in the Tajin ball court panels, the carved round columns, and the *palmas*—have closer parallels in Cotzumalhuapa art than any other single style. While the overall styles of execution differ, the content is so overwhelmingly similar that the expectation of communication between these extremes of the Coastal Lowlands is quite high. Discrete style traits and motifs also link the two art styles (appendix, items D-1, 2, 3, 4, 5, 9, 10).

This south-to-north diffusion is supported by the intermediate sites of Tonala on the Chiapas coast and Cerro de las Mesas on the Gulf coast. These sites have acknowledged Middle Classic components (as well as components from earlier phases). For example, Stelae 6 and 8 at Cerro de las Mesas have early ninth-Cycle bar-and-dot inscriptions (Stirling 1943, pp. 35–42). And Ferdon (1953, p. 112) makes the following assessment of Tonala:

> At the close of the Early Classic and beginning of the Late Classic period a strong central Mexican influence is seen to arrive at the site as is especially manifested in the building of temple enclosures or precincts and single room temples with side-wall porches. The arrival of this Mexican influence appears to have stimulated building activity, but, in the end, may also have been the cause for a rather abrupt abandonment of the site.

In the early Middle Classic period, Tonala also evinces contact with Cerro de las Mesas in the posture and detail of Stela 9 (Ferdon 1953, pl. 20a-d). Fifth-and sixth-century Cerro de las Mesas stela carving, in turn, shows definite Izapan archaisms, having much in common with the Cycle 7, Stela 1 at El Baul, for example.

But what we wish to emphasize here is that during the late Middle Classic period (i.e., the seventh century), both sites show evidence of the Cotzumalhuapa art style diffusing northward. Two stelae and one carved altar from the Tonala vicinity (Ferdon 1953, pls. 24d-f, 21a-d) reflect this influence, as does Stela 4 at Cerro de las Mesas, which is directly analogous to Monument 9 at Bilbao (Parsons 1969, pls. 36a-b). These correspondences may well be contemporary with the proposed Cotzumalhuapa contact at Tajin.

Aftermath:
The Late Classic Period

While the Middle Classic period witnessed the formative stages of Classic Veracruz and Cotzumalhuapa civilizations in the Peripheral Coastal Lowlands, the Late Classic (ca. A.D. 700–900) saw their florescence as specialized regional entities. The same observation holds true for the highland Mexican Xochicalco and Zapotec civilizations and for the lowland Puuc and Maya civilizations. In the Maya region, certain fundamental early Mexican symbolism persisted, such as Tlaloc and imbricated year-sign emblems. Further, interregional, long-distance contacts in Middle America probably did not cease altogether in the Late Classic. Southward-directed impulses from highland Mexico or the Gulf coast were resumed in the terminal Late Classic—this time on the early Toltec horizon. These movements played a part in the demise of the central lowland Maya civilization and possibly in that of the Cotzumalhuapa civilization as well.

Indeed, excavations by Harvard University at Seibal in the southern Peten have established that Toltec traits were introduced there at the end of the Late Classic period. Present are Gulf coast Fine Orange ceramics, Toltec glyphs, and late Mexican stylistic traits in stone monuments (Smith and Willey 1969). Also, we now have evidence of at least six Veracruz-type stone *palmas* in El Salvador.* In a terminal Late Classic cache at Quelepa (E. Andrews V. 1970), three plain yokes, one notched *hacha,* and two effigy *palmas* were discovered in immediate association. Considering the total apparent absence of *palmas* in southern Chiapas and Guatemala, we might have to explain their late appearance in the southern coastal extremity by means of a different trade route. This could have involved coastal navigation around the Yucatan peninsula, into El Salvador by way of the Motagua and other connecting valleys. Such a route might also explain the presence of stone yokes and Chenes architectural features on Temple 22, at Copan (Parsons 1969, p. 165). The problem of an early Mexican presence at Chichen Itza (Parsons 1969, pp. 172–84), however, I will leave to another paper in this symposium.

Although my earlier arguments conceivably may have overloaded the Middle Classic period with widespread Mexican-derived correspondences, I hope I have demonstrated the utility of a comprehensive Middle Classic horizon concept. I have also attempted to delineate the role of a Peripheral Coastal Lowland region in the Middle American

*Stanley Boggs: personal communication.

cotradition. The major burden of sorting out Teotihuacan (Middle Classic) from Toltec (Early Postclassic) in southeastern Middle America will rest in the hands of those with art-historical orientation in their research. Also, the various factors under discussion desperately need more solid footing in stratigraphic archaeology.

Appendix
Middle Classic Trait List:
Peripheral Coastal Lowlands*

A. Architecture

    1. *Talud-tablero profiles*

       [Diagnostic of Teotihuacan.] Duplicated at Matacapan, Veracruz, and Kaminaljuyu, Guatemala. Appear in modified form at Tajin, Tonala, and possibly Bilbao (Mound C-2).

    2. *Stairways with balustrades*

       [Diagnostic of Teotihuacan.] Duplicated at Matacapan and Kaminaljuyu. Also utilized at Tajin, Izapa (Group F), and Bilbao (monument plaza).

    3. *Frontal (shrine) platforms on pyramids*

       [Diagnostic of Teotihuacan.] Found at Bilbao (Mound C-2), Kaminaljuyu [and Zaculeu].

    4. *Precinct-enclosing platform temple mounds*

       [Diagnostic of Teotihuacan (Ciudadela)] Found at Tonala (Group B-1) and Kaminaljuyu ("Palangana," Esperanza phase).

    5. *Monument plaza*

       Cerro de las Mesas, Bilbao, El Baul (?), and Kaminaljuyu ("Palangana," Amatle 1 phase). *Note.* With regard to El Baul. In 1970, Edwin M. Shook and I noted a large rectangular court enclosed by low mounds immediately south of the acropolis. Given the quantity of sculpture removed from the site, and the early testimony of Eisen and others (Parsons 1969, p. 147), a monument plaza function for this enclosure seems a reasonable hypothesis. At Kaminaljuyu, the large enclosure between Mounds C-II-12 and C-II-14 (the "Palangana") was excavated by Sanders's Pennsylvania State University Project and revealed Esperanza phase structures in the middle (hence, a "precinct"). In the subsequent Amatle phase, this enclosure must have served as a monument plaza,

       considering the stone monuments left standing there (Lothrop 1926). Certainly it never functioned as a ball court.

    6. *Central acropolis*

       Izapa (Mound 125, Group F), Palo Gordo, El Baul (and many other Middle and Late Classic coastal sites), and Kaminaljuyu.

    7. *Stepped, terraced acropolis* (with divisions connected by paved ramps)

       Tonala, Bilbao, and Quelepa (eastern El Salvador). *Note.* The three sites also share the use of large cut-stone masonry blocks, and all these features seem to be early Middle Classic in origin.

    8. *Ball courts*

       Distributed from Tajin to Quelepa, but especially concentrated in the Cotzumalhuapa-Kaminaljuyu zone.

    9. *Horizontally tenoned stone heads* (fixed to architectural facades, balustrades, and ball courts)

       [Found at Teotihuacan.] Concentrated in the Cotzumalhuapa-Kaminaljuyu zone. *Note.* These sculptures typically have feather ruffs and eye scrolls, and emphasize serpent, jaguar, and death's heads during the Middle Classic. Like ball courts, the category continued in the Late Classic.

B. Artifacts

    1. *Yoke-hacha ball game complex*

       Especially characteristic of Classic Veracruz zone. Plain yokes and unnotched *hachas* also evenly distributed in the coastal Guatemala-El Salvador zone.

    2. *Slate-backed pyrite mirrors*

       Classic Veracruz zone, Bilbao, Kaminaljuyu [and Costa Rica]. *Note.* Carved mirror backs from Kaminaljuyu and Costa Rica dem-

---

*Basic references for principal sites mentioned are as follows:

  Bilbao (and other Cotzumalhuapa sites) . . . Parsons 1967–69.

  Cerro de las Mesas . . . Stirling 1943.

  Izapa . . . Lee and Lowe 1968.

  Kaminaljuyu . . . Kidder, Jennings, and Shook 1946.

Matacapan . . . Coe 1965.

Quelepa . . . Andrews 1970.

Tajin . . . Marquina 1964; Tuggle 1968.

Tonala . . . Ferdon 1953.

Zaculeu . . . Woodbury and Trik 1953.

onstrate specific late Early Classic stylistic relationships with the north. One mirror at Kaminaljuyu bears interlaced Classic Veracruz scrolls, and two mirrors reported from Costa Rica show both Early Classic Maya and Teotihuacanoid affinities (Kidder, Jennings, and Shook 1946, pp. 234, 235; Stone and Balser 1965).

   3. *Large spheroid stone balls*

Cerro de las Mesas, Tonala, La Violeta (coastal Chiapas; Termer 1964), Bilbao, El Castillo, [Zaculeu, and Costa Rica]. (Parsons 1969, p. 79.) *Note.* Function unknown, but possibly symbolic of the rubber ball game.

   4. *Mold-made figurines* (plus vessel molding stamping)

[Diagnostic of Teotihuacan.] Technology diffused through the Gulf coast and Pacific coast (where applied to Tiquisate ware). (See also von Winning 1965b.)

   5. *Teotihuacan ceramic complex* (Thin Orange ware, cylindrical tripod vases, *floreros,* pitchers, *candeleros,* and incense burners) Distribution amply documented in the literature. See text for late Middle Classic incense burner distribution.

   6. *Animal effigy clay toys with wheels and axles*

Gulf coast (Remojadas style) and Pacific coast of El Salvador (Stone 1972, p. 190).

C. Art Styles and Themes

   1. *Teotihuacan III–IV stone mask and figurine style*

Gulf coast Remojadas figurines and Pacific coast Tiquisate ware figurines. Also evident in some Cotzumalhuapa and Kaminaljuyu stone sculpture (Parsons 1969, p. 138).

   2. *Narrative composition*

Classic Veracruz and Cotzumalhuapa styles.

   3. *Human sacrifice* (decapitation, heart removal, and limb amputation)

Classic Veracruz style (ball court panels, round columns, and stone *palmas*); Cotzumalhuapa style (pervasive theme).

   4. *Death* (including death manikins and death's heads)

Classic Veracruz and Remojadas styles (common theme); Cotzumalhuapa style (pervasive theme).

   5. *Trophy head cult*

Classic Veracruz style (*palma* 5, Proskouriakoff 1954; scene G, round columns, Tuggle 1968); Tonala (Parsons 1969, pl. 61d); Cotzumalhuapa style (common theme); Kaminaljuyu (Esperanza tombs, Kidder, Jennings, and Shook 1946, p. 90).

   6. *Ball game rituals* (associated with human sacrifice)

Tajin (ball court panels; scenes A and G, round columns, Tuggle 1968); Tonala (Parsons 1969, pl. 61d); Cotzumalhuapa style (common theme). (See discussion, Parsons 1969, p. 102.)

   7. *Diving god* (associated with supplicating figures or sacrificial offerings)

Classic Veracruz style (ball court panels, round columns, stone *palmas*); Cotzumalhuapa style (common theme).

   8. *Eagle and jaguar complex*

Classic Veracruz style (*palma* 9, Proskouriakoff 1954; scene H, round columns, Tuggle 1968); Cotzumalhuapa style (Monument 19, Bilbao, and Monument 4, El Baul).

   9. *Eagle or vulture receiving sacrificial offerings*

Classic Veracruz style (ball court panels, round columns, stone *palmas*); Cotzumalhuapa style (Monuments 16 and 17, Bilbao). *Note.* These are also associated with sun symbols.

  10. *"Tree of life" emanating from death figure*

Tajin (Scene D, round columns, Tuggle 1968); Cotzumalhuapa (Monument 21, Bilbao). *Note.* The main luxurient flowering vine in the latter composition grows from a death's head emblem on the torso of the central figure. (This emblem may also be a surrogate for a stone *hacha.*)

  11. *Consulting, gesticulating figures with attendants*

Classic Veracruz style (ball court panels, round columns, stone *palmas*); Cotzumalhuapa style (pervasive theme). *Note.* Phallic jaguar attendants are found both on the round columns at Tajin (scene C, Tuggle 1968), and on Monument 19 at Bilbao.

D. Style Traits and Motifs

   1. *Body outlining*

[Xochicalco], Tajin, Tonala, El Baul (Parsons 1969, p. 166).

   2. *Prowling jaguars*

[Teotihuacan], Tajin (Proskouriakoff, 1954, fig. 9a), Cotzumalhuapa style (Parsons 1969, p. 140).

   3. *Large knotted sashes*

Tajin (round columns), Tonala (Ferdon 1953, pls. 24e,f), Cotzumalhuapa style (diagnostic).

   4. *Ollin symbol*

[Teotihuacan], Tajin (scenes G, H, round columns, Tuggle 1968), Cotzumalhuapa style (Parsons 1969, p. 141).

   5. *Sun disk*

[Teotihuacan; Marquina 1964, p. 100], Tajin (scene H, round columns, Tuggle 1968), Cotzumalhuapa style (Monuments 16 and 17, Bilbao). *Note.* At Teotihuacan and Tajin it surrounds the Ollin symbol.

   6. *Rattlesnake tail*

[Teotihuacan], Bilbao, Kaminaljuyu, Cara Sucia (El Salvador). (Parsons 1969, p. 126; Lothrop 1933, fig. 52.)

7. *Raised rectangular border frames*

[Teotihuacan], Matacanela, Cotzumalhuapa style (Parsons 1969, p. 140).

8. *Framed rings*

[Teotihuacan], Matacanela, El Baul (Parsons 1969, p. 140).

9. *Stepped fret*

[Teotihuacan], Tajin, El Castillo (Parsons 1969, p. 140).

10. *Cacao*

Tajin (Marquina 1964, p. 449), Cotzumalhuapa style (common motif).

11. *Tabbed speech scrolls*

[Teotihuacan], Cotzumalhuapa style (common motif).

E. Deities

(All appear first at Teotihuacan and reappear in the Cotzumalhuapa style; Parsons 1969, p. 141.)

1. *Tlaloc*
2. *Xipe*
3. *Ehecatl-Quetzalcoatl*
4. *Huehueteotl*

WILLIAM T. SANDERS

ethnographic analogy and the teotihuacan horizon style

The Problem

OVER THE LONG SPAN of their respective developments, a characteristic shared by both areas of New World civilization, Mesoamerica and the Central Andes, was an intense internal cultural regionalism. At various points in the history of each area, however, specific local art styles and themes were widely diffused, if not over the entire culture area, at least over extensive portions of it. A major preoccupation of both Central Andean and Mesoamerican specialists has been to explain these "horizon styles."

We can define at least three major horizon styles in Mesoamerica: the Olmec (1100–900 B.C.); the Teotihuacan (A.D. 400–600); and the Mexica-Puebla, this last with two pulses (A.D. 1000–1200 and A.D. 1427–1521). In this paper I will attempt to explain the Teotihuacan horizon in terms of a series of ethnographic-structural models.

In recent years, archaeologists have become increasingly interested in applying ethnographic analogues to prehistoric institutions. Another interest, both current and previous, has been in cultural dif-
fusion as a dynamic process, but only rarely have archaeologists attempted to understand diffusion in terms of the socioeconomic institutions of the groups involved. I do not mean to say that most of us are not aware of the fact that cultural contact between, say, hunting and gathering societies occurs in a very different social context than such contact between urban civilizations. Very rarely, however, do archaeologists think explicitly in socioeconomic terms when discussing social contact situations. Let us take, for example, the case to be discussed in this paper: the impact of Teotihuacan on Kaminaljuyu. Theoretically, a group of people from Kaminaljuyu and Teotihuacan could have met at some intermediate locality, exchanged wives, had a sexual orgy, conducted a puberty ceremony, and returned home in typical Arunta fashion. I doubt that any Mesoamerican specialist seriously entertains such a possibility, but, nevertheless, there is very little discussion in the literature about the possible institutional context of social contact.

In this paper, I will first offer a variety of models of interaction between the personnel of chiefdoms or the state levels of sociopolitical integration, after which I will summarize the archaeological data from the recent research at Kaminaljuyu. In the concluding portion, I will attempt to apply one of the models to the data. The models are presented below in outline form:

A. Indirect diffusion of cultural ideas between the people of Teotihuacan and Kaminaljuyu through intermediate populations, with no face-to-face contacts between the two groups.
B. Nonperiodic occasional contacts—exploration parties, casual or directed, primarily with economic objectives; unorganized trade; initial contacts for missionization programs.
C. Periodic, frequent contacts.
   1. Trading expeditions—important aspects would be specifics as to the status of the merchants and their home country, degree of subsocietal differentiation of the two interacting societies, kinds of products traded, frequency and duration of visits, and the sociopolitical level of the two societies in contact.
   2. Conquest—political incorporation followed by tribute collecting through indirect rule, i.e., the native chiefs. The model here is one in which no actual transfer of the administrative or military personnel is involved.
D. Full-time residents in foreign communities.
   1. Foreign merchants acting as representatives or factors for home corporations.
   2. Immigrant craft groups, integrated within a native socioreligious system.
   3. Religious missions.
   4. Conquest—followed by political incorporation, involving direct rule through exported administrative and/or military personnel.

Although this outline does not include all the conceivable cultural contact situations, it probably does embrace all of those that could fit the Teotihuacan-Kaminaljuyu case.

The Kaminaljuyu Case:
Archaeological Data

The Pennsylvania State University Kaminaljuyu Project, directed by Joseph Michels and myself, is still in the data-processing stage. Therefore, some of the statements made here may require drastic revision,

and, while not definitive, some ideas may be offered with the data on hand.

Thirty years ago, the Carnegie Instituion excavated a number of structures at Kaminaljuyu (Kidder, Jennings, and Shook 1946). Some of these dated from the Terminal Formative period, others from the period of Teotihuacan contact. Briefly, these excavations revealed that in the final few centuries of the Formative period, a highly evolved culture existed at Kaminaljuyu. This culture included monumental architecture and widespread, large-scale trading contacts. There were obviously very important distinctions in rank and prestige within Kaminaljuyu society, as indicated by the tomb offerings. Kaminaljuyu was a rich, local culture with its own styles in sculpture, pottery, figurines, and architecture. E-III-3, a temple platform built of earth, was the key structure excavated (Shook and Kidder 1952).

Also excavated were two additional temple platforms, Mounds A and B, with tombs dating from the Middle Classic period. Within the tombs were many offerings—some in pure Teotihuacan style, others a close imitation of that style—including the diagnostic tripod vase, an artifact found all over Middle Classic Mesoamerica.

The most impressive discovery, however, was the architectural style of the platforms themselves. Mound A had eight superimposed platforms, Mound B had five. The final structures in both were constructed in pure Teotihuacan style, using techniques that were a close adaptation of those from Teotihuacan. The presence of monumental architecture in foreign style suggests something very different from the simple movement of portable goods.

Since Carnegie's initial excavations, the Kaminaljuyu site has been excavated intermittently by Shook (1950–51), Berlin (1952), Borhegyi (1965), Vivian Broman, Susan Miles, and Gustavo Espinoza. The Pennsylvania State University Project included three field seasons between 1968 and 1970. It involved large-scale excavations in 10 mounds, test pits in 30 additional mounds, and the excavation of 550 test pits in the residential area of the site (Bebrich n.d.; Brown n.d.; Cheek n.d.; Kirsch n.d.; Reynolds n.d.; Sanders and Michels 1969). Of the 200 or so mounds plotted on the Carnegie map, we have, all told, some data from at least half (fig. 1).

On the basis of this data, the following picture of the Middle Clas-

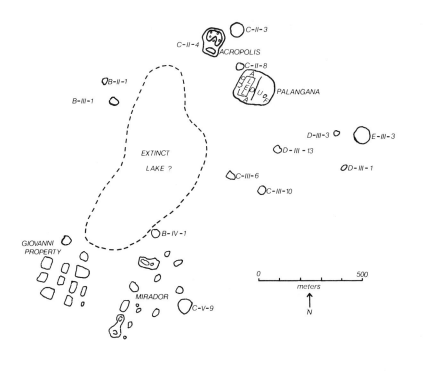

1. Plan of Kaminaljuyu, Guatemala.

sic period at Kaminaljuyu emerges. With respect to residential patterns and household artifacts (it should be noted here that, on the basis of research at Teotihuacan and in Teotihuacan rural settlements, we now have abundant documentation for the comparison), Sanders 1965), the situation appears to be as follows. Of the over 1 million pot sherds collected by the project, at least 20 to 30 percent date from the Middle Classic period. At least 200,000 obsidian artifacts were collected, and a substantial percentage of these date from the Middle Classic period. Virtually none of the pottery from the residential area is Teotihuacan in style, and apparently only tombs contain Teotihuacan-type pottery. Virtually all of the Kaminaljuyu obsidian objects consist of

cylindrical cores, rectangular blades flaked from these cores, and detritus resulting from their manufacture. At Teotihuacan, a substantial percentage of the obsidian consists of this same type of artifact, but also includes bifacially flaked projectile points and scrapers. Scrapers are completely absent at Kaminaljuyu, and points are very rare and limited to the Late Classic and Postclassic periods. Indeed, in the entire range of household artifacts, nothing distinctively Teotihuacan appears in the residential portions of the site.

Of even greater interest and significance is the virtual absence at the residential areas of Kaminaljuyu of a variety of religious artifacts used in household ceremonies at Teotihuacan. These include the stone Huehueteotl censers (this god was apparently the god of the family at Teotihuacan), and ceramic censers and figurines. For example, among the thousands of figurines collected at Kaminaljuyu, only two or three have a Teotihuacanoid appearance.

Finally, with respect to residential architecture, there is nothing at Kaminaljuyu that approximates the large Teotihuacan-type compound, with its central ceremonial courtyard, apartment patio complexes, and stone and plaster construction. At Teotihuacan, these structures covered an entire city block, averaging 3,600 square meters, and they housed from fifty to sixty people. Instead, typical lower-class residences at Kaminaljuyu, throughout the history of the town, consisted of small pole-and-thatched dwellings with dirt floors and grouped around courtyards, some of which had prepared floors. The maximal residential unit at Kaminaljuyu was clearly the small extended family.

On the other hand, with respect to overall planning—distribution of residences and civic buildings—and the architectural style of public buildings—the period of Teotihuacan contact at Kaminaljuyu is associated with substantial, even revolutionary, changes.

During the Terminal Formative period, there were approximately fourteen plaza complexes of civic buildings on the site. Each complex consisted of one or more terraced pyramid temples; an elite residence or two, placed on a lower terraced platform, and several smaller platforms or mounds of unknown functions; all grouped around a squarish plaza. Attached to each of these apparent administrative centers was a small, compact, densely settled residential area. These wards were well spaced from each other, and we suspect that the total population of the site did not exceed 10,000 persons, and was probably closer to 5,000.

There are some chronological problems concerning events immediately before and during the period of Teotihuacan contact. The following discussion is based on a Ph.D. dissertation by Cheek (n.d.) (fig. 2).

According to Cheek, the span of Teotihuacan contact was A.D. 400–600. Between A.D. 400–450, a number of typical Terminal-Formative-type centers continued to function, one of which was located at a place on the site referred to in the literature as the "Palangana." Today, this complex appears as a huge double compound, but the construction of the compound dates from the Late Classic period. Approximately 1,500 meters southeast of the Palangana—and hundreds of meters from the nearest Terminal Formative civic center—a complex of small platforms, which apparently functioned as shrines, was constructed in Terminal Formative style and technique, but with tombs containing Teotihuacan ceramics. Two of these platforms are referred to as Mounds A and B.

Between A.D. 450–500 the construction pattern continues, but with substantial increments in the size of the buildings at the Palangana and at Mounds A and B. In the latter two cases, the shrines become temples. There was also a gradual adoption of Teotihuacan stylistic elements and construction techniques, as well as a continuing use of Teotihuacan ceramics in the tombs. Between A.D. 500–550, the Mound A-B group reached its climax in terms of building size, and by then the buildings were in pure Teotihuacan style. This is also the period of the most spectacular tombs, all of which included the standard Teotihuacan tripod vases. The structures at the Palangana also become completely Teotihuacan in style.

Between A.D. 550–600, revolutionary changes in settlement patterns occurred at Kaminaljuyu. First, the Mound A-B complex was abandoned as a civic center. The Palangana temple complex continued to function, but, approximately 200 meters northwest of it, a massive acropolis-like complex of buildings in pure Teotihuacan style was constructed. Of particular interest is the fact that Kaminaljuyu's widespread contacts with the outside, particularly with Teotihuacan, seemed to diminish. What few tombs have been found contain fewer

| | Chronological Sequences | | Structures | | Construction Stages | | | | | | |
DATE	Architectural Period	Ceramic Phase	Mounds A	B	E	L	C	A	D	U	Acropolis
1000		?				L6				U3	
	Post-	A M A T L E III			E6						
900											
800	Teotihuacan	?			E5						
	Contact	A M A T L E II									
700											
600					E4	L5	C3	Al	D3	U2	
	Withdrawal Phase 2	E A S M P A E T R L A E N I Z A			E3-c				D2-c		C-II-4
	"Teotihuacan"		A8 A7	B5 B4	E3-b E3-a	L4-c			D2-b	U1	
500	Integration Phase 1		A6 A5 A4	B3 B2	E2	L4-b			D2-a?		
	Contact		A3 A2 A1	B1	E1	L4-a					
400		A U R O R A					C2				
300	Pre-					L3	C1		D1		
200	Teotihuacan						L2				
100	Contact	A R E N A L									
AD/BC		V E R B E N A				L1					
100											
200											

2. Interrelationship of the construction stages at the Palangana, Kaminaljuyu.

exotic goods, and the locally manufactured ceramics are not of exceptional quality. The style of many of these ceramics is clearly derived from Teotihuacan, but is actually what an art historian would call an Epigonal version of the Teotihuacan style. Associated with the acropolis is the abandonment of all outlying civic centers and the massing of population around that huge construction. There is no evidence, however, of any substantial increase in the total population. These changes clearly reflect the evolution of the Kaminaljuyu political system, from one that was aristocratic but decentralized, to one that was highly centralized. In a previous paper, I have suggested that these changes reflect the shift from a chiefdom to a state type of political system.

A major type of Teotihuacan artifact that did become part of the local Kaminaljuyu culture in Middle Classic times was the ceramic incense burner, with modeled gods in Teotihuacan style. The patron god Tlaloc is frequently represented on the incense burners found at Kaminaljuyu. Unlike the situation at Teotihuacan, however, where these incense burners were used in residential structures, at Kaminaljuyu, they were used in public ritual. Great numbers of them were found by Borhegyi (1956) in the bed of Lake Amatitlan, where they had been cast as ceremonial offerings. At Teotihuacan itself, Tlaloc is never represented in the household censers. Another interesting phenomenon at Kaminaljuyu, noted by Borhegyi (1965), is a temporary cessation in the manufacture of a series of ceremonial objects typical of the Terminal Formative and Early Classic periods. These objects included mushroom stones, three-pronged incense burners, figurines, frog effigy altars, and stelae with relief carvings in the Izapa-Kaminaljuyu style. What stone carving persists is in the form of simple stelae with carved representations of Teotihuacan deities.

Of interest also is the fact that, through the Terminal Formative, Early Classic, and various phases of the Middle Classic, there was a decline of interest in funerary cults and offerings at Kaminaljuyu, again suggesting major changes in structure of the political system there.

Our data suggests that there were also major changes in the production system of at least one major commodity, obsidian, and possibly others as well. Approximately 1,200 meters south of the acropolis, near the Terminal Formative C-V-9 group, is an area where there is an enormous concentration of obsidian detritus and artifacts, clearly a workshop area. The *barrio* or ward attached to the C-V-9 center was probably inhabited by specialists in obsidian blade core manufacture. In Middle Classic times, this workshop area expanded enormously and was unassociated with a civic center. Most of the obsidian is from El Chayal, only twenty-five kilometers north of Kaminaljuyu, and this resource was presumably directly controlled by the elite of that town. It is interesting to note that the contemporary hamlets for both time periods have very few rectangular blades and the artifact complex consists of irregular flakes. Apparently, the rectangular blades were produced for use within the town and for foreign export, and obsidian was distributed to the rural hamlets in bulk form, for local processing. This evidence also checks well with data from the Maya lowlands, where a steady increase in the use of Chayal obsidian is demonstrated between the Terminal Formative and Middle Classic periods. The absence of a civic center associated with the workshops in Middle Classic times suggests a more centralized control of production.

Finally, the data from the sustaining area of Kaminaljuyu is of considerable relevance to our problem. In the Teotihuacan valley—as Teotihuacan emerged and then expanded in size—the rural population was either nucleated at the growing center or placed in large, planned villages and towns. When we initiated the Kaminaljuyu project, we suspected that a comparable process of nucleation might have accompanied Teotihuacan contact with Kaminaljuyu. In fact, what we saw was the centralization of the population *within* the town, but no substantial *increase* in that population, while the rural population continued to reside in the typical Terminal Formative hamlet of 50 to 100 inhabitants. Indeed, the Middle Classic period witnessed an increase in the number of hamlets. Furthermore, and of particular interest, is the presence of small civic centers throughout the sustaining area during the Middle Classic. These consisted of a chief's residential compound (formed by a plaza delimited by low platforms and one or two small pyramids) attached to a ball court. This type of small civic center became very common in the Late Classic period. Teotihuacan construction techniques and stylistic features are absent, and so we have an interesting case of two distinct styles of elite architecture in the valley of Guatemala, contemporary in date.

The Kaminaljuyu Case:
Testing the Model

In reviewing the data on the Middle Classic period at Kaminaljuyu by phase, a rather clear picture emerges of the processes and possible mechanisms of contact.

First, both the wide, irregular spacing of the distribution of Teotihuacan portable artifacts throughout Mesoamerica as a whole, and the very close resemblances between Teotihuacan artifacts and architecture and those of sites hundreds of miles away, argue for face-to-face contact between Teotihuacanos and local populations. In the initial phase of the Middle Classic at Kaminaljuyu, small shrines, in local style, with tombs containing Teotihuacan ceramics, probably relate to a phase of periodic, frequent, and short-term Teotihuacan residence at the site—our type C contact situation. Even at this time, the Teotihuacanos may have been permanent residents but their status was apparently not high enough for them to obtain access to local labor. Prior to this, in the Terminal Formative and Early Classic periods, there is evidence of scattered stylistic attributes or traits in local pottery, which might reflect our type B contact—nonperiodic, occasional. During phases 2 and 3 however, when the small shrines expanded into substantial pyramid temples, and particularly during phase III, when they were constructed in pure Teotihuacan style, the implication is not only that Teotihuacanos were permanent residents, but also that they were able to obtain local labor for temple construction. Presumably they occupied a separate ward or *barrio* of the town.

A major problem in this assumption is the lack of evidence of Teotihuacan residential technology. There are two possible explanations for this. One relates to the economic structure of Teotihuacan itself. On the basis of Millon's recent studies, we can assume that the city was characterized by intense internal craft specialization and even subspecialization. Millon has identified at least 500 craftsmen's compounds among the 2,000 or so compounds occupied during the Xolalpan phase. The actual number was probably higher, since many crafts are difficult to detect archaeologically. If household technology was produced by professional craftsmen, and the resident Teotihuacan group at Kaminaljuyu did not include craftsmen, then the necessary skills for the manufacture of household technology was lacking. A sec-

ond possibility (and in fact both explanations could apply) is that only Teotihuacan men were at Kaminaljuyu, and they either married local women or had families back at Teotihuacan. We think the possibility of intermarriage is more probable. Even if the residential Teotihuacan families used local tools, we would be hard put to explain the absence of household religious technology. Supporting our general argument of actual personnel being transferred to the area is the ethnohistoric evidence of Nahua-speaking wards in towns in the valley of Guatemala during the sixteenth century (Feldman n.d.).

Assuming that this progression of degree of contact is correct, the next question is that of its purpose. The evidence of a heavy focus on religious concepts—temple architecture, the introduction of the patron god Tlaloc, and the use of Teotihuacan-style ceramics for burials—indicates a missionizing colony. This concept could also be supported by the fact that much of the native religious tradition disappeared. My major objection to this interpretation is that proselytizing religions are a relatively rare phenomenon in human history, and they are associated primarily with Iron Age states in the Old World, which had political, social, and economic institutions that were much more evolved than most Mesoamerican specialists believe such institutions could have been in pre-Hispanic Mesoamerica. Much more common among cultures at the institutional level of Teotihuacan are patron gods related to sociopolitical systems and subsystems. Furthermore, overt missionization very rarely occurs outside of direct political control, and if it does occur outside of such control, it is usually a secondary objective. For example, Islam has been introduced into Hausa towns in northern Nigeria primarily by Arab merchants, married to native women. Because of their wealth and prestige, these merchants tended to marry high in the local social scale, and the spread of Islam has been accomplished as a social rather than a political process (Nadel 1942).

The model we heavily favored at the initiation of the project was that of conquest and increasingly tighter political incorporation. Our specific model was the Aztec empire. This model could still be adapted to the Kaminaljuyu archaeological situation, in terms of the phasing of the degrees of contact. For example, phase 1 could represent the initial conquest—regularized tribute collecting but indirect rule and no Teotihuacan resident administrators. Phases 2 through 4 would represent a period of direct rule by resident administrators. There are, however, several major objections to this model. First, evidence of Teotihuacan influence in Mesoamerica in the form of elite architecture (and we have argued that this is the key fact to suggest resident Teothihuacanos) is very widely scattered. In fact, the only known cases of such architecture—in pure Teotihuacan style—outside of the central plateau, are from Matacapan, Veracruz, and Kaminaljuyu. The famous structure 5-D-43 at Tikal, which is cited as an example of Teotihuacan architectural style, was actually constructed after Teotihuacan influence at the site (in the form of ceramics) had ended; in fact, the building is stylistically much more similar to Xochicalco. There are, of course, stylistic attributes of Teotihuacan origin in the architecture of many Mesoamerican centers, but they do not necessarily suggest Teotihuacan rule or residence.

When we began the settlement pattern surveys of the basin of Mexico, I expected to find that the Teotihuacan period population was as large and as dense as the Aztec. In fact, it could not have been more than one-quarter of the Aztec population in 1519. With this fact in mind, it is difficult to understand how Teotihuacan could have maintained political control over an area as large as their stylistic influence in ceramics and other portable artifacts would suggest.

It is also difficult, to understand how Teotihuacan could have maintained direct, coercive control over a few widely spaced communities, without controlling large, intervening areas as well. We noted that even within a small area like the valley of Guatemala, Teotihuacan influence seems to have been confined to a few select settlements.

Finally, if we apply the analogues from Aztec or Inca provincial administrative centers, then the archaeological situation at Kaminaljuyu does not replicate the situation found at such centers as Oztuma in Guerrero (Armillas 1944), or Huanuco in Peru (Morris n.d.). In each of these centers, colonies of complete families were established, and the whole range of hometown artifacts is represented along with—at least in Huanuco—foreign residential architecture.

A model we favor is that of trade as the motivation for the contact situation and professional Teotihuacan merchants as the agents. The evidence, from the tombs, of the movement of exotic goods over con-

siderable distances and the widespread distribution of El Chayal obsidian, provides direct support for this hypothesis. Indirect support may be found in the fact that there were large-scale craft specialization and a specialized class of merchants in Teotihuacan. There is also evidence that at least one foreign enclave (from Oaxaca) lived at Teotihuacan, which suggests that Mesoamerican centers were as cosmopolitan in this sense as the ethnohistoric data demonstrates they were at the time of the Spanish conquest.

One of the reasons why we find this model particularly attractive is because we have a direct ethnographic analogue from the period of the Spanish conquest. The Aztec Pochteca were a professional merchant class, with their own guild organization and religious cult, and they apparently had extraterritorial status at the home city, at least in the resolution of internal legal disputes (Acosta Saignes 1945). They were also—and this is a key point—a high status group with close economic (in the sense that much of the merchandise they moved was restricted to consumption by the elite class) and social relationships to the noble and warrior classes. They organized large trading caravans, which included personnel from a number of towns in the central plateau, and they were frequently absent on trading expeditions for several years at a time. In addition, they established permanent colonies at strategic trade centers to act as factors for the caravans; the sources specifically mention the towns of Tochtepec in Oaxaca and Naco in Honduras (Chapman 1959).

A major consideration of the political status of the Pochteca was their relationship to the home state. While on expeditions, they frequently transported the ruler's goods and acted as his agent in their sale. In the cases of large, expanding, militaristic states, like the Aztec, they acted as intelligence agents in foreign areas, preparatory to military campaigns.

On the other hand, sources indicate that the Pochteca acted as middlemen between foreign towns and that much of their trade did not involve the home city at all. There is perhaps a far-fetched parallel here to the contemporary Norwegian merchant marine. At any rate, much of the Pochteca's trade was for private gain, and they were, in essence, professional middlemen. Many of their expeditions involved movement through hostile territory, and merchant caravans traveled well armed. There are frequent allusions to the Pochteca as military men, and Sahagun even reports that they conquered a town in Chiapas. Very often, as I pointed out previously, trade was often the first phase of contact with foreign areas, and it was followed by military conquest by the rulers of the home city, political incorporation into the home city, and regularized taxation.

This entire process could conceivably have occurred at Kaminaljuyu in Middle Classic times, with type B contacts dating from Early Classic-Terminal Formative times; C dating to the first two phases of the Middle Classic, with regularized expeditions but no resident factors; D to the third phase, with resident factors; and phase 4 correlated with political incorporation. Accepting this model, Mound groups A and B would have been the center, first of the temporary and ultimately of the permanent residences of the Pochteca. The absence of Teotihuacan houses, household technology, and ritual would suggest that only men were involved (this apparently was the case with the Aztec Pochteca). Either they maintained families at Teotihuacan and personnel were rotated on a regular basis, or they married local women. We favor the latter choice for two reasons. First, the scattered data we have on residence in the Mound A-B *barrio* suggest family residence. In addition, this model provides us with a convenient explanation for the diffusion of Teotihuacan religious ideas into the Kaminaljuyu community. Our model here would be the previously noted Arab merchant in a Hausa town.

Apparently Teotihuacan *men* organized for *public* rather than *household* worship of the Teotihuacan patron god Tlaloc. The apparent focus on religion among the migrants is not surprising. The Aztec Pochteca were closely linked to the elite level of Aztec culture and, if anything, the data from Teotihuacan show a more pervasive influence of religion in the total cultural system. Furthermore, using the Middle East as an example, religion frequently serves as a device for maintaining the ethnicity of groups living in foreign communities. In a fascinating study of Hausa merchants from northern Nigeria living in Yoruba towns in southern Nigeria, Cohen (1969) demonstrated an increase in the intensity of religious behavior on the part of the Moslem Hausa living in the foreign communities.

Considering also the disparity in size and, at least, in indirect political power between Teotihuacan and Kaminaljuyu, it would be surprising if the merchants did not occupy a high position in the local social system and therefore what intermarriage that did occur would most likely be with the local elite. Because of this social leverage, the merchants apparently were not only able to influence the religious system of the entire town, but also were able to obtain access to sufficient local labor to construct substantial temples.

The reported Oaxaca *barrio* at Teotihuacan offers some interesting parallels and differences. Like the Teotihuacan *barrio* at Kaminaljuyu, this group lived in native-type residences, used primarily local household technology, but maintained its own religious traditions. At the Oaxacan *barrio*, however, there are no Oaxacan temples, only tomb furnishings and household ceremonial vessels in Zapotec style, and, furthermore, the Zapotec religious system did not diffuse throughout the general Teotihuacan society. These differences undoubtedly relate to the fact that the Teotihuacanos at Kaminaljuyu exercised greater political power than did the people of Oaxaca at Teotihuacan.

In a provocative article, Borhegyi (1971) makes an additional point about the diffusion of Teotihuacan religion. He argues that the religion of the lowland Maya, and most probably the highland Guatemalan population as well (who may or may not have been Maya at this time), involved a predominant focus on ancestor cults. Temples were constructed in honor of mythical elite lineage ancestors or deified rulers, and as such, the symbols had little relevance for foreigners. At Teotihuacan, however, the temples were built to high gods, who ruled over such major areas of human activity as agriculture, rain, warfare, etc., and hence would have universal relevance. (We suggest that ancestor cults were probably present at Teotihuacan but involved mostly household ritual, a factor that might further explain their absence among the Teotihuacan colony at Kaminaljuyu.)

Pasztory (1974) has pointed out in a convincing paper that the patron god of Teotihuacan—Tlaloc, the rain god—is portrayed in two different ways, and that one variant is rarely found outside Teotihuacan. Presumably the god represents the internal affairs of the city. The second variant is found in all of the foreign communities where Teotihuacan contact has been established archaeologically, and he is at times depicted on a shield held by a warrior. He may well be the god of the Warrior-Pochteca class.

I am not arguing here for a proselytising religion at Teotihuacan. I am saying only that when people like professional merchants move, they take their gods with them. If they marry into the native elite and are generally a prestigious element in the local social system, the possibility for the diffusion of the cult of their god is very high. The fact that the cult did not spread outside of the community where Teotihuacanos resided is further evidence of its nonproselyting nature and its elitist function.

A major question is whether or not the fourth phase of the Middle Classic at Kaminaljuyu, the phase when the community was reorganized and the acropolis constructed, represents the direct political incorporation of the town into a Teotihuacan empire. The apparent cessation of direct Kaminaljuyu contact with Teotihuacan, evidenced by tomb furnishings, would seem to argue against such incorporation, as does the absence of evidence of a special administrative military class.

I feel that a better explanation is that the phase 4 equates with a time of dramatic reduction of Teotihuacan power in the central plateau, the breaking off of relationships between the city of Teotihuacan and the merchants living in foreign centers, and ultimately the taking over of the Kaminaljuyu community by this foreign merchant colony as a private political venture.

One of our problems is sorting out these events is our tenuous hold on the absolute chronology of events at both sites. We know that Teotihuacan suffered a substantial reduction of population (from 125,000 to 85,000 people) between the Late Xolalpan and the Metepec phases, and that the latter phase also coincides with a general reduction of Teotihuacan's political power and cultural influence. If we could show a correspondence in time between the Metepec and Middle Classic phase 4 at Kaminaljuyu, then the case would be demonstrated. At the moment, most researchers think that the Metepec phase dates from the seventh century. Primarily on the basis of ties between Kaminaljuyu and the Maya lowlands, Cheek (n.d.) would date phase 4 at A.D. 550–600. There are C_{14} dates from Teotihuacan that might suggest a somewhat earlier dating of the various phases, and they could be adjusted to Cheek's chronology (fig. 2).

The model proposed here could easily be adapted to the archaeological evidence. From evidence presented by Millon (1973), we know that Teotihuacan was a major production and trade center. The highly selective nature of Teotihuacan influence would link in some way with major trade routes and the location of the key points, or nodes, in the trade network. The degree of Teotihuacan influence in foreign centers would in part tie in with the relative size and prestige of the two interacting communities and hence the ability of the residential Pochteca to intervene in local political affairs. With its insufficient demographic base, Teotihuacan, instead of attempting a political empire, apparently created a commercial empire and exercised substantial control over the direction and movement of trade throughout Mesoamerica. In part, Teotihuacanos simply took over the preexisting Formative trade network, not only expanding the volume of goods moving along it but also establishing new networks in those areas, such as the Peten, that were outside of the Formative systems.

The specific objective of the Teotihuacan Pochteca at Kaminaljuyu was probably to secure a hold on the trade between environmentally diverse areas such as the Pacific Coast, the Pacific piedmont, the Guatemalan highlands, and the Peten lowlands. Kaminaljuyu is situated in a critical topographic position with respect to the flow of a great number of goods such as obsidian, cacao, copal, seashell, jade, chicle, cotton cloth, tropical bird feathers, animal skins, salt, and basalt. How much of this trade was conducted by the merchants on a private level, as opposed to an official relationship to Teotihuacan is a question. With our Pochteca model, either one or both could be the case. The widespread nature of Teotihuacan contacts and the integrity of the horizon style suggests both a single network centered at Teotihuacan and a process involving the establishment of colonies at a number of selected nodes in the network as points of redistribution. Tikal, for example, was apparently the center for the redistribution of obsidian and other highland materials to the other lowland Maya centers, so the Teotihuacanos apparently established a colony only at the one Tikal site.

The primary lever by which Teotihuacan achieved this mercantile imperialism probably rested in its institutional structure. First, the process of massive nucleation of much of the population (perhaps one-half to one-third) into a single physical community undoubtedly permitted a level of control of people and resources not approximated by other contemporary Mesoamerican centers. Second, the emergence of a market system as opposed to chiefly redistribution networks, of special institutions of production, such as the compound production units, and of distribution, such as a professional merchant class (even at the time of the conquest, trade among many Mesoamerican people was conducted by nobles as a secondary activity) provided the city with a competitive advantage in the production and distribution of goods along the international trade network.

JOHN PADDOCK

the middle classic period in oaxaca

NEARLY ALL OF the many overviews of Mesoamerica published from 1940 to the present refer to Monte Alban and Teotihuacan as each having a Classic period, or as having participated in a pan-Mesoamerican Classic period. At Monte Alban, this is designated period III; at Teotihuacan, it includes periods II and III and, with some reservations, period IV.

There has been a nearly unanimous tendency to see at both capitals a "classic" sequence of stylistic development:

	Teotihuacan periods	Monte Alban periods
Decline	IV	IV
Baroque	III	IIIb
Classic	II	IIIa
Experimental	I	I & II

Further divisions of these periods, and the substitution of names for numbers, have not fundamentally affected this developmental scheme.

At Monte Alban, we have long had a Classic period divided into Early (IIIa), Middle (Transition IIIa–IIIb), and Late (IIIb) (Caso and Bernal 1965, pp. 871–72). Monte Alban IV was defined as the time when local tradition disintegrated after the abandonment of the capital, just as Teotihuacan IV[1] represented the period of disintegration after the abandonment of that capital.

That a style with a powerful identity did evolve locally, through a series of stages rather reasonably characterized as something like archaic-classic-baroque-decadent, at both Monte Alban and Teotihuacan, seems undeniable. But the concept of a Middle Classic period as stated by Parsons (1969) has forced us to face up to a problem of terminology, if not of conceptualization, which has been stubbornly ignored for years, in spite of the pleas of a few for reform (Paddock 1966c, pp. 111–12, 116; 1972b; n.d.a).[2]

Because Teotihuacan is intimately involved in Parsons's definition of the Middle Classic period, he says confidently that its periods III and IV (Xolalpan and Metepec) are not only typical of the Middle Clas-

1. Monte Alban Transition II–III period urn. Museo Frissell de Arte Zapoteca, Mitla. Drawing by Trudy Oppenheimer.

2. Teotihuacan II figurine. Drawing by Trudy Oppenheimer.

sic, but, in a sense, the origin of it. However, in the terms used by nearly all the authors whose ideas are being read daily in our libraries, periods III and IV at Teotihuacan are times of quantitative abundance, qualitative decline, and approaching abandonment. Period IV is *Terminal* Classic at Teotihuacan. How can it also be Middle Classic, and early Middle at that? Parsons forces a dilemma upon our attention. Something has to give way, and for the good of us all, we hope it will not be Parsons. The case of Monte Alban will strengthen his argument.

Had Parsons not specified the dates A.D. 400–700, we might have puzzled long over what represents his Middle Classic at Monte Alban. Surely research at Monte Alban alone would never have led to formulation of the Middle Classic concept as stated by Parsons. As Bernal long noted (1958), after a time of contact with Teotihuacan—the signs of which help to define Transition II–III and IIIa—Monte Alban in IIIb seems isolationist, strangely cut off from the busy Mesoamerican world around it (Bernal 1965a, p. 805). He proposed that the abandonment of Teotihuacan had ended its contacts with Monte Alban, and the large number of radiocarbon dates that coincide in suggesting an early end for Teotihuacan made this proposal persuasive (M. Coe 1962; Acosta 1964, p. 55; Bernal 1965c; Pendergast 1971; Johnson and Mac-Neish 1972).

Many years ago, Caso hypothesized that the beginning of Teotihuacan contacts in Transition II–III at Monte Alban had occurred during Teotihuacan II. In preradiocarbon days, the bases for Caso's theory were necessarily stylistic. For example, he noted that the large "lampshade" headdress of the Transition urn (fig. 1; Paddock 1966c, figs. 91, 93, 95, 97), if flattened from front to back, would result in the sort of broad-band headdress (fig. 2; Covarrubias 1957, p. 129 center) typical of many Teotihuacan II figurines (Caso 1965b, p. 856; Caso, Bernal, and Acosta 1967, p. 306).[3] The surprisingly small number of objects imported from Teotihuacan that have turned up in excavations at Monte Alban does, in fact, include some from Teotihuacan II. And excavations made in the Oaxaca *barrio* at Teotihuacan in 1966–67 showed that occupation there had occurred (I now believe exclusively) during Transition II–III of Monte Alban (Millon 1967c; Paddock 1967, pp. 426–27; 1968, pp. 125–26; in press b.) Unhappily, the area had been thoroughly churned up during ancient reconstructions. As a result, it is possible to say with confidence of the associated Teotihuacan materials only that they range from Early Tlamimilolpa (initial III) to Late Xolalpan (final III) or even Metepec (IV).* Some Oaxaca-style materials were definitely on the *tepetate*, and may represent the first occupation at this locality.

Our traditional view of Teotihuacan-Monte Alban contacts by periods might be summarized as follows:

Teotihuacan periods	Monte Alban periods
	abandonment
	IIIb
abandonment	Transition IIIa–IIIb
IV	late IIIa
III	early IIIa
II	Transition II–III

Attempts to add absolute dates to this scheme, however, face severe problems. Parsons has adopted A.D. 400–550 for Teotihuacan III–IV, significantly earlier than the Millon chronology (Millon 1967a, p. 10), but in fair accord with the available radiocarbon dates (which do, in fact, also permit a much earlier dating).

As for the Monte Alban column, until 1975 we had only one radiocarbon date for Monte Alban itself, and that was one of the very early University of Chicago dates, related to period II (Libby 1955, p. C-425). Recent dates on other valley of Oaxaca materials, and a new dating of the Yucunudahui tomb that Caso and Bernal tied stylistically to Transition IIIa-IIIb (Caso 1938, p. 50; Caso and Bernal 1965, p. 889), suggest that this transition occurs around A.D. 300–400. One new date, on materials from a period IIIb context at Monte Alban, is pertinent: A.D. 740.[4]

In other words, it appears that Monte Alban IIIb can justifiably be given a provisional placement around A.D. 400–700, though there are complications as noted. Like Teotihuacan III–IV, Monte Alban IIIb is the time of quantitative prosperity, gradually declining standards of all kinds, and final abandonment. The interesting developmental par-

*Evelyn Rattray 1974: personal communication.

3a and b. Mayoid figurines from the Isthmus of Tehuantepec. Museo Frissell de Arte Zapoteca, Mitla.

allel with Teotihuacan does not, however, justify an inference of chronological equivalence; dating should be left to objective methods.

Millon's excellent data (1967b) on the population and area of Teotihuacan as they varied through the centuries force upon us an important correction: the abandonment of Teotihuacan was not a single event, but rather a long process. Once the great capital has begun declining from its zenith of wealth, population, and power (whose peaks do not necessarily coincide), it ceases at some point to function as an exporter of ideas to distant capitals. This may be long before its final extinction.[5]

Reports of the excavation process at Monte Alban have long been scheduled for a separate volume in the series that began with a study of Oaxaca "urns" (Caso and Bernal 1952). But in the volume on the ceramics, there is a point where Caso[6] gives a detailed account of excavations in one area (Caso, Bernal, and Acosta 1967, pp. 381–85, 440–44). He did this in order to clarify exactly how he made the distinction between Monte Alban IIIb and IV.

In several places at Monte Alban, ceramic offerings were found in the rubble of ruined buildings, often far enough above the last floor to indicate that they had been placed when the rubble was already rather deep. In other cases, burials and offerings had been placed after the rubble was dug through and old floors broken through, clearly without knowledge of what was there. Nevertheless, even though the people making the offerings did so at a time when these areas were in ruins and the city presumably abandoned, the pottery they offered was not significantly different from that of the last offerings made when construction was still going on, i.e., that pottery found under the last intact floors.

In spite of the fact that the ceramics did not show signs of a new period beginning, Caso reasoned that the abandonment of Monte Alban was an event of such importance that it must have represented, for the society concerned, a change of the magnitude acheologists recognize in defining a new period. From the narrow view of archeology based on ceramics alone, then, periods IIIb and IV are continuous; but from the broader view that takes in the whole culture, they are separate—according to Caso. Naturally, the abandonment of the city was the basis for his definition of the difference.

This difference between IIIb and IV is important to us also because Caso, as was probably inevitable then,[7] believed that the end of IIIb and of Monte Alban as a functioning city was also the end of the Classic period in central Oaxaca; period IV was thus defined as Postclassic.

The logic of all this is impeccable, as befits the work of a former professor of the philosophy of law. But translating this logic into archeological terms presents formidable difficulties. First, having been found (by definition) only in a handful of burials and offerings made in the rubble of Monte Alban, period IV remains only vaguely known. Second, as Caso himself believed, "Perhaps . . . the city was not abandoned all at once, but rather some palaces and temples fell into ruins slowly, while others remained in use and in some areas new tombs were being built and new buildings placed over them" (Caso, Bernal, and Acosta 1967, p. 381). This opinion has been amply confirmed by the discoveries of recent years in valley of Oaxaca sites where, in contrast to Monte Alban, the full culture of period IV once existed.

Individual buildings are abandoned in any city from time to time. There is a cyclical growth-decline of which few participants are aware, in the absence of statistics, until it forms an obvious trend. Even a decline to near zero population, or to nonurban status, does not look important when it begins. For example, a person living in Monte Alban takes a job in Etla. He neither rents nor sells his Monte Alban house because, for the moment, there is no tempting offer, and in any case he vaguely plans to move back some day. But he never does, because the city is declining all the while, and finally his house falls into ruins.

The sudden abandonment of Monte Alban would almost necessarily have been caused by a catastrophe, and that, presumably, would have left traces—of which there are none to be seen. The possibility of a sudden abandonment is not totally ruled out, however, and only a large number of objective dates, collected from the last occupation layer all over the mountain, can resolve the question.

With the Monte Alban excavations ended, Bernal (1965a, p. 804) began searching for a site that would provide data on the nature of period IV beyond the very scanty information gained from the few offerings discovered at Monte Alban. In several excavations, however, he failed to hit upon a fully satisfactory site. It was only in 1961, when work began under my supervision (with Charles Wicke) at Lambityeco, that the right place was located; and even there it was not until 1967, when we returned to begin an intensive study, that we realized we had at last found a place where period IV culture could be seen in detail.

Lambityeco is a limited area within a large site, called Yeguih. What sets Lambityeco apart is the fact that it was occupied only during early Monte Alban IV, whereas other sectors of Yeguih show signs of occupation from before the foundation of Monte Alban down to the Spanish conquest. The reasons for our confidence that Lambityeco belongs in period IV are many: it has all the period IV diagnostics that had been found at Monte Alban years before; it shows the surviving traits of IIIb, with the predictable declining quality; and it has given us many previously unidentified diagnostics of IV. These last are traits not found at all in Monte Alban, but occurring—sometimes abundantly—in Lambityeco and other valley sites, and identifiable by stratigraphy, associations, and objective dating as being late.

The radiocarbon dates from Lambityeco were startling. So tightly clustered that in themselves they must be given great weight, these dates were confirmed by the dating of similar materials from other sites (Rabin 1970, pp. 14–15). The earliest constructions we studied at Lambityeco are already associated with period IV diagnostics. The last constructions, which were abandoned to fall into ruin, are dated in the first half of the eighth century A.D. (A.D. 700, 720, 730, 755).

This period is considerably before the date Caso applied to the abandonment of Monte Alban. Because Tohil Plumbate, Y Fine Orange, and Carved Slate had been found at Monte Alban in contexts that in some cases were definable as IIIb—that is, in intact structures—Caso had dated the abandonment around A.D. 1000.[8] Is there a contradiction here?

Not really. The seemingly early radiocarbon dates for Lambityeco are confirmed by the association of Balancan (Z) Fine Orange with the buildings, and the absence of Plumbate and the later Y Fine Orange; that is, some of the Monte Alban remains that are dated in IIIb solely on the basis of their having an intact floor over them really are later

4. Lambityeco stucco-covered clay bust of Cocijo.

than the period IV remains of Lambityeco. The seeming contradiction is only a difference in the basis of definition: whereas we are using a variety of remains to define period IV at Lambityeco, Caso, of necessity, used a somewhat arbitrary criterion—the abandonment of Monte Alban—and he did not have the means to date that. Now we know that period IV had begun in Lambityeco well before the last constructions occurred at Monte Alban.

Just as Caso suspected, the abandonment of Monte Alban (like that of Teotihuacan) must have been a process rather than an event—and a process that took decades, or even a century or more. Caso's explorations were largely limited to the central part of the city. It is easily possible that certain temples and elite residences in the center were kept up for decades after the city had lost its position as the regional capital, and even after it had lost the attributes of a city. The Monte Alban ceramics report itself gives convincing evidence for a situation something like this. Vessels of a ware called G-3M, a diagnostic of period V—not IV, but V—were found as "exotics" in otherwise IIIb

5. *Hacha* **from the Isthmus of Tehuantepec. Museo Frissell de Arte Zapoteca, Mitla.**

tinuation of IIIb with only gradual changes; and that offerings at Monte Alban in early IV might well have included a considerable proportion of heirlooms. Finally, if a family took the body of a person born at Monte Alban back there for burial after the abandonment, and reopened an old tomb (a common practice) or built a new one, perhaps laying a new floor over it, we would have an artificially prolonged IIIb, or the creation of a small new IIIb enclave, by Caso's definition, after the city had been abandoned.

That IV and V are at least partially contemporary has long been believed by Caso and his collaborators; that IIIb overlaps both of them in some degree is no great new complication.

Having dealt, however, awkwardly, with the inescapably awkward situation of late Middle Classic times in Oaxaca, we may proceed to examine the Parsons Middle Classic, as it may appear in Monte Alban and its immediate area.

As art, the works of Teotihuacan, Monte Alban, Peten Maya, and Bilbao seem to me strikingly different, each from the other. They produce in me an impression somewhat like that produced by four very divergent personalities—contemporaries perhaps, all native speakers of the same language, common possessors not only of what is universally human but also of some single cultural substrate, yet differing profoundly from each other in attitudes, tastes, reactions, and propensities.

In contrast, Bilbao seems to *share* with Tajin and Tula some characteristics of precisely the kind that set it so starkly apart from Teotihuacan, Monte Alban, and Peten Maya. This sharing is not total, just as the differentiation is not total.

Parsons has commended to our special attention the human faces represented in the masks and figurines of Teotihuacan III–IV (Covarrubias 1957, pls. XXVII, XXIX). When I compare them with the human faces of Monte Alban "urns," and the faces in the Peten Maya reliefs and the reliefs of Bilbao, I find four contrasting views of human nature.[10]

Somebody once told me that, if we are unable to point to specific shared traits, we ought not to talk of stylistic similarity linking two traditions or works. Much as I am inclined to accept this proposal, a trait-list approach to the Middle Classic question produces in Oaxaca

contexts. The report (Caso, Bernal, and Acosta 1967, p. 383) lists no less than twenty-three places (tombs, burials, and offerings) where this diagnostic trait of period V turned up in contexts defined as IIIb.[9]

Three factors enter into this definition of the context as IIIb: a) an intact floor or floors over the place; b) the presence of IIIb-style items; c) the absence of pieces recognizable as belonging to IV. It is possible that now, with the Lambityeco data in hand, some of these offerings might be reclassified as of IV style, but I have not been able to look at them since the Lambityeco excavations. In any case, it appears that period IV had begun elsewhere while period IIIb had not yet ended at Monte Alban. This situation need not seem so anomalous if we reflect that a group of conservatives holding out at Monte Alban would be inclined to cling to old ways in any case; that in most ways IV is a con-

results that I find disconcerting. Subjectively, I cannot see (would it be better to say feel?) in Monte Alban the Middle Classicness that Parsons believes is shared by Teotihuacan III-IV and Bilbao. But Parsons has a list of shared traits that I cannot deny, even though I might argue the meanings of some of them.

Further, the trait list that Parsons applied to Monte Alban (see appendix) produces a peak at exactly the time he implies it should—that is, the traits of Middle Classic seem to be most common at Monte Alban in period IIIb, which coresponds rather closely in time to the Laguneta phase that defines Middle Classic at Bilbao.

We are now accustomed to accepting as real the microbes, atoms, and remote stars that we cannot see or feel. Should we accept the Middle Classicness of Monte Alban IIIb? As a statistical demonstration, my accompanying trait list is primitive. The technical problems of trait lists are many and familiar.[11] But there is something to be said in favor of this one. First, the trait list has produced a result contrary to what I expected. Unable to perceive Middle Classic style at Monte Alban, I am surprised that the trait list so plainly indicates that it is there—though far from complete—and there at the right time as well. Second, having listened patiently for many years to the trait-list expositions of diffusionists without being moved toward their conclusions, I am hardly likely to be led too far by this trait count. And third, as will be seen, I have given this list a very skeptical going-over, which may invalidate some items on it but surely argues in favor of those that survive. Therefore I accept my trait list as indicating the existence of an entity—the Parsons Middle Classic—at Monte Alban, even though I remain unable to see or feel it there (of course I perceive it at Bilbao).[12]

The list of Middle Classic trait totals by periods suggests at once that the appearance of a handful of them in Monte Alban I and II is anticipatory, i.e., that these are Oaxaca traits destined to turn up later in Teotihuacan, and a glance at their identity confirms the impression. The sharp upturn in Monte Alban IIIa is, of course, a reflection of the familiar (but invariably overestimated) Teotihuacan "influence" at Monte Alban. As indicated above, what is most striking here is not the presence but rather the scarcity of actual imports from Teotihuacan at a contemporary, wealthy capital like Monte Alban.[13]

6. Ballplayer figurine. Collection of Howard Leigh, Mitla.

The peak in IIIb is a strong indication that in "Middle Classic" Parsons has defined a meaningful entity, however inappropriate that term may be for Monte Alban's terminal phase. If we had fattened the trait list by including individually all the Teotihuacan traits Parsons listed in 1969 (table 5, p. 196), we should have increased slightly the totals in Transition II–III and IIIa. The considerable survival of Middle Classic traits in Monte Alban IV is natural in a time when no radical changes were occurring, when elements carried over from IIIb were slowly declining in quality and a moderate number of new elements were appearing. The continued survival, and in part revival, in period V may be a reflection of the long-familiar fact that the Mixteca, whose influence is powerful at this time, was, in a way, a reservoir of Teotihuacan culture.

7. Dainzu ballplayer relief.

9. Dainzu relief of priest making an offering.

8. Dainzu death's head or skull relief.

The graph (fig. 10) shows, at the bottom of each bar, the number of traits I consider firm at Monte Alban for each period. Above those traits are those I checked as present, but with reservations, either because of scarcity or because a rather liberal interpretation was required to allow the decision of presence. Added at the top of each bar is the number of traits that merited only a question mark. It is notable, and reassuring, that the resulting curve has the same form in all three cases, and that the absences add a fourth. A detailed discussion of the materials resulting in this graph will be found in the appendix.

One detail, however, is so sharply contrary to all this painful analyzing, defining, and counting that it merits special mention. Monument 27 of El Baul (Parsons 1969, pp. 133–34, pl. 52d, e) is so conspicuously similar in various ways to the Dainzu reliefs (fig. 9; Bernal 1968a, b) that it really belongs apart from the trait list and graph.

The ballplayers of Dainzu and of El Baul have much in common. Probably the most striking trait is the heavily mitted hand grasping a ball. The strange, fingerless hand, the size of the ball, the awkward way the ball is clutched, and the way in which the mitt is tied on the forearm are represented almost identically at the two places. The pants that come to just below the knees are another highly peculiar shared trait, which was also known at Monte Alban in period II (Paddock 1966c, figs. 57, 58). The violent posture of the falling figure at El Baul is like that of the Dainzu players (and Dainzu has one standing figure). At both places the players use thick cords to tie their costumes. And at both they wear protective masks, though of differing forms.

At Dainzu—and at Monte Alban (Caso 1969, fig. 8)—the masks are simple, barred face protectors. At El Baul they are, at least on the perhaps somewhat idealized stela, effigies of monkey heads. Perhaps the quite simian skull at Dainzu (fig. 8) is related.

In spite of the great similarity, the Dainzu reliefs may be significantly earlier. Bernal dates them tentatively as very early in Monte Alban II, perhaps 100–200 B.C. I have dated them, for several reasons that are far short of conclusive, as of Transition II–III, perhaps around A.D. 100–200.

And Parsons, while placing Monument 27 in Middle Classic (1969; p. 133), tends to date it early in the period, in the Narrative division (1969, p. 141), associated with the Laguneta ceramic phase (1969, p. 142). Further, he notes that it was found so close to Stela 1 as to suggest an association. But stela 1 is of Izapa style, which Parsons places in Protoclassic, dated about 100 B.C.–A.D. 100. He believes that stela 1 was reset, along with later monuments such as Monument 27, in front of a Middle Classic mound. And, of course, we already know of Izapa-Monte Alban II similarities. Since Transition II–III consists in large part of period II traits, this is plausible.

The dating question is interesting with respect to another Oaxaca monument, the Nuine stone at Tequixtepec del Rey, which may be partially explained by relation to those of Dainzu and El Baul. A figure in violent posture, with strange hooklike or mittened hands, appears—along with a circular cartouche—on a Nuine stone at Tequixtepec del Rey (Paddock 1966c, fig. 213). While this stone has been moved to the town plaza and thus is of unknown context, its style is consistent with that of other monuments in the area, which would suggest early Middle Urban, equivalent to Middle Classic. Nevertheless, its simplicity would allow an earlier dating, and nothing in it

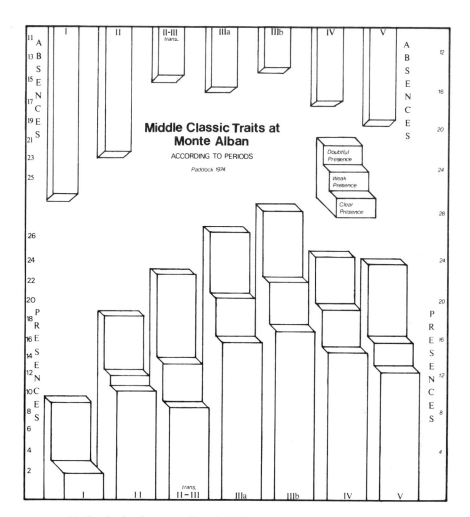

10. Graph showing a number of Middle Classic traits present at Monte Alban.

would prohibit placement in the times of Izapa-Monte Alban II or Transition II–III. The scanty evidence we have indicates activity in the Nuine region during those times. But this discussion has taken us far from Monte Alban and the immediately surrounding valley of Oaxaca.

The orbit of Monte Alban does not include all of Oaxaca. What can we say of the rest of the area? The Isthmus of Tehuantepec is, at one time and in some degree, an extension of Monte Alban culture, but that occurs in late times when Mixtec invasions in the valley of Oaxaca have made it prudent for the Zapotec rulers to move their capi-

11. **Stone relief of "tree of life." Museo Regional, Oaxaca.**

tal to Tehuantepec (Paddock 1966, p. 375). In Middle Classic times, centuries earlier, the Isthmus is included in the area covered by Parsons (this volume), though he does not deal specifically with it. Several items that are barely present, or completely absent, in the Monte Alban area seem to be clearly present in the Isthmus during Middle Classic period. Speaking from personal acquaintance with the Frissell Museum in Mitla, which includes a considerable amount of material purchased in the Isthmus over twenty years ago, I can point out several items of interest.

We know nothing of architecture in that area (referring to the south, or Pacific, side of the Isthmus) in Middle Classic times. But the yoke-*hacha* complex, in the form of *hachas* at least, seems to be rather well represented, while at Monte Alban it is virtually absent. Wallrath (1967, fig. 83) shows a *hacha* in the form of a death's head. Working with an extremely limited amount of material, Wallrath must have missed some diagnostics that larger-scale excavations would have revealed. Nevertheless, he defined an "Early Tixum Sub-phase" that he considers (1967, p. 158) to be "transitional between the Early Classic and the Late Classic," and dated (exclusively by cross relations) to perhaps A.D. 500 to 700. Some Middle Classic diagnostics seem to have appeared during the preceding phase as well, which would be expected; and there are plain signs of links with Monte Alban IIIb, unfortunately from surface collections. The ceramic piece that shows a trophy head ritual (fig. 3a; Leigh 1961; fig. 6; Moser 1973; fig. 27), in the Frissell collection, is one of a number of examples I have called "Mayoid" figurines, though they have southern Veracruz traits as well. Wallrath used the same term for this type of figurines (1967, figs. 70, 71), which he places in the "Late Tixum Sub-phase," of Early Postclassic.

Parsons has not explained why the Oaxaca coast is not included in his Peripheral Coastal Lowlands; Lack of data is the most likely explanation. But there has been a survey of the area by Brockington and others (1974) that will make it possible to consider the problem. The Oaxaca coast seems to have been a genuine cultural backwater for centuries, producing Formative-style figurines (as may have been the case in the Isthmus as well) until Late Classic times, when a Putun Maya contact and an abrupt awakening occurred. This period was followed by Mixtec invasions and the establishment of the major Mixtec capital of Tututepec (Smith 1973, pp. 84–88). But the possibility remains that the Oaxaca coast was all but unaware of the Middle Classic and its times of turmoil.

The Mixtec region, whose low-lying northwest area constitutes the Nuine, is a very different matter. Late Teotihuacan is so important to the Nuine that one is tempted to propose the area as a major region of refuge for people in flight from the Teotihuacan debacle. Links had been durable and important, the Nuine having exported many thousands of pieces of Thin Orange pottery to Teotihuacan during two or three centuries at least. Indeed, a considerable number of Nuine Mixtecs or, preferably, Tetlamixtecas, (Paddock 1966c, p. 200; 1966b, p. 380) may have resided in Teotihuacan while the trade was prospering. But the Nuine—"Hot Land," the Mixtec term for the Mixteca Baja—was not ruined by the collapse of Teotihuacan trade. On the contrary, it flowered. Combining a large ingredient of Teotihuacan derivation with some touches of Monte Alban and some plain evidences of contact with El Tajin, the Nuine became an important regional variant of Middle Classic, its glyphic system showing some overlap with that of Xochicalco (Caso 1962; Paddock 1966c, pp. 174–200;[14] 1970a; Pasztory 1976).

During these times, the Mixteca Alta, a cool highland that borders the valley of Oaxaca on the west and hence was more affected by Monte Alban, was in a phase of modest growth that gave no indication of the importance the area would have a few centuries later. With the Nuine on one side and Monte Alban on the other, the Mixteca Alta was a retarded area in relation to its flourishing neighbors. Spores (1972) has designated a phase called "Las Flores"—which he dates at A.D. 500–1000–1100 (and which I would place earlier)—as Late Classic in the valley of Nochixtlan-Yanhuitlan. The Yucunudahui tomb, in this same valley, which was related (Caso 1938, p. 50; Caso and Bernal 1965, p. 889) to Transition IIIa–IIIb at Monte Alban and radiocarbon dated to A.D. 300–400 (Rabin 1970, p. 14) belongs to this phase. Middle Classic would seem to have had a negative effect on the Mixteca Alta. But, when the rivals on both sides faded (with the end of Middle Classic or of Middle Urban, we lack the data to decide), the Mixteca Alta became dynamic in its turn.

12. Urn of period IIIb with a Tlaloc-Dzahui mask in its headdress. Provenance and location unknown.

13. Stone relief inscription in circular cartouche. Museo Frissell de Arte Zapoteca, Mitla.

"when many towns in the valley were definitely ruled by Mixtec caciques" (MacNeish, Peterson, and Flannery 1970, p. 209); and even the valley of Oaxaca, after Monte Alban was out of the way, became in many respects a Tetlamixteca province.

Bernal's characterization of Monte Alban IIIb as isolationist still seems valid, even after finding plain signs in the period that Middle Classic ways were known and some of them thoroughly accepted. The capitals of the Middle Classic period, the dynamic places that formed its character and were, for a time, the creative centers of Mesoamerica, do not include Monte Alban. Its period of creativity was long past, in periods I and II (the definitive formalization of its tradition in Transicion and IIIa might be considered a last small creative movement). In the world of Middle Classic, though it may have been prosperous, Monte Alban was out of place, passive, an antiquated and quietly declining survivor of an earlier age.

Simply by surviving, however, the tradition of Monte Alban again played a dynamic role. The powerful individuality of Monte Alban culture, never embarrassed by the presence of ugly imitations of Teotihuacan monuments—such as those that somehow were installed at faraway Maya sites during the expansive florescence of Teotihuacan—was still a significant force when the Mixtecs arrived. We do not yet understand the mechanisms, but it appears almost undeniable that the major resurgence that makes Monte Alban V so radical a turnabout from IIIb and IV involves more than the arrival on scene of a new people bearing a culture at a dynamic stage of development. Though many traits of the now-bedraggled old tradition were quickly rejected, some were incorporated in the brilliant new synthesis, and these include several markers of the Middle Classic.

In the Postclassic or Late Urban, expansion from bases in the Mixteca Alta brought the coast of Oaxaca under the area's aegis (Smith 1973, 84–88). Tetlamixteca style replaced that of Monte Alban in the Tehuacan valley at this time also (Chadwick and MacNeish 1967),

Notes

1. Vaillant (1941, p. 67) called this stage period V.

2. Some specialists are openly impatient with further discussions of this problem, but major publications continue to appear that take no notice of it.

3. The capes worn by these personages increase the resemblance; and the occurrence of the same two traits in Remojadas figurines of Veracruz makes Caso's Teotihuacan II theory seem even more valid (Covarrubias 1957, fig. 85, upper right; Medellin Zenil 1960, pls. 38, 39).

4. TX-1815, A.D. 740 ± 100, from Feature 19 at Monte Alban.* The IIIb materials from this area at Monte Alban seem to me to be virtually indistinguishable from period IV materials found at Lambityeco.

Also helpful are TX-1919, 520 B.C. ± 50, and TX-1921, 580 B.C. ± 50, obtained on materials from Monte Alban trash pits of early period I (Winter n.d.)

Even though the Lambityeco remains are firmly dated, their complex relationship to Monte Alban requires careful statement. The Lambityeco area was not in use before

*Marcus Winter 1975: personal communication.

period IIIb or afterwards; that is, the first constructions there occurred after IIIb had begun, but abandonment took place before Monte Alban IIIb had ended at Monte Alban itself. Nevertheless, from beginning to end, the Lamityeco remains are plainly characterized by the traits of Monte Alban IV. There is a mass of evidence, treated at length elsewhere (Paddock in press a, c), to confirm that the early period IV occupation at Lambityeco and some other valley of Oaxaca sites is contemporaneous with late IIIb at Monte Alban. Radiocarbon dates have confirmed this seeming anomaly (Rabin 1970, pp. 14–15), which is entirely comprehensible if viewed in the context of declining control by a conservative group at Monte Alban and increasing independence, with new traits that define period IV, at outlying places such as Lambityeco and Miahuatlan.

Because Lambityeco was abandoned after so short an occupation, we have no detailed knowledge of period IV except in its very early phase. Thus, while we date the beginning of IV with confidence as well before A.D. 700, we have no dates for late IV. And, at Monte Alban and nearby sites, IIIb continues until A.D. 800 or so.

5. Another important point is that certain outflows of Teotihuacan ideas and people may be evidence, not of prosperity and power, but of conflict and the flight of one party, or of breakdown and exodus. The impressive wave of Veracruz-Tabasco traits that reached central Chiapas, the Isthmus of Tehuantepec, and the eastern Oaxaca coast at the end of the Maya Classic—a wave so clear that Brockington believes it may even have some immigration—surely is not a sign of Maya expansion and empire building, but of quite the opposite (Brockington and Long 1974). When the social system breaks down, and life must go forward on a lower level of organization and productivity, large segments of the population must flee or starve.

6. Having translated and edited a number of Caso's works, I can recognize easily his personal style of writing here.

7. Though it bears a publication date of 1967, the study of Monte Alban ceramics had been finished by 1952, and it was not significantly changed after that date.

8. Most probably Monte Albán was not abandoned suddenly, but rather the new centers of attraction created in the Valley caused people to leave Monte Albán a few at a time, so that the temples and palaces they no longer used were left without upkeep. Thus, if we conceive period IV as that of Monte Albán's abandonment, at Monte Albán itself it is not distinguishable from IIIb. It is only because of the appearance in the Valley of objects not found in Monte Albán that we can conclude the period after abandonment [and before the conquest] is a rather long one.

The final abandonment of Monte Albán certainly is not caused by a Toltec conquest. We do not know whether the people who brought about the destruction of the Toltec Empire also provoked the abandonment of Monte Albán,

Further, if we consider the traits of Toltec sculpture as seen at Tula and Chichén, only one of them appears in Monte Albán: the jaguar wearing a necklace and walking. The element appears twice in Monte Albán—once on the South Platform and again in the building that forms the portico of the north stairway in the Patio Hundido of the North Platform. There are traces of a third—only the claws—in one of the buildings of the Vertice Geodesico complex [on the North Platform]. Walking felines appear also, in painting, on Tomb 125.

But we should keep in mind that the jaguar seems to be the tribal deity of Monte Albán, and in a [colonial] map of Xoxo [Xoxocotlan, at the foot of Monte Alban on the east] the South Platform is called Hill of the Jaguar [Smith, M. 1973, p. 338].

Again, we see the absence of Toltec traits in the ceramics. There is not a single fragment of Mazapan, Coyotlatelco, or Aztec I, If it were not for the presence of

Plumbate and Fine Orange vessels in some tombs [47 and 50, according to Caso 1965a, p. 908, 1965b, p. 868], we would lack any direct evidence that the site had been occupied during Toltec times. Tobacco pipes, so typical of that period, are likewise absent.

Therefore we may conclude that Monte Albán seems to have been finally abandoned at a time that cannot be very long before the 10th century A.D., and not after the 12th.

(Caso, Bernal, and Acosta 1967, p. 84.)

9. One trait doth not a period make; like those of most periods almost everywhere, I assume that the diagnostics of Monte Alban V appeared one by one.

10. What are insistently referred to as Teotihuacan traits in Peten Maya sculpture seem to me to be remote from the spirit of Teotihuacan.

11. Though unresolved, these issues have been set aside (with appropriate rationalizations) by many. Decades of competent discussion, in which Boas and Kroeber might be cited as early leaders, left us with important theoretical questions unanswered and, paradoxically, with a number of plainly sound works produced in defiance of this apparently shaky theoretical foundation. For example, what is one trait? An automobile, or a tire, or a tire valve, or a valve core? If we define what constitutes one trait, how then can we count traits? Are some traits more significant than others? What is the importance of absent traits? When we check *present* for some trait at Bilbao and Monte Alban, are we talking about two entities that are the same, or only about a similarity created by our own definition? (Carried to an extreme, this caution makes comparison of any two cultures impossible.) If we find the trait once at Bilbao and 1,000 times at Monte Alban, we say "present." If it is present 100,000 times at each site, we check the same square the same way. If we have no example above ground, we indicate the trait as absent, helplessly aware that one or more traits may be turned up tomorrow. And so on—yet this time it worked, as it has worked many times before. One important reason for that, of course, is that we are treating contemporary phenomena in contiguous areas; no diffusionism is involved.

12. Accumulating facts that he found impossible to accommodate in the formidably entrenched concept of the Maya Classic, Early and Late, forced Parsons to develop the Middle Classic concept. The same dilemma of accumulating data that refuse to fit into existing categories—plus my having already defined an Early and a Late Urban to replace Classic and Postclassic for non-Maya Mesoamerica—forced me likewise (and without consulting Parsons) to promulgate a Middle: the Middle Urban (Paddock 1973; n.d.b.). The two periods are entirely different. Middle Classic is the middle of the Maya Classic; Middle Urban is the middle of the entire span of all Mesoamerican civilization, from the first urbanism to the Spanish conquest. Thus, Middle Urban is not restricted either to the Maya region or to the time span of Maya Classic. Middle Urban begins with the latter part of Middle Classic, includes the following Late Maya Classic and contemporaneous phenomena elsewhere, and extends down to the beginning of the Toltec period, thus incorporating the Jimenez Moreno "Epiclassic" (Jiminez Moreno 1959; 1966). For an especially lucid, forceful discussion of Epiclassic and what I have now named Middle Urban, see Webb (1973). The outstanding centers of Middle Urban are Tajin, Cholula, Xochicalco, the Nuine, Uxmal, and Bilbao.

13. Blanton reports that in his survey of well over 2,000 residential terraces on Monte Alban, he has identified no materials imported from Teotihuacan.*

*Richard E. Blanton 1975: personal communication.

14. Whereas in 1966 I placed Nuine style in Early Urban, and had not then formulated the Middle Urban concept, I now conceive Nuine as a diagnostic facet of Middle Urban (n. 10, above; Paddock 1973; n.d.b) as well as of Middle Classic. The Middle Urban concept was first presented to an informal meeting of archeologists in Oaxaca in August 1972.

Appendix

This trait list is taken (the numbers beyond 9 are added) from the appendix of the Parsons paper in this volume. Some of these traits are discussed more fully in the Bilbao publication (Parsons 1967b; 1969).

A full-scale search of the literature being out of the question for various reasons, I have had to rely on a search of memory, aided at some points by the memories of others. Therefore it is likely that some pertinent item has been overlooked in one or more categories.

Looking at the Bilbao monuments from a Oaxacan's point of view, what is there that is familiar and not on the Parsons list? What might he have added?

The result of reviewing the Bilbao materials for this purpose is to be struck all over again with how different these materials are from their Monte Alban counterparts—and to be struck with the fact that often there are no real counterparts. Thus, we have had to look in different contexts to find more or less similar traits.

Because the present state of exploration in Oaxaca does not give us enough data to make a meaningful list of traits, this list ignores all areas of Oaxaca except Monte Alban and the surrounding valley of Oaxaca.

MIDDLE CLASSIC TRAIT LIST: MONTE ALBAN-VALLEY OF OAXACA

	Monte Alban periods						
	I	II	Tr	IIIa	IIIb	IV	V
1. *Talud-Tablero* profiles		+	?	+	+	+	+
2. Stairways with balustrades		+	?	+	+	−	−
3. Frontal platforms on pyramids				−	−	−	w
4. Temple mounds in closed precinct	+	+	+	+	+	?	−
5. Monument plaza	+	+	+	+	+	−	−
6. Central acropolis	+	+	+	+	+	+	+
7. Stepped, terraced acropolis with ramps	−	−	−	−	−	−	−
8. Ball courts		+	+	+	+	+	+
9. Horizontally tenoned stone heads	−	−	−	w	?	w	w
10. Yoke-*hacha* ball game complex	−	−	w	w	?	?	−
11. Slate-backed pyrite mirrors	−	−	−	−	−	−	−
12. Large spheroid stone balls	−	−	−	−	−	−	−
13. Mold-made figurines (or effigies)	−	w	w	w	+	+	?
14. Teotihuacan ceramic complex	−	−	+	+	−	−	−
15. Wheeled animal effigy toys	−	−	−	−	−	+	−
16. Teotihuacan III–IV mask and figurine style	−	−	w	w	w	−	−
17. Narrative composition in stone reliefs	?	?		+	+	+	+
18. Human sacrifice depicted	−	−	−	−	−	−	−
19. Death (skeletal depictions)	−	−	w	−	w	−	w
20. Trophy head cult	−	−	?	−	+	+	−
21. Ball game rituals	−	+	+	+	−	−	+
22. Diving god	−	−	−	−	−	−	−
23. Eagle and jaguar complex	−	−	−	?	?	w	?
24. Eagle receiving sacrificial offerings	−	−	−	−	−	−	−
25. "Tree of life"	−	−	−	−	w	w	−
26. Consulting, gesticulating figures	?	?		+	+	+	+
27. Body outlining (double lines)	−	−		−	−	?	−
28. Prowling jaguars	?	?	?	+	+	?	?
29. Large knotted sashes	?	+	+	+	+	+	?
30. *Ollin* symbol	?	?	?	?	?	?	?
31. Sun disk	−	−	−	−	−	?	+
32. Rattlesnake tail (naturalistic)	−	−	−	?	?	−	?
33. Raised rectangular border (*tablero*) frames		+	?	+	+	+	+
34. Framed rings (in *tablero*)	−	+	?	?	?	−	+
35. Stepped-fret (*greca*)	−	+	+	?	+	+	+
36. Cacao representations	−	−	−	−	−	−	−
37. Tabbed speech scrolls				+	+	+	?
38. Tlaloc (Dzahui)	−	−	+	+	w	+	+
39. Xipe	?	?	?	?	+	+	+
40. Ehecatl-Quetzalcoatl	?	?	?	?	?	?	?
41. Huehueteotl	−	−	−	−	−	−	−
42. Circular cartouche	−	−	−	−	w	w	−

Results:

	I	II	Tr	IIIa	IIIb	IV	V
present (+)	3	11	9	15	16	14	12
weak (w)	0	1	4	4	5	4	3
sum of above	3	12	13	19	21	18	15
doubtful (?)	7	6	9	7	7	6	8
sum of above	10	18	22	26	28	24	23
absent (−)	26	22	15	16	14	17	19
no data: blank							

1. If we admit the altered proportions used at Mitla and Yagul, the *talud-tablero* profile survives, with its several distinctive Oaxaca traits, until the conquest. In Monte Alban I, the known buildings lack it; but they are too few to justify a statement of absence (Acosta 1965; Hartung 1970). We do not know any buildings datable to Transition II–III.

2. The known stairways of Monte Alban I lack balustrades, but they are few; hence the doubts.

3. Frontal platforms are plainly lacking on Oaxaca pyramids, though there are too few early examples known to justify a statement of absence. In IIIb and IV there are small chambers and tablelike arrangements built into some stairways, at the bottom center, at Monte Alban and Lambityeco; these might be functionally similar to frontal platforms, but they surely cannot be classed as the same trait. The presumably civil "palace" and "council hall" buildings of period V in Yagul and Mitla have ample aprons in front that might well function as frontal platforms, but the buildings are not pyramids, and the aprons run the full width of the fronts and around the sides (Marquina 1951, p. 330; Acosta 1965, p. 825; Bernal 1965b, 1966).

4. Little as it may resemble that of Bilbao, the enormous central plaza of Monte Alban is counted here as a precinct because it is closed and has temple mounds both within it and atop its enclosing walls, like a more complex Teotihuacan "Ciudadela." Within this major precinct there are two miniature precincts (Systems M and IV), each having a temple pyramid at the rear, a plain platform in front, and walls on the sides, with an *adoratorio* in the center. Similar systems occur at Lambityeco and Guiengola. The Patio Hundido of the North Platform at Monte Alban, bounding the main plaza, is another precinct with *adoratorio* Marquina 1951, p. 315; Acosta 1965, p. 815; Paddock 1966c, pp. 155, 163, 167, 223–24).

5. The great plaza of Monte Alban is counted as a monument plaza. The concentration of monuments here may be in some degree a consequence of the mountaintop location, but there is no doubt that a number of stelae, from several periods, were placed both in walls bounding the plaza and standing free in it (Batres 1902, map; Paddock 1966c, pp. 145–48).

6. The great plaza of Monte Alban is counted as a central acropolis. Guiengola has an acropolis on its slope, probably assignable to period IV, but it is in the Isthmus—in Parsons's Peripheral Lowlands. Yagul is a clear case for period V, probably for IV, and perhaps earlier (Bernal 1965b, p. 842; 1966, pp. 352–54; Paddock 1966c, p. 217).

7. The stepped, terraced acropolis with ramps seems to be absent. Yagul and Guiengola have several levels in their acropolises, but Guiengola has steps connecting them and Yagul has steps in some cases, though in many cases the evidence to decide between stairs and ramps is lacking.

Large stones are conspicuous in the constructions of Monte Alban I and II. Later use of smaller stones might have been determined simply by the exhaustion of the supply of nearby large blocks (Acosta 1965, p. 820; Paddock 1966c, p. 111).

8. Ball courts may well have been in use in the valley of Oaxaca from period II or before (e.g., Dainzu), but both the game and the court may have been different from those referred to here. Monte Alban ball courts go back at least to IIIb, perhaps to period II; the Yagul court to IIIb or IV. The Yagul court and a similar one at Dainzu were in use in period V (Wicke 1957; Bernal 1968a, b). A newly excavated court at San Jose Mogote is attributed to period II.*

9. Horizontal-tenoned heads of period V at Yagul (Paddock 1955, fig. 26; Wicke 1966) are quite different from the gigantic (serpent? Cipactli?) head reused in a ball court wall at Yagul (Oliver 1955, pp. 64–65). This example, here assigned to period IV, has the same general form, with a tenon at the rear, but it is too heavy by tons to have been cantilevered. Parallel examples occur, also in period V, at Mitla (Rickards 1910, pp. 96, 97; Wicke 1966, p. 340). The serpent head on the facade of Tomb 123 at Monte Alban (Caso 1965b, pp. 867, 869) is assiged here to period IV. The T-forms that accompany it are like the inverted ones of period IV at Lambityeco (fig. 4). Horizontally tenoned (Cipactli? serpent?) heads of modest size, highly conventionalized and probably asignable to IIIa, are also known (Easby and Scott 1970, no. 166). None of the above is of Teotihuacan style or has a ruffed collar.

10. One *hacha* was found at Monte Alban, in a IIIb or IV context (Caso 1938, p. 22). They are much better known from the Isthmus of Tehuantepec (fig. 5). Yokes are not known, though two small ceramic figures may be wearing them (fig. 6; Boos 1966b, p. 469). These figures are probably of IIIa, though both might easily be of Transition II-III.

11. Absence of the mirrors seems clear.

12. Stone balls are rare, perhaps absent, though small ones were found at Dainzu in the area of the ballplayer reliefs,* and the players in the reliefs hold balls of about the same size in their hands (fig. 7).

13. Extremely rare in Monte Alban II, the use of molds is still rare in Transition, not common in IIIa, but it becomes overwhelmingly dominant in IIIb, not only for figurines, but for other uses as well. There is some revival of hand modeling in IV, perhaps because mold techniques had become intolerably poor. The known valley figurines of period V are of stone—identical with the penates of the Mixteca—and the effigies are hand modeled.

14. The Teotihuacan ceramic complex is a defining trait of Transition II–III and IIIa. It should be noted, however, that Monte Alban I figurines are totally different from those of Teotihuacan; there are no figurines in Monte Alban II, and extremely few in IIIa. There is a handful of imported Teotihuacan vessels, and their forms are not uncommonly adapted to Oaxaca wares even though literal copies are rare. Thus, if the traits of the Teotihuacan ceramic complex were listed here one by one, we should have several cases of

*Kent Flannery: personal communication.
*Ignacio Bernal: personal communication.

"present" rather than a single case. The chart misses an important qualifier: in view of known contacts and the distance involved—a third of that to the Maya sites—the Teotihuacan culture had significantly little impact at Monte Alban (Paddock 1972a, pp. 237–38).

15. While no bodies of wheeled animal toys have been found, perforated ceramic disks like those found with them elsewhere are known at Lambityeco, and a niche in Tomb 6 contained over fifty of them. These are not worked sherds or spindle whorls.

16. Teotihuacan stone masks, or similar masks, are conspicuously absent. The extent to which the naturalistic faces on Monte Alban "urns" may be considered similar to the faces of Teotihuacan figurines (or, perhaps more appropriately, *braseros*) is best judged from some examples. No one would mistake the Monte Alban faces for the Teotihuacan ones, but they do have something in common. The significance of this occurrence seems to lie in the definition. There are no Monte Alban figurines that have faces like those of the Teotihuacan figurines; and the "urn" is a form absent in Teotihuacan culture.

17. Narrative composition occurs on Stela 7 at Monte Alban (Caso 1928, pp. 85–87, 144–45; 1965b, pp. 856–57), and, perhaps on another portion of the same stela, the "Estela lisa" (Acosta 1959, pp. 14–21, figs. 14–17; Caso 1965b, p. 856); several other stelae, of IIIa or IIIb, show single scenes with single personages but seem to be historical. If the "Danzantes" of period I were properly grouped, they would emphatically form scenes of lively interaction (Paddock 1966c, pp. 103–10), but those remaining in place are not very suggestive of this. We have no proof that their present placement, dating from Monte Alban I in and adjacent to Building L at Monte Alban, is their first use. In period IV the stone inscriptions do not usually involve attendants, but they do almost invariably show interaction of pairs of humans (Caso 1965b, fig. 16; 1965c, fig. 18; Paddock 1966c, pp. 220–22; Easby and Scott 1970, no. 167).

18. No scenes of human sacrifice are depicted, though there are depictions of decapitated heads, perhaps consequent on sacrifice (see nos. 20, 39 below; fig. 3; Leigh 1961; Moser 1973). Figurines with animal helmets (jaguars?) and holding what look like sacrificial knives are known from Monte Alban IV. The standing figures on some Monte Alban stelae, which are dressed in animal costumes and apparently have their arms tied, may be prisoners destined for sacrifice. What Caso interprets as a sacrificer's costume is worn by one personage of period V in Zaachila Tomb 1 (Paddock 1966a, pl. 15). But none of these is a depiction of the act. Scenes of sacrifice in the Mixtec codices are not counted here because none of them seems to come from the valley of Oaxaca; they are contemporary with Monte Alban V.

19. Unequivoval death figures are extremely rare. The huge, monkey-like skull of Dainzu is here placed in Transition (fig. 8). Caso (1969, fig. 7) shows a stone death's head from Monte Alban, of undetermined period and here placed in IIIb. There is another skull stone, probably late, in the Frissell Museum. Also of period V are the Zaachila examples (Paddock 1966a, pls. 16, 17, p. 326).

20. Trophy heads are plainly present in IIIb, when Xipe figures carry them (Caso and Bernal 1952, pp. 249–57; Paddock 1966c, p. 173) and in period IV when "warrior" figures carry or wear them (Moser 1973, fig. 21, pl. XVI). Small heads worn on necklaces or belts of sculptured and painted figures probably represent jade ornaments, not actual heads. At San Luis Beltran (a Monte Alban IV site), Bernal found a circle of large plates, each with a human skull and the top two vertebrae.* The clear depiction of a ritual involving a head (fig. 3a; Leigh 1961, fig. 6; Moser 1973, fig. 27) is from the Isthmus of Tehuantepec.

21. Whether or not the game played is the same, at Dainzu there are stone relief figures of what seem to be priests making offerings (fig. 9; Bernal 1968a, b). The majority of stones in this large group show ballplayers in action. Because the ballplayers and some of the associated offerings are of period II style, while the priest figures seem to be of IIIa, I have placed all the reliefs in Transition II–III. Small figures of seated personages wearing what might be yokes (fig. 6; Boos 1966b, p. 469) are of Transition or IIIa and may indicate a ceremony. A period V gold piece from Tomb 7 at Monte Alban (Caso 1965a, fig. 55; 1969, pp. 95–97) shows a ball court, perhaps a ceremony associated with death, and below it a sun disk. But there is nothing that resembles the elaborate ceremonial activities of costumed ballplayers at Bilbao, nor is human sacrifice depicted. On the other hand, if I proposed—as I certainly do not—that all scenes of ceremonial activity and all ritually costumed figures of Monte Alban were connected with the ball game, it would be impossible to refute the idea. This is slippery ground indeed.

22. 23. 24. 25. To this striking little group of absent or barely and dubiously present traits should be added 3, 7, 11, 12, 18, 27, 30, 32, 36, 40, and 41. That is, absences may be worth counting (fig. 10). Unless the diving god appears in some other guise, he is unknown. As for the eagle-jaguar complex, bird helmets are fairly common in II, III, and IV, but almost always identifiable as clearly not eagles (Caso and Bernal 1952; Paddock 1966c). Jaguar helmets are rather common on figurines of IIIb, and very common in those of IV, but to what extent this implies military orders of eagle and jaguar knights is an open question. Eagles receiving offerings are missing. The "tree of life" motif is very doubtfully present in the form of a tree or flowering plant shown on a stone in the Museo Regional of Oaxaca (fig. 11; Caso 1928, p. 120), and in a painting on Tomb 123 of Monte Alban (Caso 1965b, p. 869). Neither of these figures is associated with a death figure. The

*Ignacio Bernal: personal communication.

stone, which has been in the museum for about a century, is of unknown provenience. It seems to be an ignimbrite of the type common in the valley of Oaxaca. The style suggests IIIb or IV; I have placed it in IIb because the known stones of IV are of a highly distinctive style and content different from this one. The Tomb 123 paintings, placed in IIIb by Caso, I would suspect might be better dated, in view of what we now know, to Monte Alban IV.

26. One might argue for interpreting the "Danzantes" of Monte Alban I (and II) as gesticulating and, with less confidence, as consulting. Although phallicism occurs among the "Danzantes," they surely cannot be said to resemble the Bilbao reliefs. No monuments are assignable to Transition, though there is no reason to think none were carved; we just have no way of dating them. The Monte Alban stelae of IIIa and IIIb, like the interacting pairs (spouses?) of IV, may be included with somewhat more confidence, though here again the difference in visual impact—and content—from the Bilbao monuments is conspicuous. The Mitla murals of period V seem to belong here, and there might be other remains of the period that should be added, such as painted figures on polychrome pottery (some of which probably was made in the valley). But attendants and phallicism are usually lacking throughout after Monte Alban II.

27. Parallel lines around the bodies of relief figures are not known. In period IV, such lines do occur on some glyphs and garments, but this does not fit the definition of the trait.

28. Jaguar representations—more exactly, large felines—are extremely common in the valley, especially in pottery. The standing or walking feline is unmistakable in some Monte Alban stone carvings of period III and in pottery figures of the same times (Caso 1938, p. 6; Paddock 1966c, p. 173).

29. Whether they should be classed as the same trait is perhaps moot, but rather large knotted sashes are very common on the "urns" because they were used constantly by women, rarely by men, to hold up skirts; men used them at times for other purposes. While the Bilbao representations are much more flowing and those of Monte Alban always neatly in place, this may be because the Bilbao examples, which were on stone reliefs, were not subject to the practical restrictions of the Monte Alban examples, which were almost always on pottery figures. Even those shown on stone at Monte Alban are never represented as windblown or moving as a result of the figure's movements, though that occurs among the Dainzu ballplayers, but this may be only a reflection of the overall more static quality of the Monte Alban representations (Paddock 1966c, figs. 121, 124, 150, 174).

30. It may be that this trait should be marked present in all periods. The question is whether Glyph L of Monte Alban is the same as the *ollin* sign. The two lines often shown as painted or tattooed vertically across each eye may, Caso thought, be a mark of Xipe (see no. 39, below). This trait, whatever it is, occurs from beginning to end of Monte Alban culture, and

(in Mixtec style) in period V as well (Caso and Bernal 1952, pp. 249–57).

31. In general, the sun disk is conspicuously absent. It occurs, with a figure in Mixtec codex style, on the door stone of Tomb 11 at Yagul (Paddock 1955, p. 38), now in the Museo Regional of Oaxaca. Another example, of the same period, is in the Mitla murals (Seler 1904). A second stone, undated and also in the Museo Regional, is a polychromed sun disk, perforated in the center and carved on both sides. The period V examples in gold from Monte Alban (no. 21, above) and Zaachila (Caso 1966b, p. 328) are well known.

32. While there may be some stylized symbols that represent snake rattles, there are no unquestionable, easily recognizable ones (Caso 1965b, fig. 17 shows a typically dubious, overlong one). At times a snake may be shown complete, but with no indication of rattles. Serpent symbols are, of course, omnipresent, but they are strongly conventionalized and often totally unrecognizable as such, e.g., in carved decoration of IIIa pottery (Bernal 1949; n.d.; Caso and Bernal 1965, fig. 14; Caso et al 1967) and in the Mitla mosaics (Caso and Bernal 1952, pp. 145–62).

33. Monte Alban-style frames lack the bottom and are double on top and sides, but they are obviously related to the Teotihuacan form of plain rectangle, apparently as a source of it since they appear in Monte Alban II (Acosta 1965, p. 818), when they sometimes framed circular motifs as was also the case later at Teotihuacan. As noted above (no. 1), this trait survives after Monte Alban and flourishes at Mitla (Hartung 1970).

34. Framed rings are seen in Monte Alban II (see no. 33, above). Monte Alban *tableros* probably had some painted rings like those of Teotihuacan in IIa and IIIb, but the paint has not survived. The trait is clear in the Mitla murals of period V.

35. The valley of Oaxaca seems to be the place where the stepped-fret first occurs in Mesoamerica (Paddock 1966c, figs. 63, 69). It is used in architecture here for the first time in IIIb at Atzompa, a part of Monte Alban (Sharp 1970, n.d.). In period IV it occurs at Lambityeco, and in V at Mitla and Yagul. Although the Mitla friezes represent the highest development of the stepped-fret, they appeared much later than what might be called the "*greca* horizon," when Tajin and Uxmal are outstanding examples of the motif's widespread use.

36. Unless, like the snake rattles, the cacao trait occurs as a presently unrecognized symbol, it is not known. A town in the Etla valley, just north of Monte Alban, now bears the Nahuatl name of Cacaotepec; it may have had a Zapotec or Mixtec equivalent of this name earlier.

37. Speech scrolls are fairly common, and tabs occur on a few, as will have been noted in illustrations to which I have already referred.

38. Tlaloc—in the valley of Oaxaca more probably the neighboring Mixtec rain god Dzahui—does not occur very early. With Transition there come Tlaloc vases from Teotihuacan (Caso and Bernal 1952, p. 36; 1965, fig. 12),

and there is a Transition I-III "urn" that almost transforms the Monte Alban Cocijo into a Tlaloc-Dzahui (Boos 1966b, p. 49). This form remains very rare through IIIb, though I have a photograph of a period IIIb urn that has a Tlaloc-Dzahui in the headdress (fig. 12). In IV there are a few examples from Lambityeco and elsewhere—quite possibly in times when Mixtec invasions, peacable or otherwise, were beginning (Kowalewski and Truell 1970). In period V some stone figurines of Mixtec style (penates) are of this deity (Easby and Scott 1970, no. 267).

39. Unless we accept any human face having vertical lines across the eyes as a Xipe, this deity is not identifiable here before the large ceramic effigies of IIIb and IV (Caso and Bernal 1952, pp. 247–60; Paddock 1966c, figs. 90, 140, 175, 181). The common tiny Teotihuacan figurine with three circular depressions to represent eyes and mouth is unknown, though one of the examples cited, a hollow figure, has circular features. There is a famous period V gold Xipe from Tomb 7 of Monte Alban (Caso 1965a, p. 927; 1969, pp. 97–99), but of course this might have been made elsewhere.

40. Similarly, if we assume that the deity with a serpent mask or headdress is Quetzalcoatl, he is common in and around Monte Alban from periods I through IV, but there is nothing in the valley of Oaxaca that really resembles the wind god of late Central Mexico. Caso and Bernal (1952, pp. 142–62) were so doubtful of the identification of their Dios con Mascara Bucal de Serpiente with Quetzalcoatl that they used the name "Quetzalcoatl" only in a subheading of their long discussion and in a phrase at the end. Ehecatl is in any case a rather thorough transformation of Quetzalcoatl, and that the two terms are synonymous before Toltec times seems doubtful.

41. While there are many representations of old personages, male and female, a number of them more or less clearly identifiable as one or another deity, *braseros* are not among them. Therefore I conclude that Huehueteotl is unknown, or at least not represented in any durable material, in the valley of Oaxaca (one unmistakable stone one was found in the Mixteca Alta).

42. The circular cartouche that encloses a number of Bilbao inscriptions is not on Parsons's list, but I will add it. This is not because it occurs in the Nuine, but because there is one (fig. 13) in the Frissell Museum at Mitla. While the provenience of the cartouche is unknown, it is plainly in valley of Oaxaca style, probably of period IIIb. A period IV stone in the Museo Nacional de Antropologia (Caso 1928, p. 84) is the only other circular one I know of in valley of Oaxaca style.

ARTHUR G. MILLER

a brief outline of the artistic evidence for classic period cultural contact between maya lowlands and central mexican highlands

CULTURE CONTACT between highland and lowland Mesoamerica can be more clearly viewed in extant artistic evidence than in any other form of archaeological data from which inferences are drawn. The following outline is a brief compilation of the most salient iconographic and stylistic features of certain artistic remains that suggest that the lowland Maya area and the Central Mexican highland area were in cultural contact during the Classic period.

Before presenting some of the evidence for Classic period contact between the lowland Maya and highland Mexican cultures, a short statement about the intrinsic differences in the artistic expression of these two areas is in order. If we compare a mural from Bonampak (fig. 1) with a mural from Teotihuacan (fig. 2), we can see some obvious contrasts that are characteristic of the artistic canons of the two areas. First of all, in the Maya example, the subject matter is clearly narrative, whereas in the Teotihuacan example, it is presentational. In figure 1, a story—perhaps unclear to us, but clearly a story nevertheless—is being illustrated while in figure 2, a mass of symbolic images

is being presented in the form of a complex costume and setting. In figure 2 we see a plethora of visual imagery representing an elaborately dressed priest kneeling, or perhaps dancing, on a path leading to a "jaguar" temple. By contrast, the figures in the Bonampak mural are acting out a linear scenario—a historical event—involving the presentation of an important infant to a group of "elders." The Bonampak scene is a visual depiction of an event in time, whereas in the images of the Teotihuacan mural, there is a timeless symbolic quality. The emphasis in that mural is on what the priest symbolizes as seen in the details of his costume and in his attitude in front of the temple.

The clarity of the figures shown silhouetted against the plain light ground in the Maya mural is in marked contrast to the merging of the figure and the background in the Teotihuacan mural. This contrast is principally due to the particular use of color values in the two murals. In the Bonampak mural, color values in the figure-ground relationships are far apart, and they are close together in the Teotihuacan example. Thus, color serves to suggest a stagelike space in the Maya

1. Mural from Bonampak. After Kubler 1969, fig. 6a.

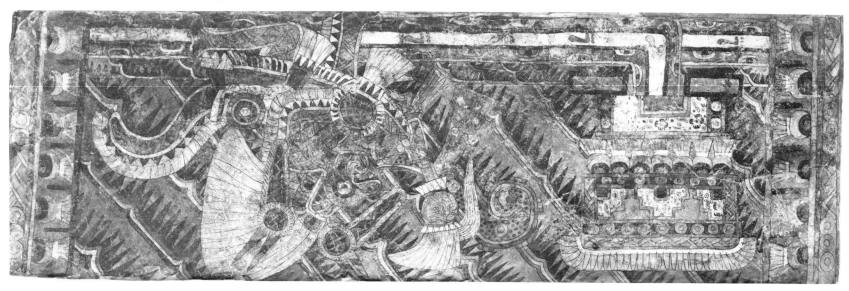

2. Teotihuacan mural from Tetitla. Courtesy of Dumbarton Oaks Collection, Washington, D.C.

mural, while it is used to deny any sense of space in the Teotihuacan mural. The marked differences of figure-ground relationships can be appreciated in the black-and-white illustrations in which color values are visible without their hues. We can see clearly the figures standing in figure 1, while in figure 2 it is difficult to make out just where the figure ends and the ground begins.

Some Examples of Artistic Contact
between Lowland Maya and Highland Mexicans

For some time now, our knowledge of artistic connections between the Maya area and Teotihuacan has been based on the finds of Teotihuacan-style objects and architecture found at the Classic Maya centers. In the 1930s and 1940s, Kidder, Jennings, and Shook (1946) excavated the site of Kaminaljuyu in the vicinity of Guatemala City and found Teotihuacan-style pottery in Mounds A and B. They noted that this Esperanza phase pottery was similar to some Teotihuacan pottery of the Tlamimilolpa and Xolalpan phases. The presence at Kaminaljuyu of Teotihuacan-style architecture, Thin Orange pottery, *floreros*, and *candeleros*, as well as the distinctive cylindrical tripod vessels, was interpreted as evidence of contact with the great metropolis of Teotihuacan located over 800 miles to the northwest. In addition to these Teotihuacan-style pottery wares, Mounds A and B also contained lowland Maya ceramics of the Tzakol phase.

The excavations of the Tikal Project from 1955 to 1964 produced some interesting finds that also appear to have been influenced by Teotihuacan. I am referring to the so-called Tlaloc face carved in low relief (Moholy-Nagy 1962) and to Stela 31, which shows alleged Teotihuacan warriors carrying square shields and Mexican *atlatls* flanking the main Maya figure (W. Coe 1965). Many pottery vessels reminiscent of highland Mexican ceramics were also found at Tikal. Most spectacular of all was the unearthing of a structure (5D-43) that reminded the excavators of Teotihuacan architecture so much that it was dubbed "the Teotihuacan structure" (W. Coe 1965).

There are Teotihuacan-related traits in the interior and exterior sculpture of Temples I and IV at Tikal. In a recent paper, Kubler (1976) has noted many Teotihuacan motifs on the lintels of these temples, the most significant of which is a mosaic-serpent helmet. A similar helmet

3. West wall of Structure 5D-57, Central Acropolis, Tikal. Courtesy of the Tikal Project, University Museum, University of Pennsylvania.

with platelike disk decoration appears on the roofcomb of Temple I. The Teotihuacan-associated mosaic-serpent helmet is found on Lintel 2 of Temple I and on Lintel 3 of Temple IV. Kubler suggests that the appearance of this motif further inside the temple on Temple IV asso-

4. East end, upper zone of Structure 5D-57, Central Acropolis, Tikal. Courtesy of the Tikal Project, University Museum, University of Pennsylvania.

ciates the ruler shown here more closely with Teotihuacan than the ruler shown on Temple II. "In effect, the Teotihuacan trait of the mosaic-serpent helmet in Temple IV has been promoted from the outer to the inner position, and from the profile presentation to a frontal one, suggesting an increase in importance for Mexican highland lineage in this generation at Tikal" (Kubler 1976).

Excavation in the Central Acropolis of Tikal revealed two Classic period buildings whose exterior upper end walls are decorated with sculpture having non-Maya stylistic and iconographic characteristics, which ultimately point to highland Mexico as a source. On one building, called Structure 5D-57, the west wall consists of deeply carved masonry with a thin application of stucco that was originally painted. The most salient features of this remarkable exterior sculpture are the masklike face and the shape and ornamentation of the feather head-dress (fig. 3). The overall shape of the head and the shape of the eyes, nose, and mouth bear a striking resemblance to the numerous stone masks associated with highland cultures influenced by Classic period Teotihuacan. Structure 5D-57 is dated Tepeu I according to the manner of construction; a radiocarbon date for the building has been read at A.D. 621.*

On Structure 5D-57 there is a facade sculpture on the east end that also consists of deeply carved masonry covered with thin stucco. The east end sculpture (fig. 4) shows a human figure with splayed feet. The figure is extraordinarily rigid in appearance because of the quantity of

* Peter D. Harrison 1973: personal communication.

iconographic detail that covers the entire body, leaving only the face bare; this manner of decoration is in itself a Teotihuacan characteristic, as can be seen in the sculpture and mural painting from the site (Miller 1973). This central figure assumes a top-heavy crosslike configuration. The figure's right hand is extended and holds a knot that ties the arms behind the back of a seated and nearly naked captive figure shown in profile. Flanking the scene of the frontal figure and profile captive figure are two inverted L-shaped glyph panels, which are in the process of being deciphered. The glyphs in the panels are Maya. The seated, bound, profile figure, the cross-legged pose, and the few items of clothing are all Maya traits in art. The facial features of the figure and the general soft, roundness of the body outline are also Maya artistic and physical traits.

In strong contrast to these Maya elements in the east end sculpture is the central figure that dominates the scene. This rigid, standing, frontal figure is angular. The visual juxtaposition of angularity and curvilinearity is a very effective formal device to distinguish captor from captive. In this regard, it is significant to note that general curvilinearity of visual forms is a Maya characteristic and angularity a Teotihuacan characteristic. The dominant central figure of this composition is replete with Teotihuacan iconography. Most striking is the masklike face flanked by huge ear plugs. This face is similar to the one shown in the figure 3 sculpture. The trilobe motif in the headdress, the asymmetrical bird of the headdress—reminiscent of the birds decorating the headdresses of late Teotihuacan figurines from Amantla—are some of the most obvious Teotihuacan iconographic motifs in this figure.

A discussion of the Teotihuacan presence at Tikal has been published by W. Coe (1972). In this paper, Coe outlines and discusses the implications of the most salient artistic traits found at Tikal. More recently, Teotihuacan-style objects have been found elsewhere in the Maya area. An unusual offering, associated with a cache in a substructure at Becan in the Rio Bec region of the Yucatan peninsula and dating from the Classic period, was excavated under the direction of the late Andrews IV of the Middle American Research Institute at Tulane University (fig. 5). The offering consists of a brown-slipped, carved, cylindrical tripod vase in which a two-piece, hollow figurine of Teoti-

5. Cylindrical tripod vase from Rio Bec.

huacan style was placed (Ball 1974a). Inside the hollow figurine were ten small solid figurines also of characteristic Teotihuacan style and iconography. The carving on the cylindrical tripod vessel in which the figurine was placed is in Maya style. The figurine represented on the vessel may be the Maya God B of the codices (more commonly known as Chaac), the lowland Maya equivalent of the highland Mexican Tlaloc.

Stela 11 from the Classic site of Yaxha in the department of Peten, Guatemala (Morley 1937–38, pl. 161b; Proskouriakoff 1950, p. 180) has recently been described as a carving that ". . . depicts Tlaloc fullface in Teotihuacan guise" (W. Coe 1972, p. 259).

Excavating at the Classic Maya site of Altun Ha, Belize, Pendergast (1971) recently found a temple structure containing a ceremonial offering of worked green obsidian of a type that comes from Central Mexico. Some of the worked obsidian was in a style similar to that of the obsidian "gingerbread man" found by Millon and his associates inside the Pyramid of the Sun at Teotihuacan (Millon 1961; 1965; Pendergast 1971, pp. 457–58). The date assigned by Pendergast to the Altun Ha cache is A.D. 150–200, which is contemporary with the dates for the Miccaotli phase at Teotihuacan (Millon 1967, p. 10). Rovner (n.d.) of the Becan Project goes so far as to state that the lithic evidence of green obsidian from the Yucatan peninsula (some of it in the Teotihuacan "gingerbread man" form) indicates a peninsula-wide Teotihuacan influence during the second century A.D.

A discovery made at Teotihuacan in 1971 may contribute to the accumulating data for artistic and cultural Mexican traits found in the Maya area. A cave, which once may have contained a spring, was found underneath the Pyramid of the Sun. Slate disks, beautifully engraved with anthropomorphic figures—one dressed in a jaguar costume, another dressed as a bird—were found inside the cave. These disks appear to have both Gulf coast and Maya stylistic influences (Heyden 1975). At least one underground cave containing water in Yucatan has been securely linked to highland Mexican influence: the cave of Balankanche near Chichen-Itza contained Tlaloc effigy vessels and was reported as being a "Toltec" sacred spot in use in A.D. 800 E. Andrews IV 1970). Underground cave water sources associated with Mexican traits have been reported from Xelha in Quintana Roo, and I have described Mexican traits in the Tancah Cenote cave, which is also in Quintana Roo (Miller 1974, p. 140). The full significance of the association of Mexican traits with underground water sources needs to be investigated further. In the meantime, the presence of such Mexican traits in the Maya area suggests cultural influence from the central highlands.

But what about influence in the other direction? Did Classic Maya style and iconography diffuse to highland Mexico? Do we find examples of Maya style and iconography at Teotihuacan? There are scattered hints of Maya trade relations with Teotihuacan, for which the best evidence is a Nebaj-style jade that was said to have been purchased at Teotihuacan. Maya pictorial designs may have reached Teotihuacan by means of painted ceramics. Kolb (n.d.) has shown that Linne (1942) and Millon (1964) both found sherds of the Early Classic Tzakol phase at the extreme eastern edge of the Teotihuacan site near Linne's Tlamimilolpa excavation. Kolb further discusses Teotihuacan's possible relationships with Barton Ramie, Tikal, and Monte Alban.

Some Evidence for Maya Influence in the Mural Painting of Teotihuacan

The so-called Pinturas Realistas mural fragments, said to come from Tetitla (Villagra 1952, pp. 70, 72–76, figs. 2–6), which is one of many fifty-seven-square-meter one-story apartment compounds at Teotihuacan (Millon 1970, p. 1077), show Maya personages and Maya glyphs. Hall (n.d., pp. 81–83, 85) has rightly pointed out that these paintings are more related to Kaminaljuyu art in the Guatemala highlands than to lowland Maya art. Several, lesser-known examples of Maya influence are to be found on other Tetitla paintings. First, the subject matter of the Tetitla Room 7 paintings is unusual and perhaps indicative of Maya influence. They represent old men emerging from shells, a theme more common in Maya than in Teotihuacan art (Miller 1973, pp. 134–36), and the depiction of beards on the figures is a trait also more frequent in Maya than in Teotihuacan representation.

The unusual shade of red employed in these Room 7 paintings at Tetitla (Miller 1973, fig. 269) is a yellow red, which results from mixing light red and ochre. The sash and part of the shell from which the man emerges are conspicuously painted with this pigment. The pigment is not found in any other Teotihuacan mural painting and is not to be confused with the common orange red found in the mural art of an earlier period at Teotihuacan. Such yellow reds are common on Tepeu phase ceramics of the Maya, and Maya trade pottery may have been the source of the influence on the color scheme of Teotihuacan art.

Room 27 at Tetitla shows another atypical Teotihuacan mural

(Miller 1973, p. 137). A seated figure in profile is shown with his legs crossed, a pose characteristic of Maya art. The figure is placed on the extreme right part of a wall facing the doorway. Whereas most Teotihuacan painting exhibits *horror vacui*, this wall has a large open space with the profile figure placed asymmetrically on it. Such a figure on a plain background is reminiscent of Maya pictorial compositions.

A figure swimming through stylized waves is depicted on the walls of Portico 26 at Tetitla (Miller 1973, p. 136). The subject matter of this mural is unusual because the figure is shown collecting marine shells in a net, despite the fact that Teotihuacan is 250 miles from the nearest sea. This mural, plus the presence of many actual marine shells and stone and ceramic models of shells, decorated pottery representing shells, and the numerous representations of shells in such monumental art forms as sculpture and painting, indicate that shells had a special significance at Teotihuacan. One particular type of shell depicted in Teotihuacan mural painting has been identified as *Strombus gigas* (Miller 1973, figs. 253–54), and in Mesoamerica, this shell is found only on the east coast of Yucatan (E. Andrews IV 1969, p. 9).

Another atypical example of Teotihuacan mural painting can be seen in a mural now in the Saenz Collection in Mexico City. The Saenz mural fragment shows two profile figures in dancing postures, both facing the same direction, dressed in complicated costumes. Although the Saenz mural is unmistakably Teotihuacan in such fundamental aspects as pictorial composition, style, and painting technique, it is blatantly non-Teotihuacan in the forms of the costumes and hats and in its possibly Maya subject matter. Curiously, the style has traits of what Robertson (1969) has described as the International Style of the Late Postclassic, as seen in the mural paintings of Tulum, Quintana Roo, and Santa Rita in British Honduras. The posture of the dancers is similar to postures in the Mixteca-Puebla codices. The obvious time gap between the Late Postclassic of the east coast of Yucatan and the Classic period of Teotihuacan (the Saenz mural must have been painted before A.D. 700) does not permit us to consider influences between Postclassic lowland Maya and highland Teotihuacan. Nevertheless, the late Maya elements of the Saenz mural may indicate some earlier Maya Influence at Teotihuacan.

The Mesoamerican Ball Game and Teotihuacan

The Mesoamerican ritual ball game is traditionally associated with Classic Maya and especially with Classic Veracruz centers. Evidence for the existence of the ball game during the Classic period—in the form of ball courts, ball-playing gear, and representations of ballplayers and ritual games—is found throughout Mesoamerica, with the notable exception of Teotihuacan. Evidence for the presence of a ritual ball game at Teotihuacan is restricted to two cases. One is the representation of a ball game in progress in the mural paintings of Patio 2 at Tepantitla (Miller 1973, figs. 162, 165). Two posts with *talud* and *tablero* bases and circular tops are shown lying on their sides. The posts demark an area where animated figures are playing ball with decorated sticks. The ball game represented is more reminiscent of North American lacrosse than of what we have come to know as the Mesoamerican rubber ball game, with its distinctive architecture and playing gear. The other indication of a ball game at Teotihuacan is an actual ball game marker found at La Ventilla (Aveleyra Arroyo de Anda 1963) similar to the markers depicted in the Tepantitla mural. The La Ventilla marker consists of four connected parts and was found inside a typical Teotihuacan-style miniature platform that occupied the center of an important patio in a multi-room domestic complex (Aveleyra Arroyo de Anda 1963).

The distribution of Teotihuacan figurines, currently under analysis, indicates that figurines of foreign origin, possibly Maya, come from certain *barrios* of Teotihuacan, particularly those of Tepantitla and La Ventilla.* An unusual figurine, with a head that is interchangeable with the head of an old man, is said to have come from the *barrio* of La Ventilla (Sejourne 1966a, pls. 25, 26). This figurine appears to be a Teotihuacan version of a Remojadas or possibly Jaina figurine. The head of the old man as an iconographic theme may be related to Maya art. These foreign surface finds in association with references to the ball game and the Tepantitla mural may all indicate Maya influences at Teotihuacan.

*Warren Barbour 1972: personal communication.

Summary

That there was artistic contact between the Maya lowlands and the Mexican highlands during the Classic period is demonstrated by the extant visual data. Clear evidence of Teotihuacan influence in the Maya area can be seen at Tikal, Becan, Yaxha, and Altun Ha. Mural painting provides good evidence for Maya artistic influence at Teotihuacan. Secondarily, ball-game-related representation, paraphernalia, and figurines, may also reflect a Maya presence at Teotihuacan. The fact that Teotihuacan painting is so rich and varied in style and iconography is surely partially the result of contact with foreign, particularly Maya, painting traditions. The accumulating tangible evidence of contact between lowland and highland peoples suggests a vast body of ideas—intellectual and practical—that the Maya and the people of Teotihuacan shared, but for which we have no direct archaeological evidence. We should be able to infer, therefore, contact of, say, poetry, when the only archaeological evidence we have of artistic contact is mural painting. Maya architectural forms that are influenced by Teotihuacan architectural forms can suggest that there were contacts between Maya and Teotihuacan astronomical thought. Ultimately, we must recognize the fact that there are vast categories of human activities that leave no archaeological trace but are as transferable as those that result in endurable material objects.

NICHOLAS HELLMUTH

teotihuacan art in the escuintla, guatemala region

DURING THE LAST six years, grave robbers have unearthed hundreds of Teotihuacan-related artifacts throughout the Tiquisate region of the Guatemalan department of Escuintla. The dozens of ornately decorated Teotihuacan-style incense burners, cylindrical tripods, *candeleros,* and figurines from this region make up the most extensive corpus of Teotihuacan-influenced artifacts in all Mesoamerica. The previously unsuspected intensity of Teotihuacan influence so far from Central Mexico will necessitate the formulation of new hypotheses regarding the nature and degree of Teotihuacan expansion in ancient Mesoamerica.

I first encountered Teotihuacan-related pottery in the private collection of Enrique Salazar in 1970. Later, in the private collection of Dr. Guillermo Mata, I found one decorated cylinder tripod. Dr. Mata introduced me to other collectors who allowed me to take the photographs that illustrate this report. During the past six years, I have photographed several hundred ceramic artifacts from the Tiquisate region. Such a quantity of Middle Classic material from Escuintla came as a surprise, for in the published literature, only a handful of Teoti-

huacan-style cylinder tripods and one or two *incensarios* from the Pacific coastal plain are illustrated (Kidder 1943, figs. 90v, w, 91j, k; Thompson 1948, figs. 26e, 46e; Kidder 1954, figs. 19a–h; R. Smith 1955, fig, 1h; Tozzer 1957, vol. 12, fig. 489; Shook 1965, figs, 2b–f; Parsons 1967b, pls. 14b, 16f–g).

The Tiquisate region of Escuintla is situated between Guatemala City and the black volcanic sand beaches of the Pacific Ocean (fig. 1). Shook has surveyed the region and provided the names of the sites from which he believes most of the Teotihuacan-related material is derived. At one site, Finca San Antonio Rio Seco, Shook noticed that hundreds of Teotihuacan-style sherds littered the freshly ploughed surface of a two-meter-high mound. A day of salvage excavation yielded the only controlled recorded find of such pottery in situ (C.I.W. files, Peabody Museum, Harvard University). Most of the pottery illustrated in this report comes from private collections that have no stratigraphic or other archaeological provenience.[1]

This report has the following aims: to describe the unsuspected

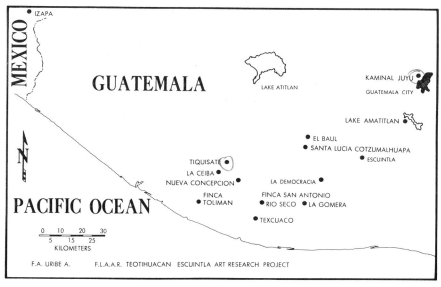

1. Map of the Escuintla* region.

*Escuintla is a department (state) of Guatemala; the departmental capital has the same name. Here, and throughout this report, "Escuintla" refers not to the capital but solely to the coastal half of the department from Tiquisate to the Pacific Ocean.

quantity of Teotihuacan-related pottery from the coastal plain of Guatemala; to analyze the decorative motifs of that pottery in order to interpret the nature (military, economic, religious) and degree of Teotihuacan influence on coastal Guatemala; to show that the Teotihuacan outposts throughout the Tiquisate region were one part of the sources of "Teotihuacan" influence at Tikal, Uaxactun, Tres Islas, Yaxha, and the rest of the Peten; to indicate that Veracruz influence coexisted with that of Teotihuacan; to suggest a new source for the origins of the Cotzumalhuapa (Bilbao) art style; and to present new evidence to support the idea of a relationship between the supposedly "Toltec" art of Chichen Itza and Middle Classic coastal Guatemalan art.

Incense Burners

Incense burners were the most complex artifacts made by the Middle Classic potters of Escuintla. A complete Teotihuacan-type *incensario*

ideally consists of two basic sections: an hourglass-shaped base and an elaborate chimney lid. The complete *incensario* is sometimes more than half a meter high (fig. 2). More than 120 Escuintla *incensarios* are known to me.[2] This number is considerably greater than the less than 25 published examples known from Teotihuacan itself.[3] In other words, more Teotihuacan-related *incensarios* have been recorded for the Tiquisate region than for Teotihuacan itself. In addition, more than 200 hourglass *incensario* bases have been brought up from the bottom of Lake Amatitlan (Borhegyi 1965).

The Tiquisate region incense burners have an hourglass-shaped base with a separate chimney lid. Whereas some Teotihuacan, Monte Alban, and Tikal hourglass bases are adorned, the Tiquisate and Lake Amatitlan bases are generally plain with at most a *talud-tablero* nose plaque motif, earspools, and a necklace (fig. 2). Since the Tiquisate bases are generally devoid of decoration, collectors are not interested in them. The looters simply leave the fragments of the bases scattered behind in their backdirt. Shook salvaged approximately five complete bases and fragments of another fifteen—all from a single mound at Finca Rio Seco. His unpublished photos show plain base types in a cache. Fragments of ornate chimney lids were found on the ploughed surface of the mound. Among the many chimney lids found to date, the following provisional types can be distinguished: male torso lids, seashell lids, flower-adorned lids, female figurine lids, and unique lids.

Male Torso Lids. The male torso lids are essentially provincial copies of Teotihuacan prototypes. The individual *adornos* are so similar to Teotihuacan *adornos* that they may have been made from molds brought from Teotihuacan. Although the overall *incensario* is complex, it is actually composed of several simple distinct parts, and each part is made separately from a small mold. While each mold may have been brought from Teotihuacan, the parts were apparently assembled locally. As a lot, Tiquisate *incensarios* look more like one another than they do any Teotihuacan prototypes. Comparison between the *incensarios* of the two regions is complicated by the fact that virtually all published Teotihuacan specimens have been reconstructed by antiquities dealers who sometimes used whatever fragments they had around.[4]

Several varieties of Escuintla male torso lids may be defined. An attractive kind has an individual rising up on butterfly wings, with a butterfly face and antennae in his headdress. A unique example of this type shows the butterfly deity rising from ripe cacao pods (fig. 3). Archaeologists have long presumed that Teotihuacan was interested in controlling the agricultural products of the fertile Tiquisate coast and the obsidian mines of the adjacent highlands. This remarkable *incensario* may indicate the importance of cacao growing to Teotihuacan colonists. Cacao plants are also shown on Tiquisate region slab-foot cylinder tripods (Photo Archives of Foundation for Latin American Anthropological Research).

A second common variety of male *incensario* lid is the "weapons-bundle" carrier (Hellmuth 1975, pls. 23, 24, 32). The "weapons" are usually only the decorated spear ends in sets of three or four. Spear points are usually not shown. It is nevertheless clear that the tasseled ball and diamond shape is the symbol of a special Teotihuacan spear. In certain owl and weapon representations (von Winning 1948), the whole spear is shown with this symbol at one end. On Tiquisate *incensarios,* the spear bundles are held in the hand or represented in the butterfly headdress. In a few Escuintla *incensarios,* the spear sets are contained within a heavily outlined frame (that coincidentally looks like an Olmec "knuckle duster"). Several other kinds of objects are held by these *incensario* personages (Hellmuth 1975, pls. 23 left, 25, 28, 29, 32, inside front cover). They include feathered rectangular shields represented in profile or some other unidentified object. Since most of the personages carrying these objects have spear-end decorations in their headdresses, these objects are probably items of armament or they relate to warrior symbolism.

The weapon-holding figure of the *incensarios* is also found represented on cylinder tripods (fig. 5). On the tripod vessel the figure has ringed eyes and wears the so-called tassel headdress. C. Millon (1973) has shown that this headdress was generally associated with warrior images. Pasztory (1974) has suggested that ring-eyed deities do not necessarily represent Tlaloc the rain deity but could represent warrior gods.

The Teotihuacan-related *incensarios* of Escuintla have other interesting traits. The Reptile Eye (RE) glyph, common at Teotihuacan, is

2. Escuintla *incensario* with hourglass base.

5. Escuintla ceramic tripod.

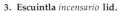

3. Escuintla *incensario* lid.

4. Escuintla *incensario* lid.

present on the chest medallions of several figures (fig. 4) (Hellmuth 1975, front cover, pls. 26, 27, 28, 32, 33, 37). It is tempting to associate the RE glyph with butterfly images, because the two types frequently occur together both at Teotihuacan on cylinder tripods and at Tiquisate on *incensarios*. But the RE glyph is so ubiquitous, that it is hard to connect with any one set of symbols.[5]

Most of the Tiquisate male *incensario* lids have *talud-tablero* nose plaques (figs. 2, 3). Other lids have ornate butterfly nose plaques (fig. 4). One unique specimen has a complete butterfly framed by a *talud-tablero* as a nose ornament. The *talud-tablero* nosepiece is not necessarily a stylized butterfly.

The source for the iconography of virtually all Tiquisate region male *incensarios* is clearly Teotihuacan.[6] Several Tiquisate region male *incensario* figures carry strap bags similar to those illustrated in the murals at Teotihuacan (Kubler 1967, fig. 45). These Tiquisate strap bags are usually of one variety, with side attachments and lacking a long pendant. Teotihuacan priests may have introduced this accessory

74   MIDDLE CLASSIC CONCEPT

into coastal Guatemala and Kaminaljuyu (Kidder, Jennings, and Shook 1946, fig. 204). From either Kaminaljuyu or the Tiquisate region, the bag was introduced to Tikal and the other Peten Maya sites. The Maya eventually adapted this bag as part of their own ritual accessories. Even in the Late Classic period, however, such bags still carried Teotihuacan symbolism—in the form of Tlaloc ring eyes—as decoration (Tikal Stela 16). The ceramic art of Tiquisate provides one missing link between Teotihuacan and the Peten Maya area.

Female Figurine Torso Lids. A type of *incensario* lid that consists of a large, three-dimensional, hollow, mold-made female figurine seated on an upside-down bowl, is completely distinct from the male *incensario* lid (fig. 6). The bowl is open towards the bottom and fits the top of the hourglass-shaped lower half. The figurine is usually so poorly bonded to the top of the vessel that the bowl does not survive excavation or transport. The figurines that sit on the *incensarios* are essentially identical to free-standing Escuintla figurines except for their larger size (they are twenty-five to thirty-five centimeters high). (When examining a free-standing figurine, one should always examine the bottom to see if the figurine was once attached to an *incensario* upper half.)

These Escuintla female figurines are characterized by their seated position—elbows free from the body, well-defined hands on knees or lap, with clothing and body well modeled on the sides and back as well as the front. The figure often holds a bowl, bird, or cacao pod. This figurine type is not widespread in Teotihuacan art, as far as can be judged from the published photographs.[7] The absence of this figurine type in Central Mexico is paralleled by the absence of the figurine *incensario* at Teotihuacan, and the form may therefore be a local Escuintla one. A few of the Escuintla figurine headdresses and the clipped hair bangs have parallels in Teotihuacan art (Sejourne 1966a, fig. 37 bottom left; *Artes de Mexico* 1970, p. 90).

Some Mesoamericanists have said that they detected Veracruz stylistic features in the Escuintla *incensarios*,* but the comments were informal with no specific references to actual published pieces. Full three-dimensionality is characteristic of Veracruz figurines, as it is of

*Harold McBride 1973: personal communication; Esther Pasztory 1973: personal communication.

6. **Escuintla female** *incensario* **lid.**

the Escuintla figurines, and a number of details are also shared. The manner of interweaving the hair (McBride 1971, pl. 28), the open-centered earplugs (Anton 1969, p. 163; Xirau 1973, pp. 120, 129, 157), and the clipped bangs (McBride 1971, photos 69, 72). One of the stranger features of the Escuintla figurines consists of the circlets on the shoulders. Somewhat similar bumps are present in the same place in Veracruz ceramic art (McBride 1971, pls. 33, 34, 37; Xirau 1973, pp. 114, 148). Similar shoulder markings on any Teotihuacan figures are not known to me.

A single feature that sets the Escuintla *incensario* figurines apart from northern Mesoamerican styles is the presence of nose-beads. This ornament is quite common in the south, in the Esperanza phase art of Kaminaljuyu (Kidder, Jennings, and Shook 1946, figs. 178c, 205f, and on Tzakol phase faces from the site of Holmul in the Peten. A rare and distinct type of Lake Amatitlan *incensario* that does not resemble the Escuintla type, also has the double nose-bead. This definite link between Escuintla and Lake Amatitlan *incensarios* is hard to explain, for otherwise the *incensarios* of the two regions are noticeably different. Amatitlan *incensarios* are far less pure Teotihuacan.

The urns of Monte Alban resemble the Escuintla braziers in several ways. First, and most important, they share the same boxlike, undefined rendering of the crossed feet. The actual toes are usually hidden by the long skirt and rarely stick out. Each Escuintla *incensario* foot variety has a Monte Alban counterpart: toes protruding (Caso and Bernal 1952, fig. 134); no feet at all (Caso and Bernal 1952, fig. 223); the toes of one foot protruding in the middle (Caso and Bernal 1952, fig. 36). Another trait shared with Monte Alban urns is the curled representation of the inner part of the upper ear above the earplug (Caso and Bernal 1952, fig. 345). The interwoven hair of Monte Alban urns is of the same general type as on the Escuintla figurines (Caso and Bernal 1952, figs. 436, 437). A striking feature of the Escuintla figures is that they hold offering bowls, birds, or cacao pods. Such offerings are on occasion held by Monte Alban urn figures as well (Boos 1964b; pls. XXIV, XXIII; von Winning 1968, pl. 227).

The art of coastal Chiapas and Oaxaca is still largely unexplored archaeologically, but one fine effigy vessel, from Santa Rosa Chiapas (Brockington 1967, fig. 24), is definitely a product of the general tradi-tion to be found at Escuintla. Although the spout on the back and certain minor details of costume of the Santa Rosa vessel are different, the large size, the twin nose-bead, and the boxlike base obscuring the anatomical detail of the legs is related. It is worth noting that this effigy vessel and its two companion pieces were unique at Santa Rosa. In this context, Brockington's comments on this rare piece are interesting:

As Delgado notes, the figure has a ". . . general aspect of Teotihuacan III" . . . It also bears considerable resemblance to Early Classic Monte Alban pieces, specifically Boos' "Deity with the Headdress Composed of a Horizontal Band," which is characterized by a ". . . horizontal band across the forehead of the feminine figure . . . a wreath or circle composed of overlapping feathers with a jade ornament . . . in the center . . ." [Boos 1966, p. 442] . . .

Bernal examined the Santa Rosa piece and, while agreeing that it has a definite Monte Alban aspect, sees no close resemblances. He pointed out that the nose ring never occurs at Monte Alban (personal communication).

We have a superb example of prehispanic sculpture that apparently represents a distinct but successful and confident integration of several known regional styles. Such an integration may have been the product of a yet unknown cultural center." [Brockington 1967, pp. 21–22].

Cylindrical Tripods

Ballplayers and Executioners. Ballplayers and executioners are frequently pictured in mold-impressed scenes on Tiquisate region cylindrical tripods. Seven almost identical scenes of single "decapitators" have been photographed (Hellmuth 1975, pl. 10). Tozzer (1957, vol. 12, fig. 489) illustrated one of the same kind. The identification of these personages as ball game players is based, first of all, on their position—down on one knee, the other leg bent—which is thought to be a typical ballplayer pose. A Chinkultic ball court marker, Edzna Stela 6, and a Copan ball court marker all show actual ballplayers in similar poses (Tozzer 1957, vol. 12, figs. 478, 485, 486). This pose is so peculiar and consistent that its association with some aspect of the ball game may be accepted. The relation of this pose to the ball game is stressed because, with one exception, the Escuintla scenes do not show any ball, ball court, *palmas,* or a traditional kind of yoke that would identify the figure unquestionably as a ball game player. The lack of padding in particular, might indicate that the celebrant is depicting a pre- or postgame activity in which the ball itself was not used. Before we seek to determine precisely what this nonplaying activity was, let us demonstrate more conclusively that the ritual association is with the ball game.

On two different Escuintla tripods, a thick belt is worn by the figure (fig. 7). The belt is outlined by a simple rectangular frame, with a row of disks in its interior. Similar belts are worn by the ball game players represented on the sides of the Great Ball Court of Chichen Itza (Tozzer 1957, vol. 12, fig. 474). It seems fair to assume that this belt with disks was a type of ball game yoke, of evidently a southern variety, since no such yokes are known from Veracruz (Proskouriakoff 1954; Kampen 1972). The other belt type on the Escuintla players consists of a human head on the right and a serpent head on the left (fig. 8). The discrepancy in size between the large human head and the squat and elongated serpent head may indicate that the two are separate entities stuck onto the waist or held separately. In the related art of Cotzumalhuapa, a human head is often carried, but not worn, at waist level (Tozzer 1957, vol. 12, fig. 487). On the Tajin ball court scenes, a human head is occasionally found in the waist-back position (Kampen 1972, fig. 22b). It is suggested that the head may be real, and is not a *hacha,* or a thin stone head, or any other artifact. Judging from another scene on an Escuintla vessel (fig. 11), the Chicken Itza ball court scene, and Cotzumalhuapa Stela 1, the head was probably freshly cut from an unfortunate victim.

The other portion of the Escuintla belt has a Mexican-style snake head with a long, thick eye scroll. If the human head is indeed separate, then the serpent head can more easily be recognized as a yoke of the Cotzumalhuapa type. Bilbao Monuments 1 and 3 show serpent heads on ballplayer yokes, although differences exist in the delineation of the fangs and the lack of pronounced eye scrolls (Parsons 1969, pls. 32a, 34a). It should also be noted that the Bilbao serpent heads face backward, not forward as on the Escuintla figures. The semi-

kneeling position and probable belt yokes are enough to show the association of these personages with some aspect of the ball game. The depiction of the actual ball in two different scenes is convincing proof of this argument.

The Escuintla ballplayers are not similar to the known representations of ballplayers in either Teotihuacan or Maya art. Borhegyi (1965, pp. 21–28; 1971, p. 87) has implied that the ball game was introduced into Guatemala by the people of Teotihuacan, a claim so far not supported by the Escuintla evidence. Yet the Escuintla ballplayers are represented on Teotihuacan-derived cylindrical tripods, and they may have been found in association with tripods that do have obvious Teotihuacan symbols. Despite the presence of Classic Veracruz-style scrolls on the Escuintla vessels, Veracruz is also not necessarily the source for the ballplayer figures. None of the Tajin ball game scenes show yokes of the Escuintla type. Mold-made scenes from the Rio Blanco region of central Veracruz are the closest in style and content, although many differences exist as well. Von Winning classifies the Rio Blanco scenes as having "design elements from El Tajin sculptures, from Teotihuacan and Maya art . . ." (1971, p. 34).[8] The belts, and especially the waist-level serpent heads of Rio Blanco, are similar to the Escuintla rectangular belts (fig. 10). These serpents, with their eye curls, are of the general Escuintla type, one difference being that the heads face up.

Several of the Rio Blanco celebrants are in the supposed "ballplayer pose," down on one knee. Their actual connection with ball playing is questionable, unless the circular heads near their feet are meant to represent balls decorated with faces. The animal heads at the waists of the Rio Blanco figures are definitely separate from any yoke-belt actually worn. Could these detachable animal heads be the same objects that are carried by the figures on the Chichen Itza ball court sculptures? Borhegyi identifies the Chichen hand objects as "jaguars," but the nature of the animals is irrelevant. Since the Rio Blanco scene shows these animal heads only loosely attached to the belt, perhaps the lack of animal heads on the Chichen ballplayer belts can be attributed to the simple fact that the heads are being carried. The large eye scrolls on the Rio Blanco and Escuintla heads could have functioned as handles.

7. Drawing from Escuintla tripod vessel.

9. Escuintla ceramic tripod. Denver Art Museum.

8. Escuintla ceramic tripod.

10. Rio-Blanco-style vessel. After von Winning, 1971, fig. 2a.

Until prototypes can be found elsewhere, the seven single-person scenes must be judged to be largely of local Escuintla inspiration. The Rio Blanco region of central Veracruz may have been one major source of inspiration, but the Rio Blanco style seems to have been modified during the long passage between coastal Veracruz and coastal Escuintla, which was on the other side of the continent. The Teotihuacan butterfly wings and "flames" on one of these Escuintla fragments show that Central Mexican art styles were known to the makers of the seven ballplayer pots, but the overall iconography is distinctly different from anything so far known at Teotihuacan.

The Decapitation Scene. One feature of the seven pots that was not mentioned is the unhafted stone knife in the upraised left hand. The unhafted knife is clearly shown in the Chichen Itza and Tajin ball game decapitation scenes and on Bilbao Monument 1. An unusual Escuintla cylinder tripod gives a rare view of this scene from Guatemala (fig. 11). The scene is sloppily presented in three main sections that consist of a striding executioner, a headless human body with serpents issuing from its bloody neck, and a rare hieroglyph from which volutes are emerging. The executor holds an unhafted stone knife in one hand and a bleeding head in the other. Although this type of knife was undoubtedly used in many situations unconnected with the ball game, the yokes worn by the figures and the tower of serpents rising from the neck of the victim suggest that a post-ball-game ritual is being commemorated, similar to the one seen at Chichen Itza. Aside from his thick belt, the Escuintla executioner's clothing is indistinct, due to sloppy casting from the mold. His headdress features some kind of bird or serpent monster with butterfly antennae in the front. Bird and serpent headdresses with butterfly symbols are also found on another Escuintla vessel showing a ball game scene with the players dressed as butterflies (fig. 12). Serpents are characteristic of the headdresses of the seven identical ballplayers discussed above. The executioner figure on the decapitation scene vessel appears to be of local inspiration, since at this time no definite foreign model can be found for it. The speech scroll in front of his mouth is not of the long, flowing Teotihuacan type with bumps, but is rather an inverted version that reminds one of the abbreviated El Tajin variety (Kampen 1972, fig. 22). Other specifically Classic Veracruz or Rio Blanco motifs are not obvious on the vessel.

The middle section of the vessel consists of the headless male body of a victim, still clothed, with a tower of serpents issuing from his neck. The thick belt of the Escuintla victim is of the type worn by the Chichen Itza ballplayers. The Chichen Itza representation also shows the decapitated ballplayer with six serpents and a vine emerging from his neck. Although the Chichen Itza scene has vaguely Classic Veracruz-style scrolls, the Escuintla scene does not. The horizontally arranged serpents are more naturalistically depicted than the single vertical serpent. The head of the vertical serpent is rendered in a general Teotihuacan manner, but the whole configuration of the serpent column is not typical of Teotihuacan art. Actually, the use of the cylinder tripod ceramic shape is the only indicator of a relationship to any Central Mexican cultural inspiration. The overall manner of depiction would have to be labeled local Escuintla, especially the careless rendering of the feet, the unnaturalistic, chunky appearance of the hands, as well as the sloppy workmanship of the whole scene.

Section three of the decapitation scene vessel consists of a stand supporting a head glyph in a thick cartouche, four liquid volutes, and five curls, each shaped like a fat "6." These Escuintla liquid volutes are distinguished from volutes in Izapan art, such as Izapa Stela 5, and from other renditions of water, by a bump on the upper part. However, similar bumped volutes are found on Izapan Stelae 21 and 23 and on the early Temple of Agriculture murals at Teotihuacan. Water symbolism is not particularly noticeable in the art of Bilbao. Curiously, on Izapa Stelae 23 and 24, the bumped curls issue from incense burners like smoke. The fat curls shaped like "6's" are usually called "flames," yet are often directly associated with shellfish and waves (von Winning 1948, fig. 10; Sejourne 1966b, fig. 85). This curl usually stands by itself as a design unit, but it is suspiciously similar to the body portion of a Teotihuacan conch shell (Sejourne 1966b, fig. 38). Like the bumped volutes mentioned earlier, the "6's" seem to be equally at home in water scenes and as "flames." The important feature is that both the volute and the "6" curl are apparently derived from Teotihuacan art. The "6" curl is also present in the art style of Bilbao (Parsons 1969, pl. 63i). The presence of both these designs in supposedly Pre-or Protoclassic Izapan art has not yet been explained by traditional historical sequences. Perhaps Izapa is the source both for Teotihuacan to the north and Escuintla to the south. Thus, the contemporaneous pres-

11. Drawing from Escuintla tripod vessel.

12. Drawing from Escuintla tripod vessel.

ence at both Teotihuacan and Escuintla may not mean contact between these two centers, but merely a common source of origin. The dates of the Izapan monuments are not yet satisfactorily documented in the literature. We can hope that the publications of the New World Archaeological Foundation will shed light on this important question.

The head glyph in the medallion bordered by the volutes is not related to any Teotihuacan representations. The type of head and the size and shape of the cartouche also rule out the Classic Maya as a source. The motif is most similar to heads in Monte Alban and Xochicalco glyphs. The Escuintla head is similar to the decapitated heads of the ball game scenes and to the bloody head held by the executioner on the same vessel. Could this glyph signify the decapitated head? This and other Escuintla glyphs are vaguely similar to the Cotzumalhuapa glyphs, as illustrated by Thompson (1948, fig. 62). They are not identical, however, and perhaps in Escuintla we have the rare opportunity to study a hieroglyphic system hitherto totally unknown in Mesoamerica. Since Cotzumalhuapa is situated in the same general region as Escuintla, we might look to that tradition as the source of the glyphs. The dates of Cotzumalhuapa art are possibly a century or so later than the majority of Teotihuacan manifestations. The early dates for Cotzumalhuapa art proposed in the literature have not been generally accepted, partially because the art of several time periods is found in Cotzumalhuapa, and the differing styles are confused in the literature. Stylistic evidence favors a date of Tepeu 1 or 2 equivalent for most of the Bilbao stelae, slightly later than the Tzakol 3 Esperanza date of the Escuintla ceramic art.

We have, then, on one cylinder tripod from Escuintla, motifs from Teotihuacan, Chichen Itza, Cotzumalhuapa, Monte Alban, or Xochicalco. The contemporaneity of these motifs from diverse Mesoamerican regions is amply demonstrated by the fact that the motifs are all on the same pot. This combination of otherwise regionally distinct art styles is the most noticeable feature of the ceramic art of Escuintla.

Star-belt Personage and Tlaloc Scene. In 1971, an antiquities seller loaned me, for one afternoon, two large slab-footed tripods to study. One was bulbous rather than strictly cylindrical in shape (figs. 13, 14), and its slab-feet tripod supports had been knocked off long ago. My photographs, taken in cramped quarters, were overexposed, and there

was not enough time available to draw the scene carefully. The drawing published here is a rough sketch and only outlines the main features of the scene: a head glyph with arms over a trimountain symbol, a Tlaloc seated inside a temple with a bleeding heart in front, and a stylized personage wearing a star design on his belt. The following brief description attempts to show the diverse origins of the motifs on this one pot.

The head glyph is of the same general tradition as the other glyphs on Escuintla pottery—definitely not Maya or Teotihuacan— closest to Xochicalco, Cotzumalhuapa, or Monte Alban. The "6's" around the glyph are similar to the flame or water designs seen on the pot with the decapitation scene. The trimountain symbol, the butterfly wing on the right, the "6's" and the treble-scroll designs are taken from Teotihuacan art, whereas the glyph and the hands are definitely local Escuintla in style. The curious rendition of the hands is similar to hands shown on later (?) Cotzumalhuapa stelae (Thompson 1948, figs. 2–8). The feet of the Escuintla personages are not similar to the abnormally crooked feet of the figures on the Cotzumalhuapa stelae. It is reasonable to suppose, at least on the grounds of geographic and temporal proximity, that there was some form of connection with later Cotzumalhuapa art. The origins of Cotzumalhuapa art may not derive directly from Teotihuacan, but rather from the Middle Classic ceramic art of Escuintla.

Three other motifs on the Escuintla vessel are of Teotihuacan derivation: the butterfly wing, the bleeding heart, and the treble-scroll symbol. The lines on the far right of the scene outline a butterfly wing of Teotihuacan type. Although this identification is not immediately evident, a perusal of Teotihuacan art quickly shows it to be correct.[9] The bleeding heart in front of the goggle-eyed personage and the trimountain symbol are both obvious copies of Teotihuacan art. In a thorough examination, minor stylistic differences can be noted, and the Escuintla artist may have borrowed these motifs from a Teotihuacan provincial outpost rather than directly from Teotihuacan. (That the bleeding heart really represents a heart has never been documented, but the name is a convenient one.) Above the butterfly wing is a "water blob" that is quite common in Teotihuacan art (Sejourne 1966b, figs. 12, 28, 66). Another water blob is to the left of the star-belt

13. Escuintla tripod vessel.

14. Drawing of Escuintla tripod vessel.

personage. The tail marks this as distinct from the usual treble-scroll symbol (von Winning 1946).

The striding figure shown on the left of the scene is virtually unique in Mesoamerican art and is, therefore, difficult to discuss in a comparative framework. The headdress is poorly molded, but what little is visible looks strange. The arm has a curl at the shoulder of unknown significance. Similar shoulder curls are occasionally shown on Teotihuacan jaguars (von Winning 1948, fig. 10). The hand holds what appears to be a ball with an appendage of some sort on top. The feet are barely impressed in the clay, but they appear to be flat on the ground and not in the upturned Cotzumalhuapa position. The clothing is simple and unlike the generally elaborate Teotihuacan costumes. The giant star in the round cartouche that covers the whole midsection of the body is an unusual form. Whereas stars are common at Teotihuacan (either starfish or a sectional view of a conch shell), only rarely is the Teotihuacan star used in what might be construed as a glyphic context (Sejourne 1966b, fig. 84). Only one other known Tiquisate scene has a similar star in a context related to military symbolism (fig. 15). Some coastal Oaxaca Rio Grande stelae and a Veracruz mural (Gendrop 1971, pl. 123) have glyph cartouches on the midsection of a male figure, but these representations may not all be related.

The ring-eyed personage seated inside a temple has the facial features of a traditional Teotihuacan Tlaloc (fig. 16), but the setting of the profile bust inside a temple is not characteristic of Teotihuacan art (but rather of Postclassic Mixtec codices). In Tajin art, profile figures are shown inside buildings, but they do not resemble the Tiquisate scene. A Tikal cylindrical tripod, in so-called Teotihuacan style, shows humans in temples in profile, but this vase may be a locally made Guatemala artifact. R. Millon has indicated that this vessel shape is not typical of Teotihuacan.* Two types of ring-eyed deities are found in Middle Classic Tiquisate art, the rain deity (fig. 16) and the war deity (fig. 5). One cylindrical tripod from Tiquisate represents a frontal Tlaloc with a lightning bolt in one hand and a Tlaloc effigy in the other.[10] The ring-eyed deity with the tassel headdress is undoubtedly the prototype for the warrior images of Yaxha Stela 11 and Tikal Stelae

* Rene Millon 1972: personal communication.

15. Drawing of Escuintla tripod vessel.

31 and 32. The political implications of the prominence of the warrior deity and absence of the rain deity in the lowland Maya area need to be further investigated.

Second Star-belt Scene. A cylinder tripod of related interest is illustrated in figure 15. The arrangement of the figures, the rendering of the designs in a convoluted, swirling manner, differ from the geometric Teotihuacan style. Such motifs as ringed eyes and speech scrolls, however, are of Central Mexican origin. The overcrowded composition and the manner of modeling whereby lines are not continuous create a complex interweaving of lines in which individual designs are dif-

16. Drawing of Escuintla tripod vessel.

ficult to isolate from the overall pattern. A somewhat similar composition is evident on the Rio Blanco scenes from Veracruz.

One possible parallel to the star-belt at Teotihuacan is a star glyph represented on the body of a feline (Gendrop 1971, fig. 49). On this feline (or possibly coyote), the star is clearly a heraldic emblem. Chichen Itza has by far the greatest known variety of star-belts. Most of these pointed designs are clearly derived from a spiny seashell (Tozzer 1957, vol. 12, figs. 183, 287–89, 474, 597). The only other place so far where glyph-belts appear frequently is in the little-known art of coastal Oaxaca. Here, Brockington (1969) has found a fascinating new stela. Although no actual stars are shown inside the cartouches, the location of the glyph on the belt and the geographic proximity of coastal Oaxaca to coastal Escuintla would indicate that there was a direct connection between the two regions. Since a number of Oaxaca traits were borrowed in Escuintla art—a curl nose deity on cylinder tripods, the feet forms of the figurine *incensarios*—other artistic connections may come to light. Since neither coastal Oaxaca nor coastal Escuintla is well known archaeologically, glyph-belts eventually may be discovered on new monuments. The origins, interregional diffusion, and symbolism of the glyph-belts need further discussion. At this point, the only conclusion that can be made is that on the Escuintla glyph-belt vessels, motifs from more than one regional tradition are to be found side by side.

Escuintla appears to be quite different from areas such as the central Peten that at times were culturally isolationist. Once we recognize the degree to which Escuintla had contact with the outside, historians can begin to study the ways in which outside stimulus may have influenced sixth- to eighth-century Escuintla in areas other than the ceramic arts. Political organization, warfare, trade, and religion may also have been enriched by new ideas from Veracruz, Teotihuacan, and Oaxaca. Curiously, we have not found any influences from the south, but since the archaeology of coastal El Salvador is poorly known, such influences could be present in Escuintla, and we would have no way to detect them.

Notes

1. Thick rain forest vegetation used to protect the many sites of Escuintla, but in the last four decades, the forest was cut down to provide farming and cattle-grazing land. Since the mounds get in the way of efficient ploughing and planting, the owners do not object to their workers bulldozing the mounds to make level ground. In this process vast quantities of pottery are ripped out of the ground. The local workers supplement their meager income by selling artifacts found on the surface. The men eventually initiated their own moonlit diggings to find whole pottery. Since neither local police nor landowners had much concern for simple adobe mounds, the looting has increased steadily. Although I have repeatedly reported this looting to the Instituto de Antropologia e Historia, no effective salvage studies or protection has been forthcoming. Since the National Museum has not collected any of this important material, one is forced to photograph the pottery wherever it is found—in antiquities shops or in local private collections.

2. The photograph archives of the Foundation for Latin American Anthropological Research include about ten hourglass bases, twenty-five male torso chimney lids, eight seashell-flower-adorned frame chimney lids, ten female figurine chimney lids, and more than twenty large fragments of various types. In addition, I estimate that another forty whole *incensario* lids have been smuggled to the United States and Europe (especially Belgium) within the last six years. About thirty *incensarios* exist in private collections in Guatemala, which I have not yet photographed.

3. *Artes de Mexico* 1957, pl. 60; Seler 1960, vol. 5, pls. XXXIV-2, XXXV, XXXVI-a, LI, LXIV; Dockstader 1964, fig. 35; Fondo 1964, pls. 321–23, 394–96; Sejourne 1966b, figs. 13, 23–28, 30, lams. 9–13; Anton 1969, pl. 183; von Winning 1968, p. 222; *Artes de Mexico* 1970, pp. 90, 91, 110; Xirau 1973, pls. 62–65.

4. Dealers will save up fragments from various sources until they have enough parts to create an entire *incensario* lid. The Tiquisate *incensarios* are usually found intact; minimal enhancing is practiced by the local restorers.

5. In my opinion, it is more prudent to await additional discoveries than to undertake a detailed study of the hundreds of known representations of the RE glyph. Earlier published observations on this symbol are unacceptable because today much more new evidence is available.

6. Only one Guatemalan coastal *incensario* differs from these norms, showing possible Monte Alban traits. This brazier, in the Joslyn Museum, Omaha, is listed in the museum catalog as being from Antigua, Guatemala. Antigua is located in the highlands, about twenty kilometers from Escuintla. Escuintla pottery is often brought to be sold in antiquities shops in Antigua.

7. I do not have available the figurine collections from Teotihuacan that are being studied by Charles Kolb and Warren Barbour, so I cannot yet judge whether this Escuintla type is actually absent at Teotihuacan.

8. These pots deserve a separate style name in order not to term them "Classic Veracruz." Despite their source of origin in the state of Veracruz, the lack of overwhelming scroll interlace designs, the presence of Teotihuacan elements, and their own

marked regionality, demand a special name to distinguish them from the Tajin and traditional Classic Veracruz art works. "Rio Blanco" appears to be the most appropriate name.

9. The artists of Teotihuacan painted colorful butterflies on their murals (Kubler 1967, figs. 3, 4) and on their pottery (Seler 1960, vol. 5, p. 479, fig. 90, p. 502, fig. 148b, p. 515, fig. 167, p. 525, figs. 178–180; Sejourne 1966b, figs. 12, 39, 93, 121, Kubler 1967, figs. 42–43). Butterflies in association with Reptile Eye glyphs are also frequent (Sejourne 1966b, fig. 36). Butterflies are common on Teotihuacan incense burners (Sejourne 1966b, figs. 25, 28).

10. The vessel is in the collection of General Carlos Arana Osorio, former president of Guatemala.

MARVIN COHODAS

Diverse architectural styles and the Ball game cult: the late middle classic period in yucatan [1]

THE MIDDLE CLASSIC PERIOD (A.D. 400–700) as defined by Parsons (1969), appears to have been a time of intensive interaction among the regional cultures of Mesoamerica. Much of this interregional contact was certainly stimulated by trading relationships, which probably were as elaborate and far-reaching as those of the Aztecs. This trade is evidenced by the widespread diffusion and acceptance of art motifs, techniques, and entire cults throughout Mesoamerica. In Yucatan, the intensive mercantile interaction of the Middle Classic period, and its resultant economic prosperity, stimulated the spread of the ball game cult and the development and/or elaboration of at least four distinct architectural styles.

Parsons divides the Middle Classic period into a Teotihuacan phase (A.D. 400–550) and a Teotihuacanoid phase (A.D. 550–700). The early phase is distinguished by the widespread influence of the Teotihuacan culture in trading relationships, settlement patterns, architecture, ceramics, and other arts. The later phase is characterized by the absorption of Teotihuacan traits and their subsequent use in the for-

mulation of several distinct new art styles throughout Mesoamerica. It is this later phase that will be discussed in the following analysis of Yucatan prehistory.

While the influence of Teotihuacan in the early Middle Classic period is well known and easily recognized, especially at sites such as Kaminaljuyu and Tikal, the effects of this influence on the art styles of the succeeding period are not well understood. Parsons found that the most distinctive traits of the late Middle Classic period were elaborated primarily in art styles that had not previously been dated to this period. The most important of these are the Xochicalco and Cotzumalhuapa styles. Similarly, the present definition of the late Middle Classic culture in Yucatan relies in part on the analysis of art and architectural styles that are not widely accepted as Middle Classic in date. This problem is most apparent in the redating of some Toltec-related architecture at Chichen Itza—formerly considered Postclassic—to the Middle Classic period. However, this redating of Chichen-Toltec architecture appears valid, especially because of the architecture's relationship to other Middle Classic manifestations of the ball game cult.

The following discussion will consist of both an analysis of ball-game-related art in Yucatan and a definition of the late Middle Classic Yucatan architectural styles. Several Yucatec ballplayer sculptures will be identified and examined through comparison with similar representations from the southern Maya lowlands in order to determine their Middle Classic affiliations and significance. The architectural styles that existed in Yucatan during the late Middle Classic period will be identified on the basis of probable dating and then defined according to their stylistic and technical characteristics. It will be shown that while a uniform manner of representing ballplayers is found throughout Yucatan during the late Middle Classic period, the architectural styles located in the same regions remained distinct. Finally, the changes that these architectural styles underwent during the final decades of the Middle Classic period will be described. These discussions of Middle Classic culture in Yucatan will include the related site of Coba, in Quintana Roo.

Ballplayer Representations

Both Pasztory (1972) and Parsons (1969) suggest that the ball game achieved great importance and widespread acceptance in the Middle Classic period. Pasztory demonstrates that the ball game achieved the status of a state cult in Mesoamerica only during this time. This suggests that an analysis of the diffusion and elaboration of the ball game cult during the Middle Classic period should contribute to a better understanding of the nature of the commercial relationships and interchanges of ideas that produced the Middle Classic horizon.

The spread of the ball game cult throughout Mesoamerica during the late Middle Classic period appears to have been directly related to trade (Pasztory 1972; Cohodas 1975). For example, in the Maya area, representations of ballplayers in the stone sculpture of the southern Lowlands cluster near the rivers (Usumacinta, Pasion, Sarstoon), which were used as the primary trade routes across the base of the Yucatan peninsula (and also in areas on the east and west, as at Copan and Chinkultik, which are intermediary between the highland and lowland Maya environments). Furthermore, there is a constant association between cacao, which in Aztec times was used as currency, and ballplayers in both the sculpture of the Cotzumalhuapa region and in ballplayer figurines of Jaina (Campeche) and Lubaantun (British Honduras) in the Maya lowlands. The depiction of cacao pods in Classic period representations of ballplayers is significant in view of Sanders and Price's suggestion that Teotihuacan expansion in the Middle Classic period may have been related to the acquisition of cacao resources (1968). This relationship between the ball game and trade was retained in Aztec times. According to Sahagun (1950–71, bk. 2, pp. 133–34), the merchants of Tenochtitlan were called upon to perform the human sacrifices (Panquetzaliztli ceremony) in the Teotlachtli, or Ball Court of the Gods.

It thus appears that two primary characteristics of the Middle Classic horizon—the importance of trade and the emphasis on the ball game cult—are linked in terms of cause and effect. This suggestion explains why major late Middle Classic trading centers, such as Bilbao in the Cotzumalhuapa region and Tajin in central Veracruz, devoted most of their art to representations of ballplayers or the ball game. It will also be shown that the economic ties that involve Yucatan in the late Middle Classic period bring the same emphasis on the ball game cult, as seen especially in sculpture of the Puuc region and at Chichen Itza.

Most of the Maya ballplayer sculptures that are dated by inscription are from the southern lowlands. By examining these dated sculptures, it is possible to determine that they occur in two phases of the Late Classic period: during the seventh century, or late Middle Classic, and during the period from A.D. 780–810. It will be shown that a completely distinct type of ballplayer representation is employed in each of these two phases, and that this differentiation of ballplayer types allows the identification of late Middle Classic ballplayer representations in Yucatan.

In the southern Maya lowlands, the seventh-century sculptures of ballplayers occur on ball court markers that are usually placed in sets of three along the midline of the ball court playing field. Those markers, which have been dated, include the Chinkultik relief, dated by inscription to A.D. 590, and the preserved set of Copan markers that

Proskouriakoff (1950, p. 116) has dated to the middle of the seventh century (A.D. 652–62). As may be seen on the Copan markers, players in action are depicted in a half-kneeling posture that in frontal view takes on a distinctive squared-leg appearance. The ball is shown in a disproportionately large scale between two confronting players. This representation of the playing ball is usually decorated with hieroglyphs or with the head of a deity. Other features that appear on

1. Stela from La Amelia.

markers bearing this type of ballplayer are vine motifs, as on the Copan markers, and the representations of ball court architecture as on the markers from Lubaantun (Morley 1937–38, vol. 5, pls. 162 a, b, c) and from an unidentified Usumacinta River site (not published). The consistent features of the late Middle Classic Maya ballplayer representations are the confronting ballplayers, the half-kneeling pose that shows squared legs in frontal view, the large ball with hieroglyphs or the head of a deity, and the frequent inclusion of vine motifs and ball court architecture.

The second type of Maya ball player representation occurs on sculptures dated to the period A.D. 780–810, which are found only in the Pasion-Chixoy River drainage, with the exception of a relief from Piedras Negras (Morley 1937–38, vol. 3, fig. 97). Stelae 5 and 7 from Seibal (dated A.D. 780 according to Greene et al [1972, pp. 222, 226] and A.D. 800 according to Graham [1971, p. 153]) and La Amelia (fig. 1) are examples of this type. In these sculptures, ballplayers usually appear on paired stelae rather than on markers. The players always stand, with one heel raised, and one player is shown dorsally. The ball is not shown—with the exception of the Cancuen altar (Morley 1937–38, vol. 5, pl. 96b) on which no glyphs or deity head appear—and ball court architecture never appears. These later ballplayers are thus easily distinguished from the seventh-century players on the basis of the standing pose with one raised heel, the dorsal view, and the absence of the depiction of the playing ball, half-kneeling posture, or ball court architecture.

All representations of ballplayers in the northern Maya lowlands conform to the seventh-century type as defined above. In addition, many of these sculptures may be dated to the seventh century on the basis of archaelogical information. Before examining the representations of ballplayers in Yucatan, two ballplayer reliefs from other areas of the northern lowlands will be mentioned. Altar 2 at Uxul (Ruppert and Denison 1943, pl. 59) in Campeche is one of the best-dated ballplayer sculptures, with an inscription that clearly records a date corresponding to A.D. 692. The sculpture includes confronting ballplayers in the square-leg posture, however the representation of the playing ball appears to have been defaced. Stela 6 at Etzna (Tozzer 1957, vol. 12, fig. 485) displays a half-kneeling player who rests against

2. Bench relief from the Great Ball Court, Chichen Itza.

a ball court profile, including the bench, playing wall, and tenoned ring. This profile does not correspond to the actual ball court at Etzna; rather it is most similar to the ball court type occurring at Chichen Itza and Uxmal (Tozzer 1957, vol. 11, p. 138) as will be discussed shortly.

Ballplayers are represented in Yucatan at such sites as Ichmul, Labna, Uxmal, and Chichen Itza. The undated Ichmul reliefs (Proskouriakoff 1950, fig. 82) display the consistent features of the seventh-century type, with half-kneeling figures confronting the ball decorated with hieroglyphs.[2] The representation of ballplayers at Labna occurs on a now-destroyed section of the flying facade, on the pyramid-temple known as the Mirador. Stephens's (1963, pp. 30–31) illustration and description of this temple show that the stucco relief over the central door consists of two squared-leg players confronting a ball. As will be explained subsequently, the architectural features of the Mirador are appropriate to a seventh-century date for this relief. Finally, a three-dimensional stone sculpture of a ballplayer in squared-leg posture is known from Uxmal. On the basis of circumstantial evidence, a

3. Red House platform superposed over ruined ball court, Chichen Itza.

possible date may be suggested for this sculpture. The ballplayer lies in a pile of sculpture that is said to have come from the North Building of the Monjas Quadrangle,* a structure that is dated by C_{14} to A.D. 653 ± 100 (Foncerrada de Molina 1965, p. 168). All of these ballplayers conform to the seventh-century type as seen in the southern lowlands. While none of them can be securely dated, there is no evidence to suggest a date later than the seventh century or late Middle Classic period.

At Chichen Itza, the bench reliefs of the Great Ball Court, the Monjas Ball Court (Bolles n.d.), and the Red House Ball Court (Ruppert 1952) all contain elaborate depictions of seventh-century ballplayers. The panels in all three ball courts are identical in format (fig. 2). In each panel, two lines of players confront a ball that is decorated with the head of a deity. The first players in one of the two lines is depicted in the half-kneeling pose, and from his severed neck sprouts a vine. The confronting players, the half-kneeling posture, decoration of the ball with the head of a deity, and the vine motif conform to the seventh-century ballplayer type as seen at Copan.

None of these Chichen Itza reliefs can be securely dated. All three ball courts have been considered to date to the Early Postclassic period (A.D. 900–1200) because the reliefs are carved in the so-called Toltec style of Chichen Itza. There is no concrete evidence to suggest such a late date for these reliefs. Rather, the evidence suggests a Classic period date. Both the Red House Ball Court and the Monjas Ball Court structurally underlie the Classic period (Florescent or Chichen Maya style) structures known as the Red House and Monjas second-story structure, respectively. This sequence of the Red House group, which was suggested by Folan (1968, p. 50) is confirmed by a recent clearing of the west bench of the ball court, revealing the superimposition of the Red House platform above it (fig. 3). The early placement of the Monjas Ball Court was discovered by Bolles (n.d.) and Brainerd (1958, p. 43). The Monjas Ball Court was found to underlie the pyramid on which the second-story structure is placed. These stratigraphic records clearly demonstrate the Classic period dating of the Chichen Itza ball court reliefs. Furthermore, the ball game cult is entirely absent from all

*Edward Lifschitz 1974: personal communication.

known Postclassic sites in the Maya lowlands. Since the Chichen Itza reliefs are Classic in date, and since they conform to the Middle Classic type of ballplayer representation, it may be suggested that they date to the late Middle Classic period, contemporary with the other Yucatan ballplayer representations.

With the identification and tentative dating of these representations of ballplayers in Yucatan, some conclusions may be offered. First, the seventh-century ballplayer type is consistently employed for ballplayer representations in both the southern and northern sections of the lowland Maya area. This indicates that during the seventh century, or late Middle Classic period, all lowland Maya sites drew on the same standardized type for the representations of ballplayers. The standardization of the type, and the rapidity with which it spread, are clear evidence of intensive trade relations between all regions of the Maya lowlands during the late Middle Classic period.

The second conclusion supports Pasztory's (1972) suggestion that as a state cult the ball game was limited to the Middle Classic period in Mesoamerica. The majority of Maya stone sculptures representing ballplayers were carved during that period. These sculptures are not only more numerous than those dated from A.D. 780–810, but they are also more widespread and carry more complex symbolism. Furthermore, the majority of the seventh-century representations in the southern lowlands occur on ball court markers, while those of the later period are found on stelae. The importance of the ball game cult in the Middle Classic period is also evident at Chichen Itza, where nine ball courts were constructed of which the Great Ball Court is the largest structure at the site and the largest in Mesoamerica. This situation is paralleled in other regions of Mesoamerica. Tajin, in Veracruz, contains at least seven ball courts, while the sculptures of both Tajin and the Cotzumalhuapa region are devoted primarily to the ball game cult. These two conclusions again support the premise that trade relationships were directly linked to the spread and elaboration of the ball game during the Middle Classic period in Mesoamerica. Furthermore, the importance of, the ball game cult in the Puuc region, as at Uxmal and Labna, and at Chichen Itza, demonstrate the participation of Yucatec culture in the major trends of the Middle Classic period.

While the Middle Classic of ballplayer representations in the

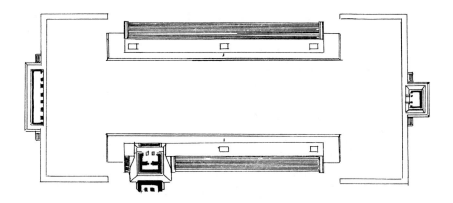

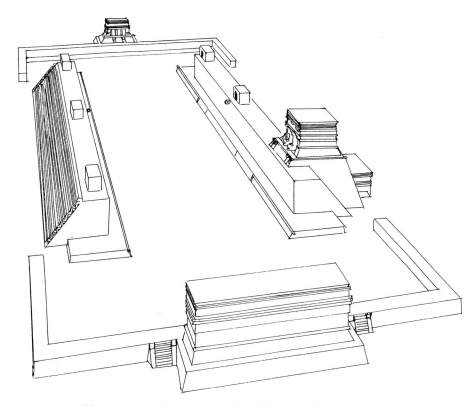

4. Plan and perspective view of the Great Ball Court, Chichen Itza.

northern and southern Maya lowlands are similar in configuration, the difference in sculpture type is marked. The ball court marker is the dominant form of ballplayer representation in the southern lowlands area that surrounds the major river systems. From the Peten northward, such a standardization of form is absent. Each site in the north appears to have chosen a medium appropriate to its own sculptural and architectural interests. For example, ballplayers occur on an altar at Uxul, relief panels at Ichmul, a stela at Etzna, in architectural sculpture at Labna and Uxmal in the Puuc region, and on ball court bench reliefs at Chichen Itza.[3] This diversity of form, which occurs particularly in the northern lowlands, is one aspect of the diversity of artistic traditions in the late Middle Classic period, as will be discussed in the analysis of Yucatan architectural styles.

In Yucatan, a particular ball court type appears to have spread with the standard form of ballplayer representation. This type is distinguished by vertical playing walls, sloping benches, and tenoned rings. Both ball courts at the metropolis of Coba (Thompson et al 1932), in Quintana Roo, were built with short playing walls and large sloping benches similar to the ball courts at Copan. By contrast the Coba courts display tenoned stone rings used as goals rather than the tenoned serpent and bird heads that are common in the Copan region. Both Coba courts are dated to the seventh century on the basis of inscribed dates on associated stelae (Thompson et al 1932).

The ball court at Uxmal (Ruz Lhuillier 1958) has a higher vertical playing wall, which is decorated with reliefs of feathered serpents. The two tenoned rings from this Uxmal court are carved with inscriptions that date the court to A.D. 649. The three ball courts at Chichen Itza (fig. 4), mentioned above, display the same profile, tenoned rings, and feathered serpent decorations.[4] The Uxmal and Chichen Itza type of ball court, with the high playing wall, corresponds to the ball court depicted on Etzna Stela 6. It appears that a specific type of ball court with vertical playing walls and tenoned rings was dispersed in Yucatan contemporary with the spread of the seventh-century type of ballplayer representation.

In summary, it would appear that ball game iconography was accepted in Yucatan at the same time and in the same standardized form as in the southern lowlands. All of the ballplayer representations in

Yucatan belong to the seventh century or late Middle Classic type, and there is no archaeological evidence to suggest a later date for these sculptures. The ball game appears to have received the same emphasis in late Middle Classic art outside of the Maya lowlands, especially in Veracruz and the Cotzumalhuapa region. Through identification and tentative dating of these ballplayer representations, it has been possible to show that Yucatec culture participated fully in the major trends that characterize the late Middle Classic period throughout Mesoamerica.

Late Middle Classic
Architectural Styles in Yucatan

Four architectural styles appear to have coexisted in the central regions of Yucatan during the seventh century or late Middle Classic period. They are: 1. the Puuc style, restricted during the late Middle Classic period to the Puuc hills of southeastern Yucatan, and including such sites as Uxmal, Kabah, Labna, and Sayil; 2. the Chichen Maya style, restricted to Chichen Itza; 3. the Chichen Toltec style also restricted to Chichen Itza; and 4. an unnamed but widespread style that was elaborated in most of the other major Yucatan sites and in Coba, Quintana Roo. Because this fourth style developed during the Regional or Early Classic phase in Yucatan, it will be called the Regional style.

Since the dating of these four architectural styles is problematic, the evidence for assigning them to the late Middle Classic period will be considered in some detail before they are defined in terms of style and technology. It may be stated as initial support for the present dating, that seventh-century type ballplayers occur at Puuc (Labna and Uxmal) and Regional (Ichmul) sites as well as in the Chichen Toltec architecture of Chichen Itza. The ball court with vertical playing wall and tenoned rings is associated with the same three styles. It will be shown that, although the four styles mentioned above are not confined to the late Middle Classic period, they are contemporaneous during this period.

The dating of these four architectural styles is dependent on the dating of that phase of Yucatec prehistory known as the Florescent phase. Florescent phase architecture is distinguished by the technique of veneer masonry in which thin, well-dressed facing stones are tenoned into a load-bearing, concretelike hearting. The Puuc style of architecture, which has been considered typical of the Florescent period, is further recognized by an architectural decoration formed of stone elements tenoned into the facade and fitted together like a mosaic to form geometric patterns and depictions of long-snouted deities (the so-called mosaic masks). Most of these decorations are found on the upper facades of Puuc buildings, which are vertical in contrast to the sloping upper facades that are prominent in the southern lowlands.

Since the beginning of the present century, the chronological placement of the Florescent period in general, and the Puuc remains in specific, has been the subject of extended debate. The source of the debate is the lack of precise correlation between ceramic phases in Yucatan and the ceramic sequence in the southern lowlands. The southern lowland ceramics are securely dated by their relation to the Maya inscriptions recording long-count dates that can be fixed in relation to the Christian calendar. By contrast, there are no long-count dates in the Yucatan region that are associated with Florescent-style remains. To further confuse the issue, there is also no agreement on the chronological relationships between the subregions of the northern lowlands, including the Chenes (Campeche), Puuc, Regional, and Chichen Itza areas.

While disagreement on the dating of the northern lowland architectural styles in relation to those of the southern Maya is still strong, there is enough evidence to support a correlation between the Florescent phase with the Late Classic period (A.D. 600–900) in the southern lowlands. This dating was first supported by Thompson, who, in 1937, suggested a method by which the cyclic Maya dates that occur on inscriptions in the Puuc area and at Chichen Itza could be fixed in relation to the long-count dates used in the south. He suggested that all inscribed dates in Yucatan that are associated with Florescent remains occur between the years A.D. 600 and 900. Although this dating method has not been accepted, in 1941, Thompson was able to cite further evidence for a Late Classic-Florescent correlation. He found that the ceramic trade wares known as Plumbate and X-Fine Orange, which were known to be Postclassic in date and which occur at Chichen Itza, are not found in Puuc sites. Since Thompson's analyses, several C_{14} dates have been analyzed from Florescent structures at Uxmal, and they confirm Thompson's opinion that the Florescent phase began by A.D. 600. Foncerrada de Molina (1965) has further demonstrated the validity of Thompson's dating through an analysis of these C_{14} dates and a comparison of Uxmal architecture with the Late Classic architectural styles of the southern lowlands. Finally, in his synthesis of lowland Maya architectural styles, Pollock (1965) retained Thompson's dating of the Florescent phase from A.D. 600–900.

Within the last two decades, an increasing tide of disagreement with Thompson's dating of the Florescent period has arisen. Many North American scholars believe that the Florescent phase began later than the southern lowland Late Classic period. In his analysis of Yucatan ceramics, Brainerd (1958) attempted to date the Florescent phase on the basis of dated trade-ware ceramics from the Peten region of the southern lowlands. Since finds of trade wares in the Puuc area were scant and poorly documented, Brainerd based his dating on the appearance of Puuc architectural technique (veneer masonry) and ceramics (slate wares) at sites outside the core Puuc area (the Regional sites), arriving at a date of A.D. 700 for the start of the Florescent phase.

More recently, Smith (1971) and E. Andrews IV (1965b) have suggested that the Florescent phase does not begin until A.D. 800. Smith bases his dating on the fact that the technique of carving designs in elite ceramics, which is characteristic of the Florescent slate wares, does not become popular in the Peten until the ninth century. Andrews based his dating on the appearance of veneer masonry at Dzibilchaltun, a large but provincial Regional site in northern Yucatan.

Brainerd, Andrews, and more recently, Ball (1974b) have attempted to support this later dating of the Florescent phase on the basis of a single example of architectural stratigraphy at Uxmal. The Chenes architectural style, which dominated Campeche during the Late Classic period, is known to have begun by A.D. 600. Since the Puuc-style Governor's Palace rests on a platform that is built over a Chenes-influenced structure (Pollock 1970), these authors have suggested that the Puuc style is at least somewhat later than the Chenes style, and that it must therefore begin after A.D. 600. This argument

may be questionable, since the Governor's Palace is acknowledged by most authors (Kubler 1962, p. 149; Foncerrada de Molina 1965, p. 169; Pollock 1970, p. 85; E. Andrews V*) to be a late structure in the Uxmal sequence. Consequently the Chenes-derived structure that preceeds it could easily postdate earlier Puuc-style structures at Uxmal.

The ceramic analyses that Brainerd, Andrews, and Smith use to prove a later date for the beginning of the Florescent phase also seem insufficient. Brainerd and Andrews rely on the appearance of Puuc architecture and ceramics outside of the core Puuc area. Brainerd himself suggests the probability of a time lag in the diffusion of these traits, but both he and Andrews ignore this caution in their analyses. Finally, Smith ignores the possibility of carved ceramics becoming popular in the Peten after long use in Yucatan, although current investigations at Altar de Sacrificios and Seibal (Ball 1974b) point to significant Yucatan influence in the southern lowlands, especially during the ninth century.

In order to resolve the conflicting opinions presented above, and to incorporate the information presented in the analysis of ball game representations in Yucatan, it is suggested that the Florescent phase is contemporary with the Late Classic phase in the Peten, and that it begins by A.D. 600. It also appears that the Puuc architectural style that distinguishes the Florescent phase did not spread out of the core Puuc area until A.D. 700. This suggestion allows for a century of Puuc development contemporary with the other architectural traditions in Yucatan and accounts for the first appearances of the Puuc tradition at Regional sites in around A.D. 700. This dating indicates that during the seventh century, the Puuc and Regional styles coexisted in Yucatan, and explains the appearance of the seventh-century type ball court at both Uxmal and Coba.

The above analysis suggests the existence of an Early Puuc phase that is primarily confined to the area of the Puuc hills and that dates to the seventh century or late Middle Classic period. The definition of this Early Puuc style is based on Pollock's (1965, p. 431) analysis of Puuc architectural development and on C_{14} dates. Pollock suggests that the pyramid-temple, and the roof comb or flying facade[5] with stucco

---

* E. Wyllys Andrews V 1974: personal communication.

decoration that usually appear on such temples, are Early Puuc characteristics. The Labna Mirador is an example of such a pyramid-temple. As mentioned above, the stucco decoration on the Temple's flying facade includes a representation of seventh-century-type ballplayers.

The first stage of the Magician Pyramid at Uxmal, also known as the Magician I Temple, is an Early Puuc structure (fig. 5). This temple, the earliest of five construction stages in the Magician Pyramid, is built with a roof comb and has a C_{14} date of A.D. 569 ± 70 (Foncerrada de Molina 1965, p. 168). The Magician I Temple (Saenz 1972, pl. 1) displays many decorative features that appear to be characteristic of the seventh-century or Early Puuc style. Some of these decorations are the spools, simple lattice panels, attached colonnettes with spools at the center, *tau*-shaped pendants, double step-frets, masks with heavy convex eye bands, serpent heads with human heads between the jaws, the rounding of temple corners with attached columns, and the decoration of the lower facade flanking the doorways. All of these traits consistently appear as a complex on many structures in the Puuc area. For example, the arch at Labna (fig. 6) is decorated with attached corner columns, double step-frets, simple lattice designs, *tau* pendants, and a roof comb. The serrated molding band that occurs on this arch appears also to be an Early Puuc trait.

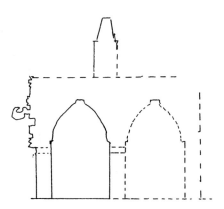

5. Magician Pyramid at Uxmal, cross section and details.

6. Arch at Labna. After Marquina 1964, photo 360.

The decorations on both the Magician I Temple and the Labna arch are formed of stone mosaic rather than the carved stucco used on the Labna Mirador, but they share a simplicity and boldness that differ from later Puuc decorations. More importantly, they depend for aesthetic effect on the contrast between distinct areas of light and pockets of shadow. This effect is particularly evident in the arrangement of the *tau* pendants and lattice pattern, but it is also true of the composition of the other ornaments. For example, the heavy eye bands on mosaic masks make the eye area appear as a pocket of deep shadow.

The North Building of the Monjas Quadrangle at Uxmal (Marquina 1951, photo 376) may also be considered a seventh-century structure because of its early placement in the Monjas sequence (Kubler 1962, p. 149) and because of its C_{14} date of 653 ± 100 (Foncerrada de Molina 1965, p. 168). The decorations on the North Building parallel those of the Magician I Temple even to the extent of repeating the Tlaloc-like heads with trapeze-and-ray signs. In addition, the North Building employs another method of giving height to the facade. Instead of adding a flying facade or roof comb, mask panels are made to project above the roof line.

Three-dimensional sculptures are attached to the facade of the North Building. Among those sculptures no longer in situ that are said to come from this structure, and that include the ballplayer mentioned above, are life-sized standing human figures. These figures wear loincloths decorated with *tau* pendants (c.f. Chinkultic marker) and are carved in a style similar to that of the seventh-century stelae from Tonina in the southern Maya region (Blom and La Farge 1926–27). A similar figure may be seen in the facade of the east wing of the Labna palace (fig. 7), one of the finest examples of Early Puuc architecture. The Labna facade also includes several other characteristics of the seventh-century Puuc style, including the decoration of the lower part of the facade, the *tau* pendants, colonnettes with spools, rounded corners, a serpent with a human head in its jaws, and a bold, three-dimensional mosaic mask with convex eye bands. The contrast of the shadowy pockets and areas of highlight is especially evident in the mask form, *tau* band, and lattice background.

The style of seventh-century Puuc architecture is to be charac-

7. Labna palace. After Marquina 1964, photo 362.

ized by the use of veneer masonry, pyramid platforms, roof combs, flying facades, roof projections composed of masks, both temple- and range-type buildings, and both stucco and stone decorations. The decorative motifs that are characteristic of the early phase stone facades include spools, colonnettes with spools, attached columns or colonnettes used to round the corners, pendant *taus*, double step-frets, simple lattices, masks with convex eye bands, serpents with human heads in their jaws, and serrated moldings. The Early Puuc aesthetic relies on simple, repetitive forms in projecting and recessed patterns that give bold contrasts of light and shade. The Early Puuc style includes a wider range of ideas than is found in later Puuc architecture. For example, both pyramid-temples and range-type buildings are constructed, both stucco and stone are used for decoration, and these decorations occur on the lower facades, upper facades, flying facades and roof combs. By contrast, later Puuc architecture is more restricted, since it consists only of range-type buildings that lack roof projections, flying facades, or roof combs, that are decorated only in stone and only on the upper facade, and that have more intricate and fussy decorations.

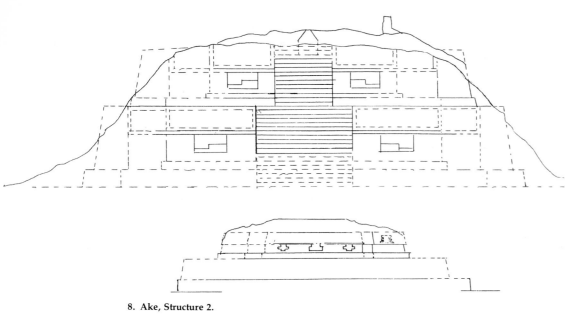

8. Ake, Structure 2.

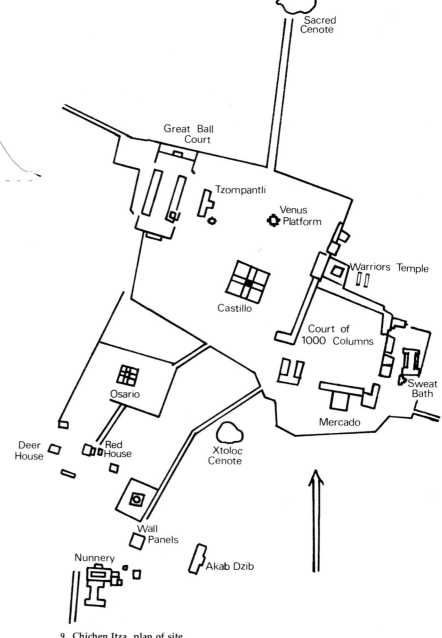

9. Chichen Itza, plan of site.

The Regional architectural tradition developed during the Early Classic period at sites such as Ake, Izamal, Oxkintok, and Yaxuna. The evidence for the continuation of this architectural style through the seventh century is strongest at Oxkintok (Brainerd 1956, p. 15) and Coba (Thompson et al 1932). Many of these sites also show Puuc-style structures that are small and stratigraphically later than the Regional-style structures.

While the poor preservation of Regional-style structures precludes an analysis of their decorative style, the technological features may be easily summarized. Regional structures are built in a block masonry technique in which the heavy facing stones are load bearing, in contrast to the veneer facing used in the Puuc area. At some sites (Ake, Izamal, and Coba), this block masonry reaches megalithic proportions. The ruins of Ake (fig. 8) and the Regional-style remains at Oxkintok (Shook 1940) are the best-studied Regional sites. As in the Puuc sites, Regional-style temples are often built on steep pyramids; however, they lack roof combs or flying facades. Decoration is only in the stucco medium and consists of figural motifs. The platforms are decorated with recessed panels and the temple walls are frequently pierced by window openings. All of the important sites with Regional-style architecture contain elaborate systems of causeways that are used for intrasite communication as well as for communication between widely separated sites (for example, Coba to Yaxuna and Izamal to Ake).

The last two architectural styles of the late Middle Classic period in Yucatan are both limited to Chichen Itza (fig. 9). The Chichen Maya architectural style consists of multi-room, range-type buildings built in the block masonry tradition, and often decorated with mosaic designs. The Chichen Toltec style consists of one- or two-room structures built in the veneer masonry technique. The most elaborate of the Chichen Toltec structures also include multiple columns that are used as interior supports or to form grand colonnades. Decorative traits characteristic of the Chichen Toltec style are feathered serpents carved as entrance columns or balustrade reliefs. The differences in form and technique between Chichen Toltec and Chicken Maya structures have led scholars to postulate different dates for each style. It will be shown in this section, however, that the two Chichen Itza styles were contemporary during the late Middle Classic period.

Thompson's (1937) dating of the Puuc and Chichen Maya (i.e., Florescent) structures to the Late Classic period included the assignment of all Chichen Toltec architecture to the Postclassic period. The evidence for this dating is based on the similarity between some Chichen Toltec structures and the architecture of Tula, Hidalgo—the primary Central Mexican site of the Early Postclassic period—as well as the association of the Toltec king Quetzalcoatl (Maya Kukulcan) with both sites. It has been assumed that Quetzalcoatl conquered Chichen Itza, displacing the local Maya population that was responsible for the Chichen Maya architectural style, and introducing the Chichen Toltec style of architecture.

While this Postclassic dating of the Chichen Toltec remains has until recently enjoyed universal acceptance, new information (Parsons 1969) suggests that the Chichen Toltec style began during the seventh century, contemporary with the beginnings of the Chichen Maya and Puuc styles. Parsons has presented much of the evidence for this dating, and Pollock (1965, p. 393) has also voiced discontent with the Postclassic dating of Chichen Toltec architecture at Chichen Itza.

Rather than repeat Parsons's arguments, this discussion will focus on the inconsistencies and questionable interpretations that have supported the Postclassic dating.

The evidence that has been employed to support this dating is in three forms: legendary, ceramic, and architectural. The arguments corresponding to each of those forms will be analyzed briefly, and it will be shown that there is, in fact, no shred of secure evidence for the traditional Postclassic dating of Chichen Toltec architecture.

The Mexican chronicles of the conquest period relate the story of Quetzalcoatl, a priest-king and culture hero who was exiled from his capital, Tula, because, after living a pure and chaste life, he was tempted into sin. According to most of the chronicles, Quetzalcoatl journeyed south with his followers, then immolated himself and rose to heaven as the morning star. However, the Spanish Friar Sahagun reported that Quetzalcoatl sailed eastward from Veracruz instead of immolating himself (Tozzer 1957, vol. 11, p. 28). Jimenez Moreno (1941) suggested that this voyage led him to Yucatan whereupon, as Kukulcan, he conquered Chichen Itza and performed other deeds recorded in the chronicles of Yucatan.

The Aztec tale of Quetzalcoatl's sin and punishment is paralleled by events described in the Yucatec chronicles. Three brothers are said to have shared the rulership of Chichen Itza. They were virtuous and celibate until one of them died or went away, whereupon the other two sank into sin and debauchery and were put to death by their subjects (Tozzer 1957, vol. 11, p. 31). These three brothers are credited with the construction of the Castillo of Chichen Itza, a temple that Landa (Tozzer 1957, vol. 11, p. 31) also ascribes to the worship of Kukulcan. The association of the Castillo with both the three ruling brothers and Quetzalcoatl-Kukulcan, and the parallel tales of each as sinful rulers, suggest that both the Maya and Mexican legends are elaborations of a single mythic theme. If this is true, then these two different versions of the theme cannot both be accepted as historical fact. However, the acceptance of Quetzalcoatl's exile from Tula is the crucial link in dating Chichen Toltec architecture to the Postclassic period.

It may also be shown that the Yucatec chronicles are consistently interpreted as recording events that they do not, in fact, record. The traditional interpretation of the portions of the chronicles dealing with Quetzalcoatl-Kukulcan and with Chichen Itza is as follows: in 987, Kukulcan, the exiled Toltec king, conquered Chichen Itza and displaced the local Maya population, the builders of the Chichen Maya temples. Actually, the chronicles record that the Itza inhabited Chichen Itza, not that they conquered it. The chronicles do not specify that the Itza were led by Kukulcan, although he is sometimes mentioned in connection with them. Finally, the chronicles do not mention a local population at Chichen Itza, but rather suggest that Chichen Itza was not inhabited before the arrival of the Itza (Tozzer 1957, vol. 11, pp. 36–39). In short, the conquest of Chichen Itza by Kukulcan, and his displacement of the local Maya population is a hypothetical event that is not recorded in the Maya chronicles of Yucatan.

The Yucatec chronicles known as the *Chilam Balam* record the arrival of the Itza at Chichen Itza in a *katun* 4 *ahau*. In Maya calendrics, the *katun* is a 20-year period that is named for the *ahau* day—from 1 to 13 *ahau*—on which it ends. The total cycle of the 13 *ahau katuns,* or the *katun* round, requires 260 years, so a *katun* 4 *ahau* occurs every 260 years. The date 987 was chosen as the beginning of the *katun* 4 *ahau,* which was closest to the end of the Classic Maya culture. This choice was based on the preconceived idea that Kukulcan and the Itza arrived after Maya culture had ceased to flourish. In order to correlate this dated event with the exile of Quetzalcoatl from Tula, Jimenez Moreno (1941) chose one of the many disparate dates given in the various Aztec chronicles of Quetzalcoatl that, by adding two calendar round cycles of 52 years, would reach A.D. 986. Again a prejudgment was used to manufacture historical fact out of legendary evidence.

These related choices of late tenth-century dates for the beginning of the Toltec epoch in Yucatan are accompanied by even further uses of legendary material as historical fact. The books of *Chilam Balam* actually record the events of all *katuns* from several centuries before to many years after the conquest. Since the 260-year *katun* round is a cyclic calendar, many *katuns* 4 *ahau* are included. Other passages in these texts show that each of the thirteen *katuns* in the *katun* round carries a symbolic or prophetic meaning, and this meaning is applied to the *katun* histories. For example, in the *Chilam Balam* of Chumayel, which is concerned primarily with the history of the Itza, several *katuns* 4 *ahau* in the historical series are associated with arrivals: two *katuns* 4 *ahau* record arrivals of the Itza at Chichen Itza and a third records the arrival of the Spaniards. Similarly, *katuns* 8 *ahau* carry an evil portent. For this reason, most *katuns* 8 *ahau* in the Chumayel series are associated with an abandonment or destruction related to Chichen Itza or the Itza (Tozzer 1957, vol. 11, p. 245). The Chumayel chroniclers, writing up to two centuries after the conquest, recorded oral traditions that had, through long centuries of retelling, already been changed and elaborated in order to fit into the symbolic pattern of the *katun* round.

Therefore, it appears that the suggestion of the date A.D. 987 for the arrival of the Itza is suspect on two counts. First, *katun* 4 *ahau* is a cyclic date that can occur every 260 years, so that the determination of the proper *katun* 4 *ahau* for the arrival of the Itza is subjective. Second, the fitting of history into prophetic time cycles invalidates the acceptance of any *katun* 4 *ahau* as the actual date of a historical event. To return to the conventional interpretation of the chronicles—that Kukulcan conquered Chichen Itza in A.D. 987—it has been shown that the chronicles do not record this conquest and that the date A.D. 987 cannot be accepted as historically correct, even for the arrival of the Itza. Consequently, if the chronicles are to be used in the interpretation of Yucatan prehistory, they must be interpreted objectively and not stretched to fit a preconceived conclusion.

The ceramics of Chichen Itza have been studied primarily by Brainerd, who (1958, p. 31) states that "although no certain stratigraphic evidence for the sequence from Florescent to Early Mexican ceramics is yet available, architectural stratigraphy is definite between the two styles in the Caracol and Monjas complexes at Chichen Itza, and is accompanied by documenting ceramics." The first part of Brainerd's statement still holds true: as yet, no stratigraphic evidence for a Florescent to Toltec ceramic sequence has been found, since Florescent slatewares are always found mixed with the Mexican (supposedly Toltec period) slate wares (Brainerd 1958, pp. 36–38; Smith 1971).

The second part of Brainerd's statement, concerning definite architectural stratigraphy and documenting ceramics, is based on supposition rather than proof. First, there is no definite Maya to Toltec architectural stratigraphy at Chichen Itza. In the Caracol Complex,

Chichen Toltec annexes are thought to postdate the primary structure, which is considered to be transitional Maya-Toltec. Ruppert's (1935) excavations found no proof for this hypothetical sequence.[6] Similarly, two Chichen Toltec annexes in the Southeast Court of the Monjas Complex are presumed to postdate the Chichen Maya structures on the same court. However, Bolles (n.d., p. 518) clearly states that there is no evidence for this supposition. By contrast, the opposite sequence from Chichen Toltec to Chichen Maya is undisputably present in the Red House (see above) and Monjas complexes (Brainerd 1958, p. 43). In short, architectural stratigraphy does not confirm a sequence from Chichen Maya to Chichen Toltec architecture.

Finally, Brainerd's analysis of documenting ceramics may also be questioned. He (1958, p. 37) dates the lower Caracol platform to the Florescent phase on the basis of a single sherd from a Florescent slate ware bowl. He dates the upper Caracol platform to the Toltec period on the basis of a single Early Mexican slate ware sherd, in spite of the fact that both platforms combine Chichen Maya block masonry construction and Chichen Toltec balustrade decorations of feathered serpents. The dating of two similar architectural constructions to different cultural epochs on the basis of two sherds is no longer an admissible interpretation.

In the Monjas Complex, ceramics were recovered both from room fills and from a sealed deposit under the floor of the Chichen Toltec ball court. The ceramics were mixed in both samples. For example, the sealed deposit contained four Florescent and two Early Mexican sherds (Brainerd 1958, p. 43). Again, the evidence does not warrant the conclusion that Chichen Toltec architecture and Early Mexican slate wares replace Chichen Maya architecture and Florescent slate wares.

It appears that legendary, architectural, and ceramic evidence has been distorted to prove a preconceived Maya to Toltec sequence at Chichen Itza, with the Toltec epoch dated to the Postclassic period. The only fact that has supported the Postclassic dating of the Chichen Toltec style is the relationship between the architecture of Chichen Itza and Tula. As Kubler (1962) has shown, however, and as I (Cohodas n.d.) have analyzed elsewhere, these relationships only correspond to the latest activity at Chichen Itza. Consequently, the evidence only shows that Chichen Toltec architecture existed in the Postclassic period, but not that it originated in that period. Finally, the clear evidence of the superimpositions of Chichen Maya buildings over Chichen Toltec ball courts argues conclusively for a period of contemporaneity between Chichen Toltec and Chichen Maya architecture that must date, in part, to the late Middle Classic period. The associations of some Chichen Toltec remains with seventh-century ballplayer representations, with Maya architecture, and with the architecture of Tula, indicate that the Chichen Toltec style began in the seventh century and continued to flourish into the Postclassic period.

Since there are no secure dates for Chichen Toltec architecture, the only structures that may be isolated as Middle Classic remains are the ball courts with seventh-century-type ballplayer reliefs and their associated temples. The construction features of these ball courts have already been considered, so this discussion will be limited to an analysis of the ball court temples as examples of late Middle Classic Chichen Toltec temple structures. The best-preserved of these temples are all part of the Great Ball Court Complex and are known as the Lower Temple of the Jaguars, and the North and South Temples of the Great Ball Court.

These three Late Middle Classic temples of the Chichen Toltec style share certain features of form and decoration. All are single-chambered structures with two or six columns in the entrance.[7] The columns, jambs, and interior surfaces in these temples are carved with elaborate multifigure compositions in painted relief. These relief carvings, like those of the ball court benches, are distinguished from later Chichen Toltec reliefs by their high, flat relief and emphasis on precision and clarity, as well as by their emphasis on figures in motion.[8] In contrast to the lavish interior decorations, the exteriors of these three temples are undecorated. They also share with Puuc-style architecture the technique of veneer masonry and three-part or *atadura* moldings.

It appears that Chichen Toltec architecture of the late Middle Classic period is characterized by ball courts with high playing walls, tenoned rings, and bench reliefs of ballplayers, and by single-chamber temples with columnated entrances, interior reliefs, and undecorated facades. The carving style in late Middle Classic Chichen Toltec art emphasizes figural motion, clarity, and precision, and is executed in a high, flat relief. These structures are constructed in the veneer masonry technique as in Early Puuc style. Finally, there is no evidence of pyramidal platforms or roof decorations in use during this phase. It would appear that the full development of Chichen Toltec architecture, as seen in the Castillo with its roof *adornos,* high pyramidal platform, and feathered serpent columns, belongs to a later phase of the Classic period.

The late Middle Classic phase of the Chichen Maya architectural style may be represented by only two structures. The East Wing of the Monjas Complex was begun in the earliest surviving phase of construction of that complex, and appears to be contemporary with the Monjas Ball Court (Bolles n.d.; Cohodas n.d.). Only the lower walls of the structure—with the exception of the east facade—represent the original construction (Bolles n.d., p. 283). These lower walls are decorated with simple lattice panels as in Early Puuc architecture. The plan of the East Wing consists of parallel ranges of rooms with transverse rooms at either end. This plan is shared by the Magician I Temple at Uxmal. The same plan occurs on the Temple of the Phalli at Chichen Itza, which is the second probable late Middle Classic Chichen Maya structure. This temple is also the earliest in its complex (Vaillant 1952). Like the Monjas East Wing, it rests on a round-cornered plinth. Its original decorations, if any, consisted of reliefs of fan-shaped objects. As is typical of Chichen Maya architecture, both buildings are constructed in the block masonry technique.

The late Middle Classic structures in the Chichen Maya style are thus characterized by a specific room plan (the most complex arrangement found at Chichen Itza), block masonry, and simply decorated facades. Both structures lack the mosaic mask ornaments and veneer masonry that are typical of Puuc architecture. However, it appears that this early phase of the Chichen Maya style results from the execution of an Early Puuc temple plan and certain Early Puuc decorative traits (decoration of the lower facade and simple lattice panels) in the block masonry of the Regional style.

Evidence has been presented to show the coexistence of four distinct architectural styles during the late Middle Classic period in Yucatan. The early phase of the Puuc style is distinguished by the use of veneer masonry and the development of stone mosaic facade decorations. Unique features of the Early Puuc style include the use of

pyramid-temples with roof combs or flying facades decorated with stucco ornaments. The early style of mosaic decoration includes decoration of the lower facades, and the use of such ornaments as spools, *tau* pendants, and serrated moldings, to give bold contrasts of light and shadow. The structures of the Regional style employ block masonry rather than veneer masonry, and consist of pyramid-temples decorated by sunken panels and figural sculpture executed in stucco. Elaborate systems of causeways are also particular to Regional sites.

Like the Puuc style, the Chichen Toltec style employs veneer masonry. However, during the late Middle Classic phase, the decorations consist of figural reliefs rather than geometric mosaics, and they are confined to the temple interiors, rather than to exterior facades. Furthermore, these temples are small structures composed of a single chamber. The tall pyramids, mosaic ornaments, and roof decorations that distinguish many Chichen Toltec structures do not appear until the succeeding phase. By contrast, the Chichen Maya structures employ block masonry and are almost completely undecorated. These structures display a complex room plan in contrast to the single-room Chichen Toltec structures. The Chichen Maya style may be characterized as a simplified reproduction of Puuc architecture in the block masonry technique. It appears, then, that a primary difference among these four styles is in the mode of decoration. While the Puuc style emphasizes geometric mosaics, the Regional style emphasizes figural reliefs in stucco, and the Chichen Toltec style relies on stone figural reliefs, whereas the Chichen Maya style lacks architectural decoration almost completely.

The reasons for the distinctiveness of these four styles in the late Middle Classic period must now be tentatively explained. It may be noted that two of the styles, the Early Puuc and Chichen Toltec, are characterized by the use of veneer masonry, while the Regional and Chichen Maya styles employ block masonry. These two masonry techniques are characteristic of two different phases in Yucatan prehistory. Block masonry is an important trait of the Regional or Early Classic period in Yucatan, while veneer masonry is characteristic of the Florescent or Late Classic period. The late Middle Classic period thus represents a phase of transition during which block masonry was gradually replaced by veneer masonry.

Andrews V suggests that this transition takes place simultaneously at all sites in Yucatan. However, when veneer masonry appears at Regional sites, it appears after A.D. 700 and occurs with characteristically Puuc forms of decoration. This suggests that the Puuc region was a center of origin for the veneer masonry technique in Yucatan. Ceramic data (Brainerd 1958; Smith 1971) suggest that the Puuc region was practically uninhabited before the start of the Florescent phase. Chichen Itza was also uninhabited (Brainerd 1958; Smith 1971) before the advent of the Chichen Toltec veneer masonry style. Consequently, the two first appearances of the veneer masonry technique in Yucatan occurred in areas that lacked a strong tradition of Regional or block masonry architecture. Since the first appearances of veneer masonry in Yucatan did not occur at any Regional site, that technique could not immediately have replaced the block masonry technique, as most scholars have supposed. Thus, a period of overlap occurs, which fills the gap between the origins of the Puuc style, around A.D. 600, and its spread to the Regional sites, after A.D. 700. For this reason, the block and veneer masonry techniques were employed simultaneously in Yucatan for at least a century.

While only two masonry techniques were employed in Yucatan during the late Middle Classic period, four different architectural styles were elaborated. For example, the Puuc style applied the veneer technique to geometric mosaic decoration on building facades, while the Chichen Toltec style emphasized figural reliefs on temple interiors. Cultural differences have usually been cited to explain the uniqueness of the Chichen Toltec style, but there is no proof for this distinction. The reasons for the development of the block masonry Chichen Maya style also remain unexplained.

The Terminal Middle
Classic Period in Yucatan

The final decades of the Middle Classic period in Yucatan may be distinguished as a separate phase. At Chichen Itza, where the distinctions between the late Middle Classic period and this terminal Middle Classic phase are most apparent, there is evidence to date the terminal phase to approximately A.D. 690–720 (Cohodas n.d.). The major trends of this short terminal Middle Classic phase are: 1. the replacement of the ball game cult with a new martial cult, and 2. the spread of the Early Puuc style to Chichen Itza. The following analysis will emphasize the importance of the distinction between the late and terminal Middle Classic phases in Yucatan.

The waning of the ball game cult in Yucatan may be demonstrated by the absence of ballplayer reliefs, and probably also of ball courts, after the seventh century. The new martial cult that takes its place is represented in art by scenes of battle and depictions of a raptorial bird. Mural paintings representing battles occur at Chichen Itza in both the Chichen-Toltec-style Upper Temple of the Jaguars (Gendrop 1971, pp. 82–83) and in the Chichen-Maya style second-story building of the Monjas Complex (Tozzer 1957, vol. 12, fig. 684). Both of these structures are built on pyramids that overlie late Middle Classic Chichen Toltec ball courts, thus suggesting a possible sequence from ball game cult to martial cult. The image of the raptorial bird is present along with battle scenes on the gold disks from the Sacred Cenote (Lothrop 1952). The two sets of murals and the gold disks are all related to the style of the earlier Chichen Toltec reliefs characterized by multifigure compositions, figural motion, and narrative depictions.

In the Puuc region, the raptorial bird is represented in the facade decorations of the Great Pyramid at Uxmal.* Battle scenes occur in the murals of the painted temple at Mul Chic (Gendrop 1971, pp. 56–61), and the carved jambs of the Codz Poop at Kabah (Tozzer 1957, vol. 12, fig. 603). The evidence for the contemporaneity of these Chichen Itza and Puuc region manifestations of the martial cult derives from shared architectural features, as explained below.

The terminal Middle Classic architecture of the Puuc region is distinguished by the continuation of the early Puuc style with the addition of a baroque form of facade decoration. Early Puuc traits that occur on the Puuc temples mentioned above are the roof comb and stucco decoration on the Mul Chic temple (Pina Chan 1962); the serrated molding, mosaic masks with convex eye bands, and roof comb on the Codz Poop at Kabah (fig. 10); and the same early form of mosaic mask on the Great Pyramid at Uxmal. More importantly, the

---

* Personal observation.

10. **Codz Poop at Kabah. From** *Maya Cities: Placemaking and Urbanization,* **by George F. Andrews. Copyright 1975 by the University of Oklahoma Press.**

Uxmal and Kabah structures share a decoration of the lower facade that receives an emphasis equal to that of the upper facade. In both structures, there is a sense of the ornament overcoming its boundaries and spilling out into space that qualifies the style as baroque.

During the terminal Middle Classic phase, the Early Puuc architectural style spreads to Chichen Itza, where Early Puuc architectural forms and decorations occur on both Chichen Maya and Chichen Toltec structures. This incorporation of Early Puuc decorations in the Chichen architectural styles clearly distinguishes the terminal Middle Classic structures at Chichen Itza from those of the late Middle Classic period. As will be shown, this Early Puuc influence occurs on the same structures that were mentioned above in connection with the change to the martial cult.

The Upper Temple of the Jaguars (fig. 11) clearly shows the influence of the Early Puuc architectural style. The temple is raised on a steep pyramidal platform, an architectural device employed in the Puuc area but previously unknown at Chichen Itza. The facade of the temple is elaborately decorated with stone reliefs. Again, the decoration of building exteriors had not previously been employed in Chichen Toltec architecture. Furthermore, among the facade decorations on this temple are the Early Puuc spool ornaments. Finally, the use of roof *adornos* in the Upper Temple of the Jaguars may be a Chichen Tol-

tec response to the Early Puuc emphasis on heightening the facade. Thus, while only the spool ornaments in the Upper Temple of the Jaguars facade are specifically Early Puuc in origin, the impetus towards the raising of the temple on a pyramid, the decoration of the facade, and the use of ornamental devices to add height to the facade may all derive from the Early Puuc style.

The Chichen Maya structures of the terminal Middle Classic phase are distinguished by a complete change to Early Puuc forms of architectural decoration. Two of these structures, the Red House and the Monjas annex known as the Iglesia (fig. 13) employ several characteristic Early Puuc decorative devices, including the flying facade. The Red House (fig. 12) actually combines several methods of adding height to the facade, since it has a roof comb and Chichen-Toltec-style roof *adornos* in addition to the flying facade. The extreme similarity between the decorations of these two structures should indicate a contemporaneity that is supported by C_{14} dates.[9] Again, the evidence for the sequence from late Middle Classic to terminal Middle Classic is indicated by the superimposition of the Red House platform over the Chichen Toltec ball court.

The Iglesia and Red House share another distinct architectural trait, which may be called five-part molding. On the Iglesia, (fig. 13), the lower section of the upper facade consists of a sunken central panel with vertical and diagonal moldings both above and below, forming a five-part structure. The identical configuration appears in the uppermost section of the Upper Temple of the Jaguars facade. On the Red House, this pattern is expanded so that the central section becomes the entire upper facade, with medial and superior moldings each formed of a vertical and diagonal member to complete the five-part arrangement. In addition, stone rings are tenoned into the Red House facade. The similarity of the Red House to the temple in the Cemetary Group at Uxmal, which is also a three-room structure with a roof comb, an expanded five-part molding, and stone rings tenoned into the facade,* again indicates the strong relationship between terminal Middle Classic architecture at Chichen Itza and Early Puuc architecture.

*Personal observation.

11. Upper Temple of the Jaguars, Chichen Itza. After Kelemen 1969, vol. 1, pl. 40a.

13. Iglesia, Chichen Itza. After Maudslay 1889–1902, vol. 3, pl. 17.

14. East Wing of the Monjas, Chichen Itza.

12. Red House, Chichen Itza. After Marquina 1964, photo 419.

15. Temple of the Seven Dolls, Dzibilchaltun. After E. Andrews IV 1965b, fig. 10.

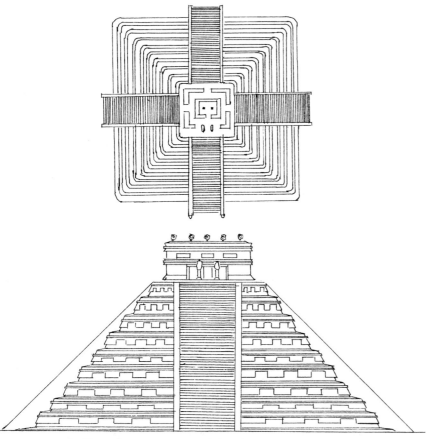

16. Castillo at Chichen Itza, plan and elevation.

Two structures of the Monjas Complex show the influence of Early Puuc architectural decoration. The second-story building, which contains battle murals, is decorated on the lower facade with simple lattices and colonettes (Marquina 1951, pp. 851–54) as in Early Puuc style. The east facade of the East Wing of the Monjas (fig. 14) is known (Bolles n.d., p. 283) to have been built at a later time than the late Middle Classic portion of the East Wing discussed above. The east facade is decorated with Early Puuc-style serpents with human heads in their mouths, serrated moldings, and *tau* decorations. Furthermore, the lower facade receives an emphasis equal to that of the upper facade, and both contain massive mosaic masks giving a baroque effect identical to that of the Codz Poop at Kabah and the Magician Pyramid at Uxmal. The presence of this type of facade decoration at Chichen Itza confirms the importance of the baroque decorative style as an indicator of the terminal Middle Classic period.

An interesting conclusion may be drawn from this analysis. Observation will show that all Chichen Maya structures, except for the two late Middle Classic constructions discussed previously, are closely related and all are decorated in the Early Puuc manner. None of the Chichen Maya structures can be shown to reflect later developments in the Puuc style. This may indicate that the Chichen Maya architectural style ceased to exist after the end of the terminal Middle Classic phase.

In the same way that a fashion for a specific type of ball court spread throughout Yucatan during the seventh century, a new architectural type may have been in fashion during the terminal Middle Classic phase. This type of structure is a sanctuary temple in which an inner sanctuary is surrounded by a corridor whose vaults are made to turn the corners. This type of sanctuary temple is common in the southern lowlands at Palenque, where it was first introduced at the dedication, in A.D. 692, of the triad of Temples of the Sun, Cross, and Foliated Cross (de la Fuente 1965, p. 136). The Temple of the Seven Dolls, located at the Regional site of Dzibilchaltun (fig. 15) is a Yucatec example of the sanctuary temple. Andrews V dates this temple to A.D. 700 on ceramic grounds and suggests that the sanctuary form was directly derived from Palenque.* The facade of the Temple of the Seven

* E. Wyllys Andrews V: personal communication.

Dolls may illustrate a further spread of Early Puuc-style decorations, since it displays deity masks, *tau* pendants, and other designs carved in stucco.

The Castillo at Chichen Itza (Marquina 1951, pp. 849–55) is also a sanctuary temple that incorporates Puuc-style mosaic masks into its facade decoration, and is raised on a tall pyramid (fig. 16). Since the figural reliefs in the interior of the Castillo are carved in the Early Chichen Toltec relief style, the Castillo may also date to the terminal Middle Classic phase.[10]

While the distinctive character of the terminal Middle Classic phase is evident in all regions of Yucatan, the evidence for a sequence from late to terminal Middle Classic is present only at Chichen Itza.[11] Both the late and terminal Middle Classic phases are also most distinctive at Chichen Itza, and there is secure evidence there of their sequential relationship. The late Middle Classic phase is characterized by two architectural styles, the Chichen Toltec and Chichen Maya, which during this phase lack Early Puuc-style decorations. Among these structures are three ball courts that show the prominence of the ball game cult at Chichen Itza during the late Middle Classic phase.

By contrast, structures of the terminal Middle Classic phase at Chichen Itza combine influence of the Early Puuc style with the development of the new martial cult. The evidence for this sequence derives from the building of three terminal Middle Classic temples (the Upper Temple of the Jaguars, the Red House, and Monjas second-story) above Late Middle Classic ball courts. In addition, the Iglesia and east facade of the Monjas East Wing, are both known to postdate the late Middle Classic section (lower walls) of the Monjas structure (Bolles n.d.). Finally, the evidence for the replacement of the ball game cult by the martial cult is seen in the battle murals of two structures (the Upper Temple of the Jaguars and the Monjas second-story), which again postdate the ball courts. It thus appears that a phase during which no Puuc decorations are employed[12] and the ball game dominates, is followed at Chichen Itza by a phase in which Puuc influence is prominent and the martial cult is introduced, and that these two phases are related in a stratigraphic sequence.

This discussion has served to highlight both the similarities and the differences between the late Middle Classic period and the short terminal Middle Classic phase in Yucatan. The similarity is the evidence of interaction between the regionally distinct styles, as seen especially in the cult developments in the Puuc region and at Chichen Itza.

There are several differences between the two periods. First, the ball game is the prominent cult in the late Middle Classic, but it is replaced by a martial cult in the terminal Middle Classic. This change appears to have occurred contemporaneously at Chichen Itza and in the Puuc region. Second, the four architectural styles of Yucatan are distinguished by both technique and decoration in the late Middle Classic, whereas the distinctions among the terminal Middle Classic styles are primarily those of technique. The primary reason for this difference is that during the late Middle Classic period, the Puuc style was confined to the Puuc region, while in the terminal Middle Classic phase the Puuc style spread to and influenced the architectural styles of Chichen Itza. Consequently, a specific form of baroque ornamentation was employed in both areas simultaneously. Third, both phases include fashions for certain architectural forms. The ball court with vertical playing walls was used in all regions during the late Middle Classic period, while in the terminal Middle Classic phase, the sanctuary temple was the most widespread architectural form. All of these differences suggest an important change in Yucatan culture and in its interregional relationships.

The importance of the terminal Middle Classic phase in this discussion of Yucatan prehistory lies primarily in the significance of the spread of the Puuc style. This spread is the second step in the transition between the Early Classic and Late Classic periods in Yucatan, or between the period of block masonry construction and the period of veneer masonry construction. In the preceeding section, it was shown that the elaboration of veneer masonry architecture first occurred in two areas, the Puuc and Chichen Itza, both of which lacked strong traditions of Regional style or block masonry architecture. This circumstance helps to explain the century of overlap between the block masonry construction employed at the Regional sites and the veneer masonry first developed in two localized areas.

During the Late Classic period in Yucatan, or after A.D. 700, the Puuc architectural style eventually replaces the Regional style, causing the complete replacement of the Early Classic block masonry tradition by the Late Classic Puuc tradition. In order for this change to occur, the Puuc style had to spread outward. The first evidence of this spread is the appearance, during the terminal Middle Classic phase, of the Puuc style at Chichen Itza. Subsequently the Puuc style spread to the Regional sites and completely replaced the Regional block masonry tradition. Similarly, the Chichen Maya block masonry style was subsequently discontinued leaving only the Chichen Toltec style at Chichen Itza. Consequently, after the terminal Middle Classic period, only two architectural styles were elaborated in Yucatan: the Chichen Toltec and the Puuc. Since both these styles are characterized by veneer masonry construction, the full Late Classic period in Yucatan signals the replacement of the block masonry tradition by the veneer masonry tradition.

In conclusion, I have attempted to show that the late Middle Classic and terminal Middle Classic phases in Yucatan represent two steps in the transition between the Early Classic (or Regional phase) and the Late Classic (or Florescent phase) periods, as expressed in the transition from the block masonry to the veneer masonry architectural traditions. A primary reason for this century of transition appears to have been the development of veneer masonry at sites that were not heavily inhabited previously and that lacked a strong block masonry tradition.

Veneer masonry could not immediately replace the block masonry tradition, since at the inception of the former, the two traditions were spacially separated. The eventual replacement of one with the other appears to have required three steps. The first step was the development of two architectural styles, the Puuc and Chichen Toltec, which elaborated the veneer construction through decorations appropriate to the technique. This step occurs during the late Middle Classic period, when these two styles develop independently and are related only through their emphasis on the ball game cult. The second step is the

initial diffusion of the Puuc style beyond the boundaries of the Puuc region. This step occurs during the terminal Middle Classic phase when characteristic Early Puuc decorations are employed in the final codification of the Chichen Maya and Chichen Toltec architectural styles. As before, the Puuc and Chichen areas simultaneously accept a new cult orientation, represented in the terminal Middle Classic by the introduction of the martial cult. The third step is the spread of the Puuc style to the Regional sites and the termination of the Chichen Maya style. With this development, only the Chichen Toltec and Puuc styles remain in major Yucatan sites, and the transformation to the Late Classic period is complete.

By characterizing the sequence in which the Puuc style replaced the Regional architectural style in Yucatan during the Middle Classic period, the earlier dating of the beginning of the Chichen Toltec style has received further confirmation. In all three steps, the developments at Chichen Itza parallel those of other regions of Yucatan. Thus, the development of the veneer masonry style in the Puuc region during the seventh century, and the contemporary elaboration of the ball game cult, are paralleled at Chichen Itza by the development of the Chichen Toltec veneer masonry style coinciding with the major elaboration of the ball game cult. The change to a martial cult and emphasis on baroque facade ornamentation that occurred in the Puuc region during the terminal Middle Classic phase also occurred at Chichen Itza. Finally, the replacement of the Regional block masonry style by the Puuc veneer masonry style in most areas of Yucatan is paralleled at Chichen Itza by the cessation of the Chichen Maya block masonry style resulting in the dominance of the Chichen Toltec style. These close parallels between the Puuc region and Chichen Itza argue convincingly for the contemporaneity of the Puuc and Chichen Toltec architectural styles during the Late Classic period or A.D. 600–900.

Notes

1. This research was carried out under a grant from the Kress Foundation, 1973–74.
2. Proskouriakoff (1950, p. 189) considers the Ichmul reliefs to date to her dynamic sculptural phase (A.D. 750–810), because of the energetic postures of the ballplayers. However, Proskouriakoff characterizes the dynamic style by compositional, not figural, motion (1950, p. 138). The absence of compositional motion on the Ichmul panels supports the earlier date suggested here.

3. Further examples are the ballplayer figurines from Jaina in Campeche and the grafitto on Structure 5D-43, at Tikal.*

4. One of the original tenoned rings from the Great Ball Court was also inscribed with a date. Unfortunately, this date has never been successfully interpreted and photographs of the inscription are not available.

5. The roof comb is a vertical projection in the center or rear of the roof, while the flying facade is a similar projection at the front edge of the roof.

6. Ruppert (1935) states that only the first stage of the construction of the primary Caracol structure is definitely earlier than the annexes.

7. The Red House Ball Court Temple, which is not preserved, was a single chamber with six columns in the entrance, the same plan as the South Temple of the Great Ball Court.

8. The interior reliefs of the Lower Temple of the Jaguars consist of processional figures organized into registers, which are defined by a twined-serpent guilloche. This register organization corresponds to the so-called paneled type of stela common in west-

*Nicholas Hellmuth 1973: personal communication.

ern Yucatan, of which the only dated example is Jaina Stela 1, dated A.D. 652 (Proskouriakoff 1950, p. 160). Paneled stelae are also common at Oxkintok, in a section of the site that did not postdate the seventh century (Brainerd 1958, p. 15). Two of the Oxkintok stelae (Stelae 9 and 21 in Proskouriakoff 1950, figs. 87d, 88a) employ the same guilloche to divide the registers. This similarity may support a late Middle Classic date for the Lower Temple of the Jaguars.

9. The C_{14} dates for the Iglesia are A.D. 600 ± 70 and A.D. 780 ± 70, of which the average is A.D. 690. The date for the Red House is A.D. 610 ± 70. (E. Andrews IV 1965a, p. 63.)

10. The C_{14} dates for the Castillo are A.D. 790 ± 70 and A.D. 810 ± 100. Parsons applies a 1.03 correction to reach A.D. 755 ± 70 and A.D. 776 ± 100 (Parsons 1969, p. 178).

11. Evidence of the sequence from late Middle Classic to terminal Middle Classic also occurs at Uxmal. The fourth stage of the Magician Pyramid is a single chamber with the baroque style of facade ornamentation. This chamber is built above and therefore later than the late Middle Classic Magician I Temple.

12. The lattice designs in the lower facade of the Monjas East Wing may not be specifically Puuc decorations.

ESTHER PASZTORY

artistic traditions of the middle classic period

Architecture

CEREMONIAL ARCHITECTURE in Mesoamerica underwent a major transformation during the Middle Classic period. One aspect of this change was a substantial increase in the number of centers, and in the number of buildings within those centers, after A.D. 400. The architecture of the first half of the Middle Classic was strongly influenced by Teotihuacan, and previously varied architectural forms, profiles, and ornaments became standardized and systematized. During the second half of the period, the most advanced forms of architecture appeared in regions peripheral to Teotihuacan and the lowland Maya, at the many new sites that flourished in the late sixth and early seventh centuries. The new centers appear to have been in competition with the old cities, and with each other, in the erection of impressive ceremonial precincts. Many new building types were introduced at these centers, ornamentation became varied and eclectic, and a number of technical engineering problems were resolved. The architecture of the subsequent Late Classic period, though often more unified and aesthetically harmonious, was far less innovative.

During the early Middle Classic period, Teotihuacan architecture influenced Mesoamerican ceremonial architecture. At Teotihuacan, in the Miccaotli phase, a standard manner of articulating platform profiles was developed, which consisted of alternating a sloping base (*talud*) with a projecting panel (*tablero*).[1] Prior to the development of the *talud* and *tablero* profile, most Mesoamerican platforms had either simple or composite sloping profiles. The aesthetic effect of Teotihuacan articulation is achieved through the dramatic contrast of two dissimilar forms. Direct imitations of Teotihuacan *talud* and *tablero* profiles have been uncovered at Kaminaljuyu in Guatemala, at Matacapan in Veracruz, and at Dzibilchaltun and Ake in Yucatan. The local architectural profiles in Oaxaca, Puebla, and Veracruz in the Middle Classic period were not direct imitations, but rather variations on the Teotihuacan *talud* and *tablero* theme. As at Teotihuacan, the architectural profiles of those regions became standardized and applied uniformly to all major types of civic architecture in the fourth and fifth centuries.[2]

During the seventh century, the two-part architectural profiles

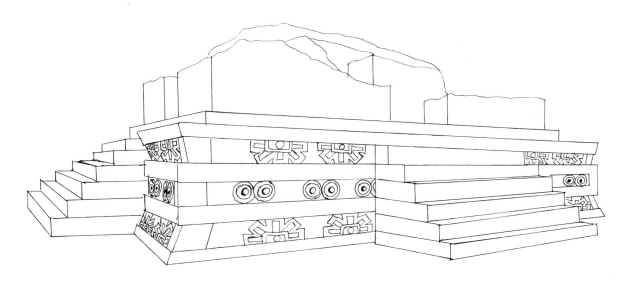

1. Tikal Structure 5D-43, drawing.

prevalent throughout Mesoamerica were elaborated by the introduction of a flaring cornice on top of the vertical panel that reverses the sloping angle of the base. With one exception, this three-part articulation is not found at Teotihuacan, but does occur in Oaxaca, Veracruz, Morelos, and Yucatan.[3] The form is so widespread in the architecture of Tajin, in Veracruz, that this site may well be the one that popularized the flaring cornice. The three-part articulation in Oaxaca appears to date from the Monte Alban IV period (Hartung 1970).[4] In the seventh-century architecture of Yucatan, the platforms of structures may have simple profiles, but the temples on top are ornamented with variations of the slope, panel, and flaring cornice. In Puuc architecture, two- or three-part moldings occur until the late seventh century, when they are standardized into a three-part molding called *atadura,* which consists of a sloping and a flaring cornice that frame a vertical band. The so-called Teotihuacan-style building erected at Tikal during the seventh century is also articulated with a three-part division of slope, panel, and flaring cornice, a combination characteristic of the architecture of the Peripheral Coastal Lowlands (fig. 1). The ball court facing this Tikal structure is also characteristic of Peripheral Coastal Lowland architecture, rather than Teotihuacan. In three-part profile articulation, the contrast between verticals and diagonals is less

dramatic than in the two-part *talud* and *tablero* design. The sloping forms mediate between verticals and horizontals, emphasizing the continuity and mergence of shapes rather than their abrupt changes of direction.

Besides flaring cornices, late Middle Classic structures are frequently characterized by vertical panels that are varied by the alternation of projecting and recessed rectangles. Recessed panels probably originated in Monte Alban architecture of the Early Classic period. During the late seventh century, they occur on some structures at Cholula, Tajin, and on the Castillo and Upper Temple of the Jaguars at Chichen Itza. While the use of recessed panels continues in the Toltec architecture of the early Postclassic period at Tula and Chichen, flaring cornices disappear after the Classic period, and two-part profiles are revived.

During the Middle Classic period, a number of specialized structures were invented or revived. These include ball courts, pyramids with four stairways, round buildings, and arches. Prior to the Classic period, the ball game was probably played in open plazas and fields. During the Classic period, however, special ball courts were erected for the game and its attendant ceremonies. Few courts are known from the Early Classic and early Middle Classic periods.[5] The largest number are to be found at Kaminaljuyu, where fifteen courts of this early date have been located so far (Brown n.d.). Parsons (1969, p. 163) has shown that at least three different types of courts coexisted at this time, indicating not only the importance of the game but also the existence of a period of experimentation with different types of structures. Chichen Itza has all three types of ball courts and is thus architecturally and iconographically one of the major centers of the ball game cult. The tradition of building masonry courts for the ceremonial ball game spread during the late Middle Classic period. Ball court construction became less varied but did continue during the Postclassic period.

Round buildings are a rarity in Mesoamerican architecture of any period. During the first half of the Classic period, most structures were erected on rectangular plans. Round buildings and curving walls become important during the late seventh century, especially in Yucatan. The Caracol of Chichen (Marquina 1964, p. 890), two structures at Edzna (G. Andrews 1969, p. 65), and a structure at Ake (Marquina 1941) are all examples of late Middle Classic buildings with stone-vaulted roofs over round plans. Round buildings were used for special functions, such as astronomic observations (Ruppert 1935; Pollock 1936).

2. Cholula Building F, reconstruction drawing. After Marquina 1970, fig. 9.

Round temple platforms had been frequent in the architecture of the Preclassic period, but they disappeared in the Early Classic period (except in the Huasteca, a provincial region where round temple platforms continued to be constructed through the Classic period). The oval Pyramid of the Magician, begun at Uxmal in the late seventh century, is part of the evidence of the renewed interest in round forms (Foncerrada de Molina 1965, p. 153). Considering the existence of long-distance trade at this time, it is not inconceivable that Yucatan merchants were familiar with Huastec architecture. While round temples and platforms were rare in the Middle Classic period, round corners or wall segments occur at a number of sites. In several early Puuc structures, such as the arch of Labna, the corners are marked by round columns, instead of meeting at sharp angles. Round corners are also to be found on the Castillo Pyramid at Chichen Itza, on Rio Bec temples, and on the North Platform of Monte Alban. The sporadic appearance of round walls, platforms, and buildings in Yucatan and Oaxaca indicates an interest in continuous, unbroken contours instead of the harsh contrasts preferred in the architecture of the early Middle Classic period. Technical problems in the building of curving masonry walls and vaults over circular plans may account for the rarity of round structures, despite their aesthetic appeal.

In Middle Classic architecture, an interest in radial design is evident not only in the presence of round buildings, but also in the presence of rectangular platforms with four stairways. An example is Tikal Structure 5D-43, the platform with the slope, panel, and flaring cornice articulation, which originally had four stairways reaching to the top. The frieze of this structure is decorated with half Maltese crosses, which are similar in form to the Maya glyph for completion. The Castillo of Chichen, another pyramid with four stairways, is ornamented with alternating recessed and projecting panels of Monte Alban derivation; there are 52 panels, the number of years in the Mesoamerican time cycle comparable to our century. It appears probable that radial buildings symbolized the completion of time cycles. There are 365 niches ornamenting the Pyramid of the Niches at Tajin, a structure that has only a single stairway, but contains temporal allusions linking it to the Tikal and Chichen structures.[6]

Another new type of structure found in the Mesoamerican architecture of the seventh century is the arch. In Yucatan, monumental archways lead to roads linking a number of sites of that period. Gates and roads between sites are not generally known in the architecture of other Mesoamerican regions. The first monumental avenues were probably the several-mile-long north-south and east-west avenues at Teotihuacan, built prior to the Middle Classic period; at Teotihuacan, however, the avenues serve to organize the interior of the city rather than to link one city with another. In the Peten region, causeways were built in the Late Classic period to connect the center of the site with outlying temple complexes. It is only in Yucatan that roads connect independent cities and are associated with monumental gates. Many of the Yucatan roads, such as the 62.3-mile-long road connecting Coba and Yaxuna, date from the Middle Classic period and were probably constructed earlier than the long Peten causeways. Considering the importance of trade in seventh-century Yucatan, it is hard to imagine these roads having only ceremonial functions. They must have contributed greatly to the speed and efficiency of overland commercial transportation. The presence of causeways at northern Mesoamerican sites, such as Xochicalco and La Quemada—both of which arose as centers at focal trading points during the Middle Classic period—probably indicate strong ties with southern and eastern Mesoamerica.

As already noted, some of the most advanced engineering solutions to architectural problems occurred during the Middle Classic period. The Maya site of Palenque is as notable for its architecture as it is for its sculpture. Corbel-vaulted passages were used there both as an aqueduct to control the Otulum River and as a bridge to cross it. A several-story tower was erected within the precincts of the Palenque palace. Such towers are a rarity in Maya architecture; the only parallels are found in Campeche (E. Andrews IV 1968b) and Yucatan (Pollock 1965, p. 429). Besides the use of vaults to regulate a stream, Palenque architecture is notable for the spaciousness of its interiors (Kubler 1962, pp. 130–34). In most lowland Maya structures, interiors are small, doorways are few, and piers are placed close together. At Palenque, the corbel-vaulted rooms are placed back to back, supporting each other, making possible a reduction in the massiveness of the walls. Interiors and doorways are considerably enlarged, and the mass of walls is further lightened by rows of trefoil niches. The emphasis in

Palenque architecture is on the framework of load-bearing walls, rather than on their overall massiveness.

The development of veneer-faced concrete architecture in Yucatan also occurred during the seventh century (Pollock 1965, p. 402). During earlier periods, Maya walls had consisted of rubble, with stone retaining walls. In western Yucatan in the late Middle Classic period, a new building technique developed: instead of rubble, the interiors of walls were made of a lime and rubble mixture that solidified into concrete. Instead of retaining walls, the concrete was faced by thin, beautifully cut veneer masonry. The resulting structures were both stronger and more refined in appearance than were earlier buildings. In the Classic period, veneer masonry spread from Yucatan to many parts of the Maya region; during the Postclassic period, however, this tradition was followed by a return to wall masonry of less finely cut blocks.

Relatively little architectural ornament from the early Middle Classic period survives. The platforms of Monte Alban and Teotihuacan were plastered and painted, but they generally lacked sculptural decoration. In the Maya area, modeled stucco designs, such as masks and figures, adorned the sides of stairways and shrines (W. Coe 1967). During the seventh century, architectural ornament became extremely complex and eclectic, particularly in the peripheral regions and in Yucatan. Relief carving, stucco modeling, and stone mosaic could be combined in one building, and naturalistic and geometric motifs could appear side by side. At Lambityeco, for example, characteristic Monte Alban profiles with recessed panels were decorated with figures modeled in stucco and with stepped-frets and T-shaped designs constructed of stone mosaic. Both stone mosaic and stucco modeling are more typical of Maya than of Monte Alban decoration and indicate a Maya influence on Oaxaca.

The most important new decorative vocabulary of the seventh century was stone mosaic. Although it occurred in Oaxaca, Veracruz, and Yucatan, it probably originated in Yucatan. The making of precisely cut stone designs that could be assembled into several separate images was probably related to the finely cut veneer masonry stones used as architectural facing in Yucatan. The stone mosaic blocks were eventually mass-produced, since individual pieces are indistinguishable from one site to another. At the same time, stone mosaic decoration had a practical and aesthetic function: pieces could be mass-produced yet assembled in new and individual contexts.

The decoration of early Puuc structures in western Yucatan was not limited to stone mosaic. On the first stage of the Pyramid of the Magician and on the north building of the Nunnery at Uxmal, mosaic masks are found in association with rows of colonettes, relief carvings—such as reclining figures holding vines and Tlaloc faces with year signs—guilloche designs, and three-dimensional carvings—such as the human face emerging from a monster maw, called the "Queen of Uxmal" (Foncerrada de Molina 1965, figs. 15, 42–46). The roofs were embellished with either roof combs or projecting crenellations. Mosaic ornament predominated on later Uxmal structures, and, although the designs were more ornate, the compositions were internally more coherent and less eclectic. The restless silhouette of flying facades and crenellations was eliminated. The contemporary structures of Chichen, the Great Ball Court with its temples and the substructure of the Castillo, were both similar to Uxmal in their eclecticism. Monte-Alban-derived, recessed panels were used at Chichen both on platform bases and on frieze panels on temple walls; colonettes, mosaic designs, and relief carvings were juxtaposed on panels between sloping bases and flaring cornices (Marquina 1964, pl. 263).

The decoration of architecture with relief designs is also characteristic of Cholula, Xochicalco, and Tajin. At Cholula, the panel of one structure was ornamented with an interwoven design of strips similar to basketry, probably related to mosaic decoration (fig. 2). At Xochicalco, the Temple of the Feathered Serpent was entirely covered with the relief design of serpents and seated figures (Marquina 1964, pl. 40). At Tajin, both relief and mosaic ornamentation are known, although generally not on the same building; relief designs occur on ball courts and a colonnaded structure, whereas mosaic decoration is found, especially on residential structures (Marquina 1964, pp. 422–50).

Another new form of architectural decoration during the late Middle Classic period involved carved columns and piers. Carved piers are found on the Metepec phase Palace of the Butterflies at Teotihuacan (Acosta 1964, p. 59), on the Building of the Columns at Tajin, and on the North Ball Court Temple of Chichen Itza.

In the architecture of the early Middle Classic period, Teotihuacan influence is evident in the trend toward greater architectural simplicity and regularity and the contrast of distinct forms juxtaposed next to one another. Rectilinear shapes and relationships predominated during this period. The simplicity of early Middle Classic architectural ornament gave way in the late Middle Classic period to highly heterogeneous and varied designs. Stark contrasts were avoided by the addition of flaring cornices to slope and panel articulation, by the multiplication of panels and cornices, and by a variety of ornamental treatment. Relief carving was widely used on the walls of platforms and buildings and on columns and piers. Stone mosaic was developed in the architecture of Yucatan and spread to all the peripheral regions of Mesoamerica. Round buildings, curving walls, and structures with four stairways had a sporadic distribution during the late Middle Classic period. Emphasis was on subtle forms and relationships that stressed fluidity and continuity, and on the coexistence of a variety of decorative vocabularies. In addition to the development of new types of ornament, technical advances are evident in architectural construction, especially in the Gulf and Yucatan areas. The presence in Yucatan of both new types of decoration and of construction indicates the growth of vigorous regional cultures that were not concerned with preserving tradition, but rather were willing to explore new scientific and artistic approaches in which the practical and the aesthetic were equally stressed.

Art Style

The heterogeneous styles of the many Classic period cultures in Mesoamerica may be divided into three basic traditions: the Teotihuacan highland, the Maya lowland, and the Peripheral Coastal lowland. Teotihuacan art is conventionalized, flat, ornamental, and heraldic in style, and its major subjects are deities, priests, and ritual action. The art works reflect two primary religious cults, one dealing with water, vegetation, and fertility, the other with warfare. Images are composed of widespread motifs used in a highly consistent manner, similar to the pictographic images in the later Mixtec codices. By contrast, lowland Maya art is individualistic, naturalistic, ornate, and elegant in style, and primarily dynastic in subject matter. Maya

3. Izapa Stela 3, drawing. After Badner 1972, fig. 44.

4. Cerro de las Mesas Stela 9, drawing. After Stirling 1943, fig. 11a. National Museum of Natural History.

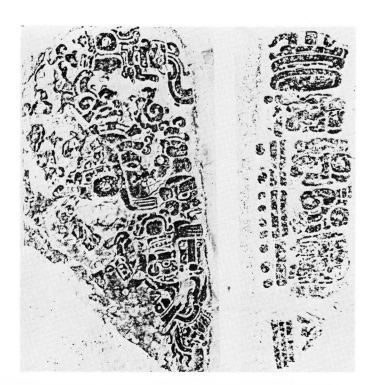

5. Tikal Stela 29, rubbing. After Greene 1972, pl. 132.

6. Monte Alban period II urn. The Cleveland Museum of Art. Gift of Hanna Fund, 54.857.

monumental art represents the accession and exploits of individual rulers surrounded by supernatural insignia and patrons. Some of the temples and carvings, and the majority of the fine-painted ceramics, were funerary in function and iconography. The composition of Maya iconography is often esoteric, and the styles could be intentionally archaistic. The rapidity of style changes and the multiplicity of contemporary styles reflect the Maya preoccupation with formal and aesthetic problems. The style of Peripheral Coastal Lowland art is between the Teotihuacan and Maya extremes, which is to be expected in view of its intermediate geographic position. This tradition is essentially naturalistic but also simple and vigorous. In iconography, both gods and humans interact in narrative and ritual scenes. The primary cult of these areas appears to have been the ball game cult, judging by the large percentage of monumental art devoted to ball game themes. The art of the Peripheral Coastal Lowlands lacks the pictographic complexity of Teotihuacan art and the esoteric richness of Maya art. Its emphasis on action, drama, and narrative, gives it an immediacy that makes it more comprehensible to the Western viewer. Historically, the Peripheral Coastal Lowland and Maya traditions were dominant in Mesoamerica during the Late Preclassic and Early Classic periods. Thereafter, between A.D. 350 and 500, the Teotihuacan artistic tradition exerted a strong influence throughout the area. Subsequently, between A.D. 500 and 700, the Peripheral Coastal Lowland tradition was again dominant.

The Late Preclassic and Early Classic styles of the Peripheral Coastal Lowlands and Maya areas are illustrated by Izapa Stela 3, Cerro de las Mesas Stela 9, Tikal Stela 29, and a Monte Alban urn from period II (figs. 3–6). Despite the differences caused by regional traditions and dates, all these works present a naturalistic interpretation of the human figure, with an emphasis on curvilinear shapes. An attempt was made by the artists to suggest the softness of flesh by modeling or by the use of rounded outlines. The Izapa and Cerro de las Mesas stelae represent figures in active postures, and the Izapa stela shows a dramatic scene taking place in water. All the low relief figures combine side and frontal views in one image. Ornament, richest on Tikal Stela 29, consists of curvilinear scrolls and masks, which cover the figure in profusion.

Most regional styles in Mesoamerica underwent major changes between A.D. 350 and 500. Throughout the area, there was a growing preference for rectilinear shapes, squat proportions, bilateral symmetry, frontal or profile postures, simplicity of composition, and the repetition of units of decorative detail of about the same size. The casual, irregular, but lively quality of the earlier styles disappeared and was replaced by a more formal, rigid, and repetitive representation. These stylistic changes were probably stimulated by some form of contact with Teotihuacan art. As has been discussed previously, Teotihuacan was at this time the major center of power and prestige in Mesoamerica. Many Teotihuacan iconographic traits and design motifs have been found in foreign contexts, and they are often cited as evidence of the degree of Teotihuacan influence at this time. More indicative than isolated motifs and themes, however, was the transformation of local styles to conform to Teotihuacan artistic conventions. It is not suggested that these styles were necessarily imposed by Teotihuacan conquerors, but merely that for both political and aesthetic reasons some aspects of Teotihuacan style were widely imitated.

A particularly characteristic aspect of Teotihuacan art influential in the Classic period was an emphasis on rectilinear forms. Strong Teotihuacan influences have been recognized in the beginning of the Classic period in the art of both Oaxaca and Veracruz (M. Coe 1965, p. 700; Paddock 1966a, p. 127). In period IIIa, Monte Alban urns became almost square in proportion: the torso is compressed so that the shoulders appear just above the knees and the legs form a square pedestal for the figure (fig. 7). The head is greater in width than in height, and the headdress extends horizontally on top of and behind the head as a flat frame. The carved ornaments consist of the repetition of identical forms, such as circles, feathers, or glyphs. At Cerro de las Mesas, there was a similar tendency towards the representation of simpler postures and rectilinear shapes, which is evident in the later stelae, such as Stela 6 (dated A.D. 468) (fig. 8). Here, the figure stands in an awkward position, and its limbs are formed by outlines that meet at sharp angles. The ornate costume may be broken down into rectilinear segments that cover the body from the chin to the knees without revealing any rounded contours.

The Teotihuacan emphasis on rectilinear forms was influential not

7. Monte Alban period III urn. After Caso and Bernal 1952, fig. 346.

8. Cerro de las Mesas Stela 6, drawing. After Stirling 1943, fig. 11b. National Museum of Natural History.

9. Carved back of pyrite mirror found at Kaminaljuyu. After Kidder, Jennings, and Shook 1946, fig. 156 top.

10. Tikal Stela 9, rubbing. After Greene 1967, pl. 8.

only on the representation of the human figure but also on the nature of ornamental designs. It is quite likely that Teotihuacan was instrumental in transforming the loose scroll decoration of Early Classic art into the more disciplined Classic Veracruz interlace design. One of the earliest dated examples of Veracruz interlace occurs on a mural painting at Teotihuacan, which is dated between A.D. 200 and 300 (Marquina 1964, pl. 27).[7] Since the design fitted into the narrow frieze panel of the *tablero*, the scrolls are arranged between horizontal and vertical bands that parallel the architectural panel. On a carved mirror back found at Kaminaljuyu, scrolls are arranged along ribbons of equal width, which pass over and under each other and are studded with little projections (fig. 9). Early Classic interlace design is similar to the grid pattern of mats or textiles that is the result of manufacturing techniques; that is, these designs have a rigid and mechanical quality quite the opposite of the fluid Preclassic scroll forms.

Teotihuacan stylistic influence is equally evident in lowland Maya art. Proskouriakoff (1950, pp. 102–06) has noted that Early Classic Maya art may be divided into two phases. The Early Classic stelae represent figures in a combination of frontal and profile postures, surrounded by scrolls and ornaments very similar to Preclassic styles. On later stelae, Maya figures are represented in a stiff profile view, and the ornament is second in importance to the human figure. At Tikal, for example, stela composition underwent a major change between the late fourth and early fifth centuries, the time corresponding to the most intense trading relationships with Teotihuacan. The ruler represented on Stela 29 (A.D. 292) stands in profile, obscured by a veritable thicket of ornament, including feathers, scrolls, and masks (fig. 5). A deity mask in profile is carved above that of the ruler. By contrast, a stela erected in A.D. 495, such as Stela 9, is striking in the severity and simplicity of its composition (fig. 10). The figure stands in a profile position, and the silhouette is raised in high relief against a plain background. The ruler is richly dressed, but the ornament is held within parallel horizontal and vertical units that divide the figure into a clearly comprehensible grid.

The selection of a strictly profile form for the representation of rulers on Maya stelae during the second half of the fifth century was probably also stimulated by Teotihuacan conventions. In prior Maya tradition, human and supernatural figures were both shown in profile. In Teotihuacan art, figures were either completely frontal or profile. The distinction between frontal and profile figures at Teotihuacan was very significant, since a frontal representation was frequently limited to supernatural images, while human figures were shown in profile. Prior to the rise of Teotihuacan, the frontal representation of deities or humans was rare in southern Mesoamerica, since both humans and deities shared the same profile pose.

The stylistic development of Tikal stelae is further complicated by archaistic trends and Teotihuacan dynastic relationships. According to Coggins's reconstruction (n.d.), the ruler on Stela 29 is the first Maya ruler ("Jaguar Paw") at Tikal to be commemorated by a stela. He is represented in a florid Maya style in profile, with a profile patron deity above his head. The next ruler represented on Stela 4 (A.D. 382) ("Curl Nose"), is an outsider and is shown in a frontal view with Teotihuacan costume elements such as a feather headdress and necklace of shells (fig. 11). This stark, frontal pose, the figure's costume divided into square elements by vertical and horizontal lines, is characteristic of Teotihuacan art. But human figures are generally not shown in a frontal pose in Teotihuacan art. That pose is restricted to deity representation. Frontal ruler representation is not continued at Tikal until the late Middle Classic period. The next ruler who combines Maya and Teotihuacan ancestry ("Stormy Sky") is shown in an archaistic Maya style on Stela 31 (A.D. 445) and on three posthumous stelae (Stelae 1, 2, and 28). On Stela 31 (fig. 12), the ruler is shown in profile, as on Stela 29. He is flanked on two sides by warriors in the contemporary simple style derived from Teotihuacan art, and they are dressed in Teotihuacan costumes. The three posthumous stelae represent Stormy Sky in a curiously contorted pose, feet and head in profile, but the torso rendered frontally (fig. 13). The style is ornamental in the extreme, with masks, feather wings, and little deity figures climbing on poles helping to obscure the human figure. The partially frontal pose and insignia may signify that the ruler has joined the gods. The next stelae to be erected, such as Stela 9 (Kan Boar) (fig. 10), are in the profile position with a plain background and without accessory masks or deities. Other late fifth- and sixth-century stelae, such as Tikal Stela 25, which represents a woman, continue this style.

A clear parallel with Teotihuacan figure types is indicated by a sixth-century stela from Yaxchilan (Stela 27, A.D. 514) which represents a ruler in a profile position scattering seeds or a liquid on an altar (Morley 1937–38, vol. 5, pl. 103a). This ritual action parallels the many representations in Teotihuacan art of profile priest figures pouring a liquid (fig. 14).[8] It appears, therefore, that in the late fifth and early sixth centuries, Maya ruler representations were closer to Teotihuacan human or priest figures than to deity representations. With the exception of Stela 4 at Tikal, frontal figure representations on stelae from Tikal (Stela 32) and Yaxha (Stela 11) confirm this conclusion: both represent not only a deity image, but also one of Teotihuacan rather than Maya origin. The switch to the representation of the ruler in a frontal position in Late Classic Maya art is therefore another highly significant reversal and may indicate a conscious attempt to associate the ruler with the supernatural rather than the human world.

In the Peripheral Coastal Lowlands area, frontal representations of figures were also rare prior to the arrival of Teotihuacan influences. In the late Preclassic art of the Pacific Slope, a frequent compositional type was the representation of a profile deity figure looking down at a profile human figure (fig. 15). Frontal deity images were introduced in the Middle Classic period. On Bilbao stelae, profile ballplayer figures are represented below frontal deity busts (fig. 16). In these reliefs, the deity images are the focus of the composition not only because they are frontal, but also because their faces are modeled in high relief, and the ballplayers are looking up and gesturing in their direction. On the Bilbao stelae, a clear hierarchy was represented: the deity figure on top, frontal and in high relief, and the human figure below, profile and in low relief. The two figures are linked by the gesture of the human figure, which is one of presenting an offering, of supplication, or of deference.

Hierarchic compositions of human and deity figures may also have originated in Teotihuacan art. In the Late Preclassic art of the Pacific Slope, profile deity figures are occasionally shown above profile human figures (fig. 15). In these instances, however, not only are both the human and deity figures in the same position, although superimposed one above the other, but also, instead of the human figure looking up at the deity, the deity is shown looking down at the human fig-

11. Tikal Stela 4, rubbing. After Greene 1972, pl. 121.

12. Tikal Stela 31, drawing. After W. Coe 1965, p. 33.

13. Tikal Stela 1, rubbing. After W. Coe 1965, p. 32.

14. Teotihuacan mural from Tepantitla. Cortesía: INAH. México.

ure with what may be interpreted as a protective glance or gesture. At Teotihuacan, the human-supernatural relationship is usually represented by a frontal deity image or emblem flanked on both sides by a profile human figure gesturing or presenting an offering (fig. 14). This bilaterally symmetrical deity image is static and passive, as though it were an inanimate object, while the human figures are active, thus reversing the earlier, Pacific Slope tradition of passive human figures and active deities. In the Pacific Slope and Bilbao examples, the human-supernatural relationship, although clearly unequal, is one to one. At Teotihuacan, two or more human figures are normally shown flanking a deity image, thus even further reducing the importance of the human individual. The clearly subordinate position of the human figure vis-à-vis the deity was, therefore, a Teotihuacan representational convention that became quite influential during the early Middle Classic period.[9]

During the fifth century, Teotihuacan influence substantially transformed regional Mesoamerican styles. To the Western observer used to admiring naturalistic representation, it is surprising to discover that the conventionalized, "primitive-looking" Teotihuacan style influenced the more "advanced," naturalistic traditions of the rest of Mesoamerica. A political explanation of this influence is not entirely satisfactory. No matter how much prestige Teotihuacan may have had, its art style would not have been influential in the reshaping of local traditions unless it had certain characteristics that were admired for aesthetic or ideological reasons. In fact, Teotihuacan provided an artistic approach that was lacking in southern Mesoamerica, an approach that could be described as "rational analysis." The Teotihuacan preference for angular rather than curvilinear lines and shapes exemplifies this approach. Teotihuacan rectilinear images are made up of the contrast of two opposites: verticals and horizontals. Each image or composition is subdivided into minor segments, which are segregated into contrasting units meeting at sharp angles. Taken to an extreme, such an analytical approach to representation ends in the subdivision of the image on a grid plan, and a horizontal-vertical grid has been noted in a number of Teotihuacan-influenced representations. The earlier compositions that emphasize curvilinear forms are not based on the contrast of opposites but on the fluid merging of one

15. Herrera stela, El Baul.

16. Bilbao Stela 3, rubbing. After Greene 1972, pl. 189.

form into another, negating opposition and emphasizing continuity. When an image appears to be subdivided by vertical and horizontal lines, it is easier to "read" and to remember and therefore appears to be much clearer and simpler than a design based on curvilinear relationships. Careful measuring and subdivision are scientific techniques, and their application in art indicates a rational, planned approach to the making of images. That this approach was first developed in Mesoamerica, at Teotihuacan is illustrated by the fact that the city of Teotihuacan was laid out on a grid plan of streets meeting at right angles, divided into house blocks of approximately the same size.[10]

Another rational characteristic of Teotihuacan art is the standardization of design motifs, which affects both style and iconography. Motifs—ranging from geometric designs to glyphic units—are so uniformly represented in a variety of contexts and media that they are often compared to words in a sentence (Kubler 1967), despite the fact that Teotihuacan had no real system of writing. Although the contemporary Maya did have a system of writing, they did not reduce glyphs to their simplest forms and apparently encouraged so much artistic variation in representation of glyphs that their deciphering is often quite difficult. Teotihuacan may not have been interested in adapting the Maya writing system because it was not practical and too esoteric. Once the Teotihuacan designs and motifs are learned, they are quite easy to recognize and to interpret. That practical considerations were significant at Teotihuacan is indicated by the development of mass production in certain arts and crafts, such as the making of figurines and incense burners. In incense burners, design units, called *adornos*, were mass-produced in molds and an appropriate selection of *adornos* was made for each particular vessel. The mass production of *adornos* was cheaper and faster than the individual manufacture of incense burners would have been, a practical rather than aesthetic consideration. Mass-produced works of art, however fine in original design, tend to be monotonous and repetitious and lack the quixotic and unexpected quality of a work made by an individual craftsman. Since the art of so much of southern Mesoamerica had emphasized a complex formal interplay and esoteric imagery for a very long time, the rational simplicity of the standardized treatment of Teotihuacan motifs was ap-

parently widely admired and imitated as being exceptionally innovative.

The third aspect of Teotihuacan influence, the representation of figures and motifs in hierarchic relationships, may also be considered a rational characteristic. For example, the separate conventions that apply to the representation of human and supernatural figures in Teotihuacan art establish a relationship that is based on opposition and contrast rather than on continuity. One characteristic of Late Preclassic and Early Classic art is that supernatural and human figures are practically indistinguishable, and thus it is difficult to judge their relative significance. In Teotihuacan art, clear distinctions are made between the human and supernatural world in figure posture and composition. The supernatural figures clearly dominate the less-significant human figures. The establishment of distinctions between several categories of beings, and the arrangement of these beings in accordance with their importance, indicates a rational approach to the ordering of phenomena. Although the supernatural figures dominate, the mere fact that a clear division is made between man and god implies a division in thought between that which is sacred and that which is secular. The conceptual separation of the sacred and secular aspects of experience is another characteristic of rational thought. The trend toward the separation of the divine and human in imagery eventually results in a greater importance being accorded to the human aspect.

Despite an emphasis on a separate secular realm, and on human figures in art, Teotihuacan art and influence cannot be described as "humanistic." There is no Teotihuacan interest in the representation of individual men, only in men as members of a group, such as priests, warriors, or traders. All the stylistic features of Teotihuacan art, such as flatness, angularity, reduction of designs to standard units, and hierarchic compositions serve to make the human figures appear inorganic and emotionally distant. On the Teotihuacan-influenced Maya stelae of the early Middle Classic period, human figures, though shorn of many of their earlier supernatural trappings, are represented with an almost abstract rigidity that expresses values contrary to those we would consider humanistic or individualistic.

During the second half of the Middle Classic period, Teotihuacan ceased to be the leading center of prestige in Mesoamerica. At this time, a number of cities peripheral to the major cities of the Early Classic period grew into competing centers and developed strongly individual and eclectic art styles. Some Teotihuacan stylistic and iconographic elements survived during the seventh century, enough to lead Parsons (1969) to use the name "Teotihuacanoid" to refer to them, but the general approach to form in these new cultures was different from that of Teotihuacan.[11] While Teotihuacan influence tended to make styles more abstract, rigid, and nonhuman, the new styles emphasized more natural and human representations, and complex poses and compositions. The corporeal quality of human figures was indicated by an emphasis on the rendering of unbroken body outlines and on the revival of three-dimensional sculpture. In posture types, the profile pose lost its popularity and was replaced by frontal or three-quarter poses. Unusual three-quarter poses, such as kneeling and reclining, are widespread in a variety of contexts. Multifigure compositions are frequent and range from the hierarchic composition associated with Teotihuacan to the representation of narrative scenes.

With the subdivision of designs along horizontal and vertical lines, the focus of early Middle Classic composition tends to be within the shapes and figures rather than on their outlines and silhouettes. During the seventh century, particularly in southern Mesoamerica, new art styles developed that emphasized the sinuous outline of the body of less rigidly clad figures. The most influential of these new styles was that of Palenque. A large percentage of Palenque art was produced during the seventh century. All Palenque figures are very scantily dressed, and, instead of emphasizing their costume and insignia, the artist was most concerned with representing elegant body outlines (fig. 17), including a natural representation of musculature. Similarly, the early stelae of Naranjo (Stela 25, A.D. 618) (fig. 18) and of Copan (Stela 2, A.D. 652) emphasize the curving outlines of shoulders and thighs. Though the Copan figure is surrounded by more ornament than is the Naranjo figure, the figure's outline is clearly visible, because the entire figure is raised in relief away from the background. At Xochicalco and Tajin, the silhouette of the figure is emphasized by the occasional addition of a double outline. The double outline was also used consistently in Classic Veracruz scroll ornament, beginning in the Early Classic period. Its use as an emphasis on the outline of

17. Palenque relief from the Palace, House E, rubbing. After Greene 1967, pl. 13.

18. Naranjo Stela 25, rubbing. After Greene 1972, pl. 156.

human figures appears to have been restricted to the late Middle Classic period. The figures on the Kaminaljuyu mirror back (fig. 9), for example, lack double outlines, while the figures on later mirrors and yokes are accented by a double line (Proskouriakoff 1954, fig. 3). The double outlines used in Veracruz and Morelos are not as subtle or naturalistic as the outlines of Palenque Maya sculpture, but both function similarly in emphasizing the curving contours of the human form.

Besides the use of an unbroken body outline, the reappearance of three-dimensional sculpture during the seventh century also heralds a renewed interest in the representation of the human body. Three-dimensional figures were introduced at a number of lowland Maya sites, such as Tonina, Copan, Piedras Negras, Palenque, Tikal, and Naachtun. In Yucatan, fine sculpture in the round is known in dated contexts from Uxmal (Foncerrada de Molina 1965, pl. XVIIb). Sculpture in the round may go back to the early Middle Classic period in the Cotzumalhuapa area, but it became more widespread during the late Middle Classic. At some sites, such as Piedras Negras, there appears to have been a slow development towards forms in greater relief. A figure of the ruler is represented in a niche and becomes more and more carved in the round. The first example of this type, Stela 25, dated A.D. 608 (fig. 19) is still shown only in relief, but the subsequent stelae show figures in increasingly three-dimensional forms. At other sites, such as Copan, three-dimensional forms appear quite suddenly and contrast with more two-dimensional representations. Stelae 1 and 6 dated A.D. 668 and 683 (fig. 20) represent figures almost in the round. They contrast with the earlier stelae in both costume and style: the figures are short in proportions, have fewer ornate decorations around them, and wear unusual turban-shaped headdresses. The style of these Copan stelae is distinguished by heavy forms and incised details, not unlike some of the simplified Yucatan renderings of three-dimensional forms. Particularly characteristic are the heavy knees, which differ from eighth-century representations showing the knee strongly constricted by a band. The three-dimensional Copan stelae share some traits with contemporary Cotzumalhuapa-style sculpture in the round (fig. 21). At Bilbao, several tenoned busts represent figures emerging from a flat background and wearing turbans, similar to that of Copan Stela 6. The development of three-dimensional sculpture

19. Piedras Negras Stela 25. After Maler 1901, pl. 22.

20. Copan Stela 6. After Maudslay 1889–1902, vol. I, pl. 105.

21. Bilbao monument 12. After Parsons 1969, pl. 60e. Milwaukee Public Museum.

22. Piedras Negras Stela 7. After Maler 1901, pl. 16.

at Copan and Bilbao in the seventh century was possibly interrelated.

Major changes are also evident in the representation of figure postures: profile figures became less frequent, while the frontal posture and a variety of three-quarter postures assume greater importance. The rigid profile stance so characteristic of the representation of human figures during the fifth century became rare. Profile figures continued to be depicted, but in essentially ancillary positions. The frontal position, which had, during the early Middle Classic period at many sites, largely been limited to deities, became standard for the representation of both human and deity images. Proskouriakoff has noted the shift to the representation of frontal ruler images in Maya art during the seventh century (1950, p. 112). Perhaps the earliest examples of these are to be found at Tikal, on Stelae 10 and 11, both of which represent frontal figures in very high relief (Proskouriakoff 1950, p. 113).[12] At Piedras Negras, the ruler is shown in two frontal postures: on the inaugural stelae, he is seated cross-legged in a niche; on stelae erected later in his life, he is standing dressed as a warrior (figs. 19, 22). In both types of representations, the body of the figure is nearly bilaterally symmetrical, the only difference being that the seated figure holds an incense bag held in its hand whereas the warrior carries a staff and shield.

What explains the shift to the frontal representation of human figures found in so much Maya art after A.D. 600? It has been shown that the representation of frontal figures was popularized by Teotihuacan, but in Teotihuacan art, the frontal position was restricted primarily to supernatural figures. Representing human figures in a posture otherwise characteristic of deities was probably intentional and may have reflected an equation of the ruler with the gods. On the Piedras Negras niche stelae, a ladder is shown leading up to the niche. Parsons (1969, p. 168, pls. 36c, 59n) has suggested that the composition of these stelae is related to the representation of ritual and mythic scenes on Cotzumalhuapa-style reliefs in which the sun deity is represented above a ladder.

Does the elevation of the ruler's status to that of a god reflect a secular or a religious trend? A comparison of the Late Preclassic and Early Classic Maya figures with seventh-century representations indicates that, despite the combination of human and divine elements in both, the intents of the two groups of sculptures were probably very different. On the early representations, the human figure is covered and surrounded by supernatural insignia and deity representations (fig. 5). On the seventh-century depictions, the ruler has a physical presence, due either to high relief, carving in the round, or the unobstructed outlines of the body, and the supernatural insignia and deity figures surround him without impinging on his person. The figure of the ruler is, therefore, not transformed into a form similar to that of the gods, but is represented as the gods' equivalent, while retaining his human appearance. The contrast between human and divine instituted at Teotihuacan is preserved, but the human figure is represented in a position as important as that of the gods.

Another indication of the changed relationship between ruler and deity is found in the headdress worn by the ruler. On many Late Preclassic and Early Classic examples, the headdress is a helmet with supernatural attributes that completely surround the face of the human figure, while on late sixth- and seventh-century representations, the headdress rests on top of the head and often leaves the neck bare. On Naranjo Stela 25 (fig. 18) and Bonampak Sculpture 1 (fig. 23) the head of the ruler is no longer encased in a supernatural frame, but is free to move. A variant of the seventh-century frontal ruler position is shown on the Bonampak panel, where the ruler is frontal and seated-cross-legged, but the head is in profile and the arms are in an asymmetrical position. The turn of the head affects the rest of the body, making one shoulder higher than the other. The figure is thus heraldic, because of the frontal posture, and human, because of the very natural representation of movement and gesture. This posture probably originated in the art of Palenque, where it first appeas on an oval relief from House E at the palace, one of the earliest structures at the site (fig. 17).[13] The combination of frontal and profile featues in a single figure was also characteristic of some Early Classic representations, but in these, the areas of transition are represented without any sense of movement or muscular stress, and they are frequently obstructed by insignia (fig. 13). In seventh-century representations, these twists of the body seem more physically possible, because of changes in the alignment of the shoulders and because the crucial area between the head and the shoulders is free of ornament.

23. Bonampak Altar 1, rubbing. After Greene 1967, pl. 52.

25. Uxmal Pyramid of the Magician, frieze of the lower temple, drawing. After Foncerrada de Molina, 1965, fig. 44.

24. Palenque Temple of the Inscriptions, sarcophagus top, rubbing. After Greene, 1967, pl. 15.

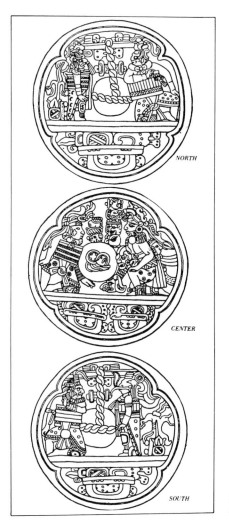

NORTH

CENTER

SOUTH

26. Copan ball court markers, drawing. After Cohodas 1974, fig. 7.

Two other widespread seventh-century postures, the reclining and the ballplayer postures, also have roots in the art of the Late Preclassic and Early Classic periods, but in the seventh century they are represented with far greater attention to verisimilitude. Reclining figures are known in the art of Palenque (fig. 24), Uxmal (fig. 25), Bilbao (Monuments 13, 14), Tajin (Great Ball Court), and Chichen Itza (Lower Temple of the Jaguars). The prominence of reclining postures in art indicates a new preference for the representation of states of transition rather than states of rest and completion.

Both the ballplayer and reclining figure types of the seventh century are probably revivals of a variety of twisted postures in Late Preclassic art. The figures represented on the monument of Dainzu, Monte Alban, and Izapa sprawl in contorted postures, without a clear reference to the ground and without any indication of the bodily balance and muscular activity necessary to bring such positions about. During the seventh century, both the reclining and the ballplayer positions seem plausible and effortless. Ballplayers are shown in kneeling postures, one leg in a squared position, one arm raised, and the other arm resting on the ground (fig. 26).

In composition, the hierarchic arrangement of a central figure or emblem flanked by profile figures continues in the seventh century, but the arrangement is often shown in a more specific setting, or it represents a moment of action. In other words, the hierarchic scene tends to be interpreted as a narrative. The three major variants of this composition depend on the nature of the central figure, which may be a more or less anthropomorphic deity, a deity glyph or emblem, or the ball used in the ball game, often with a glyph or emblem represented on it. In the murals of Tepantitla at Teotihuacan, for example, the central vegetation goddess is represented standing on a mountain above a body of water, surrounded by trees and birds (fig. 14). The deity and attendants are no longer represented against a flat red background as they had been in earlier Teotihuacan mural art, and an attempt has been made to suggest a setting. In the art of southern Mesoamerica, besides some emphasis on the setting, the attendants are often differentiated. In representations of the ball game scene, the two ballplayers flanking the ball are usually not in the same position, and the squared-leg pose is often preserved for only one of them (fig. 26).

On the Copan central marker, one figure is in profile, the other is frontal. At Palenque, deity emblems are found as central themes in hierarchic compositions on the temple panels made for the ruler Chan-Bahlum in A.D. 692 (figs. 31–33). The compositions of these panels, found in the Temples of the Sun, Cross, and Foliated Cross, are more varied than the Tepantitla composition because the attendant figures are differentiated. The pairing of a tall and a short figure has been variously interpreted, but from the point of view of composition, such a pairing assures an equal emphasis for the human figures and the deity emblems. These attendants are also shown holding a variety of emblems or offerings, which suggest that particular moments in ritual or myth are being commemorated. The emphasis on setting, the individuality of the attendants, the depiction of action, all serve to transform hierarchic compositions at Palenque into narrative scenes rather than abstract tableaux.

In the art of the seventh century, settings are also introduced in compositions in which there are only one or two figures. On the inauguration stelae of Piedras Negras, for example, the ruler is shown seated in a niche that probably represents the doorway of a structure with drapery tied up at the ceiling, and a ladder covered with a cloth leading up to him (fig. 19). This emphasis on the architectural setting is comparable to the importance of ball court representations in ball game scenes. The panels of both the south and north ball courts at Tajin show representations of a variety of buildings, including ball courts and temples, as the settings for ritual or mythic scenes (fig. 27). In art, the attempt to render a figure within an architectural structure is an attempt to achieve a degree of realistic representation.

Besides architectural settings, some seventh-century works of art represent natural or supernatural settings by surrounding the major figures with minor motifs, such as flowers, vines, fruits, glyphs, and other ritual objects. The scattering of elements on the background does not produce a coherent, illusionistic scene, but does provide more of a setting than would a plain background. Examples of such settings can be found throughout Mesoamerica. In a recently discovered mural at Teotihuacan (fig. 28), a net jaguar is surrounded by flowers, butterflies, glyphs, and even some small human figures. At Bilbao, the rock relief on Monument 21 shows three figures surrounded by a cacao

27. Tajin ball court, north-central panel, drawing. After Kampen 1972.

28. Teotihuacan mural from Zone 5A, drawing. After Miller 1973, fig. 116.

29. Teotihuacan mural from Atetelco, drawing. After Sejourne 1956, fig. 55.

30. Teotihuacan mural from Atetelco, drawing. After Kubler 1967, fig. 12.

vine and birds, as well as by other emblems (Parsons 1969, frontispiece). The representation of the three Palenque panels (figs. 31–33) and the Ruz sarcophagus top (fig. 24) are similar in concept: glyphs, jade, and water symbols are scattered throughout the empty background areas. The background filler designs are either symmetrically arranged or scattered at approximately even intervals; they neither overlap nor otherwise detract from the emphasis on the main figures. During the seventh century, not only was there increased emphasis on the representation of the human form, but also the human figures were shown against increasingly detailed backgrounds, whether architectural or natural settings, or small-scale symbolic and natural motifs.

Thus, it can be said that the art of the seventh century is characterized by an increased emphasis on the human figure, through the revival of high relief or three-dimensional sculpture, and by a greater emphasis on the sinuous outline of musculature in relief sculpture. Twisted and even contorted postures are represented in an organizationally convincing manner, and even rigid postures are enlivened by the contrasting placement of arms and a turn of the head. It is not that formal and hierarchic representations were abandoned, but that they were modified by realistic details or interesting asymmetries. In composition, rigid hierarchic compositions were modified either by variations in the individuality of attendant figures or by the greater elaboration of the setting. The compositions were often intermediate between narrative and hierarchic scenes. A patterned or ornamented treatment of background surfaces still existed, but the designs were separate from the human figures.

After the essentially simplifying Teotihuacan influence wore off, sometime during the sixth century, artistic compositions became more complex throughout Mesoamerica. But instead of a complexity similar to that of the Late Preclassic and Early Classic periods, which often involved ambiguous relationships, the seventh-century images were complex yet clear. Greater clarity was present because the images were ordered in terms of perceptual appearance, in scenes, or in panels in which there is a clear hierarchy of importance of the figures, as opposed to ornaments or background details. The more naturalistically rendered figures in seventh-century art interact with one another physically and psychologically. Scenes depict transient, though signifi-

31. Palenque Temple of the Cross, sanctuary panel, drawing. After Maudslay 1889–1902, vol. 4, pl. 76.

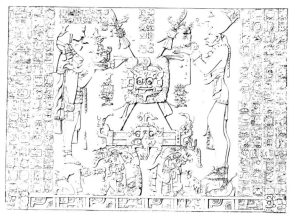

32. Palenque Temple of the Sun, sanctuary panel, drawing. After Maudslay 1889–1902, vol. 4, pl. 88.

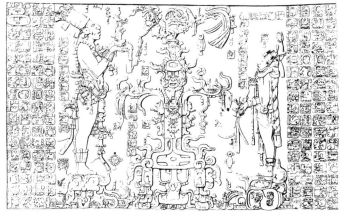

33. Palenque Temple of the Foliated Cross, sanctuary panel, drawing. After Maudslay 1889–1902, vol. 4, pl. 81.

cant, moments in ritual activity, whether the themes depicted are dynastic, ball game, or agricultural. If the art of Teotihuacan may be said to have symbolized a rigid, rational order with community values, seventh-century art symbolized life, movement, variation, and individual achievement.

Iconography

The major difference between the religious iconography of the Late Preclassic period and that of the Classic period was in the organization of the supernatural. The supernatural images of the Late Preclassic were highly variable in appearance and context, whereas those of the later period were standardized into more or less fixed categories. While the primary deities and cults changed during the course of the Classic and Postclassic periods, the highly complex framework they occupied was not radically altered. The standardization of deity features and the clear organization of the supernatural pantheon was concurrently developed at Teotihuacan and Oaxaca and eventually spread through Teotihuacan influence (Borhegyi 1971, pp. 84–88).[14] Through the process of diffusion and syncretism that occurred during the Middle Classic period, much of the religion of Mesoamerica was systematized, and this system was inherited by the peoples of the Postclassic period.

Six major image clusters can be distinguished in Middle Classic iconography, and they probably corresponded to major cults: agricultural fertility, warfare, ball game, dynastic ruler, burial, and titular patron.[15] These six cults were not necessarily mutually exclusive, since one could combine the aspects of several others. Nevertheless, each corresponded to a relatively discreet cluster in imagery and sometimes in medium.

The agricultural fertility cult was the most widespread, and its myths and deities were probably the most ancient. The deities associated with this cluster were the gods of the earth, rain, water, crops, sun, and moon. The primary myths of the agricultural cult concerned the cycle of the dry and rainy seasons, described as the descent and death of the sun deity in the underworld and his rebirth and transformation into the maize god. Although agricultural cult activity was probably found in all areas of Classic Mesoamerica, this cult was a state cult only in Central Mexico during the Middle Classic period. Elsewhere, the gods and emblems of the agricultural cults were incorporated into funerary or dynastic cult imagery.

The warrior cult developed during the Middle Classic period and became especially important at its very end. The cult's primary deities were those of the sun and the planet Venus, and the cult was associated particularly with sacrifice through the removal of the heart. The warrior cult was developed at Teotihuacan and spread throughout Mesoamerica during the Late Classic and Postclassic periods.

The ball game cult was probably much older than the fully developed warrior cult, since, in some forms, it was already present in the Middle Preclassic period. The ball game cult was most important however, during the Middle Classic period in the Pacific Slope, the Guatemala highlands, Veracruz, and Yucatan. The major deities of the ball game cult were also the sun, moon, and the planet Venus, but sacrifice by beheading was more characteristic. Both the warrior cult and the ball game cult assured the continued cosmic cycle of the sun and the renewal of fertility during the rainy season, and as such overlapped with the agricultural fertility cults.

The cult of the dynastic ruler was most characteristic of the iconography of the lowland Maya and Oaxaca. Ruling dynasties were linked with the supernatural through divine ancestry and the rituals of accession. Dynastic iconography could include scenes of accession, conquest, marriage, ritual, or funeral. Rulers could be associated with a variety of supernaturals, the most prominent being the solar and fertility gods.

Burial cult imagery occurred in both dynastic and nonhistoric contexts. A large percentage of the ceramic and terra-cotta art of Teotihuacan, Oaxaca, Veracruz, and the Maya was made for funerary offerings. In Oaxaca and the Maya area, mural painting and sculpture were used to ornament tombs. Burial iconography deals with the underworld gods who were both death and fertility deities. In some instances, funeral iconography was nearly identical with that of the agricultural fertility cults. This is because the cyclical rebirth of nature was a parallel to the death and birth of individuals within the continuity of the human community.

The cult of patron deities was especially adopted by societies in which the major state cult was not that of the dynastic ruler. The nature and function of patron deities is best known from the Postclassic period, but patron deities also may be identified in the iconography of Classic period Teotihuacan. Both the Aztec and Teotihuacan patron gods combined the features of a number of significant deities, particularly of the solar, fertility, and warrior groups.

All six of the major Classic period cults functioned to assure the continuation of the cosmic cycles of the sun, moon, and planets, and the alternation of the dry and rainy seasons. Since the aim of all the cults was the furthering of agricultural and natural fertility—a general preoccupation in Mesoamerica—to some extent the deities of the agricultural cults played important roles in all the other cults. Many of the myths of the agricultural cycle, the ball game, and the warrior cult deal with the theme of transformation through death and rebirth. The primary metaphor for all transformation was the diurnal cycle of the sun. The sun was believed to die every night at sunset as it descended into the underworld, and to be reborn every morning as it emerged from the earth. Because the transformation took place in the underworld, that area had a very important place in Mesoamerican mythology. In contrast to the wide spread of underworld imagery in Classic Mesoamerican art, there was much less imagery that dealt with the upperworld or with the daytime sky.

The six Middle Classic cults and their associated imagery did not exist in the Late Preclassic or Early Classic periods. There is no evidence in art of warrior or patron deity cults prior to the Middle Classic period. Dynastic and burial cults existed quite early, but the imagery associated with them was much more limited and less elaborate. Some representations that seem to deal with myth or ritual may relate to agricultural fertility cults, but the supernaturals represented are much less standardized and therefore harder to distinguish from one another. Similarly, there are a few representations of ball game ceremonials, but the costumes, postures, and associated symbols vary greatly from one composition to another. While the sources of the Middle Classic cult imagery originated in Late Preclassic and Early Classic art, much of the content and organization of Middle Classic imagery was new.

By contrast to the richness of invention and variation in Middle Classic iconography, the iconography of the eighth century indicates a period of consolidation. Few new iconographic themes were introduced; instead, the forms inherited from the previous century were elaborated and refined. During the Postclassic period, there was a reduction in the number and variety of iconographic complexes in monumental art. After the fall of the Classic Maya in the tenth century, the cult of the dynastic ruler played only a minor role in northern Maya iconography. Similarly, in Oaxaca, Postclassic dynastic art was limited to marriage panels, and it lacked the variety of Classic period art. Dynastic themes occurred occasionally in Toltec and Aztec sculpture, but the cult of the dynastic ruler was never again a state cult in Mesoamerica. The ball game cult was also reduced in importance. Ball-game-related art disappeared almost entirely from the Maya lowlands and Yucatan. In the rest of Mesoamerica, there were a few reliefs representing ballplayers and some ornamental rings and ball court markers, but there were no richly decorated courts comparable to those at Tajin or Chichen Itza. With the exception of the Mixtec area, where decorated tombs and lavish burials continued until the time of the conquest, burials in Mesoamerica were less iconographically complex during the Postclassic period. The two cults that continued and spread at the expense of the others were the agricultural fertility and warrior cults. A large proportion of the monumental art of the Toltecs, Aztecs, and Postclassic Maya represent warriors and those supernatural and animal figures associated with the warrior cult. Monuments representing the deities of the agricultural fertility cults were also widely distributed. They were frequently smaller in size and less complex in iconography. than the monuments associated with the warrior cults. The deities of the agricultural cycle appear to have been represented in art on both the court and folk level.

Teotihuacan had a more profound influence on cult imagery than the distribution of specific Teotihuacan motifs would indicate. Teotihuacan was the source of the warrior and patron deity cults and was the first culture in Mesoamerica to turn the agricultural fertility cult into a state cult. The general standardization of the attributes of supernaturals and the greater distinction between gods and humans, which characterized cult iconography of the Middle Classic period throughout Mesoamerica, was stimulated by contact with Teotihuacan.

As has been noted, Teotihuacan was the first Mesoamerican civilization to make the agricultural fertility cult a state cult of the first importance. It is obvious that, in an agricultural society, considerable ceremonialism would be associated with the changing seasons and the growing of crops. The sixteenth-century ethnohistoric accounts of religion indicate that a large majority of the gods and much of the yearly cycle of rituals in Mesoamerica were devoted to the agricultural fertility cults. In the Postclassic period, deities had their own cults, priests, and rituals, so one cannot talk of a single cult but only of a ritual cycle of interrelated cults. Quite possibly, a similar pattern already existed in the Classic period, but only a small percentage of the monumental arts was made for the agricultural cults in both the Classic and Postclassic periods. This may have been due in part to a tradition of making deity images out of impermanent materials, such as the cornmeal dough used in the Postclassic period, but more generally it was due to the fact that the monumental arts were made for other purposes, such as burial or dynastic commemoration. The deities of the agricultural fertility complex frequently appeared in funerary and dynastic contexts. In Teotihuacan art, however, the gods of fertility—the rain, sun, and earth deities—were represented in sculpture and more often on mural paintings. The deities are shown surrounded by priests or other humans making offerings or pouring libations. The costume, insignia, and behaviour of these deities was standardized.

The major deities of the Teotihuacan agricultural fertility cult were the rain gods, the sun gods, and the earth goddesses, all of whom were represented as giving something to humanity. At Teotihuacan, there were at least two rain gods who had different animal associations (Pasztory 1974). One, called the Crocodile Tlaloc, is represented carrying a vessel of water and a spear that probably symbolized rain and lightning. He is also shown swimming in water and biting the stem of a water lily. The other rain deity, called the Jaguar Tlaloc, differs in not having the staff and vessel, and, instead of the water lily in his mouth, he has a long bifurcated tongue. The second type of Tlaloc is frequently found in association with felines, particularly the net jaguar.

The deities comparable in importance to the rain gods were the fertility deities, who assured the growth of crops. The most significant of these were the earth goddesses, the sun gods, and the maize gods. In Postclassic Mesoamerican belief, the sun descended to the underworld where he married the earth goddess. The god of maize was born of this union. The god of maize, however, was not really an entirely separate deity, since he was the sun reborn in a new aspect. The sun god had two facets: during the dry season he was a deity of the sky and the day; during the rainy season he was a deity of the underworld and the night. As the night sun, the god was associated with water and fertility. He was believed to die in the underworld and to be reborn as the god of maize. He was, therefore, associated with symbols of death and sacrifice as well as with symbols of birth and fertility. As the night sun, the deity was associated with the jaguar; as the day, or sometimes descending sun, he was associated with a raptorial bird.

In the Teotihuacan art, the sun god in the underworld was probably represented by the net jaguar (fig. 28). The net jaguar is shown in water and fertility contexts in mural painting, which suggests the underworld during the rainy season. In the murals of Teopancaxco, the net emblem of the jaguar is flanked by priests (Kubler 1967, fig. 45). The serrated edge of the emblem is similar to the edges of a number of Middle Classic sun disks. The net design is similar to, and possibly derived from, the glyph movement (*ollin*) associated with the descending aspect of the sun deity in Postclassic iconography. In the Palace of the Jaguars mural, baby net jaguars held in yellow hands represent the rebirth of the sun in the underworld (Miller 1973, fig. 40). The yellow hands are the emblems of the earth goddess.

The earth goddess, like her spouse the sun god, was a major agricultural fertility deity in Teotihuacan art (Pasztory 1973). Her form was more frequently anthropomorphic than was that of the sun deity, and her accessory animal emblem was a bird, such as the quetzal or owl. At Teotihuacan, the earth goddess is represented as a yellow figure with a bird headdress, from whose outstretched arms seeds and riches flow (fig. 14). The goddess was represented in abbreviated form by isolated yellow hands holding precious items.

Judging by the ethnohistoric accounts of the sixteenth century, agricultural rituals in Mesoamerica were performed throughout the year, but especially during the growing season, from March to October. The chronicles describe an unending series of private and public rituals, including sacrifices, communal feasts, and theatrical reenactments of myths. Most likely, many of these rituals had ancient sources and similar rites existed during the Classic period. In the iconography of the art of both the Postclassic and Classic periods, however, few agricultural rituals are represented. One ritual that was clearly related to the fertility deities, and frequently represented in Teotihuacan art, involved the sprinkling of a liquid—water or pulque—or the casting of maize kernels. This ritual act was performed by priests and by the gods themselves. Priests shown sprinkling usually carry an incense bag, which identifies the activity as ritual (fig. 14).

Second in importance to the agricultural fertility imagery in Teotihuacan monumental art was imagery associated with the warrior cult. It is generally assumed that the warrior cult—and a preoccupation with military imagery—began only after A.D. 900. However, a warrior cult, ancestral to the Postclassic warrior cult, clearly existed in Middle Classic Teotihuacan.

The Postclassic warrior cult was based on a solar mythology. The sun was believed to have been created by the self-sacrifice of a deformed god, Nanautzin, who threw himself into a fire to become the sun. The sun was thought to die every night and to be reborn every morning, after a cosmic battle with the forces of darkness, for which he had to be strengthened by human sacrifices. The orders of the eagle and jaguar knights, composed of a rank of elite warriors, were charged with supplying the sun with sacrificial victims. In the Postclassic period, the unarmed victim was tied to a stone on a platform and had to fight fully armed eagle and jaguar knights. Such gladiatorial combats may have functioned as dramatic spectacles in the warrior cults, comparable to the playing of the ball game in the ball game cult.

The major iconographic themes of the Teotihuacan warrior cult include: the sun god as a raptorial bird and as a feline (but not a net jaguar); a deformed figure; a heart sacrifice; warriors in animal disguise; and the owl and weapon symbol (von Winning 1948; Kubler 1967, 9–10). In warrior cult contexts, the solar god rarely appears in the form of a net jaguar, which represented the night sun as a god of fertility. Instead, the deity is represented as a raptorial bird or feline,

shown with drops of blood or a heart near its mouth. In one apartment at Tetitla, raptorial birds with large drops of blood in their beaks are shown on the three sides of a patio, and a dog is represented on the fourth side (Miller 1973, figs. 281–85). The dog was a symbol of descent to the underworld, and the birds probably represented the sun in the sky.

A human figure with deformed limbs represented a deity similar to Nanautzin, the god who was transformed into the sun in Postclassic belief. The earliest examples of deformed figures occurred in the warrior cult iconography of Teotihuacan (fig. 29). At Atetelco, deformed figures are represented on the western entrance passageway to a courtyard, while the iconography of two of the three structures deals exclusively with warriors in animal disguise and with a heart sacrifice. The murals of the south structure represent anthropomorphic coyotes carrying spears and spear throwers surrounded by flames and sparks (Miller 1973, fig. 336). The murals of the north structure represent anthropomorphic bird warriors on one wall and masked warriors about to sacrifice birds on another wall (Miller 1973, figs. 342–43). The pairing of coyote and bird warriors was not as standard at Teotihuacan as the eagle and jaguar warriors of the Postclassic period.

The sacrifice of a heart is not usually depicted in Teotihuacan art; it is suggested by the presence of hearts and blood in the mouths of deities or of hearts or blood on sacrificial knives held in the hands of priests and warriors. The lower wall of the north structure at Atetelco represents a figure on a temple platform carrying a knife and heart (fig. 30). Although heart excision was a practice not necessarily limited to the warrior cult at Teotihuacan, the cult and the practice were intimately related.

The primary supernatural image in Teotihuacan warrior iconography was the raptorial bird aspect of the sun deity. Bird images were also important as warrior disguises and as martial emblems. Feline and coyote figures were of secondary importance. This warrior cult iconography at Teotihuacan dated only to the Xolalpan period, and warrior imagery became more frequent and elaborate during the Xolalpan and Metepec phases.

The obvious importance of warrior cult iconography in Teotihuacan art raises the possibility that a military organization with an elite corps of warriors, fulfilling sacred and ritual functions as well as secular and martial ones, existed during the Middle Classic period at Teotihuacan.[16] The cult was apparently dedicated to the sun deity, and its rituals involved the reenactment of the battles the sun deity fought against the forces of darkness, at its descent to and ascent from the underworld.

Another Middle Classic cult that originated at Teotihuacan was the patron deity cult. Sixteenth-century ethnohistoric accounts reveal the importance of titulary patron gods of towns and ethnic groups, the most famous of whom was Huitzilopochtli, the patron god of the Aztecs of Tenochtitlan. Patron gods usually shared the aspects of certain major cosmic deities, but they were also associated with a deified tribal ancestor or the first founder of a social group. To the extent that the patron deities combined the characteristics of several gods with the personality of a deified mortal, their iconographies were as composite as those of dynastic rulers. Huitzilopochtli, for example, was a version of the solar deity as the god of war and sacrifice, and his cult was related to the warrior cult (Brotherston 1974). He was also represented by dough images in fertility rituals, which paralleled the rituals of solar fertility gods such as Xochipilli. Patron deity and dynastic ruler cults fulfilled similar functions in different social settings. They both combined social, political, and religious features in a single personage, who had divine and human characteristics. Patron deity cults were particularly important in societies where the state cult was not that of the dynastic ruler.

The patron deity of Teotihuacan could have been a figure characterized by a headdress with three hanging tassels. This deity is represented in mural painting at Teotihuacan, but is especially frequent on Teotihuacan-influenced representations outside of Teotihuacan. At Tikal, the images on the shields of the warriors on Stela 31 (fig. 12), on Stela 34, and on Yaxha Stela 11 all represent this deity in a martial context. The god is usually identified as Tlaloc, the rain god, because of the rings surrounding his eyes, even though he does not have the other features characteristic of Tlaloc. In fact, this figure is a curiously hybrid image. He has some of the traits of the jaguar Tlaloc images at Teotihuacan, which referred to the sun as a water and fertility deity in the underworld, but not the crocodilian Tlaloc of the earth. Both the rings over the eyes and the martial symbolism link this deity with war and sacrifice imagery as represented on the mural paintings of Atetelco at Teotihuacan. C. Millon (1973) has concluded that the tassel headdress represents a social group of high rank from the city controlling, perhaps, both trade and foreign relations. The identification of this deity, and of the tassel headdress, as the patron deity of Teotihuacan is an extension of Millon's hypothesis. The deity with the tassel headdress combines features of solar and fertility gods and of the agricultural and sacrificial warrior cults. The headdress was worn by human figures as well as by gods. This deity could have been the patron of the ruling dynasty, or of the city, or of both. When the human rather than the deity figure wore this headdress, the reference was probably to the elite of Teotihuacan. That the significance of this deity was primarily political, and not cosmic is evident in the number of representations outside of Teotihuacan in which it occurs in military or historic contexts.

Teotihuacan influence on Middle Classic iconography was noteworthy in the representation of ritual rather than in the depiction of deities. This was especially evident in Maya dynastic art, where, after Teotihuacan contact, rulers were shown in ritual actions, many of which have Teotihuacan prototypes. The scenes of humans holding offerings and flanking a deity emblem, on the temple panels of Palenque (figs. 31–33), are similar to many Teotihuacan mural paintings of the sixth and seventh centuries (fig. 14). The same composition also occurs on the Tomb 104 murals at Monte Alban, in association with Teotihuacan-style costumes (Covarrubias 1957, facing p. 148). The ritual sprinkling of a liquid was new in Middle Classic Maya art and was derived from Teotihuacan representations of priests and gods pouring precious streams. During the late Middle Classic period, Maya rulers were frequently dressed as conquering warriors. Many of the emblems they wore were derived from Teotihuacan warrior cult imagery.

The most significant Teotihuacan influences on Middle Classic iconography were the systematization of deity features and the division between gods and humans in representation. The systematization of deity features is especially evident in Oaxaca, where, during the Late Preclassic and Early Classic periods, a large number of supernaturals were represented on urns intended for burial. These deities had few costume or facial details that could be used to distinguish them (fig. 6). During the Middle Classic period, the number of individual Monte Alban deities increased; the gods acquired characteristic facial features, headdresses, pectoral ornaments, earplugs, and, often, glyphs (fig. 7). The identifying insignia almost completely covered the bodies of the deities, as they did in Teotihuacan. In some instances, the insignia of Monte Alban and Teotihuacan deities was quite similar, as in the case of the Goddess IF (Boos 1966a, pl. XC), whose quetzal headdress resembled that of the Teotihuacan earth goddess. As the gods became more numerous and more standardized *acompanantes*— human figures without supernatural insignia in poses of respect and subordination—were frequently represented on funerary urns (Caso and Bernal 1952, pp. 119–31). The deity and *acompanante* figures represented the polarity between human and divine, which was so emphasized in Teotihuacan iconography.

Teotihuacan's influence on Mesoamerican iconography was a stimulus to organize many local spirits of visually indistinct form into classes of readily recognizable deities. The emphasis appears to have been on classification, since in almost all art influenced by Teotihuacan, the gods merely displayed their insignia but did not interact with one another. As the deities were classified, human beings too were represented as typical members of groups—such as priests, worshippers, or warriors—who performed routine rituals.

After the decline of Teotihuacan influence, a new element appears in Mesoamerican iconography: a preoccupation with the passage of time. Early Middle Classic art was essentially concerned with the representation of static figures outside a temporal context. The temporal aspect of late Middle Classic art is evident in the representation of ritual cycles or narratives unfolding in time, and in the commemoration of calendric cycles. The factor of time was expressed by figures represented in transient states of action, by the changing of background elaboration, by narratives where the same person was shown in scenes before and after, and in sets of separate but interrelated monuments that could only be examined one at a time.

The focus on individual persons and their history is to be found in the cult of the dynastic ruler, which was widespread in Oaxaca and the Maya area, and which had its sources in Preclassic art. Dynastic iconography is usually a hybrid mixture of other cult iconographies. When the ruler was represented as a warrior, the iconography could share some of the details of the warrior cults; when the ruler was shown performing a ritual, the iconography could be similar to that of the agricultural cults. In the Early Classic and early Middle Classic periods the Maya ruler was represented holding his insignia of office, surrounded by supernaturals (fig. 5). During the Early Classic period, the symbol of office in the Maya area was the ceremonial bar, a double-headed serpent with deities emerging from both heads.[17] The deities were frequently the rain and fertility deities, such as the gods B and K (Spinden 1913, pp. 62–64), who were similar to the Teotihuacan Tlaloc and to the jaguar gods of the underworld. After A.D. 600, a new royal emblem, the manikin scepter, was introduced at Palenque and spread through much of the Maya area. The manikin scepter was similar to the ceremonial bar, since it too represented a divinity in the form of an adze, which was primarily associated with rain and fertility. Since the Maya symbol of rulership represented the gods of agricultural fertility, Maya rulers probably claimed to have a special relationship with these gods. It is not yet clear whether these insignia signified divine descent, another form of supernatural patronage, or exclusive control over some rituals essential to agricultural activity.

Prior to the late sixth and seventh centuries, Maya rulers were usually represented without any references to specific events and times. During the seventh century, new dynastic imagery is seen in the art of Piedras Negras, Palenque, and Bonampak (Figs. 17, 19, 23), which commemorates the accession of rulers.[18] The accession theme differed from that of the ruler holding his insignia in that the ruler was shown in the accession theme either in a specifice place or performing a particular ritual with the assistance of other personages. By contrast, the earlier tradition of the iconic image of the ruler existed without a particular spatial or ritual framework. The narrative quality of accession imagery may have been part of the general emphasis on narrative representation during the seventh century, but it may also have had a more specific meaning. During the late sixth century, few dynastic monuments were erected in the Maya area, although none of the centers was abandoned. The cessation of monument erection is associated with an upheaval among the Maya ruling class resulting from changed relationships with Teotihuacan and other centers. Seventh-century accession iconography emphasized the conferral of dynastic rulership on a particular individual who may not have belonged to an accepted ancient lineage. The elevation of rulers who were not from the old ruling lineages may also explain the representation of women on accession monuments (fig. 17). Women were not shown with their husbands or sons in Early Classic Maya art. Their presence in seventh-century art indicates the importance of relationships established through marriage, as well as lineal descent. Accession imagery at Piedras Negras stressed both ritual and location. The ruler is shown seated in a niche on top of a ladder (fig. 19). The roof and sides of the structure are surrounded by a supernatural image that represented the sky on top and the earth below. On Stela 33, an attendant (perhaps a woman) is shown offering a headdress to the ruler seated on a high platform (Greene 1972, p. 55). It is clear that the Piedras Negras accession stelae represent the process whereby the ruler was elevated into the realm of the supernatural. At Palenque, Bonampak, and Piedras Negras, one or more persons are shown assisting at the accession of the ruler, in scenes that are represented as events more political than sacred.

After his accession, the Maya ruler was represented at some sites as a conquering warrior. During the early Middle Classic period, the representation of prisoners or of warrior rulers was infrequent.[19] At Tikal, on Stela 31 (fig. 12), dated ca. A.D. 500, warriors are represented flanking the figure of the ruler, but the ruler is shown with only ceremonial insignia. The warriors are dressed in Teotihuacan costume and carry the image of the patron deity of Teotihuacan on their shields; thus, they could be clearly identified as foreigners. Another sixth-century representation of a Maya ruler in a martial context is on Lintel 2 from Piedras Negras (Maler 1902, pl. XXXI). The ruler is shown facing a group of six kneeling warriors, and a seventh attendant stands behind him. Several costume traits, in addition to the rectangular shields, were similar to Teotihuacan designs, as seen on Stela 31 at Tikal. On Lacanha Stela 1, dated A.D. 593, the ruler wears the costume of a warrior and carries a rectangular shield. The figure inscribed on the shield wears a Teotihuacan year sign in its headdress and carries a shield with a Teotihuacan glyph on it (Greene 1972, p. 165).

During the early Middle Classic period, martial themes were infrequent in Maya dynastic iconography, and where they did occur, they were often associated with motifs from Teotihuacan imagery.

During the late sixth and seventh centuries, the incidence of martial themes in dynastic contexts increased. At Tikal, the conquest theme occurred on Stela 10, in association with the frontal position and high relief representation that was characteristic of the new style after the hiatus (Proskouriakoff 1950, fig. 47c). Kubler (1976), Miller (1976), and Coggins (n.d.) have studied the Teotihuacanoid style of two stucco figures on the Central Acropolis at Tikal (Structure 5D-57), dated ca. A.D. 700. Located on the east end of the structure, a rigidly frontal and rectilinear figure dressed as a warrior holds the rope tied around a Maya-style kneeling prisoner. The frontal figure probably represents Ruler A, and the rigidity of the figure may have been an attempt to represent him as continuing a Teotihuacan-Maya dynasty. However, while on Stela 31 the ruler is in Maya style, accompanied by Teotihuacan warriors, here the relationship is reversed: the ruler is in Teotihuacan guise and his conquest is Maya. Actually, the relief is much more extreme in rectalinearity than similar human or deity images at Teotihuacan. The frontal warrior is most reminiscent of Piedras Negras warrior stelae of the late Middle Classic and of Stela 4 at Tikal. What the Tikal reliefs indicate is not direct contact with Teotihuacan, as in the early Middle Classic, but an attempt to represent a work in what might be an archaistic "Teotihuacan" style, of significance mainly to Tikal's ruling dynasty.

Martial themes were especially important in the seventh-century art of Piedras Negras, where the ruler is usually represented as a conquering warrior some years after his accession (fig. 22). The Piedras Negras warrior-ruler wears a mosaic headdress that represents the upper jaw of a monster, and he carries a rectangular shield and spear. On Stela 7, the ruler wears the Teotihuacan year sign in his headdress. A blood glyph is inscribed in the year sign and on the pectoral ornament. An upside-down owl stands on his shield. Both the upside down owl and the blood glyph were characteristic warrior cult emblems at Teotihuacan. The frequent association of Teotihuacan images with Maya dynastic warriors may either indicate that certain aspects of martial ceremonialism were stimulated by the warrior cult of Teotihuacan, or that some dynastic relationship between the Maya and Teotihuacan ruling classes was recognized.

The only other region in Middle Classic Mesoamerica where dynastic iconography was important in monumental art was Oaxaca. Three Monte Alban stelae (1, 4, and 11) represent a richly dressed individual standing or seated on a platform with a place glyph (Caso 1928). The individuals on these stelae are identified by large cartouches in front of their bodies, although only the name of the figure on Stela 4, 8 Deer, can be determined. All three figures are shown carrying weapons and may represent the ruler as conquering warrior.

During the seventh century, a new theme was introduced into the dynastic art of Oaxaca—the marriage of elite personages. At Lambityeco, male and female pairs are found in both tomb and platform decorations. On the facade of Tomb 6, the portrait of a man and a woman, probably representing the occupants of the tomb, was modeled in stucco (Rabin 1970). A Lambityeco patio wall was ornamented with a stucco frieze representing reclining male and female figures facing each other. They too were associated with identifying glyphs. The representation of the wives of the elite or ruling group as the equals of their husbands was new in Oaxaca iconography and indicates a preoccupation with dynastic relationships contracted through marriage. The appearance of women and the representation of marriage relations in the monumental art of both Oaxaca and the Maya area indicate changes in the royal lineages in the seventh century and the establishment of new ties.

In Maya art, as the stages in the life of the ruler came to be commemorated by specific types of representation, funeral imagery also became more elaborate. The deceased individual was not usually represented; instead, the major themes of funerary art concerned the descent of supernaturals to the underworld, populated with monstrous creatures, and the supernaturals' death and rebirth. At Palenque, Pacal, the first great ruler of the site, was buried in the Temple of the Inscriptions. Two rows of underworld deities surrounded the body of the king in the sarcophagus. The nine stucco figures modeled on the crypt walls represent the nine lords of the underworld. The ten figures carved on the side of the sarcophagus represent the youthful maize gods emerging from the earth. On the sarcophagus lid, a reclining human figure is shown seated on a skull (fig. 24). A cross of jeweled serpents rises above him. The reclining figure may have been a rare representation of the soul of the ruler in the underworld. The sarcophagus lid design is nearly identical to that on the central panel of the Temple of the Cross (fig. 31), the only major difference being that the human figure is lacking in the Temple of the Cross design. The Temple of the Cross panel represents the sun and foreshadowes his rebirth. On the sarcophagus, the maize gods are represented as emerging from the earth at the moment of their birth. The spirit of the ruler on the sarcophagus may have been equated with the sun in the underworld, with the implication that the ruler too would rise up again among the immortals. The reclining figure posture in Classic art was especially characteristic of humans and deities about to die in a sacrificial or ceremonial context. Since dying gods and mortals who died on the sacrificial altar were subsequently reborn, the posture may have symbolized both death and rebirth.

On the plaster reliefs of the pillars on the exterior of the Temple of the Inscriptions, four human figures are shown holding manikin scepter deities in the highly unusual form of infants (de la Fuente 1965, pls. 16, 17). Infant images in Mesoamerica generally represent birth.[20] The child-manikin scepter combination was a graphic illustration of the rebirth of both the fertility gods and of the dynastic rulers whose insignia they had become. In the funeral iconography of the Palenque ruler, the ruler's spirit was shown to parallel the death and rebirth cycle of the sun and fertility gods (Schele 1974).

So far, no other tomb so richly ornamented has been found in the Maya area. Similar funerary iconography was frequently depicted on painted ceramics that were intended to be placed in burials. Coe (1973) has demonstrated that a large group of Maya funerary vessels depict in great detail the various gods and monsters of the underworld into whose realm the dead had to descend. Such narrative scenes on funerary pottery were not made until after A.D. 600.[21]

Besides the cult of the dynastic ruler and the funerary cults, which became more elaborate and more concerned with different events in time, the ball game cult also underwent changes in representation during the late Middle Classic period. Between A.D. 450 and 700, the ball game appears to have been the major cult of the Peripheral Coastal

Lowlands, judging by the quality and quantity of art works that deal with the subject (Pasztory 1972). The ball game cult of the Middle Classic period was essentially a sacrificial cult. The mythic aspect of the cult dealt with the descent of the sun into the underworld and the rebirth of the maize deity. However, in this myth, the sun god was not alone, but accompanied by his twin, usually associated with the planet Venus. The exploits of the twin heroes were recounted in the sixteenth-century book of the Quiche of Guatemala, the *Popol Vuh.* The iconography of the ball game indicates that myths similar to the late myth of the *Popol Vuh* existed in the Middle Classic period.

According to the *Popol Vuh,* the twin heroes, the sun and Venus, played a ball game with the lords of the underworld. The sun and Venus lost and were beheaded. The decapitated head of the sun was placed in the branches of a tree. A maiden (the earth goddess) walked by and was made pregnant by spittle from the head. She gave birth to another set of twins, who eventually grew up and, after many adventures, played another game with the underworld gods. This time the twins were victorious, and they killed the gods of death. The ball game myth recounted in the *Popol Vuh* was a version of the death and rebirth of the sun, with the emphasis on the ritual ball game in which first the sun and later the gods of the underworld were defeated. The sun god of the dry season died in order that the sun god of fertility and the rainy season could be born. The ceremonial ball game reenacted this myth: the two teams represented the sun and his brother pitted against the underworld, and the decapitation of the leader of the losing team was a reenactment of the beheading of the sun god or the death gods, depending upon whether the reference was to the first or second game.

While some of the iconography of the ball game cult shared certain characteristics with the agricultural fertility cults, there were also new images, such as a descending sun god, skeletal deities, decapitation sacrifice, trophy heads, and cacao and maguey symbolism. In ball game cult iconography of the Middle Classic period, the sun god was represented in aspects that differed from the iconography of the agricultural fertility cults.

The solar disk and the anthropomorphic representation of the sun god within the disk first appeared in Mesoamerican iconography during the Middle Classic period in the contexts of the ball game cult. At Bilbao, the sun deity was shown wearing a flaming disk pectoral (fig. 16) and at El Castillo the sun god was framed by a solar disk (Parsons 1969, fig. 59a). Solar disks occurred in the iconography of Teotihuacan [22] and Tajin, but bearing the movement glyph rather than the image of the god.

Skulls and skeletons were rare in Mesoamerican art prior to the late Preclassic period. During the Middle Classic period, they were frequently represented in the art of the Peripheral Coastal Lowlands. On Bilbao panels, skeletons assist in sacrificial scenes (fig. 16); on the Great Ball Court of Tajin, skeletons are represented in the borders and above sacrificial victims (Kampen 1972); at Chichen Itza, a skull is carved on the ball. Skeletal figures referred to either the destructive denizens of the underworld or to the death ritual, which reenacted the decapitation of the sun.

In ball game iconography, the rebirth of fertility is represented by water and plant imagery. Serpents and flowering vines are shown emerging from the severed necks of decapitated ball players, in the art of Chichen Itza and Escuintla. In the art of several Middle Classic centers, the plant shown in association with rebirth was not necessarily maize, but often maguey or cacao. The sap of the maguey was used to make *pulque,* an intoxicating drink consumed in ritual drunkenness that concluded many Mesoamerican feasts and sacrifices. Maguey plants in all stages of growth surround the figures on the central panel of the Great Ball Court at Tajin (fig. 27). Cacao was used in Mesoamerica not only to make a chocolate drink but also as a form of currency. Most of the important cacao-growing regions were located in the Peripheral Coastal Lowlands (Parsons 1969). Bilbao was in a prime cacao plantation area, and cacao pods are represented on a number of ball game monuments. Cacao was offered to the gods like the hearts of sacrificial victims, or it was shown growing on vines. It was the symbol of both fertility and mercantile activity. The ball game was probably the major cult of merchants in both the Classic and Postclassic periods.

During the early Middle Classic period, mainly small-scale stone objects and pottery designs were associated with the ball game cult. The stone objects consisted of stone replicas of the ceremonial gear used by the players. Prior to the early Middle Classic period, this gear was quite variable and simply decorated, but at that time standard forms were established for yokes and *hachas,* which were decorated with Classic Veracruz interlace designs. Ballplayer scenes represented on early Middle Classic pottery usually had the same composition: one or two players flanking the ball.

Towards the end of the sixth and the beginning of the seventh centuries, the centers where the ball game cult was of primary importance played a powerful role in Mesoamerican trade and politics. The ball game cult began to be commemorated on monuments or relief panels associated with ball courts. On these monuments, the scenes and compositions were varied and more narrative than in the previous period. At Bilbao, eight stelae were erected in two rows, each showing ballplayers making offerings to a descending deity. Because of the removal of these stelae in the nineteenth century, the actual sequence of figures cannot be reconstructed, but a narrative was probably intended. Narrative sets of ball game reliefs are known from Copan (fig. 20) and Tajin (Kampen 1972). At Copan, three round markers set in the floor of the playing alley have representations of two players in different postures flanking a ball, which represented either different moments in ball game ritual or, as has been suggested, the cosmic cycle of the death and rebirth of vegetation that the ball game enacts symbolically (Cohodas 1974). This hypothesis explains the presence of the plant on the south marker and of the foliated plant on the north marker. The most elaborate narrative ball game cult representation is found on the Great Ball Court of Chichen Itza and its four associated temples. Each temple has a different iconographic program, the Lower Temple of the Jaguars and the North Temple are carved with symbols of water and vegetation as well as those of the sky and underworld aspects of the sun deity. The symbols of the South Temple refer to death and drought (Cohodas n.d.).

The cycle of death and rebirth in nature, symbolized by the ball game cult, was expressed in the monumental arts of the seventh century by means of separate temples or monuments placed in different cardinal directions, which could be read together as a narrative. It is probable that the directional symbolism and the erection of sets of monuments in late Middle Classic art originated in the ball game cult art of the Peripheral Coastal Lowlands. Directional symbolism and sets of narrative monuments expressed so well the seventh-century preoccupation with time and cycles of events, that they were also adopted for subjects other than the ball game. The most remarkable are the three Temples of Palenque (the Temples of the Sun, the Cross, and the Foliated Cross) and the three stelae of Xochicalco. The Palenque and Xochicalco monuments are especially significant because they appear to represent the same cosmic cycle within different local cults, thus indicating the syncretism and parallelism of the seventh-century artistic traditions.

The Temples of the Sun, Cross, and Foliated Cross at Palenque are located respectively on the west, north, and east sides of a plaza and have strong directional significance (figs. 31–33). They were erected in A.D. 692 by Chan Bahlum, the successor to Pacal, who is buried in the Temple of the Inscriptions (Schele 1974). The set as a whole represents a highly unusual dynastic commemoration. On these monuments, the major stages in the rule of Chan Bahlum were apparently compared to the death and rebirth of the sun god of the agricultural cult. The sun deity is shown at its descent in the Temple of the Sun by means of martial symbols, crossed spears and a shield inscribed with the face of the jaguar sun deity; in the underworld in the Temple of the Cross, by means of a sun mask with skeletal jaws set beneath a tree of serpents associated with water and death symbols; and reborn as the god of maize in the Temple of the Foliated Cross by means of a naturalistic maize plant with a mask of the sun god at its apex. Human figures, one of whom may represent Chan Bahlum, assist at the different stages of the transformation.

Three stelae found at Xochicalco—located in a temple that had three rooms facing a central court—parallel the iconography of the three temples at Palenque (Pasztory 1976). Since the deities of Xochicalco are represented with insignia derived from Teotihuacan art, they can be readily identified. Stela 3 (fig. 34) represents the descending sun god 4 *ollin* with symbols of blood and sacrifice, which is comparable in meaning to the panel of the Temple of the Sun. Stela 2 (fig. 35) represents the night sun in the underworld as a jaguar Tlaloc image, in which symbols of death and water predominate. This stela is comparable in meaning to the Temple of the Cross panel design. Stela 1 (fig.

34. **Xochicalco Stela 3, drawing. After Marquina 1964, supplement fig. 4.**

35. **Xochicalco Stela 2, drawing. After Marquina 1964, supplement fig. 3.**

36. **Xochicalco Stela 1, drawing. After Marquina 1964, supplement fig. 2.**

36) represents the earth goddess, 7 Eye of the Reptile, who will give birth to the god of maize to complete the cycle of death and rebirth, and is comparable to the meaning of the panel of the Temple of the Foliated Cross. That the same basic myth is represented on monuments erected in sets of three both at Palenque and Xochicalco indicates the highly syncretic nature of seventh-century iconography.

Directional composition and buildings with interrelated iconographic programs are also known in the art of Teotihuacan, but the examples occurred in the context of the warrior cult. Moreover, sets of four instead of three were more characteristic at Teotihuacan. The room of the red birds at Tetitla and the White Patio of Atetelco were painted with figures from a warrior cult that was in the service of a solar mythology. The descent of the sun was represented by deformed figures or canine animals on the west, and the rise of the sun in the east was represented by a raptorial bird. As in the art of southern Mesoamerica, the south and west were associated with death and the north and east with rebirth.[23]

The Teotihuacan contribution to Middle Classic iconography was the systematization of the gods and spirits and of their worship. This order imposed on the supernatural is evident in the clarity and standardization of deity representations in works of art of the early Middle Classic period. The iconography of the peripheral centers during the seventh century departed radically from the rational, normative approach popularized by Teotihuacan. Seventh-century compositions represented phenomena seen from two points of view, the particular and holistic, which we might call the "microscopic" and the "telescopic." On the one hand, great emphasis was placed on individual persons and their unique history of births, marriages, conquests, and deaths; on the other hand, art works represented the spatial and temporal dimensions of cosmic cycles crucial to mankind. The two were brought together in the unique set of temples at Palenque, in which the individual and dynastic imagery was a counterpart of the cosmic imagery. As the peripheral cultures of Mesoamerica expanded their horizons politically and commercially during the late Middle Classic period, they also expanded their inner horizons. Instead of the simple, essentially timeless point of view characteristic of early Middle Classic Teotihuacan, a historical point of view, including a concept of nearly infinite time, counted in millions of years, emerged in the seventh century.[24]

Notes

1. The earliest two-part platform articulation in Mesoamerica is to be found in Oaxaca, and the Teotihuacan *talud* and *tablero* may derive from that. Teotihuacan, however, was the first to standardize the form and to apply it to all ceremonial structures in a highly uniform manner.

2. Little early Middle Classic architecture is known from the Maya area because later buildings generally cover the earlier ones. One of the few excavated examples is the North Acropolis of Tikal (W. Coe 1967, p. 25). Here, the platforms were articulated by overhanging sloping panels and great apron moldings. As in the architecture of Teotihuacan, the forms are large and simple and the emphasis is on the dramatic contrast of horizontal and vertical lines.

3. Teotihuacan probably retained the two-part division of platforms out of conservatism.

4. In Oaxaca, the three-part articulation is found on the late Danzantes building at Monte Alban, on several temple models in clay, and on a number of structures at Lambityeco.

5. The earliest stage of the Monte Alban ball court is supposed to be Monte Alban II in date (Acosta 1965, p. 829). The evidence for this early date is not clear. Flannery has recently excavated a ball court at San Jose Mogote which may be as early as Monte Alban II. *

6. The Pyramid of Quetzalcoatl at Teotihuacan, ornamented with 365 tenoned heads in the Miccaotli period may have been the prototype of the Tajin structure. However, the Temple of Quetzalcoatl was covered by another temple in the Xolalpan period.

7. The relationship between Teotihuacan and Veracruz has never been adequately investigated. Why is a Veracruz scroll design found on a platform so near the Avenue of the Dead at Teotihuacan? After such a prominent early occurrence of Veracruz designs, such designs do not appear in the later mural paintings of Teotihuacan.

8. Profile human figures carrying bags (presumably for incense) and wearing animal or deity headdresses are usually identified as priests in Teotihuacan iconography.

9. At Monte Alban, the mural painting of Tomb 104, showing a number of Teotihuacan-derived iconographic motifs, also has the composition of a frontal deity face with flanking profile figures (Marquina 1964; pp. 341–43).

10. The grid plan of the city of Teotihuacan was not necessarily the immediate

* John Paddock 1976: personal communication.

cause of the geometric rigidity of its art style; both may be material expressions of a particular ideological orientation.

11. Teotihuacan monumental sculpture was rare at all times. However, some carving is known from the Early, Miccaotli and Tlamimilolpa, and the Late, Metepec, phases. From the Xolalpan phase, the time of the greatest influence of the city, no firmly dated examples of sculpture are known. Three-dimensional sculptures of animals, a jaguar head, and serpent bodies decorated the seventh-century Palace of the Butterflies. As in Yucatan, sculpture in the round was associated with architecture at Teotihuacan. The revival of architectural sculpture in the seventh century in the art of Teotihuacan may have been a result of southern Mesoamerican influences.

12. Coggins (n.d.) suggests that the ruler represented on Stela 10 is an outsider and "usurper," probably from a site southeast of the Peten.

13. The oval relief of Palenque is undated but, on the basis of style, it is usually given a mid to late seventh-century date (Greene 1967, p. 13). The Palenque type of representation of the seated ruler was widespread in Mesoamerica. The pose is found on jades, shells, and vase paintings. Jade carvings representing the ruler in this posture have been found in the Guatemala highlands, at Teotihuacan, at Copan, and in the Chichen cenote. The figures seated under the arched body of the serpent on the main pyramid at Xochicalco are also in this pose, the only difference being the hand of the Xochicalco figure rests next to the body rather than being placed on the thigh.

14. Borhegyi's further speculations, that the religion of Teotihuacan might have been similar to the mystery cults of the Hellenistic period, are not accepted here.

15. This is not to mean that only six cults existed in Mesoamerica, but that six of them were associated with art works in permanent media.

16. Both Sanders and Price (1968, p. 203) and Borhegyi (1971) have suggested that Teotihuacan had some form of professional military organization.

17. Coggins (n.d.) suggests that the ceremonial bar was used at Tikal only on posthumous stelae. She suggests that the manikin scepter deity originates at Tikal and is a Maya translation of the Mexican rain god Tlaloc.

18. The accession theme was first described by Proskouriakoff (1961).

19. The theme of the ruler as conquering warrior in dynastic art probably has its origin in Olmec art. In Early Classic Maya art, there are several representations of a ruler trampling on a prisoner or dressed in a warrior's costume. The Leyden plate and Uaxactun Stela 5 illustrate these two types of representations.

20. Baby figures, separate from mother and child combinations, are rare in the art of Mesoamerica. Baby figures were important in the Olmec traditions of the Early and Middle Preclassic periods, but disappeared as major iconographic themes thereafter. Baby figures were revived in art in the seventh century. The Classic Veracruz terra-cotta baby figures may be direct revivals of Olmec baby figures modeled in clay. In Olmec iconography the baby, or baby were-jaguar, has been interpreted as the sun deity at the time of his rebirth (Hatch 1971). A parallel meaning is suggested for the Veracruz images.

21. Funerary iconography at Monte Alban represents supernatural figures related to the underworld. Painted on the walls of Tomb 105 are nine figures of old men and women, who probably stand for the nine lords of the underworld. It is probable that, as in the case of the Palenque crypt, the nine deities may actually be human god impersonators. On the murals of Tomb 104, the central representation is the mask image of the maize god, flanked by two god impersonators. The maize god is represented not only on the mural but also on the largest of the urns found in the tomb and on the glyphic emblem carved on the stone that covered the door. The maize god is symbolic of rebirth and the continuation of the cycle of life. The selection of his image in a funerary context may indicate a belief in rebirth or a continuity after death for at least some elite segments of the population.

22. A solar disk is probably represented in the mural at Teopancaxo (Kubler 1967, fig. 45).

23. The burial of a youth with four vessels with different but related designs at Alta Vista probably relates to the Teotihuacan warrior cult imagery. The raptorial birds may have represented the sun deity in its four different aspects in both spatial or temporal terms: at dawn, noon, evening and midnight, and at the east, north, west and south. Both the fourfold imagery and the prominent position of the raptorial bird in iconography relate the art of Alta Vista to Teotihuacan (see paper by Holien and Pickering in this volume).

24. Two late Middle Classic monuments, the Palenque Tablet of the Inscriptions and Tikal Stela 10, were the first to record dates that covered millions of years (Thompson 1960, pp. 314–16). Thompson suggests that the concept of time periods greater than a *baktun* (about 400 years) was invented late in Maya history. The evidence indicates that these unusually long calculations were first made in the seventh century.

PART THREE

mesoamerica between a.d. 400-700: problems and cross-cultural studies

THOMAS HOLIEN AND ROBERT B. PICKERING [1]

analogues in classic period chalchihuites culture to late mesoamerican ceremonialism

In 1971, the test excavations at the site of Alta Vista, Zacatecas, uncovered the remains of an unusual multiple interrment from the Early Classic period. This burial seems to have been the occasion for an elaborate deposition of Chalchihuites artifacts, which have not previously been found in such coherent association. In this report, we hope both to demonstrate the plausability of the "field assumption" that this was the burial of a deity impersonator, and to contribute to the evidence now available for a reappraisal of Classic period relationships between central Mesoamerica and its expanding northwestern frontier.

Alta Vista is a partly excavated ceremonial center of early Chalchihuites culture, located near the common boundary of the states of Zacatecas and Durango and within the *municipio* of Chalchihuites. At an altitude of nearly 2,300 meters above sea level, this site lies within a relatively narrow environmental and archaeological zone, which extends along the southern and southwestern margin of the high intermontaine basin of Coahuila, Chihuahua, and northern Zacatecas, and in the eastern foothills of the Sierra Madre Occidental.

The reason for the beginnings of the Chalchihuites occupation is probably not to be found in what might appear to be a population expansion into a favorable region to the north, but rather, in the rapid establishment of an exploitative colony among dispersed farming populations by a Mesoamerican elite. Exploitation of the Chalchihuites area's mines for the benefit of a relatively remote Mesoamerican imperium seems to be a useful framework for the evidence from the early phases of this culture (Canutillo phase— A.D. 1–250, Alta Vista phase—A.D. 250–500). Such a cultural intrusion is manifest in the coincident introduction of ceremonially dictated architecture into new kinds of settlements, in the establishment of intensive mining throughout most of the occupied region, and in significant additions to the material culture inventory. These revolutionary developments have been interpreted as being Teotihuacan inspired, or even Teotihuacan managed, even though they have the distinct overlay of various West Mexican cultures to the south (Kelley 1971, p. 786). Selected artifacts and architectural forms may have parallels at Teotihuacan, but they are not out of place in the complex West Mexican milieu of the Classic. None of these traits are of indisputably Teotihuacan origin, in the sense of having been transported directly from that center. This situation is most unlike that in the reported mining district in Queretaro, which yielded graves containing eastern and central Mesoamerican ceramics, including Teotihuacan cylindrical tripod vessels (Consejo de Recursos Naturales no Renovables 1970). At Chalchihuites, however, we infer a similar colonial status from the intensity of fortification, the religious centralization, the population nucleation and overall increase within a short time, and from the grand scale of the mines, which indicates production far beyond local needs (Weigand 1968, pp. 45, 59).

By the end of the Classic period, new centers had been founded, to the northwest in the Guadiana valley of Durango, while the centers of the original region were abandoned. By A.D. 1350, all Chalchihuites culture centers were in disuse, and the area was apparently inhabited by the somewhat acculturated descendants of the pre-Mesoamerican agriculturalists, a tradition called "Loma San Gabriel." Riley and Winters (1963, p. 177) have suggested that the Loma San Gabriel culture is ancestral to the historic Tepehuanes, while Maritzer (1958), Kelly and Abbott (1966, pp. 11, 18), and Kelley (1971, p. 801) indicate that there were Chalchihuites survivals in Huichol culture as well.

This account of Chalchihuites origins and history is in some disagreement with the recent generalizations that all of West Mexico lacks a Mesoamerican culture affiliation until the Postclassic period (e.g., Weaver 1972, p. 216) or that it was never incorporated into Mesoamerica. While we agree with Weaver, Bernal (1969), and M. Coe (1962, p. 127) that the lack of a Preclassic of Olmec origin had a profound influence on the cultural traditions of the west, the highland Classic does seem to have had a considerable influence in the northwest (Willey 1966, p. 174; Corona Nunez 1972; Braniff 1972; Kelley and Kelley n.d.).

Because of this connection, it seems more reasonable to project cultural analogies across the distance of some 1,000 kilometers, from Chalchihuites to the valley of Mexico. A second preliminary difficulty is the obvious objection to drawing an analogy between Classic and Postclassic religions, despite the probable disjunction of meaning, whatever the formal similarities. We hope to demonstrate, however,

that the cult that motivated this unusual burial survived, and even intensified, during later Chalchihuites phases, including those of the early Postclassic. This Alta Vista phase burial represents an early instance of a cult and cosmology that, in evolved forms, were temporally and spatially in place (since no drastic frontier intervened), to interact with the cults and cosmologies of Central Mexico.

The Alta Vista site has recently been found to have a Canutillo phase foundation, preceeding its Alta Vista phase florescence, which may have been constructed soon after the initial Mesoamerican occupation of the area. This central architectural complex includes a Hall of Columns, an adjacent sunken court with a pyramidal altar at its center, other still-buried court and platform groups, and contiguous room structures, presumably residences (fig. 1). The Hall of Columns was excavated by Gamio in 1908 (Gamio 1910, p. 481). It has since been found to have had a Canutillo construction phase sealed below Gamio's floor. A ceremonial cache was found in the southwest part of this hall, below a disturbed portion of the plastered floor (Gamio 1910, p. 486) and in the fill introduced by the Alta Vista phase renovators of the original hall. Gamio correctly observed evidence of the rebuilding and enlarging of the twenty-eight columns and the eventual filling of the hall. The burial found in the most recent excavation, and reported on here, was located below the floor exposed by Gamio and in the northern corner of the hall. There is a variety of burial types elsewhere at the site, including an infant urn burial, cremations in a cyst, and ossuary caches of selected bones, some of which show cutting marks at the muscle attachments. Butchering for food is our present supposition.

The burials in the northern corner were interred in an amorphous pit at a depth of from twenty-four to seventy-five centimeters below the broken plaster of the floor. At the base of the pit, on a layer of pebbles, lay a semiflexed skeleton without a skull. The fill was damp, due to the pattern of floor drainage, and the bone preservation was poor. An in situ analysis indicated that the individual was a male, between sixteen and twenty-two years in skeletal age. A Suchil red-on-brown *olla* had been placed on the pelvis with four goblets, or *copas*, next to it. These *copas* had either been placed in a stack, which had fallen over as the pit was filled, or they had been carefully aligned on their sides. A miniature smudge-fired *olla* lay in the area of the chest cavity. On this same deposition floor, at the skeleton's feet, were two detached disarticulated human legs, lying one above the other. It could not be determined whether the proximal portions of the femurs had deteriorated, along with much of the rest of the bone, or whether they had been absent at the time of burial.

Other bones and burial equipment lay above an intervening layer of pebbly black gumbo in the same pit. Lying on this layer of fill was a compacted mass of deteriorated bones, stacked long bones primarily. Small bones such as carpals, vertebrae, and phalanges were almost completely absent. Although the bones were in very poor condition, it was possible to identify each one as to the body part represented and the degree of symphyseal union. In most cases, the proximal and distal epiphyses were either unfused or in the process of being fused, and the iliac crests and ischial tuberosities were at a similar stage. Therefore, the individuals were from a very specific group—sixteen to twenty-two years skeletal age—and they were all males. Placed on these bone stacks were eight skulls with the mandibles disarticulated. A small turquoise bead lay among these bones. A red-slipped *tecomate* and the midsection of a large knife of black-mottled red obsidian were found to the northeast, away from the concentration of material that partly underlay the buried foundation of the column in this corner. Over the skulls lay the upper portion of a broken *copa* and part of a ceramic flute. The pit had then been filled to floor level and plastered over.

As this burial was unearthed, the presence of several key traits led to the suggestion, by J. C. Kelley, that the traits seemed to relate to the sacrifice of a Tezcatlipoca impersonator. The traits suggesting this annual sacrifice included the broken flute, the division in the tomb between a primary and eight secondary individuals, the evidence of ritual mutilation, and the exceptionally rich accompanying artifacts.

For this sacrificial ceremony, among the Mexica, a young man was selected a year in advance to personify Tezcatlipoca, and he was instructed in flute playing and courtly behavior. On the eventual day of sacrifice, the young man climbed the steps of a small and remote pyramid, breaking his set of flutes on the way, until, at the summit, he was dispatched in the usual fashion. Although his head joined others

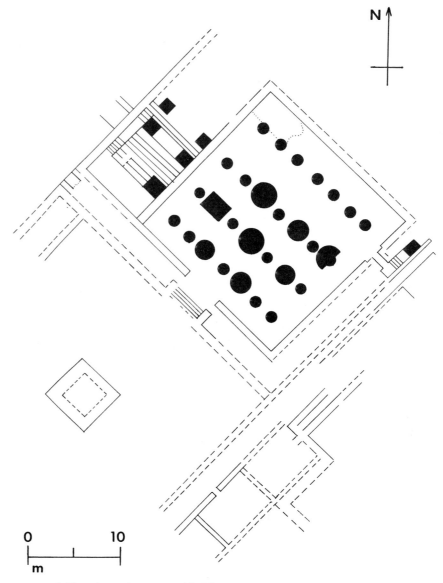

1. Plan of central structures, Alta Vista, Zacatecas.

on the skull rack, his body was treated with marked respect. Attendants were sacrificed with this god at four-year intervals. Attention then shifted to the installation of a new impersonator, and the available accounts make no further mention of the disposition of the remains of his predecessor. Both Sahagun (1950–71, vol. 3) and Duran (1971) provide summaries of this ritual, which climaxed each annual feast of Toxcatl.

Chalchihuites analogues to this Toxcatl ceremony include the presence of many of the items expected in the residue of such a sacrifice, as well as additional artifacts emblematic of Tezcatlipoca and with an iconography that is congruent to the meaning of the rite.

Analogues to the Toxcatl Sacrifice

The headless primary individual at the base of the pit is unusual in its completeness and articulation, as compared to the associated individuals and to many other interrments found at Alta Vista. In the Aztec ritual, the impersonator's body, once the head had been severed, was treated with unusual care. Sahagun's account states ". . . they did not roll it down; rather they lowered it. Four men carried it" (1950–71, vol. 3, p. 68). The head was relegated to the Tzompantli. The missing head in the Alta Vista burial could have received similar treatment, since skulls found elsewhere at the site exhibit perforations and the postmortem loss of single-rooted teeth and articulating bones that would occur in display and decomposition before burial. While this hardly demonstrates the use of a temple skull rack, it does suggest some practice of skull display, such as, perhaps, the "mobile sculpture" of skulls and bones found at Casas Grandes (Di Peso 1968a, cover plate). The decapitation of the Aztec impersonator recalls a manifestation of Tezcatlipoca in which he appears to wayfarers headless and with opening and closing doors in his chest (Sejourne 1972, p. 119).

The osteologic age of the primary individual (sixteen to twenty-two years) corresponds to the requirement, reported in Sahagun's work, that the impersonator be a very young warrior but not a juvenile, ". . . with the sutures of the crown yet soft" (1950–71, vol. 3, p. 65). The same rules for selecting an impersonator stress the importance of his physical qualities. He must have regular features, sound teeth, no deformities, etc. While the headless skeleton in this burial can be rated against few of these exactingly recorded criteria, it exhibited no pathology or trauma in an inspection routine that included an examination of every human bone encountered in these 1971 excavations.

A coincident burial of the Tezcatlipoca impersonator with his attendants is not reported in colonial documents, but such an event seems to be a reasonable projection of the sequence of the sacrificial ceremony. Duran stated that others were sacrificed with the principal every four years (Duran 1971, p. 127). These "others" were probably the eight attendants, since only they accompanied the impersonator to the pyramid of sacrifice. The additional four female attendants remained behind (Sahagun 1950–71, vol. 3, p. 68). At Alta Vista, the eight individuals represented by the deposit of skulls and large bones, above the primary burial, seem to fit several of the attributes of such attendants. They were interred as part of the same event with the putative god impersonator, but were of different status, if that can be inferred from their isolation above a layer of fill, the paucity and fragmentary condition of their burial equipment, and their skeletal dismemberment and incompleteness. In contrast, the initial burial was of an articulated skeleton, accompanied by relatively numerous and unbroken artifacts, and with an extra pair of legs. These legs, in view of what appears to have been common practice at this ceremonial center, probably constituted ritual food. In later times, Europeans were assured that the thigh was the best meat (Gillmor 1964, p. 141). This cut would be an entirely appropriate offering to the personage who, in the legends of the Toltecs, championed a cult of human sacrifice against the establishment of Topiltzin Quetzalcoatl. In Tenochtitlan, the idol Tezcatlipoca was fed with honey cake decorated with a skull and crossbones (Duran 1971, p. 107). The Alta Vista attendants, disarticulated and with small bones apparently discarded, may have constituted the provision for ritual feasting. Cutting marks at muscle attachments, which are present on bones from some other burials at Alta Vista and from the Hall of Columns burials at La Quemada, were not noted on these long bones. Thus, there is no direct evidence for intentional butchering, as opposed to exposure and decomposition before interrment. What argues against the latter possibility is that the primary individual, if killed at the same time, did not decompose to the extent of bone disarticulation.

These eight individuals can be further related to a specific ritual role, as follows. There are eight skulls laid out in two rows of four, a parallel to the division of the Aztec attendants into two groups—four who had fasted for a year in advance (priests?) and four who were warriors. "His eight young men . . ." (Sahagun 1950–71, vol. 3, p. 66) are, in this case, all within the osteologic age sixteen to twenty-two years. Moreover, we infer from Duran (1971) that they share the other physical criteria for the impersonation of the god himself since, if the original impersonator escaped, he was replaced by whichever attendant was considered most at fault. At Alta Vista, all recorded observations indicate osteological and dental normality.

The burial equipment seems to reinforce an analogy to what we know of the Tezcatlipoca sacrifice. Flutes, for instance, are generally associated with that god, as is summarized by Marti (1953), in his account of a cache of instruments found in the Tezcatlipoca-Xochipilli temple at Tizatlan. The theatricality of breaking the past year's flutes, while the impersonator ascends the pyramid steps, probably accounts for Torquemada's statement, quoted by Marti (1953, p. 148), that the flute both represents and announces the fiesta of Toxcatl. The characteristically high-pitched flute of Toxcatl, and of the Volador ceremony, was venerated as sacred (Marti 1953, p. 154). It was multitoned, yet had to be playable with one hand, since the impersonator simultaneously carried a device composed of a mirror and smoking tube.

The Alta Vista flute fragment satisfies these criteria (fig. 2a). As hypothetically reconstructed—by reference to flute fragments from other Chalchihuites sites—it may even have been pierced for suspension around the neck, in order to facilitate its constant presence in the regalia of the wearer. The Alta Vista fragment is from an instrument somewhat larger than those associated with Tezcatlipoca ceremonies from the valley of Mexico. Nevertheless, the fragment's closely spaced stops and precise construction indicate that its scale might have been doubled to produce the characteristic shrill sound played to the four directions to announce the presence of the impersonator (Duran 1971, p. 101). The fragment's special ceremonial use is indicated by its fabrication from the distinctively coarse paste of Vista Paint Cloisonné, a ware that is somewhat different from those wares compounded by skilled Chalchihuites ceramists for other ceramic types (Kelley and Kelley 1971, p. 161). At Chalchihuites, Vista Paint Cloisonné has been interpreted as a decorated ceramic with strictly ceremonial associations. Its designs are elaborate and often include depictions of ceremonialists or deities.

The broken goblet accompanying the flute as the last deposit in the grave is also of the Vista Paint Cloisonné type, and it is decorated on the interior with a personage whose face, broken out of this specimen (fig. 3), is preserved on similar *copas* from other Chalchihuites sites (figs. 4, 5). An unvarying accoutrement of this full-face figure is a pectoral disk, seemingly the *anahuatl* ring, framing a mirror, or *eltezcatl*. This is a nearly diagnostic emblem of Tezcatlipoca in codex illustrations. Although no mirror was found in this burial, the subfloor cache found by Gamio in the same Hall of Columns, and from the same construction phase, did contain such a mirror (Gamio 1910, p. 487, pl. 8).

Aztec and Cholultecan *copas*, of essentially the same form as this broken one, were called *teocaxital* and were apparently restricted to ceremonial drinking (Torquemada 1943, vol. 1; p. 266; Goncalves de Lima 1956; p. 138), a specified part of the feasting by the Tezcatlipoca impersonator during his year of elevation. Alternatively, this *copa* could have been the container for *teoctli*, or Duran's "divine wine," which some victims drank before climbing to the sacrificial block. In either case, a broken *copa* could well have joined flute fragments at the base of a Chalchihuites altar and have been conveyed to the top of the eventual burial as a memorial offering.

The red obsidian knife fragment from this upper level could have been part of the knife used in the sacrifice, or it could have been emblematic of Tezcatlipoca's manifestation as Itzli or Itzlacoliuhqui, the obsidian knife. In codical depictions, this knife is colored red (e.g., Codex Borgia 1963). The broken *tecomate*, found with the knife, has no obvious specific affinity with Tezcatlipoca. Turquoise, a ubiquitous burial offering in the Greater Southwest, is so common in Mesoamerica that the presence of a single bead in this burial is not significant, despite the inclusion of turquoise in the regalia of the impersonator (Duran 1971; pp. 98–99).

As was previously described, the primary individual in the tomb had been interred separately from the fragmentary human and artifac-

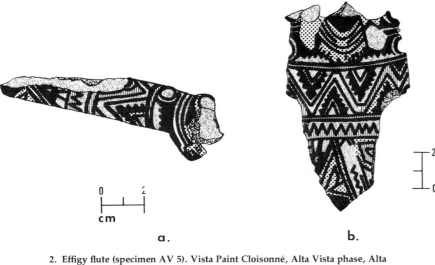

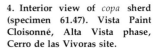

a.

b.

2. Effigy flute (specimen AV 5). Vista Paint Cloisonné, Alta Vista phase, Alta Vista site.
    a. Side view.
    b. Design.

4. Interior view of *copa* sherd (specimen 61.47). Vista Paint Cloisonné, Alta Vista phase, Cerro de las Vivoras site.

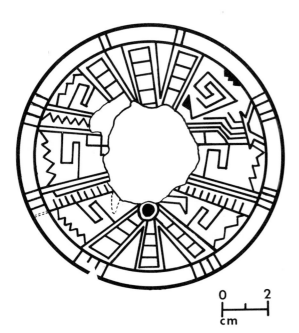

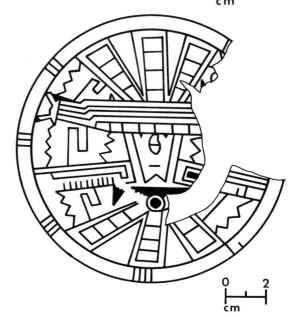

3. Interior view of *copa* (specimen AV 6). Vista Paint Cloisonné, Alta Vista phase, Alta Vista site.

5. Interior view of *copa*. Vista Paint Cloisonné, Alta Vista phase, La Escondida site.

tual debris of the suggested sacrifice. The equipment with this focal individual is not particularly suggestive of the ritual of the sacrifice, but it does seem to indicate attributes of a generic Tezcatlipoca through symbols of his associated cosmology and rites. Only the black *ollita*, with its neck and rim broken away, and placed at the chest, is presently without clear ritual implication. Other burial equipment in this lower grave is exquisite and undamaged.

While the decoration of the set of four Vista Paint Cloisonné *copas* provides most of the useful analogues in this part of the grave, it is important first to consider them as a set completed by the red-on-brown *olla*. A burial complex in West Mexico, with cloisonné-decorated *copas* and *ollas* accompanying individual inhumations, is now emerging from the refractory data of looted collections. Lumholtz (1902, p. 460) purchased dozens of *ollas, ollitas* and *copas* (with other materials), which had come from a "cemetery" at Hacienda Estanzuela, Jalisco. Their original distribution in sets is suggested by their easy segregation into lots by size, and then by the variation in workmanship among them. *Ollas* can be matched with *copas* whose bases fit the orifice of the *olla*, often seating neatly in an incised or indented groove around the rim interior. Cloisonné-decorated *ollas* from other collections frequently exhibit this groove, such as the two great *ollas* from Jiquilpan, Michoacan (Noguera 1944, figs. 15–16), and rim sherds from Totoate, Jalisco, and Potrero del Calichal near Alta Vista. In only one previous case known to us has this *copa-olla* complex been recorded in situ before sale or dispersal. In this instance an *olla*, ten *copas*, and five *ollitas*, now at the Los Angeles County Natural History Museum, were formally arranged around an extended skeleton found west of Lake Chapala in Jalisco. This complex seems at least partly contemporaneous with the shaft tomb complex and is widely distributed from Michoacan through Jalisco to as far north as La Quemada and Chalchihuites in Zacatecas. Spin-offs in the diffusion of forms and the cloisonné style of lacquer or other paint inlay are still more widely distributed in Mesoamerica and the American Southwest. The diagnostic core of this complex, the *copa* and *olla* ritual-drinking service, is as distinctive as the Japanese cup and carafe for sake or, more appropriately, the drinkers' mugs and bowls depicted in the murals at Classic Cholula.

This complex clearly influenced the Alta Vista burial, despite the lack of cloisonné investment decoration on the *olla*. The red-line decoration is probably a substitution, since this *olla* is otherwise a near duplicate in form to invested *ollas* and shows similarities to cloisonné-style geometric motifs and design layouts as well. If the ritual drink indicated by this ceramic service is *pulque,* then there is a parallel to the Aztec regard for the ritual drink as a "controlled substance" that could be appropriately used by a deity impersonator. That would be especially true of Tezcatlipoca, who "presided over feasts and banquets" (Kurath and Marti 1964, p. 198), and who used the power of *pulque* to discredit Quetzalcoatl at Tollan.

The designs applied as cloisonné-style investment to each of the various artifacts provide several analogues. The interiors of the four matched *copas* display variations on an eagle-serpent motif (fig. 6). Gamio's excavation produced at least one other *copa* of this design. The motif is strikingly like the mythological Aztec symbol, now incorporated into the flag of Mexico, and this alone may have heavily influenced Alta Vista's long-standing classification as a Postclassic site. Yet the lead provided by the Tezcatlipoca aspects of the tomb can be followed out in this case as well, and a remarkably consistent metaphor emerges.

The eagle, even more so an eagle clutching or eating a snake, can symbolize blood sacrifice. But, in Postclassic contexts, eagles also represent light, Tonatiuh, or Tezcatlipoca as the first sun Tlaltonatiuh (Caso 1958, p. 33; Peterson 1962, p. 140; Nicholson 1971, p. 399), or as creator of light in the era of the fifth sun (Nicholson 1971, p. 400). Eagles represented the sky gods of the four directional "houses of the sun" in the Tarascan Volador ceremony (Corona Nunez 1957, p. 23) and probably did so in other Mesoamerican Volador ceremonies (Kelley 1974).

Corona Nunez refers to the four directional Tezcatlipocas in explaining this Tarascan concept. The complex symbolism in the mandala of Tezcatlipoca (Codex Fejevary-Mayer 1), reproduced in Nicholson (1971, fig. 4), includes four raptorial birds at the corners, around the central Tezcatlipoca.

The underlying theme in the Volador and Toxcatl ceremonies is the renewal of the agricultural and calendric cycles by the dramatic op-

0   2
cm

a.

b.

c.

d.

6. **Interior views and exterior designs of** *copa* **set (specimens AV 7–10). Vista Paint Cloisonné, Alta Vista phase, Alta Vista site.**

position of a quadripartite sun deity with the earth, or a devouring earth monster. This aspect of the Volador, and its Classic period form in West Mexico, is documented by Kelley (1972). Toxcatl, a so-called "fixed feast" falling within our month of May, was celebrated at the zenith of the sun's influence—the height of the dry season. It was followed by twenty days of Tlaloc rain ceremonies. Seler considered Toxcatl to be the feast of the first importance (and once, the first position) in the calendric cycle (Seler 1963, p. 115). Others agree that Toxcatl is of prime importance in the calendric and ceremonial round (Caso 1946, p. 358; Duran 1971, p. 98). In this context, Tezcatlipoca is the deity of *both* sun and earth (Seler 1963, p. 115). Seler further saw the Tezcatlipoca impersonator's ascent of the pyramid at noon as a dramatization of the sun's course to the zenith. Duran (1971, p. 126) recorded it as a renewal ceremony, seemingly of the variety that Ellis, in a Southwestern context, calls "weather control" magic (1964, p. 38). Although Sahagun said that this sacrifice illustrates the end of earthly riches, we suspect that this analysis misses the point of what must be a highly magical ceremony. The impersonator's death, after having ascended the steps as the sun, suggested an end to the sun's dominance and "caused" the return of the rains.

What we have attempted to show, in this interpretation, is that much of Toxcatl's drama and "power" was carried by the contest of opposites.[2] To the Mexica, Tezcatlipoca was a composite of old tribal gods (Nicholson 1971, p. 412) and as such could at once represent the opposing earth and sun, recalling his role, with his creator twin Quetzalcoatl, in dragging the earth monster up from the primeval waters. This opposition of sun and earth monster is prominent at the head and feet of Tezcatlipoca in the mandala of Codex Fejervary-Mayer (in which the sun is seen at the top of a pyramid) and in the portrayal of a Venusian apparition called Itzcalli (Codex Borgia 1963, fold 32), in which Tezcatlipoca struggles with the earth monster. The opposition is implicit in the frequent depictions of Tezcatlipoca with one foot missing (devoured by Tlaltecuhtli or Cipactli) and replaced by a circular mirror (Covarrubias 1957, figs. 140–4; Caso 1958, pp. 29–30; Codex Borgia 1963).

If a Toxcatl ritual was commemorated at Alta Vista, it may have expressed this opposition at least as explicitly as did the Postclassic ceremony. This hypothesis depends on the correct attribution of Cipactli symbolism to the flute (fig. 2). Crocodilian monsters in the Chalchihuites depictions usually have one or two anterior legs (figs. 7, 8), and occasionally posterior legs as well (fig. 9). A multistrand necklace is common (fig. 10). Usually the head is depicted in bifurcate symmetry, often with the lower jaw missing. All of these features are present on the flute, when it is reconstructed with a head such as the mouthpiece found at a nearby site, which is decorated with white-filled incisions rather than cloisonné-style investment (fig. 11). Other Mesoamerican earth monsters tend to have, as their primary characteristic, a head depicted in bifurcate symmetry (often with the lower jaw missing), which suggests the mythic splitting of the monster by the creator twins (Nicholson 1971, p. 400).

Given this supposed identity of the Alta Vista effigy flute and the Mesoamerican Cipactli, it could hardly be more symbolic of opposition than for the Tezcatlipoca surrogate to break the flute on the ground as he ascends the temple stairway. At Chalchihuites, the monster effigy flute is represented at two sites (figs. 2, 11); the accompanying broken *copa* with the interior depiction of a personage wearing the *anahuatl*-ring mirror is known from three sites (figs. 3–5). In the subfloor cache, Gamio found a *copa* decorated with eagle and serpent, a circular mirror (with paint cloisonné decoration, pierced for suspension, and fitted with an inlaid wooden ring), and an inlaid wooden effigy, which he called "*dos figuras simétricas de alligator*," but which is probably the bifurcated head of a single monster (Gamio 1910, p. 488, pl. 8; Noguera 1930, fig. 6). The significance of the mirror, in this context, is Tezcatlipoca's association with the pectoral mirror of his regalia (Duran 1971, pp. 98–99), which is common in his depictions from central Mesoamerica (Nicholson and Berger 1968, pp. 20–21) and may be his most explicit insignia and symbol in the northwest periphery. One Hohokam mirror back depicts, in cloisonné-style investment, a probable Tezcatlipoca (Woodward 1941, pl. 1a). DiPeso (1968b, p. 53) refers to a "Tezcatlipoca pyrite mirror—cremation complex" found in part of the Greater Southwest.

The eagle design *copas* conform to the hypothesis of solar cycle ceremonialism for several reasons. If the *xicalcoliuhqui* stepped-fret motif is properly understood as signifying the fire serpent (Westheim

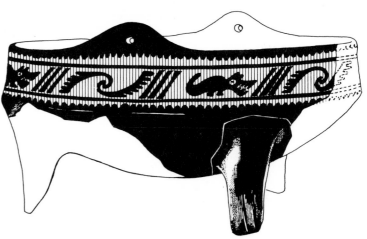

7. Interior view of a bowl. Suchil Red-on-Brown, Alta Vista phase, Alta Vista site (from the 1908 excavation). After Marquina, 1951.

9. Tripod bowl with rim tabs, champlevé decoration. Michila Red-Filled Engraved, Alta Vista phase, Cerrito de la Cofradia site.

10. Stone pendant (specimen AV 81). Alta Vista phase, Alta Vista site.

8. Small *olla.* Suchil Red-on-Brown, Alta Vista phase, Potrero del Calichal site.

11. Ceramic flute mouthpiece, black-smudged surface, incised (specimen PC 220). Alta Vista phase (?), Potrero del Calichal site.

1965, pp. 102–03), then its presence around the exterior rim and base of each *copa* is of potentially the same symbolism as the fire serpents surrounding the fifth sun of the Tenochtitlan Calendar Stone as the "serpent guide of the sun in its course" (Toscano, quoted in Westheim 1965, p. 7). While the *xicalcoliuhqui* is often seen on invested ceramics of cloisonné style in west Mexico, as in these Alta Vista specimens, it is unlikely to have been used as an arbitrary stopgap in designs of otherwise elaborate iconography, or in the occasional cases where the frets are supplied with eyes and heads.

In one Postclassic myth, a primordial couple engenders "four varicolored sons, apparently quadripartite manifestations of the omnipotent Tezcatlipoca. . . ." (Nicholson 1971, p. 398). These Tezcatlipocas could be aligned with the solar quadrants: Huitxilopochtli as "the sun at his height in the southern sky" (Burland 1967, p. 75), the Black Tezcatlipoca of the north, underworld, and midnight, etc. (Kurath and Marti 1964, p. 87). The cosmological number four is usual in Mesoamerican ritual and symbolism, and it seems to have been significantly stressed at Toxcatl. The impersonator plays his flute to four directions and is carried to each of the four sides of the temple court while incensed "in honor of the god and of the sun" (Duran 1971, p. 104). For four days preceeding the sacrifice, the impersonator sings in four locations (Sahagun 1950–71, vol. 3, p. 68). The four *copas* with the Alta Vista burial were arranged in the cup-to-base sequence, presented in the illustration from *a* through *d* (fig. 6). The "solar eagle" decorations can be tentatively assigned to divisions of the solar trajectory as follows: the top (*a*) is dawn, if the equal-armed cross glyph behind the eagle's head is Venus as the morning star; the second and third (*b* and *c*), differentiated primarily by background color (red versus white), are relegated to noon and sunset, since the fourth (*d*) is so clearly identified with the underworld by the reptilian monster behind the eagle's head. This last *copa* also differs in its construction, having a false bottom in the pedestal base, which contains a rattling pellet.

Although this equation of the sequential *copa* designs with a solar mandala may seem to lack sufficiently conjunctive evidence, it is more persuasive when considered in the context of later Chalchihuites ceremonialism. By a comparative study of ceramic decoration and forms through the Chalchihuites culture sequences, the Kelleys had previously inferred that a concern with the solar circuit was reflected in prominent types of the Las Joyas phase (A.D. 700–950) and the Rio Tunal phase (A.D. 950–1150), and that these elements are derived from prototypes in the Alta Vista Classic (Kelley and Abbott 1966, pp. 18–19; Kelley 1971; pp. 786, 794–95; Kelley and Kelley 1971, pp. 108, 118–19). They relate the perforated rim tabs of Michilia red-filled engraved tripod bowls, from the Alta Vista phase (fig. 9), to a later feature of several types, in which the rim tabs take the form of a basket handle. An occasional basket handle is modeled and painted elaborately enough to show that the prototype for this feature is a serpent with a head at each end of the handle, grasping the rim (fig. 12b). This decorative scheme indicates that the handle is the fire serpent marking the sun's trajectory across the sky and with Xolotl-like quadrupeds, eagles, human figures, or other motifs of solar association traversing its arc (fig. 12a). These sky figures enter the highly stylized jaws of the earth monster and follow one another around the decorative band (the underworld), as quadrupeds (fig. 12b), to emerge as solar symbols on the opposite end of the handle. While the Kelleys have interpreted the core deity of this cult to be a local version of Quetzalcoatl (Kelley 1971, p. 795), we concur, on the basis of data reported here, that the unifying theme throughout the Classic period in this northwestern region seems to have been a preoccupation with the continuation of the solar cycle—a decidedly Postclassic preoccupation in Central Mexico. Toxcatl was this sort of renewal ceremony, as Duran observed (1971, p. 126), but the entire institution of human sacrifice was sanctioned by the sun's need for nourishment. It may be significant that this need for sacrificial solar rejuvenation was dictated to the migrating Mexica by the legendary eagle, sitting on a cactus with a serpent in its beak (Weaver 1972, p. 239).

The foregoing should not be taken to indicate that we argue for a lineal historical connection of the Chalchihuites and Mexica cultures. These aspects of cosmology and religion had widespread distribution and development out of the Preclassic, to which the Chalchihuites culture was a legitimate heir. We have made the effort to tag consistently the leading correspondences we have observed as "analogues," which, by their conjunctive trend may constitute an analogy but not

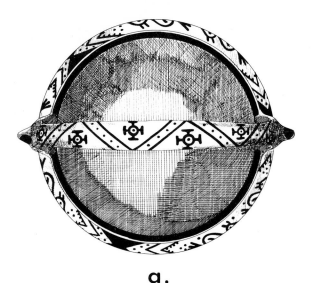

a.

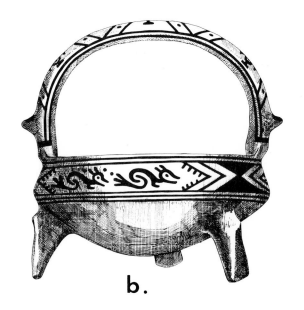

b.

12. Tripod bowl with basket handle. Neveria Red-on-Brown, Las Joyas phase, Navacoyan site, Durango.
  a. Top view.
  b. Side view.

necessarily an identity. Our "Tezcatlipoca" is so labeled for convenience, not in order to claim the "discovery" of an Aztec deity among early northern Chichimecs. In the Mesoamerican Classic, generally, there is probably the cosmological context to accommodate a Tezcatlipoca-like creator god just as there are isolated archaeological indications of such a cult. For instance, Chadwick's argument, from documentary sources, that Teotihuacan accommodated Quetzalcoatl and Tezcatlipoca dynasties, is given support by his interpretation of a differentiation in architecture and city plan in a key zone (Chadwick 1971, pp. 497–98). Sejourne (1966c, p. 207) reported a burial with a

broken flute in Zacuala, interpreting the flute as a Tezcatlipoca ritual object. Peterson (1962, p. 130) called attention to the similarity between some headless Teotihuacan figurines and apparitions of Tezcatlipoca, and Muller (1970, p. 104) identified the face painting on a Teotihuacan ceramic mask as an insignia of Tezcatlipoca. The evidence seems sparse, but it has been extracted from a complex and vast array of data. At Alta Vista, the data are relatively sparse, and it is in the relative simplicity of a frontier colony that a few religious practices may be thrown into high relief by the limited range of recoverable material culture.

Notes

1. Pickering participated in the excavation, which yielded the data reported here, and he had particular responsibility for the osteologic analyses and the crucial recording of artifact associations. Holien studied the artifacts and contributed the detail of the interpretation. We wish to thank Dr. J. Charles Kelley who, as field director and major professor, made possible our independent work on this archaeological problem. The pilot excavations, sponsored by the Cooperative Mesoamerican Research Program at Southern Illinois University, Carbondale, were financed with funds that included a grant from the American Philosophical Society. Holien has been aided by an assistantship from the Museum, Southern Illinois University, and by the use of the Museum laboratory facilities and the help of its director, Ellen A. Kelley. Use of the laboratory of

the Centro de Estudios Avanzados del Occidente de Mexico, Ajijic, Jalisco, is also appreciated. This institution presently houses the artifacts from the excavation. Illustrations are by Elaine Holien, with the addition of figures 7–9 and 12 by Sandra Rife. A preliminary version of this paper was read at the 1973 meetings of the Society for American Archaeology.

2. Another such opposition, and a case in point, is the magical function of the Mesoamerican ball game summarized by Westheim:

> It is the struggle between light and darkness. Seler explains that the movement of the ball is the path traversed by the sun from the clear half (of the sky) toward the dark half (of earth), and vice versa. . . . Xolotl is expressly designated as the god of the ball game, and the game itself should be interpreted as a combat between Xolotl, god of twilight and of the setting sun, and Quetzalcoatl, god of the morning star and of the rising sun. Preuss sees in it an *Analogiezauber* (magic practice based on analogies).
> (Westheim 1965, pp. 7–8).

At Chalchihuites, the Canutillo phase plaza at the site of Gualterio Abajo includes a ball court, excavated in 1973 by the Kelleys. Ball courts are known elsewhere in west Mexico from excavations at the Schroeder site, Amapa, and from the complex village models found in shaft tombs.

ROSEMARY SHARP

architecture as interelite communication in preconquest Oaxaca, Veracruz, and Yucatan

STRIKING SIMILARITIES in the public architectural decoration at certain sites in the valley of Oaxaca, such as Lambityeco, Yagul, and Mitla, in northern Yucatan, such as Chichen Itza, Kabah, Labna, and Xlapac, and, at El Tajin in Veracruz, suggest the presence of a widespread esthetic intercommunication system during the latter half of the Classic period and the first part of the Postclassic period in preconquest Mexico. Because this particular type of decoration, commonly called "*greca*," spread at a given time throughout Mesoamerica, and because, within the time span concerned, there was internal stylistic development, both a "*greca* horizon" and a "*greca* tradition" can be postulated (Sharp 1970, p. 11). I shall attempt here to examine this horizon and tradition, placing particular emphasis on their early phases, in order to determine how and why this intercommunication system developed.

To begin with, *greca* is unique both in form and technology. It is characterized, most notably, by intricate geometric motifs or associated patterns, which tend to be rectilinear, repetitive, and symmetrical. These motifs were set into the mosaics or carved onto the hewn stones that decorate the facades of public buildings, elite houses, and tombs. (fig. 1). Both the number and variety of component parts are limited; some common forms are rectangles, squares, trapezoids, and triangles. Finally, using Robertson's contrasting terms (1963, pp. 26–27), *greca* patterns are "unitary," i.e., composed of many discrete elements united into one form as conceived by the artist, so that each part is essential to the understanding of the whole. This is in contrast to "unified" patterns, which are constructed with a continuity of line according to the way forms are perceived in nature.

In its most developed form, *greca* technology involves many aspects that are considered characteristic of modern industry: standardization of forms and sizes; prefabrication, interchangeability of parts; and, probably, mass production. Since each facade contains hundreds, even thousands, of separate elements, it is likely that its construction required a large labor force of relatively unskilled workmen, who shaped, fitted, and secured the stones into place, rather than requiring only a few highly skilled artists or craftsmen.

It is extremely difficult to determine exactly where *greca* originated. However, some attention to one specific motif, the step-fret (fig. 1), and to the technological processes and style involved in *greca*, should help to clarify the situation.

The Step-fret

The step-fret is one of the most important *greca* motifs and a dominant symbol throughout Mesoamerican prehistory. It was used to decorate pottery, walls, and stelae long before its occurrence in stone-mosaic form, and it was widely distributed in both the Late Preclassic and Classic periods. Moreover, it is found primarily, although not exclusively (the valley of Mexico being a notable exception), in an elite context. Finally, the step-fret appears to have been inspired by a serpent model, most likely the rattlesnake (Holmes 1895–97, p. 250; Gordon 1905; Caso and Bernal 1952, pp. 111–12; Bernal 1958, p. 6; Sharp n.d., pp. 54–68). Of the many possible examples, perhaps the clearest association of step-frets and serpents is found in Murals 1 and 2 from the Palace of the Sun (Zone 5, Room 2) in Teotihuacan, a building dating to the last epoch before the fall of this great center. Here step-frets are used to decorate the dorsal areas of what appear to be stylized rattlesnakes (Millon 1967d, p. 48).

The first step-frets in Mesoamerica occurred—probably in Monte Alban II times, in Oaxaca, on pottery—as single motifs or as horizontal sequences (Caso, Bernal, and Acosta 1967, pls. III c, d, pls IV c pls. X, a, c). Although many aspects of Monte Alban II culture are still a mystery, it seems fairly certain that the culture was principally an elite manifestation, centering around 100 B.C.–A.D. 100 (Caso, Bernal and Acosta 1967, p. 74-c; Bernal 1958, pp. 4–5, 1966, p. 356; Paddock 1966a, p. 234). Step-frets are also found in a ceremonial context on pottery (Incised Dichrome) at Balankanche Cave near Chichen Itza, Yucatan, at a slightly later date (Brainerd 1958, p. 90, fig. 64), and, even later, during the Classic period at Teotihuacan (Sejourne 1966b, fig. 35).

Step-frets were also used in murals during the Classic period. At Teotihuacan, Murals 1 and 2, mentioned above, display step-frets projecting from the bodies of stylized rattlesnakes; horizontal sequences of step-frets decorate the shallow benches of the portico of the Quetzalpapalotl Palace (Zone 2) from Teotihuacan III; and, Mural 1 (Room

1. Facade, Hall of Columns, Mitla, Oaxaca.

11), Tetitla, also from Teotihuacan III, has isolated vertical motifs associated with human hands (Sejourne 1966c, fig. 148; Millon 1967a, p. 11; Miller 1973, pp. 45, 76, 316).

At Monte Alban, Oaxaca, step-frets are also found on the cloaks of certain noble figures in the murals from Tombs 105 and 106 (Gendrop 1971, p. 47, figs. 105–06). Miller believes that these particular paintings are very close to Teotihuacan murals in their two-dimensionality as well, thus providing another link between the two areas (1973, p. 27).

Finally, in the Maya area, within Structure 2, Room 2, at Bonampak, a single step-fret decorates the cloak of a noble or priestly figure; and a sequence of horizontal step-frets embellishes the narrow bench beneath the murals in Room 1 at the same site (Ruppert, Thompson,

2. Decorative heads, Pyramid of Quetzalcoatl, Teotihuacan.

and Proskouriakoff 1955, fig. 28; Kubler 1962, p. 167, pl. 86, fig. 54).

Stately or priestly figures on carved stelae within the Maya area also exhibit step-frets on their clothing or paraphernalia. For example, step-frets are present: on the belt of a male figure on a tablet from Temple 21, Palenque; on a basket at the feet of an elaborately dressed kneeling woman on Lintel 24 (Structure 23), Yaxchilan; and, on the waistband of a noble-looking man on Stela 1, Bonampak (Greene, Rands, and Graham 1972, pp. 18–19, pl. 3, 84–85, pl. 36; 148–49, pl. 68). A step-fret is also carved onto one of the stone columns at El Tajin (Building Columns, Sculpture 2). Here, the motif decorates the foot of a temple within which sits a priestly figure (Kampen 1972, pp. 82–85).

In short, the step-fret was a symbol shared by elites throughout Mesoamerica, and one that appears to have had special significance for them even before its appearance in architectural form.

Technology

The origin of many technological features involved in greca decoration, for example, standardization, prefabrication, and interchangeability of parts, may well be Teotihuacan. For example, the heads that decorate the Pyramid of Quetzalcoatl (Teotihuacan II; Stierlin 1968, p. 108) were precarved and attached to the building by long tenons that penetrated deep into the masonry. For each of the two types of heads, "goggle eyes" and "feathered serpent," the individual sculptures were almost identical, and, probably interchangeable (fig. 2).

In addition, the pillars of the portico of the Quetzalpapalotl Palace are carved with designs of butterfly-birds, one shown in front view, and one in profile facing left or right, but always facing the medial axis of a particular patio side (Acosta 1964, fig. 108; Stierlin 1968, pp. 28–29). On any one column, the total design is formed of precisely matched component parts carved onto unequal units of square-hewn stone.

Since each of these stones can occupy only one position, and since the parts of each design are so carefully matched, the implication is that the motifs must have been carved *after* the blocks were set into place (Acosta 1964, p. 62; Stierlin 1968, p. 102). This is not necessarily so. If the builders had used individual patterns for their reliefs, the figures could have been drawn on the four sides of a column, one side at a time, the component blocks distributed among many carvers, and the decorated pieces of the column reassembled later at the proper site, according to a master plan. This would have allowed for a more efficient use of time and labor than carving the columns in place, since, in the latter case, only four people could work easily on a single column at one time.

Miller has suggested that Teotihuacan murals were executed through patterns (1973, p. 32); quite possibly, carvings were also. A next logical step would have been to work with standardized blocks, so that the component parts were interchangeable. This is the system that occurred later outside of Teotihuacan with stone mosaics, although to a lesser degree in Oaxaca than in northern Yucatan.[1]

Moreover, there is evidence that Teotihuacanos *were* concerned about time- and labor-saving techniques. Prefabrication and interchangeability of parts existed in Teotihuacan in another medium to serve as a model for architecture. Molds were extensively used for making "decorative details, heads of figures, feet for tripod vessels, spindle whorls, etc" (Linne 1942, p. 166). They were commonly used to decorate braziers or *incensarios*. Linne states: "Decorative details of 'incensarios' were often made in moulds, industrialized mass-production. . . . Parts included small mask-like human faces, birds, flowers and star-shaped elements, decorated rectangles and other elongated shapes" (Linne 1942, pp. 1973, 1975; Sejourne 1966a, fig. 129, pl. 50; 1966b, fig. 23).

Style

The style associated with certain Teotihuacan murals is also similar to that seen in *greca* decoration. For example, the Offering Scene Mural from the Temple of Agriculture (Miller 1973, p. 63) is symmetrical in composition and unitary in approach. Figures are arranged between two large pyramidal forms. These figures are distinguished by outlines, and the color appears to have been applied flatly, without shading. Limbs seem to be stuck on to torsos, and there is little overlapping of one form by another. The figures are represented conventionally, and only the basic identifying features are shown.

The similarities between the art products of these different areas is not surprising, in the light of the fact that people from both Oaxaca and Veracruz were directly exposed to technological and stylistic concepts developed at Teotihuacan. A Oaxaca *barrio* lies in the western part of the city (Millon 1967d, p. 45; Paddock 1968a, pp. 122–28), which would help to explain stylistic affinities between the murals of Tombs 105 and 106 at Monte Alban and those at Teotihuacan. In addition, the presence of people from Veracruz is indicated by the Tajin-style scrolls within *tableros* in the Interlace Scroll Platform (Mural 1) on the west side of the Street of the Dead (Miller 1973, p. 90). This implies that, at least, there was bilateral sharing between Teotihuacan and each of these two other areas.

There is also evidence of communication between Oaxaca and Veracruz, which is important to the development of *greca*. From Hua-

juapan in the Nuine and the Mixteca Baja region of Oaxaca have come two very similar urns. Each has a sculptured representation of a god with his head and hands resting on the base of the urn and a firepot on his head. The firepot on one is decorated with Tajin-style scrolls, that on the other with step-frets (Paddock 1970b, pp. 4–5).

The point here is not the Teotihuacanos invented *greca* and passed it on to other areas, but that, during the middle part of the Classic period, many areas—Teotihuacan, Veracruz, Oaxaca, and others—shared ideas associated with *greca* decoration. Probably, certain technological and stylistic concepts were contributed by Teotihuacan and transmitted, very likely, by merchants, as Sanders suggests in this volume. But where the many component ideas crystallized is not known for certain. During the latter part of the Classic and Early Postclassic periods (Epi-Classic, or Middle Urban), this sharing continued, with the valley of Oaxaca, Veracruz, and northern Yucatan as outstanding participants and contributors, but there were probably others.

The Greca Tradition

Two early phases of the initial stage in the development of *greca* can be seen in Oaxaca during Monte Alban III times, a period that extends from about A.D. 100–200 to 650. First, simple inverted T-sequences, composed of flat stones of graduated sizes piled one on top of another, are recessed within *tableros* on each side of the stairway of a structure in the North Platform, Monte Alban (Hartung 1970), p. 4, fig. 8; Sharp 1970, p. 8). Similar T-sequences were present on painted stucco-covered pottery from Monte Alban II times (Caso, Bernal, and Acosta 1967, pl. XI f); and, at Teotihuacan, on pottery, in murals, and as merlons for the roofs of buildings (Sejourne 1966b, figs. 13, 26, fig. 23; 1966c, figs. 13, 23, 26). They are also present on the unique concave *taluds* around the Patio of the Altars, Cholula, Puebla (Salazar 1970, fig. 16).

Horizontal T-sequences continued to be used at Lambityeco during the following period, and they are found behind the huge plaster-sculptured masks of Cocijo, the rain-lightening god, in Mound 190, a structure from about A.D. 640 (Rabin 1970, p. 2). The only other comparable plaster sculptures at the site are the "portrait heads" on Tomb

3. Puuc-style structures, East Annex of the Nunnery, Chichen Itza.

4. Puuc-style structures, Palace, Labna.

6 of Mound 195. These have been interpreted as representing individual members of a new "secular elite who probably had their roots within the earlier theocratic society" (Rabin 1970, p. 12, fig. 18).

A similar arrangement of T-sequences in association with masks is found on Pure Florescent Puuc-style structures found in northern Yucatan, both at Chichen Itza, on the East Annex of the Nunnery, and at Labna, on the Palace (figs. 3, 4).

Although there are no portrait heads associated with *greca* in this area, human representations are present on building facades, superimposed on geometric forms. Some of these, like the Lambityeco portrait heads, suggest a secular leaning for the society. For example, at one time, many stone figures of men carrying maces or sticks in their hands were affixed to the facade of the western palace of the Nunnery Quadrangle, Uxmal (Spinden 1913, p. 7; Stierlin 1964, p. 64; fig. 88), indicating an interest in military, rather than sacred, affairs.

A second phase in the early development of architectural *greca* occurs at Atzompa, a mountaintop site adjoining Monte Alban, from Monte Alban IIIb. Here, as on the North Platform, flat stones are piled up to form a design that is recessed into a *tablero*. This motif appears within the *tableros* around a square patio. The method of construction of these designs reminds one of Tajin Chico, where flat fieldstones of similar color were also used as components for buildings.

Although the construction of the Atzompa *greca* is similar to that at Monte Alban, the design itself is more complicated. It seems to represent a simplified (or earlier) version of a more complex pattern that occurs later both at Yagul and Mitla in the valley of Oaxaca, and on the second level of the Nunnery at Chichen Itza, Yucatan. The bilaterally symmetrical Atzompa design is composed of two horizontal, downturned, and opposing rectangular hooks, separated by a T-form in the center; the T has a square hole in the top (fig. 5).

A more complicated version of this design occurs in the facade of Tomb 11, Yagul, from Monte Alban V. Here, the downturned hooks are expanded into opposing and connected step-frets, which are detached from a complete T-form (fig. 6). This basic pattern is a very common one in northern Yucatan, although it occurs there without the central T, for example, as on the palace at Xlapac (fig. 7). and the arch at Labna.

A still more complex pattern, one displaying quadrilateral symmetry, occurs on the rear wall of Building 1-N, and on the facade of Tomb 13 at Yagul, as well as within tombs at Mitla and Xaaga, a site in the eastern end of the valley at Mitla (fig. 8). Basically the same pattern, with some embellishment, decorates the second story of the Nunnery at Chichen Itza, a structure for which there is one C_{14} date of A.D. 810 ± 200 (Andrews 1965b, p. 63). However, a square is substituted for the T, and T-sequences are used as borders, in much the same way as they are at Labna (figs. 9, 4).

Returning to Oaxaca, a second stage of *greca* development for this area can be seen at Lambityeco, where, during Monte Alban IV, three types of *greca* motifs are present. First, there are the horizontal T-forms behind the Cocijo masks described earlier. Second, there are the two unique sets of opposing step-frets with upturned hooks within the east and west panels on the south side of the house patio, Mound 195-sub (Sharp 1970, pp. 5–7) (fig. 10). The third type is the step-fret with an angular scroll found in horizontal sequences on the top of the pyramid of Mound 195 (fig. 11). This motif is especially important because it is also found in both Yucatan and at El Tajin, and because variations in the motif itself appear to have chronological significance.

Chronological Implications
of the Step-fret

Within Oaxaca, the horizontal step-fret has a long tradition as architectural decoration. After Monte Alban IV times, it is found repeatedly throughout the valley in two basic forms, one without a triangular notch in the base, as in the central band from the palace at Mitla (fig. 1), and the other, with the basal notch, as in the example from Tomb 1, Zaachila (fig. 12).

Concerning this distinction, Proskouriakoff has postulated a sequential development for the step-fret on *pottery:* from the simplest figure "formed by combining a rectangular spiral with a stepped-triangle"; to the "standard step-fret," which, when used in sequence, "reproduces its own image" in the background (fig. 1); to a step-fret that has a small triangle cut out of its base so that the "self-reproducing property" of the figure is destroyed. The first forms are character-

istic of the Classic period; the last, of the Postclassic. The transition between the unnotched and notched forms comes at some "as yet undetermined" time during the Early Postclassic (Proskouriakoff 1968, pp. 10–11).

Pinpointing this transition is difficult. It is worth noting however, that Balancan (Z) Fine Orange pottery, which does not have the notch (R. Smith 1958, p. 152, fig. 1c), is associated with Pure Florescent pottery at the Puuc hill sites of Uxmal and Kabah; whereas Silho (X) Fine Orange, which does have the notch (R. Smith 1971, p. 87, fig. 59b), appears to come to Chichen Itza later during the Modified Florescent, as a trade ware (Brainerd 1958, p. 283; 39–40; R. Smith 1971, p. 162). Moreover, striking amounts of a type of pottery considered to be Balancan Fine Orange were found at Lambityeco, where the unnotched form of step-fret occurs as architectural decoration.[2]

Both unnotched and notched step-frets occur later at Mitla. The unnotched variety is the more common by far. Notched frets occur on an exterior building surface only in the case of the carved lintel of the east structure of the Patio of the Tombs, in the south area of the Group of the Columns. Notched frets also occur below this structure, within cruciform Tomb 2, and in other tombs within the general area (Tombs 4 and 5, and Xaaga; Caso and Rubin de la Borbolla 1936).

Perhaps the most interesting occurrence of the notched fret at Mitla is on the interior side of the lintel in the west room off of the rear courtyard of the Hall of the Columns. The wall surrounding the lintel is decorated with mosaic step-frets without basal notches. On the other hand, the step-frets and portions of step-frets carved onto the lintel, and carefully matched up with the surrounding mosaic design, have triangular notches in the bases (fig. 13).

Other lintels in this area are cracked, and in modern times have been buttressed with metal bars, indicating that great stress is placed on them. It seems reasonable to postulate that the original lintel for the west room was damaged and replaced in preconquest times; the notched frets were carved onto it to indicate that it was put there at a later date than the mosaic work around it.

If this hypothesis is true, the appearance of a basal notch on stone step-frets becomes a chronological marker for the Postclassic period for architecture as well as for pottery.[3]

5. Atzompa *greca,* Atzompa, Oaxaca.

7. Palace of Xlapac, Yucatan.

6. Facade, Tomb 11, Yagul, Oaxaca.

8. Facade of Tomb 13, Yagul, Oaxaca.

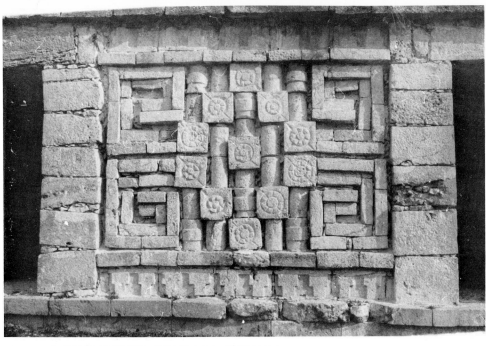

9. Facade, upper story of the Nunnery, Chichen Itza.

11. Pyramid, Mound 195, Lambityeco, Oaxaca.

12. Tomb 1, Zaachila, Oaxaca.

10. Mound 195-sub, Lambityeco, Oaxaca.

13. Group of the Columns, Mitla, Oaxaca.

14. Pyramid of the Niches, El Tajin, Veracruz.

15. Building C, Tajin Chico, Veracruz.

Outside of Oaxaca, step-frets *without* the basal notch were used at Chichen Itza in several places: on the Iglesia, where they encircle the building, for which there are two C_{14} dates: A.D. 600 ± 70 and 780 ± 70 (E. Andrews IV 1965a, p. 63); and, on the base of both the House of the Three Lintels, Old Chichen, and the East Annex of the Nunnery (Marquina 1964, p. 842, photo 415). On these latter two buildings, step-frets alternate with small columns, in groups of three. In addition, Ruppert shows step-frets on top of the Red House (Chichanchob), but their presence there is questionable (Ruppert 1952, fig. 30b; Proskouriakoff 1963, pp. 91–92). There is one C_{14} date of A.D. 610 ± 70 for this structure, which makes it roughly contemporary with the Iglesia (E. Andrews IV 1965a, p. 63), and both structures, roughly contemporary with Mound 190 at Lambityeco, in Oaxaca.

Similar sequences of step-frets are present on the rooftop of the Codz-Pop at Kabah, and at the head of the steep stairway hidden within the Pyramid of the Magician, Uxmal. Step-frets without notches are also carved in relief on the lower part of this same building, which has one C_{14} date of 560 ± 50 (E. Andrews IV 1965a, p. 63), suggesting a slightly earlier construction date than the buildings mentioned above.

At Tajin, sequences of step-frets without notches are used both vertically, to decorate the ramps bordering the staircase of the Pyramid of the Niches, possibly the oldest building on the site (Kubler 1962, p. 72), (fig. 14), and on Structure A at Tajin Chico, erected at a later date (Stierlin 1968, pp. 109–110, 115). Horizontal step-frets are much more common, an especially good example being those on Building C, Tajin Chico, a structure considered to be an "elaborate palace" (Krotser and Krotser 1973, p. 203) (fig. 15).

Serpent Stairways

Vertical stone mosaic step-frets are unique to Tajin. However, the step-frets on the Pyramid of the Niches can be considered analogous to the feathered serpent heads that decorate the ramps bordering the central staircase of the Pyramid of Quetzalcoatl at Teotihuacan, just as the niches themselves may be seen as analogous to the tiers of alternating Tlaloc and feathered serpent heads (figs. 2, 14). In support of this analogy, it has been suggested that step-frets in general represent serpents, and, it is believed that these particular step-frets represent conventionalized serpents (Garcia Payon 1967, p. 9). Moreover, it seems pertinent that of the two possible forms that occur on the Pyramid of Quetzalcoatl, only feathered serpent heads are used on the ramps.

In Yucatan, at Chichen Itza, ramps that border the stairways of particular pyramids are also decorated with serpent heads, for example, they are found on "El Castillo" (within which is an inner, *greca*-decorated structure), on the Venus Platform, and the Platform of the Tigers and Eagles (Stierlin 1968, p. 153). Many years ago, Spinden noted that "serpent stairways seem to be restricted to a definite class of pyramids, namely, those with stairways on all four sides, and to a definite period of Maya art" (1913, p. 107). Although a serpent stairway (of a slightly different kind) is found at the Caracol—a structure with stairways on only one side, also found at a Chichen Itza, such decoration does seem to be limited to the period of time in northern Yucatan now referred to as "Florescent" (E. Andrews IV 1973, p. 246). Traditionally, this period has been divided into "Pre-Toltec" and "Toltec" phases, implying that highland Mexican traits did not appear in any significant way until the latter phase. However, some authorities have noted that continental influences were present from the beginning, and that there are strong continuities between the Early and Late (Pure and Modified) phases (Proskouriakoff 1950, pp. 66, 183; E. Andrews IV. 1965b, pp. 56, 318–19; Thompson 1970b: pp. 119–20; Sharp n.d.; pp. 79–88). Moreover, Andrews recently argued that the occupation of northern Yucatan by the so-called Toltecs marked the culmination of continental influences in this area rather than their beginning (1973, pp. 253–54).

Greca decoration existed during both the Pure Florescent, when the Puuc sites were in their prime, and the Modified Florescent, when the Toltecs apparently dominated northern Yucatan from their capital at Chichen Itza and the great Puuc cities seemed to come to an end (E. Andrews IV 1965b, p. 318; 1973, p. 254; Sharp n.d., pp. 79, 85). Andrews suggests that the Toltecs dominated in a very severe way, and that the abandonment of the Puuc area at the time of the emergence of this powerful group was not coincidental (1973, p. 263).

Still, the Toltecs continued the *greca* tradition as something of their own, rather than eliminating it as something belonging to a conquered people. This suggests that the art style was, in fact, basically "Mexican" in inspiration. Like the serpent stairways from the same period, it had its conceptual roots in the highland area to the west, even though its development was outstanding in the area of northern Yucatan.[4]

Calendrical Coding

Besides serpent stairways and certain technological and stylistic concepts, one characteristic that seems to have been shared by Teotihuacan, Tajin, and northern Yucatan, was the coding of calendrical data into architecture, a tradition perhaps begun in Teotihuacan, but elaborated on later through the use of *greca*. The number of niches on the Pyramid of the Niches, of stone sculptures on the Temple of Quetzalcoatl, and of steps leading to the top of El Castillo, have all been calculated at 365, or the number of days of the solar year (Marquina 1964, pp. 87–88; Stierlin 1964, p. 149; Ruz Lhuillier 1965, pp. 22–23; Garcia Payon 1967, pp. 9–11; Stierlin 1968, pp. 100, 111; Kampen 1972, p. 6).

Other elements on these and related structures add up to: 13, 20, and 260, or the number of days in the native week, month, and year, respectively (sacred round); and 52, the number of years in the native cycle, roughly comparable to our century (calendar round). For example, the small platform in the center of the square at the top of the Temple of Quetzalcoatl has 4 staircases of 13 steps each, or a total of 52 steps in all, as does the Venus Platform at Chichen Itza (Marquina 1964, p. 886, photo 457; Stierlin 1968, pp. 45, 100). The number of step-frets on each of the central ramps at the Pyramid of Niches has been estimated at 13 (Garcia Payon 1967, pp. 9–11). There are 52 panels on El Castillo (Ruz Lhuillier 1965, pp. 22–23).

This coding process is not limited to the buildings described above, but seems to be an intrinsic part of Florescent period architecture. For example, the facade on the Palace of the Governors at Uxmal is divided by a horizontal binder over 13 doors leading to 20 vaulted chambers (Stierlin 1964, p. 65). Moreover, there are 13 step-frets on each side of the central element in the front facade of this structure.

Although it is easy to be carried away by such similarities, it seems unlikely that so many instances would have occurred purely by coincidence. It seems much more likely that intercommunication between the designers (and their patrons) in these different areas was taking place from generation to generation. This concerned particular motifs and technology, but it also involved other symbolic levels, in this case, those related to the calendar round, shared generally by Mesoamericans in all areas.

The Greca Horizon

The *greca* horizon as seen in Oaxaca, Veracruz, and Yucatan may be divided very roughly into three developmental stages, associated with three preconquest periods.

The first and preliminary stage occurs during the last half of the Classic period, when the concepts associated with stone mosaics crystallized, and architectural decoration, such as that seen on Monte Alban and at Atzompa in Oaxaca, was produced. Because of the relatively simple construction of the *greca* on the Pyramid of the Niches at El Tajin, it is possible that this structure should also belong here. Moreover, if the one C_{14} date for the lower part of the Pyramid of the Magicians at Uxmal, is correct, it too should fall within this grouping.

The second stage is associated with the Epi-Classic period, the period in which *greca* spread and flourished. Generally speaking, a marker for this stage, which is found on architecture as well as on pottery, is the step-fret without a basal notch. In the absence of published absolute dates for particular structures in the areas concerned, however, there can be no clear dividing line for them between stages one and two.

Included in the first phase of stage two are: the structures at Lambityeco in Oaxaca; perhaps, the Pyramid of the Niches, at El Tajin; and, buildings such as the Red House, Iglesia, East Annex of the Nunnery, and House of the Three Lintels at Chichen Itza, Yucatan. The second phase of stage two would include such structures as: Tombs 11 and 13 at Yagul, and most of the Mitla complex in Oaxaca; Structure A at Tajin Chico, Veracruz; and both the Palace of the Governors and the later part of the Nunnery quadrangle (dated by C_{14} at A.D. 885 ± 100) (E. Andrews IV 1965a, p. 63), Uxmal.

The third stage is associated with the Postclassic period. A step-fret with a triangular basal notch is a marker for this period; however, as far as I know, it has only been found in architectural form in Oaxaca. Included in this group would be Tomb 1 at Zaachila, and the tombs and portions of the Mitla Palace with notched frets mentioned above. In addition, structures associated with the Modified Florescent at the Toltec capital Chichen Itza, which either display a developed form of *greca,* or which clearly embody calendrical data in the manner described earlier, would also fall into this category.

In summary, *greca* represented both a horizon and a tradition, one probably reaching back to some ideological and technological concepts formulated in, and dispersed from, Teotihuacan—more specifically, certain concepts that related architecture to serpents and aspects of the calendar round, and which involved the use of a unitary, modular medium. But, above all, *greca* concerned intercommunication between people of several areas.

Interelite Communication

What specifically was the nature of this intercommunication? First, *greca* represents a culmination of esthetic effort, in short "great art." Second, it is associated primarily with elites. Last, it is secular, rather than sacred, in emphasis.

Most anthropologists would agree that "art is a universal aspect of culture" (Wolfe 1969, p. 3) and of man's social history, but truly great art is not produced by all people in all cultures. A study made by Wolfe in 1969 strongly suggests that great art is produced only when people living in certain circumstances have particular kinds of feelings, which either call for expression in art, or which can be aroused or intensified by art (1969, p. 4).

The social situation that appears to be especially crucial has two aspects. First, according to Wolfe, the men of a local community must be divided by important cleavages, such as, those that exist between debtors and creditors, or between men who are ranked on the basis of differential ownership of productive resources (1969, p. 11). Second—this aspect suggested by Fischer—the need must exist for such men to communicate on an emotional level in order to promote cooperation

toward some common economic, political, or social goals in their daily lives (1969, p. 33). Great art, then, can be seen as a form of communication that brings together people who are otherwise separated by social, economic, political, or other barriers.

In the Old World, an example of this was the International style of painting that swept across Europe during the late fourteenth and early fifteenth centuries. This was a courtly style that appealed generally to aristocratic tastes, and united people of different nations, languages, and customs on an emotional level (Cuttler 1968, p. 17).

A similar kind of widespread elite style was postulated for Mesoamerica by Brockington in his model for the Mixtecs. According to this model, a basically similar core of artistic ideas represented in metallurgy, lapidary work, fine decorative ceramics, and pictorial manuscripts appears to have spread during the Terminal Classic and Postclassic periods throughout a part of Central Mexico at the elite level. These ideas were in turn reworked at the local level and transferred on to lower levels of society in varying degrees (Brockington 1970, pp. 128–29).

The architectural decoration typical of Monte Alban IV and V in the valley of Oaxaca, of El Tajin in Veracruz, and of Chichen Itza and the Puuc sites in northern Yucatan appears to represent the same type of effort at interelite communication on an even more monumental scale.

As has already been indicated, the step-fret, an important *greca* motif, was present on pottery, painted walls, and carved stones before its use in stone-mosaic form. Moreover, it occurred primarily in an elite context, as for example, on Monte Alban II pottery, in painted sequences on the basal areas of elaborate structures or tombs in Teotihuacan and Bonampak, and as decorative trim on the cloaks of noble or priestly figures in murals, or on carved stones, in Oaxaca and the Maya area.

Later, the step-fret was used to decorate patios of elite houses, as at Atzompa and Lambityeco; facades of elite tombs, as at Yagul; or facades of monumental public buildings, as at Mitla, Tajin, the Puuc sites, and Chichen Itza.

The degree to which the comman man participated in what appears to have been principally a manifestation of the educated elite is a matter for speculation. *Greca* technology required a large labor force of relatively unskilled or semiskilled people working cooperatively. Although highly talented artists and architects must have designed the buildings, and some master craftsmen were necessary to shape particular elements, construction involved the masses, physically, and, perhaps, intellectually.

If *greca* architecture, or at least some of it, represented a coding of calendrical data, as has been suggested, to what extent did the common man understand the code? The common workmen at Tajin, and in Oaxaca and Yucatan, probably understood *greca* symbolism to a greater degree than did their counterparts in the southern Maya lowlands of the Classic period. It is simply easier to count than to read, especially if the totals could be related to commonly accepted divisions of time.

To some extent, the esoteric knowledge that was once the sole property of a religious and noble elite passed into the hands of the masses, through the *greca* motifs and *greca*-style architecture. Paradoxically, although *greca* was primarily an elite manifestation, transmitted because of elite tastes and needs, it probably served the masses as well, since it would have provided the emotional bridge between the men of any one community who were otherwise divided by social and economic differences—the major function of such great art, according to Wolfe.

Why, however, would the elite wish to share its knowledge with the masses? One explanation relates to the shift in emphasis from the sacred to the secular that appears to have begun at least by the Late Classic period. Evidence of this shift can be found in the structures and art already mentioned.

Stierlin says of the Palace of the Quetzalpapalotl that it is "an excellent example of civil architecture . . . designed purely as living quarters for the city's dignitaries." He supports his position by noting that the arrangement of the rooms in the palace annex shows that "the builders were chiefly concerned with practical quarters," and by describing the frescoes that deal with the daily lives of both dignitaries and ordinary citizens during the Classic period (rather than with religious figures and events) (1968, pp. 101–03).

The Bonampak murals also emphasize secular rather than sacred

activities. The scene in Room 1, over the repeating pattern of step-frets, has been interpreted as "a narrative sequence of Classic Maya dynastic ceremonies" (Kubler 1969, pp. 12–13). In Room 2, the scene concerns a military campaign ". . . the taking of prisoners for sacrifice" (Thompson, Ruppert, and Proskouriakoff 1955, p. 53), or the punishment of a neighboring people by a ruling group (Kubler 1969, p. 12). Although the purpose of the fighting may have had religious overtones, the fighting itself is the activity emphasized.

The Lambityeco *greca*, although associated with religious forms (Cocijos), appears historically in what has been interpreted as a secular context, that is, in the same period as portraits of members of a new secular elite. In addition, the figures of guards on the Nunnery building at Uxmal imply also an interest in secular, rather than sacred affairs.

If, as indicated by the above examples, a shift in emphasis was from the sacred to the secular occurring during the Late Classic period, then a corresponding change must also have been taking place in the composition of the ruling elite. It would be expected that more civil administrators, businessmen, warriors, and merchants would be entering its ranks, in contrast to priests, priestly nobles, and religious scribes. Moreover, the basic type of knowledge that would be important to this new elite would tend to be exoteric and pragmatic, rather than esoteric and cosmological. It is this new type of knowledge that was also more accessible to the common man, as progressively more of the peasant population were drawn into business and administrative activities. *Greca* may have symbolized not only the widening of the gulf between old and new elites, but also the closing of the gap between elite and commoner.

In conclusion, *greca*, as it appeared on elaborate and monumental buildings during the Epi-Classic period, was a great art form that provided a means of intercommunication between the elites of Oaxaca, Veracruz, and northern Yucatan. It had its roots in widespread symbolism from Late Preclassic and Classic times, and, probably, in technological and stylistic concepts present in Teotihuacan, but developed and elaborated on in other areas.

Although *greca* is associated primarily with elites, and interelite communication, it also must have served to some extent to unite elites with common men within particular areas, both because of the technical processes involved, and because of its association with the native calendar. It is also related to a shift in emphasis from the sacred to the secular, and from a religious to a more civil, military, and mercantile elite. Finally, it is possible that the popularity of *greca* architecture in various areas had as its basis, on the one hand, the need on the part of a rising secular elite to enlist support from the local common man, as well as the other new elites, in order to establish itself in power, and, on the other, the desire of the common man for a different kind of position in his world.

Notes

1. Within northern Yucatan, particular elements were clearly standardized for individual buildings, for example, the X-forms in the "latticework" on the Nunnery, Chichen Itza, and the Pyramid of the Magicians, Uxmal. Moreover, there are also striking instances of standardization and interchangeability of component parts between sites that are both near to and distant from each other. For example, sawtooth elements from Kabah and Uxmal, and banded elements from Kabah and Dzibilnoc, appear to be the same. In Oaxaca, however, the degree of standardization and interchangeability was less. *Greca* designs are first made of flat stones piled on top of each other (on Monte Alban and at Atzompa); then, of pieces of pot-sherds covered over by plaster (at Lambityeco); and, later, of stones of approximate sizes and shapes, which were individually finished at the time of construction (at Mitla). The degree of "prefabrication" at Mitla is difficult to determine. Some preparation of individual elements occurred before their final shaping at the building site. However, both the relative softness of the stone, and the tapered backs of the individual elements, made the finishing process a relatively easy task (Holmes 1895–97, pp. 233–34, 250–51; Meigs 1955, pp. 72–73; Stierlin 1964, p. 144; E. Andrews IV 1965b, pp. 309–10; Stamps n.d.; Sharp 1970, n.d., pp. 29–30).

2. Neutron activation analysis on concentrations of trace impurities in Balancan samples from Lambityeco and Tabasco-Yucatan has revealed that the clays from which the pots in the two areas were made are very different and could not have come from a single clay source.* This suggests that it was the potter who moved from place to place, and not the pots.

3. It is my personal opinion that a "notch" is, as Proskouriakoff defines it, a triangle.

*Garmon Harbottle: personal communication.

gle. Possibly the stepped notches seen in the lower tier of step-frets in figure 1 have some chronological meaning; they may indicate an intermediate stage between un-notched and triangular notched bases. However, they are unlikely to be substitutes for triangular notches, since both the stepped notch and the triangular notch appear on the carved lintel of the Hall of the Columns (fig. 13) and on the carved design within Tomb 2 discussed above.

4. The position here is that of E. Andrews IV (1973, pp. 250–52): that the Florescent tradition evolved in the north, and spread southward, rather than the other way round. However, even if this tradition did evolve in Yucatan, as Andrews claims, this does not eliminate the possibility that basic technological and stylistic concepts originated in the highland areas to the west.

EDUARDO MATOS MOCTEZUMA

the tula chronology: a revision

Previous Work

IN 1940, the work of Acosta and Moedano was initiated at Tula, following discussions that had raised the problem of Tula and the Toltecs. This work led to the first Mesa Redonda de la Sociedad Mexicana de Antropologia, held at Chapultepec on July 11–14, 1941.

Since then, one of the principal problems concerning researchers has been the chronology of Tula, which can be considered from two points of view: the archaeological and the ethnohistoric. Among the most important works in the first category are studies by Armillas (1950) and Acosta (1945, 1956–57), both of whom generally accept the founding of Tula as occurring after the fall of Teotihuacan. They characterize Tula ceramics on the basis of the material found by Acosta in stratigraphic pits and in the ceremonial center; Acosta designated these ceramics the "Tula-Mazapa-Coyotlatelco Complex," later changing this term to the "Toltec Complex." The Toltec Complex consisted of twenty-four ceramic types determined primarily by form and decoration. The types are:

1. Red decoration on brown (Coyotlatelco)
2. Incised decoration (Coyotlatelco)
3. *Ollas* with or without decoration
4. High white
5. Coarse brown
6. Red undulating lines
7. Tripods: red on brown
8. Negative decoration
9. Light brown
10. Dark brown
11. Orange on white
12. Burnished orange
13. Openwork *incensarios*
14. Incense burners
15. Cloissoné decoration
16. Champleve decoration
17. Fresco decoration
18. Tlaloc braziers
19. Small Tlaloc *ollas*
20. Pipes

21. *Comales*
22. Reddish brown on orange
23. Painted orange
24. Stamped decoration

Besides these, the ceramics known as Aztec II, III, and IV also appear.

An important distinction caused this writer to talk about two periods of Toltec ceramics: the old and the new. The first, or old, period is characterized by the Coyotlatelco ceramics, which appear in abundance on the lowest levels and the "incised decoration" ceramics (also considered Coyotlatelco), which are associated with other "Toltec" types. The second, or new, period begins with the appearance of the painted orange and stamp-decorated ceramics and is also associated with other Toltec types (fig. 3).

Since no C_{14} or other absolute dating exists, the archaeologists studying the Toltec problem relied on the chronological position of the ceramic material and on the information from historical sources, which may be relevant to the discussion. In fact, this second method of obtaining a chronology was studied by various investigators, among them Jimenez Moreno (1941) and Kirchoff (1955). Jimenez Moreno relies on the *Anales de Cuauhtitlan* or the *Codex Chimalpopoca* for his interpretation, whereas Kirchoff relies on other Toltec sources.

At first, Jimenez Moreno suggested that Tula was founded in the year A. D. 856. Subsequently, he found that the Toltec calendar functioned more like the Mixtec calendar than the Central Mexican calendar. As a result, he now thinks that the founding of Tula still remains in round numbers, about the year A. D. 900; and that the destruction of Tula occurred in about A. D. 1165.*

These dates have generally been accepted by most Mesoamerican researchers. Let us now see how the former dates suggested by Jimenez Moreno look after having taken into account the information recently obtained by the Tula Project.

Tula Project

Beginning in 1968, with the excavations of Ball Court 2, the project was able to obtain sufficient means to begin an investigation that would cover the pre-Hispanic, colonial, and modern periods. The

*Jimenez Moreno 1974: personal communication.

project's objective was to study the processes of social development that had taken place in the area. For this purpose, the investigation began with a study of the pre-Hispanic period, using two basic approaches: a study of the pre-Hispanic city and a survey of the area. This was done in order to ascertain their relationship and chronology, in relation to the center. The pre-Hispanic city was designated the "microarea" and the area was designated the "macroarea." We will consider each of these briefly.

Microarea. The work here consisted of making a superficial survey that would enable us to know the possible extensions of the city and its principle internal distribution. This last information could not have been available without the reconnaissance of Diehl (1971) and his group, who were the first to map the city limits.

The area was divided into four quadrants, and archaeological material was collected at every 100 meters, which permitted knowledge of the internal distribution of the city. The result of the surface survey will be seen in the work of Juan Yadeun, which will be published by the Tula Project (INAH). Here, we will give the general characteristics of the city in figure 1. Two stratigraphic pits were also opened in the site designated by us as Tula Chico, and the results of this action will be discussed below.

Macroarea. The archaeologists Mastache and Crespo undertook a surface survey of an area of approximately 17 kilometers, the center of which was the city of Tula. They located 106 archaeological sites, noting that the principal occupations correspond to the Early and Late Postclassic period sites, although there were Late Formative and Classic period sites as well. These surveys will be intensified in order to cover the total area.

Excavation in the Microarea:
Tula Chico

Tula Chico plaza is located to the northeast of the well-known ceremonial precinct of Tula (fig. 1). It is called Tula Chico because the arrangement of the buildings is very similar to those of the main plaza of Tula. Each mound that forms the plaza of Tula Chico received a letter of identification (fig. 2).

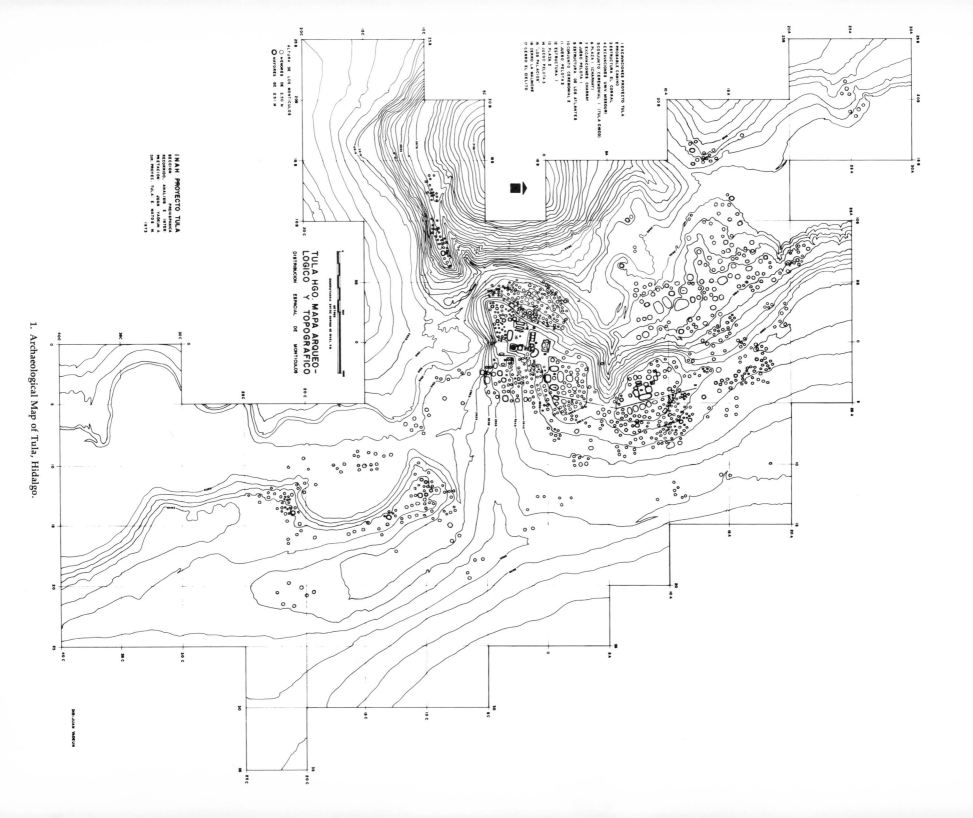

1. Archaeological Map of Tula, Hidalgo.

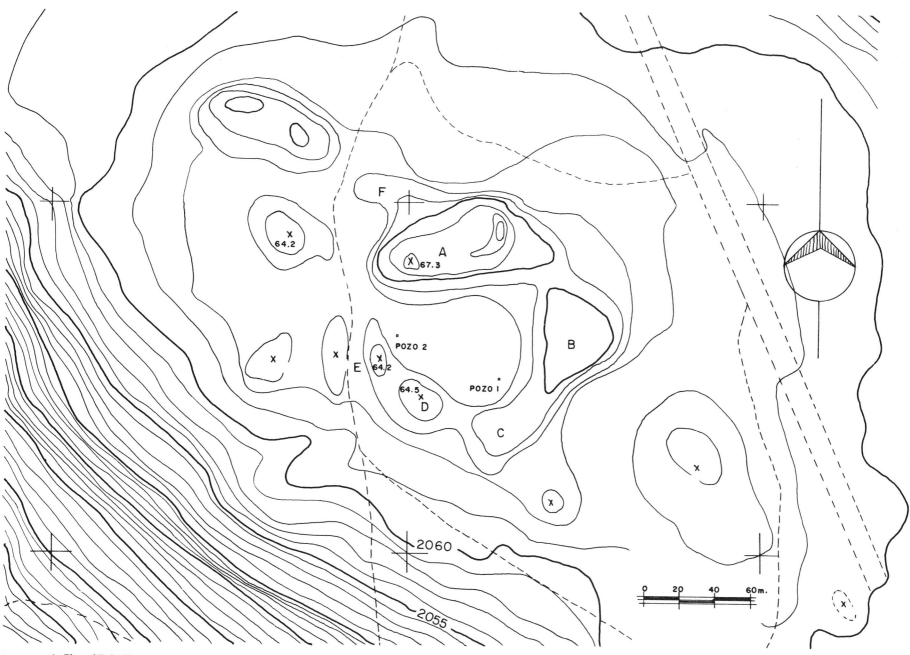

F

X
64.2

A
X 67.3

B

POZO 2

X

X
E   X
     64.2

64.5
X
D

POZO 1

C

X

X

X

2060

2055

X

0   20   40   60 m.

2. Plan of Tula Chico.

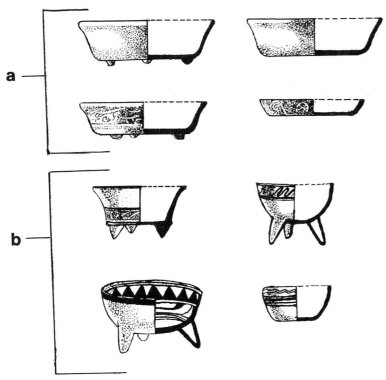

3. Toltec ceramics: a. Painted orange with stamped decoration.
b. Engraved decoration and Coyotlatelco.

In the center of the plaza, two stratigraphic pits were opened, revealing pot sherds that corresponded to the Metepec phase of Teotihuacan in the lowest level above the *tepetate*. The Incised-decorated ware of Acosta, which we will call the "Teotihuacanoid-incised" type, is very much like the Teotihuacan types, with similarities in the surface finish, technology, and decoration. There are also ceramics designated as Coyotlatelco and the Mazapa (red undulating line on brown). In the upper levels, the Coyotlatelco and Mazapa ceramics predominate, and the Teotihuacan Metepec phase ceramics disappear. The Teotihuacanoid-incised ware occurs, but with less frequency. The total absence of Aztec ceramics in the stratigraphic pits of Tula Chico

should be noted. Acosta found the same when opening pits in the areas northeast of the main plaza of the ancient city.

Discussion

We think that it is necessary to revise the chronology of Tula, since the material found from the Metepec phase, observed by Rattray, suggests two things: 1. that the plaza of Tula Chico began in the Metepec phase of Teotihuacan (A. D. 650–750), coeval with the Coyotlatelco; and 2. that this Metepec material was brought in as fill for the construction of the plaza floor, since artificial fill was brought for such purpose, and inasmuch as it is found mixed with the other types already mentioned. In addition, we have other significant information. To the immediate north of the pre-Hispanic city of Tula is found Site 83, located during the survey of the macroarea, and it is Teotihuacan in date. The material collected there by Mastache and Crespo (1974) pertains to the Tlamimilolpa and Metepec phases. It is possible that these mounds may have been utilized as fill material in Tula Chico.

There can be little doubt about the great antiquity of the plaza of Tula Chico, since the material recovered is what Acosta called "old Toltec." Moreover, neither painted orange nor Incised-decorated ceramic, which is later, is found there. This makes us suppose that Tula Chico was the initial center, and the city expanded from there.

In the ethnohistoric sources there is evidence that when the Toltecs arrived, there were groups of people already living in Tula. When Sahagun talks about the Toltecs, he states: "and from there they went out to populate the banks of a river near the town of Xicotitlan and it now has the name Tulla, and having dwelt there together, there are signs of the many works they made there (Sahagun 1956). According to this quote there used to exist a town (Xicotitlan) located next to the Tula River and as Sahagun then states that "having dwelt and lived there together," he must be referring to two different groups. The *Historia Tolteca Chichimeca* (1947) clearly tells us about the Nonohualcos and the Toltecs living together at that place. The *Anales de Cuauhtitlan* also makes reference to the proximity of the Mexicans: "When the Toltecs departed in 1 Tecpatl, at the same time the Mexicans moved towards here from far away Xicoc . . ." (*Anales de Cuauhtitlan* 1945).

Information from the sources, as well as the archaeological data discussed allows us to arrive at the following preliminary conclusions:

1. The plaza of Tula Chico reveals the presence of the Metepec phase of Teotihuacan;
2. The Metepec material is associated with Coyotlatelco and with the Incised-decorated ware of Teotihuacanoid form. Mazapa material is also found (red undulating lines on brown);
3. This plaza is the oldest known plaza in the pre-Hispanic city of Tula, and it could have been the initial nucleus of Tula;
4. The historical sources tell of the presence of two groups that began to live together at a given moment, which, on the other hand, could also indicate that the place was already occupied at the end of the Classic (Metepec phase) period.
5. During the surface survey sites of the macroarea, thirteen archaeological sites belonging to the Classic period have been located. This makes us believe that the Tula area had been under Teotihuacan control.

BIBLIOGRAPHY

Acosta, J.

1945   Las cuarta y quinta temporadas de exploraciones arqueo-logicas en Tula, Hidalgo 1943–1944. *Revista Mexicana de Estudios Antropologicos* 7: 23–64.

1956–1957   Interpretacion de algunos de los datos obtenidos en Tula relativos a la epoca tolteca. *Revista Mexicana de Estudios Antropologicos* 14: 75–110.

1959   Exploraciones arqueologicas en Monte Alban XVIIIa temporada 1958. *Revista Mexicana de Estudios Antropologicos* 15: 7–49.

1962   El Palacio de las Mariposas de Teotihuacan. *Instituto Nacional de Antropologia e Historia, Boletin* 9: 5–7.

1964   El Palacio del Quetzalpapalotl. *Instituto Nacional de Antropologia e Historia, Memorias,* no. 10.

1965   Preclassic and Classic architecture of Oaxaca. In *Handbook of Middle American Indians,* ed. R. Wauchope, vol. 3, pp. 814–36. Austin: Univ. of Texas Press.

Acosta, J., Marquina, I., and Muller, F.

1970   Teotihuacan lugar de dioses. *Artes de Mexico,* yr. 17, no. 134.

Acosta Saignes, Miguel

1945   Los Pochteca. *Acta Antropologia* 1:1.

Anales de Cuauhtitlan

1945   *Codice Chimalpopoca,* ed. and trans. P. F. Velazquez. Mexico: Universidad Nacional Autonoma.

Andrews, E. W. IV

1965a   Progress report on the 1960–1964 field seasons, National Geographic Society-Tulane University Dzilbilchaltun Project. Tulane University, *Middle American Research Institute,* pub. 31: 23–67.

1965b   Archaeology and prehistory in the northern Maya lowlands: an introduction. In *Handbook of Middle American Indians,* ed. R. Wauchope, vol. 2, pp. 288–330. Austin: Univ. of Texas Press.

1968a   Dzibilchaltun, a northern Maya metropolis. *Archaeology* 21: 36–47.

1968b   Torre cilindrica de las ruinas de Puerto Rico, Campeche. *Instituto Nacional de Antropologia e Historia, Boletin* 31: 7–13.

1969   The archaeological use and distribution of mollusca in the Maya lowlands. Tulane University, *Middle American Research Institute,* pub. 34.

1970   Balankanche, throne of the Tiger Priest. Tulane University, *Middle American Research Institute,* pub. 32.

1973   The development of Maya civilization after abandonment of the southern cities. In *The Classic Maya collapse,* ed. T. P. Culbert, pp. 243–68. Albuquerque: Univ. of New Mexico Press.

Andrews, E. W. IV, Stuart, G. E.
1968   Ruins of Ikil, Yucatan, Mexico. Tulane University, *Middle American Research Institute,* pub. 31: 69–80.

Andrews, E. W. V
1970   Excavations at Quelepa, eastern El Salvador. *Ceramica de Cultura Maya* 6: 21–40.

Andrews, G. F.
1969   *Edzna, Campeche, Mexico: settlement patterns and monumental architecture.* Eugene, Oreg.: University of Oregon.

Andrews, G. F.
1975   *Maya cities: placemaking and urbanization.* Norman, Okla.: Univ. of Oklahoma Press.

Anton, F.
1969   *Ancient Mexican art.* New York: Putnam.

Armillas, P.
1942–1944   Oztuma, Guerrero, fortaleza de los Mexicanos en la frontera de Michoacan. *Revista Mexicana de Estudios Antropologicos* 6: 165–75.

1950   Teotihuacan, Tula y los Toltecas. *Runa* 3: 37–70.

Artes de Mexico
1957   Escultura prehispanica mexicana en colecciones de los Estados Unidos, yr. 5, no. 17.

1970   Teotihuacan, lugar de los dioses, yr. 17, no. 134.

Aveleyra Arroyo de Anda, L.
1963   La estela teotihuacana de La Ventilla. *Cuadernos del Museo Nacional de Antropologia* I. Mexico: Museo Nacional de Antropologia.

Badner, M.
1972   A possible focus of Andrean artistic influence in Mesoamerica, *Studies in Pre-Columbian Art and Archaeology,* no. 9. Washington, D.C.: Dumbarton Oaks.

Ball, J. W.
1974a   A Teotihuacan-style cache from the Maya lowlands. *Archaeology* 27: 2–9.

1974b   A coordinate approach to northern Maya prehistory: A.D. 700–1200. *American Antiquity* 39(1): 85–93.

Batres, L.
1902   *Exploraciones de Monte Alban.* Mexico.

Bebrich, C. A.
n.d.   Kaminaljuyu during the terminal Formative period. Paper presented to the American Anthropological Association, New Orleans, Louisiana, 1969.

Bell, B.
1971   Archaeology of Nayarit, Jalisco, and Colima. In *Handbook of Middle American Indians,* ed. R. Wauchope, vol. 11, pp. 694–753. Austin: Univ. of Texas Press.

1974, ed.   *The archaeology of west Mexico.* Ajijic, Mexico: Sociedad de Estudios Avanzados del Occidente de Mexico.

Berlin, H.
1952   Excavaciones en Kaminaljuyu: Monticulo D-III-13. *Antropologia e Historia de Guatemala* 4(1): 3–18.

1965   The inscription of the Temple of the Cross at Palenque. *American Antiquity* 30(3): 330–42.

Bernal, I.
1949   La ceramica grabada de Monte Alban. *Instituto Nacional de Antropologia e Historia, Anales* 3: 59–77.

1958   Monte Alban and the Zapotecs. Mexico City College, *Boletin de Estudios Oaxaquenos,* no. 1: 1–9.

1963, ed.   *Teotihuacan: descubrimientos, reconstrucciones.* Mexico: Instituto Nacional de Antropologia e Historia.

1965a   Archaeological synthesis of Oaxaca. In *Handbook of Middle American Indians,* ed. R. Wauchope, vol. 3, pp. 788–813. Austin: Univ. of Texas Press.

1965b   Architecture in Oaxaca after the end of Monte Alban. Ibid., pp. 837–48.

1965c   Teotihuacan: nuevas fechas de radiocarbono y su posible significado. Universidad Autonoma de Mexico, *Sobretiro de Anales de Antropologia* 2: 27–35.

1966   The Mixtecs in the archaeology of the valley of Oaxaca. In *Ancient Oaxaca,* ed. J. Paddock, pp. 345–66. Stanford: Stanford Univ. Press.

1968a   The ball players of Dainzu. *Archaeology* 21(4): 246–51.

1968b   The Olmec presence in Oaxaca, *Mexico Quarterly Review* 3: 1.

1969   *The Olmec world,* trans. D. Heyden and F. Horcasitas. Berkeley and Los Angeles: Univ. of California Press.

n.d.   La ceramica de Monte Alban IIIa. Ph.D. dissertation, Universidad Autonoma de Mexico, 1949.

Blom, F., La Farge, O.
1926–1927   Tribes and temples. Tulane University, *Middle American Research Institute,* pub. 1. 2 vols.

Bolles, J.
n.d.   Chichen Itza: Monjas Group. Manuscript. Cambridge: Harvard University, Peabody Museum, Archives Collection.

Boos, F. H.
1964a   El dios mariposa en la cultura de Oaxaca: una revision del estado actual del conocimiento. *Instituto Nacional de Antropologia e Historia, Anales* 16: 77–97.

1964b   *Las urnas zapotecas en el Real Museo de Ontario.* Vol. 1. Mexico: Instituto Nacional de Antropologia e Historia, Corpus Antiquitatum Americanensium.

1966a   *Colecciones Leigh y Museo Frissell de arte zapoteca.* Vol. 2. Mexico: Instituto Nacional de Antropologia e Historia, Corpus Antiquitatum Americanensium.

1966b   *The ceramic sculptures of ancient Oaxaca.* New York: A.S. Barnes.

1968   *Colecciones Leigh, Museo Frissell de arte zapoteca, Smithsonian Institution, y otros.* Vol. 3. Mexico: Instituto Nacional de Antropologia e Historia, Corpus Antiquitatum Americanensium.

Borhegyi, S. F.
1956   The development of folk and complex cultures in the southern Maya area. *American Antiquity* 21(4): 343–56.

1965   Archaeological synthesis of the Guatemalan highlands. In *Handbook of Middle American Indians,* ed. R. Wauchope, vol. 2, pp. 3–57. Austin: Univ. of Texas Press.

1966   Shell offerings and the use of shell motifs at Lake Amatitlan, Guatemala, and Teotihuacan, Mexico. *36th International Congress of Americanists,* Seville, 1964, *Actas,* vol. 1, pp. 355–71.

1971   Pre-Columbian contacts—the dryland approach: the impact and influence of Teotihuacan culture on the pre-Columbian civilizations of Mesoamerica. In *Man across the sea,* ed. C. Riley, pp. 79–105. Austin: Univ. of Texas Press.

Brainerd, G. W.
1956   Changing living patterns of the Yucatan Maya. *American Antiquity* 22: 162–64.

1958   The archaeological ceramics of Yucatan. *University of California, Anthropological Records,* no. 19.

Braniff, B.
1972   Secuencias arqueologicas en Guanajuato y la Cuenca de Mexico: intento de correlacion. Sociedad Mexicana de Antropologia, *IX Mesa Redonda,* pp. 273–324.

Brockington, D.
1967   The ceramic history of Santa Rosa, Chiapas, Mexico. Brigham Young University, *New World Archaeological Foundation, Papers,* no. 23.

1969   Investigaciones arqueologicas en la costa de Oaxaca. *Instituto Nacional de Antropologia e Historia, Boletin* 38: 33–39.

1970   New evidence concerning the origins of the Mixtec ceramic tradition. *University of North Carolina, Research Laboratories of Anthropology.*

Brockington, D. L., Jorrin, M., and Long, J. R.
1974   The Oaxaca coast project reports, part 1. *Vanderbilt University Publications in Anthropology,* no. 8.

Brockington, D. L., Long, J. R.
1974   The Oaxaca coast project reports, part 2. *Vanderbilt University Publications in Anthropology,* no. 9.

Brotherston, G.
1974   Huitzilopochtli and what was made of him. In *Mesoamerican Archaeology,* ed. G. Hammond, pp. 155–66. Austin: Univ. of Texas Press.

Brown, K.
n.d.   The B-III-5 complex, Kaminaljuyu, Guatemala: new interpretations on architecture and settlement patterns during the Classic period. M.A. thesis, Pennsylvania State University, Department of Anthropology, 1972.

Burland, C. A.
1967   *The gods of Mexico.* New York: Putnam.

Byers, D. S.
1967, ed.   *The prehistory of the Tehuacan valley.* Vol. 1. Austin: Univ. of Texas Press.

Caso, A.
1928   *Las estelas zapotecas.* Mexico: Museo Nacional de Arqueologia, Historia, Ethnografia, Monografias, no. 3.

1938   Exploraciones in Oaxaca, quinta y sexta temporadas, 1936–1937. *Instituto Panamericano de Geografia y Historia,* pub. 34.

1946   Los sacrificios y otras ceremonias. In *Mexico prehispanico,* ed. J. A. Vivo, pp. 355–64. Mexico: Emma Hurtado.

1949   Una urna con el dios mariposa. *El Mexico antiguo* 7: 78–95.

1958   *The Aztecs: people of the sun.* Norman, Okla.: Univ. of Oklahoma Press.

1962   Calendario y escritura en Xochicalco. *Revista Mexicana de Estudios Antropologicos* 18: 49–79. Reprinted in 1967, pp. 166–86.

1965a   Sculpture and mural painting of Oaxaca. In *Handbook of Middle American Indians,* ed. R. Wauchope, vol. 3, pp. 849–70. Austin: Univ. of Texas Press.

1965b   Zapotec writing and calendar. Ibid., pp. 931–47.

1965c   Lapidary work, goldwork and copperwork from Oaxaca. Ibid., pp. 896–930.

1966a	Dioses y signos teotihuacanos. Sociedad Mexicana de Antropologia, *XI Mesa Redonda*, vol. 1, pp. 249–75.
1966b	The lords of Yanhuitlan. In *Ancient Oaxaca*, ed. J. Paddock, pp. 313–35. Stanford: Stanford Univ. Press.
1967	*Los calendarios prehispanicos.* Mexico: Universidad Nacional Autonoma de Mexico.
1969	El tesoro de Monte Alban. *Instituto Nacional de Antropologia e Historia, Memorias,* no. 3.

Caso, A., Bernal, I.

1952	Urnas de Oaxaca. *Instituto Nacional de Antropologia e Historia, Memorias,* no. 2.
1965	Ceramics of Oaxaca. In *Handbook of Middle American Indians,* ed. R. Wauchope, vol. 3, pp. 871–95. Austin: Univ. of Texas Press.

Caso, A., Bernal, I., and Acosta, J. R.

1967	La ceramica de Monte Alban. *Instituto Nacional de Antropologia e Historia, Memorias,* no. 13.

Caso, A., Rubin de la Borbolla, D. F.

1936	Exploraciones en Mitla: 1934–1935. *Instituto Panamericano Geografia e Historia,* pub. 21.

Chadwick, R.

1971	Native pre-Aztec history of Central Mexico. In *Handbook of Middle American Indians,* ed. R. Wauchope, vol. 11, pp. 474–504. Austin: Univ. of Texas Press.

Chadwick, R., MacNeish, R. S.

1967	Codex Borgia and the Venta Salada phase. In *The prehistory of the Tehuacan valley,* ed. D. S. Byers, vol. 1, pp. 114–31. Austin: Univ. of Texas Press.

Chapman, A. H.

1957	Port of trade enclaves in Aztec and Maya civilizations. In *Trade and market in the early empires,* ed. K. Polanyi, pp. 114–53. Glencoe, Ill.: Free Press.
1959	*Puertos de intercambio en Mesoamerica prehispanica.* Mexico: Instituto Nacional de Antropologia e Historia.

Cheek, C.

n.d.	Excavations at the Palangana, Kaminaljuyu, Guatemala. Ph.D. dissertation, University of Arizona, Department of Anthropology. 1971.

Codex Borgia

1963	*Comentarios al Codice Borgia.* Commentaries by E. Seler. Translated by M. Frenk. 3 vols. Mexico: Fondo de Cultura Economica.

Coe, M. D.

1957	Cycle 7 monuments in Middle America: a reconsideration. *American Anthropologist* 59(4): 597–611.
1962	*Mexico.* New York: Praeger.
1965	Archaeological synthesis of southern Veracruz and Tabasco. In *Handbook of Middle American Indians,* ed. R. Wauchope, vol. 3, pp. 679–715. Austin: Univ. of Texas Press.
1966	*The Maya.* New York: Praeger.
1973	*The Maya scribe and his world.* New York: Grolier Club.
n.d.	Radiocarbon dates from Teotihuacan. Mimeographed. New Haven, Conn.: Yale University, Department of Anthropology, 1962.

Coe, W. R.

1965	Tikal: ten years of study of a Maya ruin in the lowlands of Guatemala. *Expedition* 8(1): 5–56.
1967	*Tikal: a handbook of the ancient Maya ruins.* Philadelphia: The University of Pennsylvania Museum.
1972	Cultural contact between the lowland Maya and Teotihuacan as seen from Tikal, Peten, Guatemala. Sociedad Mexicana de Anthropologia, *XI Mesa Redonda,* vol. 2, pp. 257–72.

Coggins, C.

n.d.	Painting and drawing styles at Tikal: an historical and iconographic reconstruction. 2 vols. Ph.D. dissertation, Harvard University, Department of Fine Arts, 1975.

Cohen, A.

1969	*Custom and politics in urban Africa.* Los Angeles and Berkeley: Univ. of California Press.

Cohodas, M.

1974	The iconography of the panels of the Sun, Cross, and Foliated Cross at Palenque: part II. *Primera Mesa Redonda de Palenque,* ed. M. Greene, part I, pp. 95–108. Pebble Beach, Calif.: The Robert Louis Stevenson School.
1975	The symbolism and ritual function of the Middle Classic ball game in Mesoamerica. *American Indian Quarterly* 2(2): 99–130.
1976	The iconography of the panels of the Sun, Cross, and the Foliated Cross at Palenque: part III. *Segunda Mesa Redonda de Palenque,* ed. M. Greene, part 3, pp. 155–76. Pebble Beach, Calif.: The Robert Louis Stevenson School.
n.d.	The Great Ball Court at Chichen Itza, Yucatan, Mexico. Ph.D. dissertation. 2 vols. Columbia University, Department of Art History and Archaeology, 1974.

Consejo de Recursos Naturales No Renovables

1970	*Mineria prehispanica en la Sierra de Queretaro.* Mexico: Secretaria del Patrimonio Nacional.

Cook de Leonard, C.

1959, ed.	*Esplendor del Mexico Antiguo.* 2 vols. Mexico: Centro de Investigaciones Antropologios.

Corona Nunez, J.
1957   *Mitologia tarasca.* Mexico: Fondo de Cultura Economica.
1972   Los teotihuacanos en el occidente de Mexico. Sociedad Mexicana de Antropologia, *IX Mesa Redonda,* pp. 253–56.

Covarrubias, M.
1957   *Indian art of Mexico and Central America.* New York: Knopf.

Culbert, T. P.
1973, ed.   *The Classic Maya collapse.* Albuquerque: Univ. of New Mexico Press.

Cuttler, C. E.
1968   *Northern painting.* New York: Holt, Rinehart & Winston.

Diehl, R. A.
1971   *Preliminary report, University of Missouri archaeological project at Tula, Hidalgo, Mexico.* Columbia, Mo.: Univ. of Missouri.

DiPeso, C. C.
1968a   Casas Grandes, a fallen trading center of the Gran Chichimeca. *Masterkey* 42(1): 19–37.
1968b   Casas Grandes and the Gran Chichimeca. *El Palacio* 75(4): 45–61.

Dockstader, F. J.
1964   *Indian art in Middle America.* Greenwich, Conn.: New York Graphic Society.

Dumond, D. E., Muller, F.
1972   Classic to Postclassic in highland Central Mexico. *Science* 175:1208–15.

Duran, D.
1971   *Book of the gods and rites of the ancient calendar.* Ed. and trans. D. Heyden and F. Horcasitas. Norman, Okla: Univ. of Oklahoma Press.

Easby, E., Scott, J. F.
1970   *Before Cortes, sculpture of Middle America.* New York: Metropolitan Museum of Art.

Ekholm, G.
1945   A pyrite mirror from Queretaro, Mexico. *Carnegie Institution of Washington, Notes on Middle American Archaeology & Ethnology,* vol. 2, no. 58: 178–81.
1961   Puerto Rican stone 'collars' as ball-game belts. In *Essays in pre-Columbian art and archaeology,* ed. S. K. Lothrop, pp. 356–371. Cambridge, Mass.: Harvard Univ. Press.

Ellis, F. H.
1964   A reconstruction of the basic Jemez pattern of social organization, with comparisons to other Tanoan social structures. *University of New Mexico Publications in Anthropology* 11. Albuquerque: Univ. of New Mexico Press.

Feldman, L.
n.d.   A tumpline economy production and distribution systems of early central-east Guatemala. Ph.D. dissertation, Pennsylvania State University, Department of Anthropology, 1971.

Ferdon, E. N., Jr.
1953   Tonala, Mexico: an archaeological survey. Santa Fe: *School of American Research, Monographs,* no. 16.

Fischer, J. L.
1969   Comments in response to Alvin W. Wolfe's social structural bases of art. *Current Anthropology* 10: 33–34.

Folan, W. J.
1968   El Chicchan Chob y la Casa del Vendao, Chichen Itza, Yucatan. *Instituto Nacional de Antropologia e Historia, Anales* 19: 49–60.

Foncerrada de Molina, M.
1965   *La escultura de Uxmal.* Mexico: Universidad Nacional Autonoma de Mexico.

Fondo Editorial de la Plastica Mexicana
1964   *Flor y canto del arte prehispanico de Mexico.* Mexico.

de la Fuente, B.
1965   *La escultura de Palenque.* Mexico: Universidad Nacional Autonoma de Mexico, Instituto de Investigaciones Esteticas.

Gamio, M.
1910   Los monumentos arqueologicos de las inmediaciones de Chalchihuites, Zacatecas. *Museo Nacional de Arqueologia, Historia y Etnologia, Anales,* epoca 3, 2: 467–92.

Garcia Payon, J.
1962   Hallazgo de otros tableros en el centro del juego de pelota sur de El Tajin. *Instituto Nacional de Antropologia e Historia, Boletin* 8: 9–10.
1967   *Official guide to El Tajin, Mexico.* Mexico: Instituto Nacional de Antropologia e Historia.
1971   Archaeology of central Veracruz. In *Handbook of Middle American Indians,* ed. R. Wauchope, vol. 11, pp. 505–42. Austin: Univ. of Texas Press.

Gendrop, P.
1971   Murales prehispanicos. *Artes de Mexico.* vol. 18, no. 144.

Gillmor, F.
1964   *The king danced in the marketplace.* Tucson. Univ. of Arizona Press.

Girard, R.
1973   Nuevas esculturas liticas en el area Maya. *40th International Congress of Americanists,* Rome, 1972, *Proceedings,* vol. 1, pp. 195–202.

Gordon, G. B.
1905   The serpent motif in the ancient art of Central America and Mexico. *University of Pennsylvania, Department of Archaeology, Transactions* 1(1): 61–66.

Gorenstein, S.
1974, ed.   *Prehispanic America.* New York: St. Martin's.

Graham, J.
1971   Non-Classic inscriptions and sculpture at Seibal. *University of California, Archaeological Research Facility, Contributions* 13.

Greene, M.
1967   *Ancient Maya relief sculpture.* New York: The Museum of Primitive Art.

Greene, M., Rands, R. L., and Graham, J. A.
1971   *Maya sculpture from the southern lowlands, highlands and Pacific piedmont.* Berkeley: Lederer Street and Zeus.

Goncalves de Lima, O.
1956   *El maguey y el pulque en los codices mexicanos.* Mexico: Fondo de Cultura Economica.

Hall, C. S. (see also, Millon, C.)
n.d.   A chronological study of the mural art of Teotihuacan. Ph.D. dissertation, University of California at Berkeley, 1962.

Hammond, N.
1974, ed.   *Mesoamerican archaeology: new approaches.* Austin: Univ. of Texas Press.

Harbottle, G., Sayar, E. V., Meijers, P., and Abascal, R.
n.d.   Studies of ancient ceramics by neutron activation: a new tool for the archaeologist. Paper presented to the Society for American Archaeology, Norman, Oklahoma, 1971.

Hartung, H.
1970   Notes on the Oaxaca tablero. Mexico City College, *Boletin de Estudios Oaxaquenos* 27: 2–8.

Hatch, M. P.
1971   An hypothesis on Olmec astronomy with special reference to the La Venta site. *University of California, Archaeological Research Facility, Contributions* 13: 1–64.

Hellmuth, N. M.
1975   The Escuintla hoards: Teotihuacan art in Guatemala. *Foundation for Latin American Anthropological Research, Progress Reports* 1(2).

n.d.a   Mexican symbols in the Classic art of the southern Maya lowlands. M.A. thesis, Brown University, Department of Anthropology, 1969.

n.d.b   Glyphs associated with Mexican designs on Classic Maya sculpture. Manuscript. 1971.

Heyden, D.
1975   An interpretation of the cave underneath the Pyramid of the Sun in Teotihuacan, Mexico. *American Antiquity* 40: 131–47.

Historia Tolteca Chichimeca
1947   *Anales de Quauhtinchan,* eds. H. Berlin and S. Rendon. Mexico: Antigua Libreria Robredo.

Holmes, W. H.
1895–1897   Archaeological studies among the ancient cities of Mexico. *Field Columbian Museum, Anthropological Series* 1(1).

Jennings, J. D., Norbeck, E.
1964, eds.   *Prehistoric man in the New World.* Chicago: Univ. of Chicago Press.

Jimenez Moreno, W.
1941   Tula y los Toltecas segun las fuentes historicas. *Revista Mexicana de Estudios Antropologicos* 5: 79–83.

1959   Sintesis de la historia pretolteca de Mesoamerica. In *El Esplendor del Mexico Antiguo,* ed. C. Cook de Leonard, vol. 2, pp. 1019–1108. Mexico: Centro de Investigaciones Antropologicos.

1966   Mesoamerica before the Toltecs. In *Ancient Oaxaca,* ed. J. Paddock, pp. 1–82. Stanford: Stanford Univ. Press.

Johnson, F., MacNeish, R. S.
1972   Chronometric dating. In *The prehistory of the Tehuacan valley,* ed. F. Johnson, vol. 4, pp. 3–55. Austin: Univ. of Texas Press.

Kampen, M.
1972   *The sculptures of El Tajin, Veracruz, Mexico.* Gainsville, Fla.: Univ. of Florida Press.

Kelemen, P.
1969   *Medieval American art.* 2 vols. New York: Dover.

Kelley, J. C.
1971   Archaeology of the northern frontier: Zacatecas and Durango. In *Handbook of Middle American Indians,* ed. R. Wauchope, vol. 11, pp. 768–801. Austin: Univ. of Texas Press.

1974   Speculations on the culture history of north-western Mesoamerica. In *The archaeology of west Mexico,* ed. B. Bell, pp. 19–39. Ajijic, Mexico: Sociedad de Estudios Avanzados del Occidente de Mexico.

Kelley, J. C., Abbott, E.
1966   The cultural sequence on the north central frontier of Mesoamerica. *36th International Congress of Americanists,* Sevilla, 1964, *Actas,* vol. 1, pp. 325–44.

Kelley, J. C., Kelley, E. A.

1971   An introduction to the ceramics of the Chalchihuites culture of Zacatecas and Durango, Mexico, part I: the decorated wares. Southern Illinois University, *Mesoamerican Studies, Research Records of the University Museum.*

n.d.   The rise and fall of the Classic as seen from the northwestern frontier of Mesoamerica. Paper presented to the Society for American Archaeology, San Francisco, California, 1973.

Kidder, A. V.

1943   Grooved stone axes from Central America. *Carnegie Institution of Washington, Notes on Middle American Archaeology and Ethnology,* vol. 1, no. 29: 189–93.

1949   Certain archaeological specimens from Guatemala. *Carnegie Institution of Washington, Notes on Middle American Archaeology and Ethnology,* vol. 4, no. 92.

1950   Certain archaeological specimens from Guatemala, II. *Carnegie Institution of Washington, Notes on Middle American Archaeology and Ethnology,* vol. 4, no. 95.

1954   Miscellaneous archaeological specimens from Mesoamerica. *Carnegie Institution of Washington, Notes on Middle American Archaeology and Ethnology,* vol. 5, no. 117: 5–26.

Kidder, A. V., Jennings, J. D., and Shook, E. M.

1946   Excavations at Kaminaljuyu, Guatemala. *Carnegie Institution of Washington,* pub. 561.

Kirsch, R. W.

n.d.   Excavations at Kaminaljuyu: Mound A-VI-6. M.A. thesis, Pennsylvania State University, Department of Anthropology, 1972.

Kirchhoff, P.

1955   Quetzalcoatl, Huemac y el fin de Tula. *Cuadernos Americanos* 14(6): 163–96.

Knauth, L.

1961   El juego de pelota y el rito de la decapitacion. *Estudios de Cultura Maya* 1: 183–98.

Kolb, C. C.

n.d.   Lowland Mayan and Oaxacan influence at Teotihuacan, Mexico: "Dr. Rudolfo Figueroa."

Kowalewski, S., Truell, M.

1970   'Tlaloc' in the valley of Oaxaca. Mexico City College, *Boletin de Estudios Oaxaquenos,* no. 31: 2–8.

Krotser, P. H., Krotser, G. R.

1973   The life style of El Tajin. *American Antiquity* 38: 199–205.

Kubler, G.

1962   *The art and architecture of ancient America: The Mexican, Maya, and Andean peoples.* Baltimore: Penguin.

1967   The iconography of the art of Teotihuacan. *Studies in Pre-Columbian Art and Archaeology,* no. 4. Washington, D.C.: Dumbarton Oaks.

1969   *Studies in Classic Maya iconography.* New Haven, Conn.: Connecticut Academy of Arts and Sciences.

1972   Jaguars in the valley of Mexico. In *The cult of the feline,* ed. E. Benson, pp. 19–44. Washington, D.C.: Dumbarton Oaks.

1976   The double-portrait lintels at Tikal. *XXIII International Congress of the History of Art,* Granada, 1973, vol. 1, pp. 165–76.

Kurath, G. P., Marti, S.

1964   *Dances of Anahuac.* Viking Fund Publications in Anthropology 38. Chicago: Aldine.

Lee, T. A., Jr., Lowe, G. W.

1968   Situacion arqueologica de las esculturas de Izapa, Brigham Young University, *New World Archaeological Foundation.* Mexico: "Dr. Rudolfo Figueroa."

Leigh, H.

1961   Head shrinking in ancient Mesoamerica. *Science of Man* 7: 4–7.

Libby, W. F.

1955   *Radiocarbon Dating.* 2d ed. Chicago: Univ. of Chicago Press.

Linne, S.

1942   Mexican highland cultures: archaeological researches at Teotihuacan, Calpulalpan and Chalchicomula in 1934–35. *The Ethnological Museum of Sweden,* new series, pub. 7.

Lothrop, S. K.

1926   Stone sculptures from the Finca Arevalo ruins, Guatemala. Museum of the American Indian, Heye Foundation, *Indian Notes* 65(3): 147–71.

1933   Atitlan: an archaeological study of ancient remains on the borders of Lake Atitlan, Guatemala. *Carnegie Institution of Washington,* pub. 444.

1952   Metals from the Cenote of Sacrifice, Chichen Itza, Yucatan. *Harvard University, Peabody Museum, Memoirs* 10(2).

1961, ed. *Essays in pre-Columbian art and archaeology.* Cambridge, Mass.: Harvard Univ. Press.

Lumholtz, C.

1902   *Unknown Mexico.* New York: Scribners.

McBride, H.

1971   Figurine types of central and southern Veracruz. In *Ancient*

Art of Veracruz, pp. 23–30. Los Angeles: Ethnic Arts Council.

Maler, T.
1901   Researches in the central portion of the Usumatsintla valley. *Harvard University, Peabody Museum, Memoirs* 2(2).

Maritzer, L. S.
1958   A study of possible relationship between the Huichol and Chalchihuites cultures. *Southwestern Lore* 23: 51–63.

Marquina, I.
1941   Relaciones entre los monumentos de norte de Yucatan e los del Centro de Mexico. *Revista Mexicana de Estudios Antropologicos* 5: 135–50.

1951   Arquitectura prehispanica. *Instituto Nacional de Antropologia e Historia, Memorias*, no. 1.

1964   Arquitectura prehispanica. *Instituto Nacional de Antropologia e Historia, Memorias*, no. 1, 2d rev. ed.

1970, ed.   *Proyecto Cholula. Instituto Nacional de Antropologia e Historia, Investigaciones* 19.

Marti, S.
1953   Flautilla de la penitencia, fiesta grande de Tezcatlipoca. *Cuadernos Americanos* 6: 147–57.

Mastache, G., Crespo, A. M.
1974   La ocupacion prehispanica en el area de Tula, Hidalgo. In *Proyecto Tula*, ed. E. M. Matos, pp. 71–104. Mexico: Instituto Nacional de Antropologia e Historia.

Mathews, P., Schele, L.
1974   Dynastic sequence at Palenque. *Primera Mesa Redonda de Palenque*, ed. M. Greene, part 1, pp. 63–76. Pebble Beach, Calif.: The Robert Louis Stevenson School.

Maudslay, A. P.
1889–1902   *Biologia Centrali-Americana*. 5 vols. London: R. H. Porter.

Medellin Zenil, A.
1960   *Ceramicas del Totonacapan, Xalapa*. Jalapa: Universidad Veracruzana.

Meigs, C. C.
1955   Notes on the technology of greca mosaics. *Mesoamerican Notes* 4: 73.

Melgarejo Vivanco, J. L.
1960   La estela 1 de Piedra Labrada, Ver. *La Palabra y el Hombre* 16: 27–36.

Miller, A. G.
1973   *The mural painting of Teotihuacan, Mexico*. Washington, D.C.: Dumbarton Oaks.

1974   Archaeological investigations of the Quintana Roo mural project: a preliminary report of the 1973 season. *University of California, Archaeological Research Facility, Contributions* 18: 137–48.

1976   The roof-comb sculpture and the doubled-portrait lintels of Temples I and IV. *XXIII International Congress of the History of Art*, Granada, 1973, vol. 1, pp. 177–84.

Millon, C. (see also, Hall, C.)
1973   Painting, writing and polity in Teotihuacan, Mexico. *American Antiquity* 38: 294–314.

Millon, R. F.
1961   Early structures within the Pyramid of the Sun at Teotihuacan. *American Antiquity* 26: 371–80.

1964   The Teotihuacan mapping project. *American Antiquity* 29(3): 345–52.

1965   The Pyramid of the Sun at Teotihuacan: 1959 investigations. *American Philosophical Society, Transactions*, new series, vol. 55, pt. 6.

1967a   Cronologia y periodificacion: datos estratigraficos sobre periodos ceramicos y sus relaciones con la pintura mural. Sociedad Mexicana de Antropologia, *XI Mesa Redonda*, vol. 1, pp. 1–18.

1967b   Extension y poblacion de la ciudad de Teotihuacan en sus diferentes periodos: un calculo provisional. Sociedad Mexicana de Antropologia. *XI Mesa Redonda*, vol. 1, pp. 57–78.

1967c   Urna de Monte Alban IIIa encontrada en Teotihuacan. *Instituto Nacional de Antropologia e Historia, Boletin* 29: 42–44.

1967d   Teotihuacan. *Scientific American* 216(6): 38–48.

1970   Teotihuacan: completion of map of giant ancient city in the valley of Mexico. *Science* 170: 1077–82.

1973   *Urbanization at Teotihuacan, Mexico*. Vol. 1, *The Teotihuacan map*. Austin: Univ. of Texas Press.

Moholy-Nagy, H.
1962   A Tlaloc stela from Tikal. *Expedition* 4(2): 27.

Molloy, J. D., Rathje, W.
1974   Exploitation among the Late Classic Maya. In *Mesoamerican archaeology*, ed. N. Hammond, pp. 431–44. Austin: Univ. of Texas Press.

Morley, S. G.
1937–1938   The inscriptions of the Peten. *Carnegie Institution of Washington*, pub. 437.

Morris, C.
n.d.   Archaeology and ethnohistory: reconstruction patterns of craft production in the Inca economy. Manuscript.

Moser, C. L.

1973　Human decapitation in ancient Mesoamerica. *Studies in Pre-Columbian Art and Archaeology*, no. 11. Washington, D.C.: Dumbarton Oaks.

Mountjoy, J.

n.d.　The collapse of the Classic at Cholula, as seen from Cerro Zapotecas. Paper presented to the Society for American Archaeology, San Franciso, California, 1973.

Mountjoy, J., Peterson, D.

1973　Man and land at prehispanic Cholula. *Vanderbilt University, Publications in Anthropology* 4.

Muller, F.

1970　Ceramics. *Artes de Mexico*, yr. 17, no. 134: 98–101.

1973　El origen de los barrios de Cholula. *Instituto Nacional de Antropologia e Historia, Boletin* 2(5): 35–42.

Nadel, S. F.

1942　*A black Byzantium.* London: Oxford University Press.

Nicholson, H. B.

1971　Religion in pre-hispanic Central Mexico. In *Handbook of Middle American Indians,* ed. R. Wauchope, vol. 11, pp. 395–446. Austin: Univ. of Texas Press.

Nicholson, H. B., Berger, R.

1968　Two Aztec wood idols: iconographic and chronologic analysis. *Studies in Pre-Columbian Art and Archaeology,* no. 5. Washington, D.C.: Dumbarton Oaks.

Noguera, E.

1930　*Ruinas arqueologicas del norte de Mexico.* Mexico: Secretaria de Educacion Publica.

1944　Exploraciones in Jiquilpan. *Museo Michoacana, Anales* 3: 37–52.

Norman, V. G.

1973　Izapa sculpture, part 1: album. Brigham Young University, *New World Archaeological Foundation, Papers* 30.

Oliver, J. P.

1955　Architectural similarities of Mitla and Yagul. *Mesoamerican Notes* 4: 49–67.

Paddock, J.

1955　The first three seasons at Yagul. *Mesoamerican Notes* 4: 25–47.

1966a, ed.　*Ancient Oaxaca.* Stanford: Stanford Univ. Press.

1966b　Mixtec ethnohistory and Monte Alban V. Ibid., pp. 267–385.

1966c　Oaxaca in ancient Mesoamerica. Ibid., pp. 83–241.

1967　Oaxaca. *American Antiquity* 32(3): 426–27.

1968　Western Mesoamerica. *American Antiquity* 33(1): 122–28.

1970a　A beginning in the Nuine: salvage excavations at Nuyoo, Huajuapan. Mexico City College, *Boletin de Estudios Oaxaquenos* 26: 2–12.

1970b　More Nuine materials. Mexico City College, *Boletin de Estudios Oaxaquenos* 28: 2–12.

1972a　Distribucion de rasgos teotihuacanos en Mesoamerica. Sociedad Mexicana de Antropologia, *XI Mesa Redonda,* vol. 2, pp. 223–39.

1972b　El ocaso del Clasico. Sociedad Mexicana de Antropologia, *XI Mesa Redonda,* vol. 2, pp. 141–47.

1973　Review of volumes 10 and 11, *Handbook of Middle American Indians. American Anthropologist* 75: 1131–36.

n.d.a　Oaxaca after Monte Alban. Paper presented to the Society for American Archaeology, Milwaukee, Wisconsin, 1969.

n.d.b　Pristine urbanism in Mesoamerica. Paper presented to the Society for American Archaeology, San Francisco, California, 1973.

n.d.c　Mesoamerica no es el Valle de Mexico. Paper presented to the 41st International Congress of Americanists, Mexico City, Mexico, 1974.

in press[a]　The abandonment of Monte Alban. Essay contributed to a seminar at the School of American Research, ed., K. V. Flannery.

in press[b]　The 'Oaxaca barrio' at Teotihuacan. Essay contributed to a seminar at the School of American Research, ed., K. V. Flannery.

in press[c]　The rise of Lambityeco. Essay contributed to a seminar at the School of American Research, ed., K. V. Flannery.

Parsons, J. R.

1971　Prehistoric settlement patterns in the Texcoco region, Mexico. *University of Michigan, Museum of Anthropology, Memoirs* 3.

Parsons, L. A.

1967a　An early Maya stela on the Pacific Coast of Guatemala. *Estudios de Cultura Maya* 6: 171–98.

1967b　Bilbao, Guatemala: an archaeological study of the Pacific coast Cotzumalhuapa region. Milwaukee Public Museum, *Publications in Anthropology* 11.

1969　Bilbao, Guatemala: an archaeological study of the Pacific coast Cotzumalhuapa region. Milwaukee Public Museum, *Publications in Anthropology* 12.

1973   Iconographic notes on a new Izapan stela from Abaj Takalik, Guatemala. *40th International Congress of Americanists, Rome, 1972*, vol. 1, pp. 203–12.

n.d.   The Middle American co-tradition. Ph.D. dissertation, Harvard University, Department of Anthropology. 1964.

in preparation   Stylistic analysis of monumental stone sculpture: Chiapas-Guatemalan highlands and Pacific coast, with special reference to Kaminaljuyu.

Parsons, L. A., Price, B. J.
1971   Mesoamerican trade and its role in the emergence of civilization. *University of California, Archaeological Research Facility, Contributions* 11: 169–95.

Pasztory, E.
1972   The historical and religious significance of the Middle Classic ball game. Sociedad Mexicana de Antropologia, *XII Mesa Redonda*, pp. 441–55.

1973   The gods of Teotihuacan: a synthetic approach in Teotihuacan iconography. *40th International Congress of Americanists, Rome, 1972*, vol. 1, pp. 147–59.

1974   The iconography of the Teotihuacan Tlaloc. *Studies in Pre-Columbian Art and Archaeology* no. 15. Washington, D.C.: Dumbarton Oaks.

1976   The Xochicalco stelae and a Middle Classic deity triad in Mesoamerica. *XXIII International Congress of the History of Art*, Granada, 1973, vol. 1, pp. 185–15.

n.d.   The murals of Tepantitla, Teotihuacan. Ph.D. dissertation, Columbia University, Department of Art History and Archaeology, 1972.

Peterson, F.
1962   *Ancient Mexico*. New York: Capricorn Books. 2d. ed.

Pendergast, D. M.
1969   The prehistory of Actun Balam, British Honduras. *Royal Ontario Museum, Occasional Papers* 16.

1971   Evidence of early Teotihuacan-lowland Maya contact at Altun Ha. *American Antiquity* 36: 455–59.

Pina Chan, R.
1962   Informe preliminar sobre Mul Chic, Yucatan. *Instituto Nacional de Antropologia e Historia, Anales* 15(4): 99–118.

Polanyi, K., Arensberg, C. M., Pearson, H. W.
1957   *Trade and market in early empires*. Glencoe, Ill.: Free Press.

Pollock, H.
1936   Round structures of aboriginal Middle America. *Carnegie Institution of Washington* pub. 471.

1965   Architecture of the Maya Lowlands. In *Handbook of Middle American Indians*, ed. R. Wauchope, vol. 2, pp. 378–440. Austin: Univ. of Texas Press.

1970   Architectural notes on some Chenes ruins. *Harvard University, Peabody Museum, Papers* 61: 1–87.

Proskouriakoff, T.
1950   A study of Classic Maya sculpture. *Carnegie Institution of Washington*, pub. 593.

1954   Varieties of Classic central Veracruz sculpture. *Carnegie Institution of Washington*, pub. 606.

1961   Portraits of women in Maya art. In *Essays in pre-Columbian art and archaeology*, ed. S. K. Lothrop, pp. 81–99. Cambridge, Mass.: Harvard Univ. Press.

1963   *An album of Maya architecture*. Norman, Okla.: Univ. of Oklahoma Press.

1968   *Graphic designs on Mesoamerican pottery*. Washington, D.C.: Carnegie Institution of Washington.

Rabin, E.
1970   The Lambityeco friezes: notes on their content, with an appendix of carbon 14 dates. Mexico City College, *Boletin de Estudios Oaxaquenos* 33: 2–16.

Rathje, W. L.
1971   The origin and development of the lowland Classic Maya civilization. *American Antiquity* 36: 275–85.

Rattray, E.
n.d.   "Ceramic evidence on the collapse of the Classic at Teotihuacan." Paper presented to the Society of American Archaeology, San Francisco, California, 1973.

Reynolds, J. K.
n.d.   Residential architecture at Kaminaljuyu: a Formative and Classic center in highland Guatemala. M.A. thesis, Pennsylvania State University, Department of Anthropology, 1971.

Rikards, C. G.
1910   *The ruins of Mexico*. London: H. E. Shrimpton.

Riley, C. L.
1971, ed.   *Man across the sea*. Austin: Univ. of Texas Press.

Riley, C. L., Winters, H. D.
1963   The prehistoric Tepehuan of northern Mexico. *Southwestern Journal of Anthropology* 19(2): 177–85.

Robertson, D.
1963   *Pre-columbian architecture*. New York: Braziller.

1969   The international style of the Late Post-Classic. *38th Inter-*

national Congress of Americanists, Stuttgart, 1968, Proceedings, vol. 2, pp. 77–88.

Robicsek, F.
1972   Copan: home of the Mayan gods. New York: Museum of the American Indian.

Rovner, I.
n.d.   Lithics of Becan. Manuscript.

Roys, L., Shook, E. M.
1966   Preliminary report on the ruins of Ake, Yucatan. Society for American Archaeology, Memoir 20.

Ruppert, K.
1935   The Caracol at Chichen Itza, Yucatan, Mexico. Carnegie Institution of Washington, pub. 454.

1952, ed.   Chichen Itza, architectural notes and plans. Carnegie Institution of Washington, pub. 595.

n.d.   Iki, Yucatan. Manuscript. Cambridge: Harvard University, Peabody Museum, Archives Collection.

Ruppert, K., Denison, J. H., Jr.
1943   Archaeological reconnaissance in Campeche, Quintana Roo and Peten. Carnegie Institution of Washington, pub. 543.

Ruppert, K., Thompson, J. E. S., and Proskouriakoff, T.
1955   Bonampak, Chiapas, Mexico. Carnegie Institution of Washington, pub. 602.

Ruz Lhuillier, A.
1958   El juego de pelota de Uxmal. Miscellanea Paul Rivet, vol. 2, pp. 635–67. Mexico: Universidad Nacional Autonoma de Mexico.

1965   Chichen Itza: official guide. Mexico: Instituto Nacional de Antropologia e Historia.

Saenz, C. A.
1964   Las estelas de Xochicalco. 35th International Congress of Americanists, Mexico City, 1962, Proceedings, vol. 2, pp. 69–86.

1972   Exploraciones y restauraciones en Uxmal, 1970–1971. Instituto Nacional de Antropologia e Historia, Boletin 2(2): 31–40.

Sahagun, B. de
1950–1971   General history of the things of New Spain, trans. A. J. O. Anderson and C. E. Dibble. School of American Research Monographs. 12 vols. Santa Fe: School of American Research and Univ. of Utah.

1956   Historia de las cosas de la Nueva Espana. Mexico.

Salazar, P.
1970   Gran plaza suroeste. In Proyecto Cholula, ed. I. Marquina,

pp. 71–88. Mexico: Instituto Nacional de Antropologia e Historia.

Sanders, W. T.
1965   The cultural ecology of the Teotihuacan valley. Mimeographed. University Park, Pa.: Pennsylvania State University.

Sanders, W. T., Michels, J. M.
1969   The Pennsylvania State University Kaminaljuyu project: 1968 season; part 1, excavation. Pennsylvania State University, Department of Anthropology, Occasional Papers in Anthropology 2.

Sanders, W. T., Price, B. J.
1968   Mesoamerica: the evolution of a civilization. New York: Random House.

Schele, L.
1974   Observations on the cross motif at Palenque. Primera Mesa Redonda de Palenque, ed. M. Greene, part I, pp. 41–62. Pebble Beach, Calif.: The Robert Louis Stevenson School.

Sejourne, L.
1956   Burning water: thought and religion in ancient Mexico, trans. I. Nicholson. New York: Vanguard.
1966a   El lenguaje de las formas in Teotihuacan. Mexico: L. Sejourne.
1966b   Arqueologia de Teotihuacan, la ceramica. Mexico: Fondo de Cultura Economica.
1966c   Arquitectura y pintura en Teotihuacan. Mexico: Siglo Veintiuno Editores.
1972   La muerte de los dioses en la religion nahuatl. Sociedad Mexicana de Antropologia, XI Mesa Redonda, vol. 2, pp. 117–24.

Seler, E.
1904   Wall paintings of Mitla. Smithsonian Institution, Bureau of American Ethnology, Bulletin 28: 243–324.
1960   Gesammelte Abhandlungen zur Amerikanischen Sprach- und Altertumskunde. 5 vols. Graz: Akademische Druck-V. Verlagsanstalt.
1963   Comentarios al Codice Borgia, trans. M. Frenk. Mexico: Fondo de Cultura Economica.

Sharp, R.
1970   Early architectural grecas in the Valley of Oaxaca. Mexico City College, Boletin de Estudios Oaxaquenos 32: 2–12.
n.d.   Greca: an exploratory study of relationships between art, society, and personality. Ph.D. dissertation, University of North Carolina at Chapel Hill, 1972.

Shook, E. M.

1940   Explorations in the ruins of Oxkintok, Yucatan. *Revista Mexicana de Estudios Antropologicos* 4: 165–71.

1950   *Yearbook, Carnegie Institution of Washington,* no. 49: 197–98.

1951   *Yearbook, Carnegie Institution of Washington,* no. 50: 240–41.

1965   Archaeological survey of the Pacific coast of Guatemala. In *Handbook of Middle American Indians,* ed. R. Wauchope, vol. 2, pp. 180–94. Austin: Univ. of Texas Press.

Shook, E. M., Kidder, A. V.

1952   Mound E-III-3, Kaminaljuyu, Guatemala. *Carnegie Institution of Washington,* pub. 596.

Smith, A. L., Willey, G. R.

1969   Seibal, Guatemala in 1968: a brief summary of archaeological results. *38th International Congress of Americanists, Stuttgart, 1968, Proceedings,* vol. 1, pp. 151–58.

Smith, M. E.

1973   *Picture writing from ancient southern Mexico: Mixtec place signs and maps.* Norman, Okla.: Univ. of Oklahoma Press.

Smith, R. E.

1944   Archaeological specimens from Guatemala. *Carnegie Institution of Washington, Notes on Middle American Archaeology and Ethnology,* vol. 2, no. 37: 35–47.

1955   Pottery specimens from Guatemala: II. *Carnegie Institution of Washington, Notes on Middle American Archaeology and Ethnology,* vol. 5, no. 124: 75–78.

1958   The place of fine orange pottery in Mesoamerican archaeology. *American Antiquity* 24: 151–60.

1971   The pottery of Mayapan. *Harvard University, Peabody Museum, Papers* 66(2).

Spinden, H. J.

1913   A study of Maya art: its subject matter and historical development. *Harvard University, Peabody Museum, Memoirs,* vol. 6.

Spores, R.

1972   An archaeological settlement survey of the Nochixtlan valley, Oaxaca. *Vanderbilt University, Publications in Anthropology* 1.

Stamps, R. B.

n.d.   Field notes of Kabah and Dzibilnoc. Manuscript.

Stephens, J. L.

1963   *Incidents of travel in Yucatan.* 2 vols. New York: Dover.

Stierlin, H.

1964   *Living architecture: Mayan.* Fribourg: Office du Livre.

1968   *Living architecture: ancient Mexican.* Fribourg: Office du Livre.

Stirling, M. W.

1943   Stone monuments of southern Mexico. *Smithsonian Institution, Bureau of American Ethnology, Bulletin* 138.

Stone, D.

1972   *Pre-Columbian man finds Central America.* Cambridge, Mass.: Peabody Museum Press.

Stone, D., Balser, C.

1965   Incised slate disks from the Atlantic watershed of Costa Rica. *American Antiquity* 30(3): 310–29.

Termer, F.

1964   Antiguedades de 'La Violeta,' Tapachula, Chiapas. *Estudios de Cultura Maya* 4: 79–98.

Thompson, J. E. S.

1937   A new method of deciphering Yucatecan dates with special reference to Chichen Itza. *Carnegie Institution of Washington,* pub. 483.

1941   A co-ordination of the history of Chichen Itza with ceramic sequences in Central Mexico. *Revista Mexicana de Estudios Antropologicos* 5: 97–111.

1948   An archaeological reconnaissance in the Cotzumalhuapa region, Escuintla, Guatemala. *Carnegie Institution of Washington,* pub. 574.

1960   *Maya hieroglyphic writing.* 2d ed. Norman, Okla.: Univ. of Okalahoma Press.

1970a   *A catalog of Maya hieroglyphs.* Norman, Okla.: Univ. of Oklahoma Press.

1970b   *Maya history and religion.* Norman, Okla.: Univ. of Oklahoma Press.

Thompson, J. E. S., Pollock, H. E. D., and Charlot, J.

1932   A preliminary study of the ruins of Coba, Quintana Roo, Mexico. *Carnegie Institution of Washington,* pub. 424.

Thompson, J. E. S., Ruppert, K., and Proskouriakoff, T.

1955   Bonampak, Chiapas, Mexico. *Carnegie Institution of Washington,* pub. 602.

Tolstoy, P.

1974   Mesoamerica. In *Prehispanic America,* ed. S. Gorenstein, pp. 29–64. New York: St. Martin's.

Torquemada, J.

1943   *Monarquia Indiana.* 3d ed. 4 vols. Mexico: S. Chavez Hayhoe.

Tozzer, A.

1941, trans.   Landa's *Relacion de las cosas de Yucatan. Harvard University, Peabody Museum, Papers* 18.

1957   Chichen Itza and its Cenote of Sacrifice: a comparative study of contemporaneous Maya and Toltec. *Harvard University, Peabody Museum, Memoirs,* vols. 11, 12.

Tuggle, D. H.
1968   The columns of El Tajin, Veracruz, Mexico. *Ethnos* 33: 40–70.

Vaillant, G. C.
1941   *Aztecs of Mexico.* Garden City, N.Y.: Doubleday, Doran & Co.
1952   Excavations at Station No. 13. In *Chichen Itza: architectural notes and plans,* ed. K. Ruppert, pp. 157–62. *Carnegie Institution of Washington,* pub. 595.

Villacorta, C. J. A., Villacorta, C. A.
1927   *Arqueologia guatemalteca.* Guatemala: Tipografia Nacional.

Villagra, A.
1952   Trabajos realizados en Teotihuacan. *Instituto Nacional de Antropologia e Historia, Anales* 6(34): 69–78.

Vivo, J. A.
1946, ed.   *Mexico prehispanico: culturas, deidades, monumentos.* Mexico.

Vogt, E. Z.
1964   The genetic model and Maya cultural development. In *Desarrollo cultural de los Mayas,* eds. E. Z. Vogt, and A. Ruz, pp. 9–48. Mexico: Universidad Autonoma de Mexico.

Wallrath, M.
1967   Excavations in the Tehuantepec region, Mexico. *American Philosophical Society, Transactions,* new series 57: 2.

Wauchope, R.
1964–1976, ed.   *Handbook of Middle American Indians.* 16 vols. Austin: Univ. of Texas Press.

Weaver, M. P.
1972   *The Aztecs, Maya, and their predecessors.* New York: Seminar Press.

Webb, M. C.
1973   The Peten Maya decline and state formation. In *The Classic Maya collapse,* ed. T. P. Culbert, pp. 370–404. Albuquerque: Univ. of New Mexico Press.
n.d.   The significance of the 'Epi-Classic' period in Mesoamerican culture history. Paper presented to the International Congress of Anthropological and Ethnological Sciences, Chicago, Illinois, 1973.

Weigand, P. C.
1968   The mines and mining techniques of the Chalchihuites culture. *American Antiquity* 33(1): 45–61.

Westheim, P.
1965   *The art of ancient Mexico.* Garden City, N.Y.: Doubleday.

Wicke, C. R.
1957   The ball court at Yagul, Oaxaca: a comparative study. *Mesoamerican Notes* 5: 37–74.
1966   Tomb 30 at Yagul and the Zaachila tombs. In *Ancient Oaxaca,* ed. J. Paddock, pp. 336–44. Stanford: Stanford Univ. Press.

Willey, G. R.
1966   *An introduction to American archaeology.* Englewood Cliffs, N.J.: Prentice-Hall.
1974   The Classic Maya hiatus: a rehearsal for the collapse? In *Mesoamerican Archaeology,* ed. N. Hammond, pp. 417–30. Austin: Univ. of Texas Press.

Winning, H. von
1946   The treble scroll in the Teotihuacan and Zapotec Cultures. *Carnegie Institution of Washington. Notes on Middle American Archaeology and Ethnology,* vol. 3, no. 72: 82–89.
1948   The Teotihuacan owl-and-weapon symbol and its association with 'serpent head X' at Kaminaljuyu. *American Antiquity* 14(2): 129–32.
1961   Teotihuacan symbols: the reptile's eye glyph. *Ethnos* 26: 121–66.
1965a   Dual pottery molds from Mexico. *Masterkey* 39(2): 60–65.
1965b   Relief decorated pottery from central Veracruz, Mexico. *Ethnos* 30: 105–35.
1969   *Pre-Columbian art of Mexico and Central America.* New York: Abrams.
1971   Rituals depicted on Veracruz Pottery. In *Ancient art of Veracruz,* pp. 31–36. Ethnic Arts Council of Los Angeles.

Winter, M.
n.d.   Dos fechas de carbono 14 del Periodo I de Monte Alban. Manuscript.

Wolfe, A. W.
1969   Social structural bases of art. *Current Anthropology* 10: 3–44.

Woodbury, R. B., Trik, A. S.
1953   *The ruins of Zaculeu, Guatemala.* 2 vols. Richmond, Va.: William Byrd Press.

Woodward, A.
1941   Hohokam mosaic mirrors. *Quarterly, Museum Patron's Association of Los Angeles* 1(4): 6–11.

Xirau, R.
1973   *Arte prehispanico de Mexico.* Mexico: Ediciones Galeria de Arte Mesrachi.

index

Abbott, E., 146, 155
Accession theme, 136
Acosta, J., 46, 48, 50, 57n8, 59, 60, 112, 141n5, 159–61, 172, 176
Acropolis, 32, 59
Agricultural fertility cult, 130–33, 138
Ake, 13, 96
Alta Vista, 14, 19, 145–56
Altun Ha, 10, 68
Amatitlan, Lake, 39, 72, 76
American Southwest, Mesoamerican influences on, 19
Anales de Cuauhtitlan, 173, 176
Ancestor cults, 42
Andrews, E. W., IV, 5, 13, 21n7, 68, 69, 93, 107n9, 111, 163, 166–68, 170n1, 171n4
Andrews, E. W., V, 28, 31, 32, 93, 101, 104
Andrews, G., 110
Antigua basin, 30
Anton, F., 76, 84n3
Architectural settings, 127
Architecture: decoration (ornament), 111–12; as interelite communication, 158–70; Middle Classic traditions, 108–12, Middle Classic trait list, 32; Palenque, 17; seventh-century, 20–21; Teotihuacan, 9; *see also Greca* horizon and tradition; *Talud-tablero* profiles; *specific architectural features, structures, and traditions*
Architecture, Chichen Itza, *see* Chichen Itza, architectural styles
Architecture, Yucatan, *see* Yucatan, architectural styles
Armillas, P., 41, 172
Artes de Mexico, 75, 84n3
Atetelco, 133, 141
Atzompa, 162, 164, 168, 169
Aveleyra Arroyo de Anda, L., 69
Azcapotzalco, 15
Aztec: Alta Vista Tezcatlipoca sacrifice and, 148, 150, 151, 156; as Kaminaljuyu analogue, 40–42; Pochteca, 41–43

Backgrounds (settings), 127, 129
Badner, M., 28

Balakanche cave, 68, 159
Ball, J. W., 10, 11
Ball court markers, 90, 91; Copan, 76, 87–88, 139; La Ventilla, 69
Ball courts, 20, 32; in Caribbean, 19; in far north, 19; as Middle Classic tradition, 109–10; Monte Alban, 59; in Peripheral Coastal Lowlands, 29; Yucatan, 89–92; *see also* Chichen Itza
Ball game, 11, 12, 14, 17
Ball game cult, 18, 20; directional symbolism, 139; iconography, 130, 131, 137–39; limited to Middle Classic period, 90; trade and, 87, 90; waning of, in Yucatan, 101
Ball game objects, 19, 20, 22n9; La Ventilla, 69; in Peripheral Coastal Lowlands, 29, 30; *see also Hachas*; Yoke-*hacha* complex; Yokes
Ball game rituals or scenes, 30, 33, 60, 69
Ballplayers: Dainzu and El Baul, 52–53, 60; Escuintla (Tiquisate) cylindrical tripods, 76–79; poses, 76, 77, 127, 139; Yucatan, 87–92
Balls, 67, 93; stone, large spheroid, 33, 59
Balser, C., 11, 19, 33

Barbour, Warren, 69n
Batres, L., 59
Battle scenes, Yucatan, 101
Bebrich, C. A., 36
Becan, 10, 11, 67, 68
Belts: Escuintla tripod vessels, 77, 81–84; Oaxaca glyph-belts, 84
Berger, R., 153
Berlin, H., 36
Bernal, I., 45–50, 52, 53, 55, 56, 57n8, 59, 60, 76, 135, 146, 159, 161
Bilbao, 7, 8, 18, 31; backgrounds (settings), use of, 127, 129; ball game iconography, 138, 139; ballplayers, 87; decapitation scenes, 79; Middle Classic trait list, 32, 33; profile and frontal representations, 117; sculpture, 122, 125; serpent heads, 77; Teotihuacan influence, 12
Bird images, 133
Blanton, Richard E., 57n13
Bleeding-heart motif, 81
Blom, F., 29, 95
Body outlining, 33, 121–22
Bolles, J., 90, 99, 100, 104, 105
Bonampak, 125; mural, 63–65; step-fret and greca tradition, 159, 169–70
Boos, F. H., 60, 62, 76, 135
Borhegyi, S. F., 9–12, 36, 39, 42, 72, 77, 130, 142n16
Brainerd, G. W., 18, 90, 93, 96, 98, 99, 101, 107n8, 159
Braniff, B., 146
Brockington, D. L., 54, 57n5, 76, 84
Broman, Vivian, 36
Brotherston, G., 134
Brown, K., 36, 110
Burial cult: Alta Vista (Chalchihuites), 145–56; iconography, 130, 131, 137
Burland, C. A., 155
Butterfly deities, 73, 74
Butterfly wing motif, 79, 81

Cacao, 11, 34; ball game cult and, 87, 138; Escuintla region incense burners, 73; Monte Alban, 61
Cacaotepec, 61
Calendrical coding, 167
Cancuen altar, 88
Caribbean, 19
Cartouche, circular, 62, 83
Carved piers and columns, 112

Caso, A., 29, 45–50, 53, 55, 57n8, 59–62, 76, 135, 151, 153, 159, 161, 163
Catemaco, Lake, 29
Causeways (sacbe), 111; Coba, 18; La Quemada, 19
Censers, see Incense burners (incensarios)
Central America, 19
Cerro de las Mesas, 12, 31, 114, 115
Cerro Zapotecas, 16, 21n6
Chadwick, R., 19, 56, 156
Chalchihuites: Teotihuacan and, 10, 14, 145–46; see also Alta Vista
Chan Bahlum, Lord, 17
Chapman, A. H., 29, 41
Chavin culture, 28
Cheek, C., 36, 38, 43
Chiapas, 76
Chichen Itza: ball game scenes, 77, 79, 138; Castillo, 104, 105, 110; ceramic styles, 98–99; conquest of, 97–98; decapitation scenes, 79; Great Ball Court, 89–91, 99, 139; greca tradition, 162, 163, 165, 167–69; Iglesia, 102, 103; Monjas Ball Court, 90, 100; Monjas Complex, 99–101, 104, 106; plan of site, 96; Red House, 102, 103; Red House ball court, 89, 90; star-belts, 84; Upper Temple of the Jaguars, 101–03
    architectural styles: Chichen Maya and Chichen Toltec, 97–101; early Puuc style, 101–06; Puuc style, 18; radial design, 110; terminal Middle Classic period, 101–06; Toltec, 7, 18, 86–87, 97–101
Chilam Balam, 98
Chinkultik, 87; ball court marker, 76
Cholula, 109, 110, 151; chronology, 16
Cipactli, 153
Classic period, 5–8
Coastal lowlands, see Peripheral Coastal Lowlands
Coba, 18, 91, 93
Codex Borgia, 149, 153
Codz Poop (Kabah), 101–02, 104
Coe, M. D., 10, 11, 26, 29, 32, 46, 114, 137, 146
Coe, W., 16, 21n3, 65, 67, 68, 111, 141n2
Coggins, C., 10, 17, 117, 136, 142nn12, 17
Cohen, A., 42
Cohodas, M., 18, 87, 99–101, 139
Consejos de Recursos Naturales no Renovables, 146
Consulting, gesticulating figures with attendants, 30, 33, 61

Copan, 31; ball court markers, 76, 87–88, 139; ballplayer representations, 87–88; body outlining, 121; history, 17–18; sculpture, 122, 123, 125
Copas (goblets), Alta Vista, 146, 149–53, 155
Corbel vaults, 111
Cornices, flaring, 16, 19, 109
Corona Nunez, J., 146, 151
Correlation dates, 5
Costa Rica, 11, 19, 32–33
Cotzumalhuapa, 7, 17, 81, 83, 87; narrative style, 30; Peripheral Coastal Lowlands and, 28, 30, 31; trait list, 30–34; yoke, 77
Covarrubias, M., 46, 50, 56n3, 134, 153
Coyotlatelco ceramics, 173, 176
Crespo, A. M., 173, 176
Cross, Temple of the (Palenque), 137
Curls, "6"-shaped ("flames"), 79, 81
Curvilinear shapes, 114, 119–20
Cylindrical tripods, Escuintla region, 73, 76–84

Dainzu, 52–53, 59
Death, as theme, 30, 33, 60; see also Burial cult
Decapitation scenes, 76, 79–81
Deformed figures, 133
Deities: equation of rulers and, 125; Middle Classic, 34; patron, cult of, 131; systematization of features of, 134–35; see also specific deities
De la Fuente, B., 104, 137
Denison, J. H., Jr., 88
Diehl, R. A., 173
DiPeso, C. C., 148, 153
Directional symbolism, 139, 141
Diving god, 30, 33
Dockstader, F. J., 84n3
Dumond, D. E., 16
Duran, D.; 148, 149, 153, 155
Durango, 13–14
Dynastic ruler cult, iconography of, 21, 130, 131, 135–37
Dzahui, 61–62
Dzibilchaltun, 13, 93, 104–05

Eagle and jaguar complex, 30, 33
Eagle knights, 133
Earth goddess, 132
Easby, E., 59, 60, 62
Eclecticism, 8, 21
Ehecatl-Quetzalcoatl, 34, 62

Ekholm, G., 11, 19
El Baul, 31–34, 52–53
El Chayal, 39
El Salvador, 31, 33
El Tajin, *see* Tajin, El
Escuintla region, 71; eclecticism, 18; incense
    burners, 72–76; map of, 72
        cylindrical tripod vessels, 76–84; ball-
        players, 76–79; decapitation scenes, 76,
        79–81; second star-belt scene, 83–84;
        star-belt personage and Tlaloc scene,
        81–83
Espinoza, Gustavo, 36
Etzna, 88–89, 110

Feet, in Escuintla region art, 76, 81, 83
Feldman, L., 40
Ferdon, E. N., Jr., 31–33
Fertility cult, agricultural, 130–33, 138
Finca Rio Seco, 72
Fine Orange pottery, 19, 21n5, 31
Fischer, J. L., 168
Flannery, Kent, 56, 59n, 141n5
Flutes, Tezcatlipoca sacrifice and, 149, 150, 153
Folan, W. J., 90
Foncerrada de Molina, M., 18, 90, 93–95, 110, 112,
    122
Fondo Editorial de la Plastica Mexicana, 84
Framed rings, 34
Frames, raised rectangular, 34, 61
Frets, stepped, 34, 61; *greca* tradition and, 159–67
Frontal poses, 116–19, 121, 125
Funeral imagery, Maya, 137

Gamio, M., 146, 149, 151, 153
Garcia Payon, J., 18, 30, 167
Gendrop, P., 83, 101, 159
Gillmor, F., 148
Girard, R., 30
Gold, 19
Goncalves de Lima, O., 149
Gordon, G. B., 159
Graham, J., 88, 160
Greca horizon and tradition, 158–70; calendrical
    coding, 167–68; characteristics of, 158; origins
    of, 158–59; serpent stairways, 166–67; step-frets,
    159–67; technological aspects, 158, 160–61
Greene, M., 88, 136, 142n13, 160

Guerrero, 28
Guiengola, 59

Hachas: Tehuantepec Isthmus, 54; *see also*
    Yoke-*hacha* complex
Hall, C. S., 68
Harrison, Peter D., 66n
Hartung, H., 59, 109, 161
Hatch, M. P., 142n20
Hausa, 40, 42
Headdress: Escuintla, 79; rulers', 125
Head glyphs, Escuintla, 81
Heads, *see* Stone heads; Trophy head cult
Heart: bleeding, 81; sacrifice of, 133
Hellmuth, N. M., 18, 73, 74, 76, 107n3
Heyden, D., 68
Hierarchic compositions, 117, 120, 121, 127, 129
Hohokam area, 19
Holmes, W. H., 159, 170n1
Holmul site, 76
Honduras, 19
Huanuco, 41
Huasteca, 110
Huayuapan, 13
Huehueteotl, 34, 62
Huitzilopochtli, 134
Human figures, representations of, 120, 125, 127,
    129

Ichmul ballplayers, 89
Iconography, 130–41
Incense burners (*incensarios*): Escuintla region (Ti-
    quisate), 72–76; Kaminaljuyu, 39; Lake Amati-
    tlan, 76; Teotihuacan IV, 30
Infant images, 137
Innovation, 8
Inscriptions, Temple of the (Palenque), 137
Itza, 98; *see also* Chichen Itza
Izapa, 28, 32, 53, 114; volutes, 79, 81

Jaguar knights, 133
Jaguars, prowling, 33, 61
Jaina ballplayers, 87
Jennings, J. D., 9, 30, 32, 33, 36, 65, 75, 76
Jimenez Moreno, W., 12, 57n2, 97, 98, 173
Johnson, F., 46

Kabah, Codz Poop, 101–02, 104
Kaminaljuyu, 75; Aztec analogue, 40–42; chronol-
    ogy, 43; conquest by Teotihuacan, 40–41;
    ethnographic-structural models of Teotihuacan,
    impact on, 35–44; household artifacts, 37;
    household technology, 40; incense burners, 39;
    Late Preclassic period, 28; marriage with
    Teotihuacans, 40, 42, 43; merchants in, 42–44;
    Middle Classic trait list, 32, 33; as missionizing
    colony, 40; nucleation of population, 39, 44;
    obsidian artifacts, manufacture of, 39; Palan-
    gana site, 38; plan of, 37; plaza complexes,
    37–38; political integration, 43; religion, 42–43;
    residential architecture, 37; sculpture, 30;
    Teotihuacan influence, 9, 10, 43; Teotihuacan
    residents, 40–42; Terminal Formative period,
    36–39; tomb offerings, 36, 38–39; trade, 41–44
Kampen, M., 77, 79, 138, 139, 160, 167
Kelley, Ellen A., 149, 155, 156n1
Kelley, J. Charles, 13, 14, 19, 145–47, 149, 151, 153,
    155, 156n1
Kidder, A. V., 9, 30, 32, 33, 36, 65, 71, 75, 76
Kirchoff, P., 173
Kirsch, R. W., 36
Kneeling postures, 127
Kolb, C. C., 68
Kowalewski, S., 62
Krotser, G. R., 166
Krotser, P. H., 166
Kubler, G., 7, 17, 65–66, 74, 85n9, 93, 99, 111, 120,
    132, 133, 136, 166, 170
Kukulcan, 97–98
Kurath, G. P., 151, 155

La Amelia ballplayers, 88
Labna, 18; ballplayers, 89; *greca* tradition, 162,
    163; Puuc-style architecture, 94–95
La Farge, O., 29, 95
Lake Amatitlan, *see* Amatitlan, Lake
Lambityeco, 7, 13, 19–21; *greca* tradition, 161–63,
    165, 166, 168–70; period IV remains, 49, 50
La Quemada, 19
La Ventilla ball game marker, 69
Lee, T. A., Jr., 29, 32
Leigh, H., 54, 60
Libby, W. F., 47
Lifschitz, Edward, 90n
Linne, S., 68, 161

Loma San Gabriel culture, 146
Long, J. R., 57n5
Los Tuxtlas region, 29
Lothrop, S. K., 19, 32, 101
Lowe, G. W., 29, 32
Lubaantun ballplayers, 87, 88
Lumholtz, C., 151

McBride, Harold, 75n, 76
MacNeish, R. S., 46, 56
Magician, Temple of the (Uxmal), 18
Magician Pyramid (Uxmal), 94, 95, 100, 110, 112
Maler, T., 136
Maritzer, L. S., 146
Marquina, I., 13, 18, 19, 32–34, 59, 95, 104, 105, 110, 112, 116, 141n9, 166, 167
Marti, S., 149, 151, 155
Martial cult: Yucatan, 101; see also Warrior cult iconography
Masks, 33
Mastache, G., 173, 176
Mata, Guillermo, 71
Matacanela, 29
Matacapan, 11, 29
Mathews, 17
Matos, 16
Maya, 3, 75, 77; ballplayers, 87–88; chronology, 5–8; correlation dates, 5; decline and collapse, 15, 16; lowlands, 28; Peripheral Coastal Lowlands and, 28–30; pottery, 19; sculpture, 122–25; step-frets, 159–60
        art style, 112, 114; profile and frontal postures, 116–17, 125; ruler-god equation, 125
        iconography, 130, 131, 134; accession theme, 135–36; dynastic ruler cult, 135–37; funeral imagery, 137
        Teotihuacan and, 10; artistic contact, 63–70; writing system, 120; see also Peten Maya; specific Maya sites
Mazapa ceramics, 176
Medellin Zenil, A., 56n3
Meigs, C. C., 170n1
Melgarejo, 29
Mesoamerica: chronology of, 5–8; definition of, 3; map of, 4
Michels, Joseph, 36
Michoacan region, 19

Middle Classic period, xi; chronology, 7; Parsons on, 25; trait list, 32–34
Miles, Susan, 36
Miller, A. G., 17, 67–69, 132, 133, 136, 159–61
Millon, C., 73, 134
Millon, R. F., 9, 13, 15, 43, 46, 48, 68, 83, 159, 161
Mirador Temple (Labna), 89, 94
Miraflores, 28
Mirrors, slate-backed pyrite, 29, 30, 32–33
Mitla, greca tradition, 159, 162, 163, 166, 168, 169
Mixteca Alta, 55
Moholy-Nagy, H., 65
Mold-made figurines, 33, 59
Molloy, J. D., 16, 17
Monte Alban, 19, 20, 28, 72; abandonment of, 47–49, 56–57n4; art style, 114; chronology, 7; greca tradition and step-frets, 159–69; head glyphs, 81; Lambityeco and, 49, 50, 56–57n4; Middle Classic period, 45–56, trait list, 51–53, 58–62; Mixtec region and, 55–56; Postclassic or Late Urban period, 56; Teotihuacan influence, 13; Teotihuacan periods and, 45–48; urns, 76, 114, 115
Monument plazas, 32, 59
Monuments, directional symbolism of, 139, 141
Morelos, 28
Morley, S. G., 67, 88, 117
Morris, C., 41
Mosaic, stone, 18–20, 111–12
Moser, C. L., 54, 60
Mountjoy, J., 16, 21n6
Mul Chic, 101
Muller, F., 16, 156
Mural paintings, Maya and Teotihuacan, 63–65, 68–69

Nadel, S. F., 40
Nanautzin, 133
Naranjo, 121, 125
Narrative style or composition, 33, 127; Cotzumalhuapa, 30; Monte Alban, 60
Naturalistic representations, 114, 119, 129
Nicholson, H. B., 151, 153, 155
Noguera, E., 151, 153
Nose-beads, 76
Nose plaques, talud-tablero, 74
Noses, Izapan and Veracruz, 28
Nuine, 7, 19, 53–55

Oaxaca, 16, 76; barrio at Teotihuacan, 42, 46–47; glyph-belts, 84; greca tradition and step-frets, 159–69; iconography, 130, 131, 134–35, 137; Teotihuacan and, 10, 12–13, 15; see also Monte Alban and other specific sites
Oliver, J. P., 59
Ollas, Alta Vista, 146, 151
Ollin symbol, 33, 61
Olmec culture, 26, 28
Ornament, architectural, 111–12
Outlining, body, 33, 121–22
Oxkintok, 96
Oztuma, 41

Pacal, Lord, 17
Pachuca, 16
Paddock, John, 19, 21n3, 45, 46, 53–55, 57n4, 58n14, 60, 61, 114, 141n5, 159, 161
Padre Piedra, 28
Palangana, 38
Palenque, 104; architecture, 17, 111; backgrounds, use of, 129; body outlining, 121–22; directional symbolism, 139; funeral imagery, 137; hierarchic-narrative composition, 127; history, 17
Palmas, stone, 29–31
Parsons, L. A., 5, 7, 11–13, 17, 18, 21, 25, 26, 28–34, 45–47, 50–53, 57n12, 58, 71, 77, 79, 97, 110, 121, 125, 129, 138
Pasztory, Esther, 42, 55, 73, 75n, 87, 90, 132, 138, 139
Patron deities, cult of, 131, 134
Pendergast, D. M., 10, 46, 68
Peripheral Coastal Lowlands, 25–34, 54; art style, traditions, 114; art style, frontal representations, 117; ball game cult, 137–39; environmental cohesiveness, 26; geographical definition, 25–26; Late Classic period, 31–32; Late Preclassic period, 28; map of, 27; Middle Preclassic period, 26, 28; natural resources, 26; as proto-Maya, 28; seventh-century A.D. dominance, 20; Teotihuacan influence, 11–14, 29, 30; Terminal Preclassic period, 28
        Middle Classic period, 29–34; south-to-north diffusion, 30, 31; trait list, 32–34
Peten Maya, 18, 75, 77, 84; decline, 16; Teotihuacan influence, 10–11, 29; Yucatan and, 13

Peterson, D., 21n6, 56, 151, 156
Phallic cult or themes, 30, 33
Piedra Labrada, 29
Piedras Negras, 122, 127, 135, 136; history, 17–18
Piers, carved, 112
Pina Chan, R., 101
Pipil, 12
Pochteca, 41–43
Pollock, H., 93, 97, 110, 111
Popol Vuh, 138
Ports of trade, 29
Price, B. J., 9, 10, 26, 29, 87, 142n16
Profile postures, 116–19, 121, 125
Proskouriakoff, T., 28–30, 33, 67, 77, 88, 89, 106n2,
   107n8, 116, 122, 125, 136, 142n18, 160, 163, 166,
   167, 170
Puebla, 15
Puuc region, 18, 30, 101
Puuc style, 13
   architecture, 18; Chichen Itza, 18; Yucatan,
      92–95, 100–06
Pyramids, frontal platforms on, 32, 59

Quelepa, 31, 32
Queretaro, 11
Quetzalcoatl, 153, 155; conquest of Chichen Itza,
   97–98; Pyramid of (Teotihuacan), 160; *see also*
   Ehecatl-Quetzalcoatl
Quintana Roo, 68

Rabin, E., 20, 49, 57n4, 137, 161, 162
Radial design, 110
Rain deity, 83, 132; *see also* Dzahui; Tlaloc
Rands, R. L., 160
Rathje, W. L., 11, 16, 17
Rattlesnake tail, 33, 61
Rattray, Evelyn, 15, 47n, 176
Rebirth iconography, 137–39
Recessed panels, 109
Reclining figures, 127
Rectilinear forms, 114, 116, 119–20
Regional style, 92, 96–97, 100, 101, 105–06
Relief ornamentation, 112
Remojadas ceramic complex, 29, 30
Reptile Eye (RE) glyph, 29, 73–74
Reynolds, J. K., 36
Rickards, C. G., 59
Riley, C. L., 146

Ring-eyed personages, 73, 83
Rings, framed, 34, 61
Rio Blanco region, 84; ballplayer scenes, 77–79
Roads, Yucatan, 20, 111
Robertson, D., 69, 158
Robicsek, F., 17, 19
Round buildings, 110
Rovner, I., 68
Rubber, 11
Rubin de la Borbolla, D. F., 163
Ruppert, K., 88, 90, 99, 107n6, 110, 159, 166, 170
Ruz Lhuillier, A., 91, 167

Sacbe, see Causeways
Sacrifice, human, 30, 33; Monte Alban, 60; Tezcat-
   lipoca impersonator, 147–56
Saenz, C. A., 16, 94
Sahagun, B. de, 42, 87, 97, 148, 149, 153, 155, 176
Saignes Acosta, M. A., 41
Salazar, Enrique, 71, 161
Sanders, W. T., 5, 9, 10, 36, 37, 142n16
Santa Rosa Chiapas effigy vessel, 76
Sashes, large knotted, 33, 61
Sayil, 18
Schele, L., 17, 137
Schroeder site, 19
Scott, J. F., 59, 60, 62
Scrolls: Escuintla region, 77, 79; interlace design,
   116; speech, 34, 61; Veracruz-style, Classic, 16,
   19, 20, 28, 116
Secularism, 8
Seibal, 31, 88
Sejourne, L., 69, 75, 79, 81, 83, 84n3, 85n9, 148, 156,
   159, 161
Seler, E., 61, 84n3, 85n9, 153
Serpent head, 77
Serpents, 79
Serpent stairways, 166–67
Settings, 127, 129
Seven Dolls, Temple of (Dzibilchaltun), 104–05
Sharp, R., 18, 158, 163, 167, 170n1
Shook, E. M., 9, 29, 30, 32, 33, 36, 65, 71, 72, 75, 76,
   96
Skeletons and skulls in ball game iconography, 138
Smith, A. L., 31, 55, 56, 93, 98, 101
Smith, R., 71, 163
Spear bundles, 73
Spinden, H. J., 135, 162, 167

Spores, R., 55
Stairways: with balustrades, 32, 59; serpent,
   166–67
Stamps, R. B., 170n1
Star motif, 81–84
Stephens, J. L., 89
Stepped frets, *see* Frets, stepped
Stierlin, H., 160, 162, 166, 167, 169, 170n1
Stirling, M. W., 31, 32
Stone, D., 11, 19, 33
Stone balls, large spheroid, 33, 50
Stone heads, horizontally tenoned, 32, 59
Stone mosaic, 18–20, 111–12
Stormy Sky (Tikal ruler), 10, 17, 117
Strap bags, 74–75
Sun, Tezcatlipoca sacrifice and, 155
Sun deities: ball game cult and, 138; iconography,
   132–34, 138; warrior cult and, 133
Sun disk, 33, 138; Monte Alban, 61

Tajin, El, 7, 83; architecture, 18–19; art style, 127;
   ball game iconography, 138, 139; ballplayers, 87;
   calendrical coding, 167; Escuintla region ball
   court scenes, 77, 79; Great Ball Court, 138; *greca*
   tradition, 166–68; Middle Classic trait list, 32,
   33; Pyramid of the Niches, 110; sculpture, 29, 30
Talud-tablero profiles, 9, 13, 20, 32, 59, 74, 108, 109
Tancah Cenote cave, 68
Tehuacan valley, 56
Tehuantepec, Isthmus of, 54
Temple mounds, precinct-enclosing, 32, 59
Temple platforms, Kaminaljuyu, 36
Teopancaxco, 132
Teotihuacan, 17; A.D. 400–550, influence of, 9–15;
   abandonment of, 48; avenues, 111; calendrical
   coding, 167; ceramic complex, 33, 59–60;
   chronology for, 5–7; decline, 14–16, 19–20;
   Durango sites and, 13–14; in Escuintla region,
   Guatemala, 12, 71–85; Metepec phase (period
   IV), 15, 43, 45–46; Middle Classic trait list, 32–34;
   Monte Alban periods and, 45–48; mural paint-
   ing, 63–65, 68–69, 127; Oaxaca *barrio* at, 42,
   46–47; Peripheral Coastal Lowlands and, Middle
   Classic period, 29, 30; population reduction, 43;
   religion, 9–10, 42; *see also specific topics*
      architecture, 9; *talud* and *tablero*, 9, 13, 20,
      32, 59, 74, 108, 109

Teotihuacan (*Continued*)
  art style traditions, 112–21; hierarchic composition, 117, 119, 120, 121, 127; human and supernatural figures, 120; profile and frontal postures, 116–19, 125; rational characteristics, 119–20; rectilinear forms, 114, 116, 119–20; settings, 127; standardization of design motifs, 120
  ethnographic-structural models of impact on Kaminaljuyu, 35–44; archeological data, 36–39; outline of interaction models, 36; testing the model, 40–44
  iconography, 114, 130–39, 141; agricultural fertility cult, 130–33; patron deity cult, 131, 134; ritual, representations of, 134; solar disk, 138; systematization of deity features, 134–35; warrior cult, 133–34, 141
  trade (A.D. 400–550), 8–15; with Kaminaljuyu, 41–44 Zacatecas sites and, 13–14
Tepantitla, 69, 127
Tequixtepec del Rey, Nuine stone at, 53–54
Termer, F., 33
Tetitla murals, 64, 68–69, 141, 159
Tetlamixteca, 55, 59
Tezcatlipoca impersonator, sacrifice of, 147–56
Thompson, J. E. S., 71, 81, 91–93, 96, 97, 142*n*24, 159, 170
Tikal, 7; central acropolis, 66; cylindrical tripod, 83; Early Classic period, 10; profile and frontal representations, 116, 117, 125; resurgence after A.D. 700, 16–17; Teotihuacan influence, 10, 11, 16, 65; Teotihuacan-style building, 109, 110; warrior ruler iconography, 136
Tiquisate region, 71; cylindrical tripods, 73, 76–84; incense burners, 72–76
Tlaloc (rain deity), 73, 75; Balankanche cave, 68; Escuintla region cylindrical tripods, 81, 83; iconography, 132; Kaminaljuyu, 39, 42–43; Monte Alban, 61–62; patron deity cult, 134; Tikal, 65; Yaxha, 68
Tolstoy, P., 21*n*2
Toltec, 7; Chichen Itza structures, 13, 18; in Peripheral Coastal Lowlands, Late Classic period, 31; Tula chronology, 172, 173, 176
Toluquilla, 22*n*8
Tomb offerings, Kaminaljuyu, 36, 38–39
Tonala, 18, 31–33

Torquemada, J., 149
Toxcatl feast, sacrifice of Tezcatlipoca impersonator at, 148
Toys, animal-effigy clay, with wheels and axles, 33, 60
Tozzer, A., 71, 76, 77, 84, 88, 89, 97, 98, 101
Trade, 8; Aztec Pochteca, 41–42; ball game cult and, 87, 90; in late sixth and seventh centuries, 20–21; ports of, 29; Teotihuacan (A.D. 400–550), 8–15; Xochicalco, 16; Yucatan, 13
"Tree of life" motif, 30, 33, 60
Tres Zapotes, 28
Trik, A. S., 32
Trimountain symbol, Escuintla, 81
Tripod vessels, cylindrical, 73, 76–84
Trophy head cult, 30, 33, 60
Truell, M., 62
Tuggle, D. H., 30, 32, 33
Tula chronology, 16, 172–76
Tula Chico temple complex, 16
Tututepec, 55

Uaxactun, 10, 11
Ulua marbles, 19
Uxmal, 18, 122; ball courts, 89, 91, 93; ballplayers, 89–90; Great Pyramid, 101–02; *greca* tradition, 162, 163, 167, 168; Magician Pyramid, 94, 95, 100, 110, 112
Uxul ballplayers, 88

Vaillant, G. C., 56*n*1, 100
Vaults, corbel, 111
Veneer masonry, 93, 95, 111
Venus, 155; ball game cult and, 138
Veracruz, 7; art, 19, 75–77; body outline, 121–22; Cholula and, 16; *greca* tradition, 158, 161, 166, 168, 169; Peripheral Coastal Lowlands and, 28–31; scrolls, 16, 19, 20, 28, 116; Teotihuacan and, 10–12, 14; trade, 11; traits, Middle Classic period, 30–33; *see also specific sites*
Vessels: cylindrical tripod, 73, 76–84; effigy, Santa Rosa Chipas, 76
Villacorta, C. J. A., 30
Villagra, A., 11, 68
Vista Paint Cloisonné, 149–53
Vogt, E. Z., 28
Volador ceremony, 149, 151, 153

Volutes, Escuintla cylindrical tripods, 79
Von Winning, H., 29, 33, 73, 76, 77, 79, 83, 84*n*3, 133

Wallrath, M., 54
Warrior cult iconography, 130, 131, 133–34, 136–37, 141
Warrior deities, Escuintla cylindrical tripods, 83
Water blob motif, Escuintla tripods, 81, 83
"Weapons-bundle" carrier, on Escuintla region incense burners, 73
Weaver, M. P., 146, 155
Webb, M. C., 10, 15, 57*n*12
Weigand, P. C., 146
Westheim, P., 153, 157*n*2
Wicke, Charles R., 49, 59
Willey, G. R., 15, 31, 146
Winter, Marcus, 56*n*4
Wolfe, A. W., 168
Woodbury, R. B., 32
Woodward, A., 153

Xelha, 68
Xipe, 34, 61; Monte Alban, 62
Xirau, R., 76, 84*n*3
Xlapac, 162, 164
Xochicalco, 7, 8, 16, 17, 30, 112; directional symbolism, 139, 141; head glyphs, 81; Nuine and, 55
Xochicalco influence, in far north, 19

Yadeun, Juan, 173
Yagul, 59, 61, 162–64, 169
Yaxchilan, 13, 117
Yaxha: Teotihuacan influence, 67–68; warrior images, 83
Yaxuna, 18
Yeguih, 49
Yoke-*hacha* complex, 32, 59
Yokes, Escuintla ballplayers, 77
Yucatan, 5, 10; ball courts, 89–91; ball game cult, waning of, 101; calendrical coding, 167; cultural relationships, 13; *greca* tradition, 158, 161, 162, 167; history, 13, 18; martial cult, 101, 106; Middle Classic period in, 86–87; sculpture, 122; seventh-century, 20; trade, 13, 20; Yucunuda

Yucatan (*Continued*)
hui-tomb, 55; *see also* Puuc region; Puuc style; *specific sites*
architectural styles, 92–106; Chichen Maya, 97–106; Chichen Toltec, 97–106; Florescent phase, dating of, 92–93; ornaments, 111–12; Puuc style, 92–95, 100–06; Regional style, 92, 96–97, 100, 101, 105–06; round buildings, 110; stone mosaic, 111–12; Terminal Middle Classic period, 101–06; veneer masonry, 93, 95, 111
ballplayer representations in, 87–92; Maya ballplayers compared, 87–88, 90; Uxul and Etzna ballplayers compared, 88–89

Zacatecas, 13–14; *see also* Alta Vista
Zapotec, 30